Economies under Occupation

Nazi Germany and Japan occupied huge areas at least for some period during World War II, and those territories became integral parts of their war economies. The book focuses on the policies of World War II aggressors in occupied countries.

The unbalanced economic and financial relations were defined by administrative control, the implementation of institutions and a variety of military exploitation strategies. Plundering, looting and requisitions were frequent aggressive acts, but beyond these interventions by force, specific institutions were created to gain control over the occupied economies as a whole. An appropriate institutional setting was also crucial to give incentives to the companies in the occupied countries to produce munitions for the aggressors. The book explains the main fields of war exploitation (organisation and control, war financing and workforce recruitment). It substantiates these aspects in case studies of occupied countries and gives examples of the business policy of multinational companies under war conditions. The book also provides an account of differences and similarities of the two occupation systems.

Economies under Occupation will interest researchers specialising in the history of economic thought as well as in economic theory and philosophy. It will also engage readers concerned with regional European and Japanese studies and imperial histories.

Marcel Boldorf is Professor at Université Lyon 2 Lumière. His research focuses on German economic history in the twentieth century and the occupation of European countries, especially France, in World War II. Further research interests are the institutional analysis of industrialisation and social and welfare policies.

Tetsuji Okazaki is Professor of Economic History at Graduate School of Economics, The University of Tokyo. His research focuses on institutional analysis of Japanese economic development, including such topics as wartime planning and control, the role of industrial policies in the postwar period and the role of the capital market and business groups in the prewar period.

Economies under Occupation
The hegemony of Nazi Germany and Imperial Japan in World War II

Edited by Marcel Boldorf and
Tetsuji Okazaki

LONDON AND NEW YORK

First published 2015
by Routledge
2 Park Square, Milton Park, Abingdon, Oxon OX14 4RN

and by Routledge
711 Third Avenue, New York, NY 10017

Routledge is an imprint of the Taylor & Francis Group, an informa business

© 2015 Marcel Boldorf and Tetsuji Okazaki for selection and editorial matter; individual chapters their contribution

The right of the editors to be identified as the authors of the editorial material, and of the authors for their individual chapters, has been asserted in accordance with sections 77 and 78 of the Copyright, Designs and Patents Act 1988.

All rights reserved. No part of this book may be reprinted or reproduced or utilised in any form or by any electronic, mechanical, or other means, now known or hereafter invented, including photocopying and recording, or in any information storage or retrieval system, without permission in writing from the publishers.

Trademark notice: Product or corporate names may be trademarks or registered trademarks, and are used only for identification and explanation without intent to infringe.

British Library Cataloguing-in-Publication Data
A catalogue record for this book is available from the British Library

Library of Congress Cataloging-in-Publication Data
Economies under occupation : the hegemony of Nazi Germany and
   imperial Japan in World War II / edited by Marcel Boldorf, Tetsuji
   Okazaki.
      pages cm
   Includes bibliographical references and index.
   1. Germany—Economic policy—1933–1945. 2. Japan—Economic policy—1933–1945. 3. Military occupation—Economic aspects—Europe—20th century. 4. Military occupation—Economic aspects—Asia—20th century. 5. World War, 1939–1945—Occupied territories. 6. Germany—History—1933–1945. 7. Japan—History—1933–1945. I. Boldorf, Marcel. II. Okazaki, Tetsuji.
   HC286.4.E32 2015
   940.53'1–dc23
   2014040944

ISBN: 978-0-415-83533-6 (hbk)
ISBN: 978-1-315-71627-5 (ebk)

Typeset in Galliard
by Apex CoVantage, LLC

Contents

List of figures		ix
List of tables		xi
Contributors		xiii
1	**Introduction**	1
	MARCEL BOLDORF AND TETSUJI OKAZAKI	

I
The system of occupation   5

2	**European economies under National Socialist rule**	7
	MARCEL BOLDORF	
3	**Strategies and organizations for managing the 'Greater East Asia Co-Prosperity Sphere'**	24
	TETSUJI OKAZAKI	

II
War financing   37

4	**The German system of financing occupation**	39
	JONAS SCHERNER	
5	**Paying for war, 1941–1945: how Japan financed Southeast Asia's occupation**	55
	GREGG HUFF AND SHINOBU MAJIMA	

III
Exploiting the foreign labour force   71

6   Forced labour in Nazi-occupied Europe,
    1939–1945   73
    MARK SPOERER

7   Development of labour policy in 'Manchukuo'
    and its limit, 1933–1943   86
    TOSHIO KOJIMA

IV
Incorporation of territories in the war economy   97

8   The French economy under German
    occupation, 1940–1944   99
    MARCEL BOLDORF

9   German economic rule in occupied
    Belgium, 1940–1944   112
    DIRK LUYTEN

10   Nazi Germany's financial exploitation of
    Norway during the occupation, 1940–1945   130
    HANS OTTO FRØLAND

11   The incorporation of the General Government
    in the German war economy   147
    STEPHAN LEHNSTAEDT

12   The Protectorate of Bohemia and
    Moravia under German control, 1939–1944   161
    HARALD WIXFORTH

13   Development and management of the
    Manchurian economy under Japan's empire   178
    TETSUJI OKAZAKI

14   The Philippine economy during the
    Japanese occupation, 1941–1945   191
    GERARDO P. SICAT

15 The eclipse of the Indonesian economy
   under Japanese occupation   205
   J. THOMAS LINDBLAD

16 The Burmese economy under the
   Japanese occupation, 1942–1945   218
   MICHAEL W. CHARNEY AND ATSUKO NAONO

17 Indochina during World War II: an economy
   under Japanese control   232
   DELPHINE BOISSARIE

V
Multinationals acting in occupied economies   245

18 German steel industry's expansion in occupied Europe:
   business strategies and exploitation practice   247
   RALF AHRENS

19 The French opportunity: a Danish
   construction company working for the
   Germans in France, 1940–1944   262
   STEEN ANDERSEN

20 Management of the South Manchuria
   Railway Company   280
   TSUTOMU HIRAYAMA

21 Shanghai's cotton textile industry during the
   Pacific War: exploring relations with Japan
   and the transformation of the economic structure   293
   NARUMI IMAI

22 Conclusion: differences and similarities
   of the two occupation regimes   316
   MARCEL BOLDORF AND TETSUJI OKAZAKI

   Index   329

Figures

2.1	Deutsche Annexions- und Eroberungspläne 1938–1942	9
3.1	Capacity of marine shipping for civil use	35
19.1	Plan of the submarine bunker construction in Saint Nazaire	271
19.2	Plan of the submarine bunker at La Pallice	273
20.1	Rate of successful bits and weighted-average subscription price	282
20.2	Average term in office and number of middle management	286
21.1	Raw cotton initiatives of Chinese spinners	301
21.2	Establishing GARNC and reorganizing the structure of the cotton industry	305
21.3	Further reorganization of the cotton industry's structure	306
21.4	Operating profits and non-operating profits at Yong'an Cotton Mill	310

Tables

2.1	Expansion of territory under German control up to and including 1943	8
2.2	Armaments produced in and exported from the occupied territories and allied states, 1940–1944	17
2.3	Crude steel production in the territories under German control	18
3.1	Geographical area of the Greater East Asia Co-Prosperity Sphere	25
3.2	Incorporated firms in Manchuria and special corporations, 1940	26
3.3	International trade of Japan by area	28
3.4	Import of Japan by area and by category	30
3.5	Companies and cooperatives affiliated with the North China Development Co., March 1944	32
3.6	Companies affiliated with the Middle China Promotion Co., March 1945	32
3.7	Direct investment to China proper from Japan	33
4.1	Occupation tribute's spending structure in France, 1941–1944	44
4.2	Troop size, nonoccupation expenditures, and total occupation costs expenditures in France, 1941–1944	47
4.3	Occupation tributes' spending structure in Norway (%), 1940–1944	48
5.1	Southeast Asia payments to Japan, 1941–1945	58
5.2	Thailand and Indochina composition of payments to Japan, 1941–1945	59
5.3	Thailand and Indochina methods of financing government expenditure and payments to Japan, 1941–1945	60
5.4	Southeast Asia characteristics of inflation and money during the Japanese occupation, 1942–1945	62
6.1	Labour force in the Third Reich (including Austria, Sudetenland and Memel-Gebiet) in millions	74
6.2	Measures of the German Labour Deployment Administration in the occupied territories	80
8.1	Indices of French industrial production	106
9.1	Clandestine production as a percentage of total production	125

xii *Tables*

10.1	Norway's balance with Germany on clearing account during the German occupation	132
10.2	Wehrmacht booty and uncompensated requisitions	134
10.3	Accumulated German spending on the occupation account	136
10.4	Composition of Wehrmacht expenses, 1940–1944	138
10.5	Wehrmacht branches' expenditures, 1940–1944	139
11.1	Agricultural exports from the General Government to the Reich	155
13.1	Outline of the 'Five Years Plan of Manchuria Industrial Development'	181
13.2	Outline of the 'Five Years Plan of Important Industries'	182
20.1	Number of stocks and applications of transfers	283
20.2	Number of stockholders and ration of share in private stocks	283
21.1	Consumption of raw cotton by Japanese spinners in Shanghai	295
21.2	Cotton yarn and cloth output of Shenxin Mills No. 2 and No. 9	297
21.3	Cotton yarn and cloth output of Yong'an Mill No. 3	298
21.4	The stock of central China cotton investigated by ACRCC as of 30 June 1943	303
21.5	Raw cotton output and purchase by Japan in central China	311
22.1	German import structure 1940–1944	318
22.2	Shares of occupied countries on the German war production of 1943	322

Contributors

Ralf Ahrens is researcher at the Potsdam Centre for Contemporary History (Zentrum für Zeithistorische Forschung). He specialises in German economic and business history of the twentieth century.

Steen Andersen is Associate Professor at the Copenhagen Business School. His primary research areas are business history, business and war.

Delphine Boissarie, Agrégée d'Histoire, is currently writing a PhD thesis on a French business conglomerate in Indochina. She is attached to the Centre des Mondes Modernes et Contemporains at the University of Bordeaux Montaigne, France.

Marcel Boldorf is Professor at Université Lyon 2 Lumière. His research focuses on German economic history in the twentieth century and the occupation of European countries, especially France, in World War II. Further research interests are the institutional analysis of industrialisation and social and welfare policies.

Michael W. Charney is an imperial historian at the School of Oriental and African Studies, the University of London, whose research focuses on transportation, warfare and culture in Southeast Asia and Africa. During the writing of this chapter, Charney was project professor at the Institute for Advanced Studies on Asia at the University of Tokyo.

Hans Otto Frøland is Professor of Contemporary European History at Norwegian University of Science and Technology, Trondheim. His research interest lies within the field of historical political economy. He is currently directing a research project on the activities and impact of Organisation Todt in Norway during Nazi Germany's occupation.

Tsutomu Hirayama is Visiting Associate Professor, Faculty of Economics, Keio University. He is a former editor of the *Journal of Japanese Colonial Studies*.

Gregg Huff is Senior Research Fellow, Pembroke College, University of Oxford. His main research interests are the economics of war, finance, urbanisation, migration and economic development and Southeast Asia.

xiv *Contributors*

Narumi Imai is Associate Professor of Chinese Economic History at the Faculty of Education, Gunma University.

Toshio Kojima is Professor of Nagaoka University. His research field is the modern history of Japanese colonies.

Stephan Lehnstaedt is research fellow at the German Historical Institute Warsaw. His main fields of research are the history of Poland and Germany during the two World Wars, the Holocaust and its compensation after 1945.

J. Thomas Lindblad has been affiliated with the Leiden University since 1975, currently as Associate Professor in Economic History and the History of Southeast Asia.

Dirk Luyten is senior researcher at the Centre for Historical Research and Documentation on War and Contemporary Society in Brussels and guest professor at Ghent University. His research fields are punishment of economic collaboration, corporatism and social policy.

Shinobu Majima is Professor of General Economic History at Gakushuin University, Japan.

Atsuko Naono is a research associate with the Centre for South East Asian Studies at School of Oriental and Africa Studies (London) and a subject consultant at the Bodleian Library, University of Oxford. During the writing of this chapter, Naono was affiliated with the Institute for Advanced Studies on Asia at the University of Tokyo.

Tetsuji Okazaki is Professor of Economic History at Graduate School of Economics, the University of Tokyo. His research interests are in institutional analysis of Japanese economic development, the Japanese war economy during the Second World War, the role of industrial policies in postwar Japan, zaibatsu in the early twentieth century and merchant coalitions in the nineteenth century.

Jonas Scherner is Professor of Modern European Economic History at the Norwegian University of Science and Technology (NTNU), Trondheim. His current research focuses on the exploitation of occupied Europe during Nazi rule, the mobilisation and rationing of raw materials and the reconstruction of historical data.

Gerardo P. Sicat is Professor Emeritus of Economics at the University of the Philippines. He once served as Philippine Minister of Economic Planning and is a World Bank retiree.

Mark Spoerer is Professor of Economic and Social History at the University of Regensburg in Germany. He works primarily on economic and business history of the nineteenth and twentieth centuries.

Harald Wixforth is researcher in economic history at the Ruhr-University Bochum. His research interests are business history (particularly banking), occupation during World War II and regional history.

Introduction

Marcel Boldorf and Tetsuji Okazaki

In spring 1941, the German Wehrmacht prepared the attack on the Soviet Union, planning a war that should devastate the main ideological enemy in Eastern Europe.

At the same time, on 13 April 1941, the Japanese foreign minister Matsuoka travelled to Moscow in order to sign a neutrality pact with the Soviet government, thus ensuring the planned Japanese attack in the Southern Pacific.

This double decision documented that the German Reich and the allied Japanese Empire had different political and strategic aims. Their expansionist strategies directed to different areas, separating the two countries geographically and ideologically. The economic aims of creating a Greater Economic Sphere (*Grosswirtschaftsraum*) and a 'Greater East Asian Co-Prosperity Sphere' could clearly be distinguished from each other. This 'separation of the world' between the Germans and the Japanese culminated in 1942, when both empires were at the height of their power. However, conflictual points remained, such as the unsolved question of how to cope with British India. On 18 January 1942, Germany and Japan concluded a contract designating the 70th degree of Eastern length as a demarcation line between the two spheres of influence. The German Marine supervised with eagle eyes that the Japanese did respect the designated line. Moreover, the economic relations between the two powers remained rudimentary. While the German side complained that urgently needed raw materials such as rubber, quinine and tungsten were not delivered in the requested amounts, the Japanese side was disappointed at the limited supply of machinery, steel and chemicals and the like which were expected to be imported from Germany.

Although we can notice a clear separation of the two influence spheres and different modes of expansion and exploitation strategies, this book makes the attempt to compare the occupation regimes during World War II. As the literature is lacking in such Euro-Asian comparisons, the editors decided to arrange a section at the Paris International Business history conference, organised in 2012 by the European Business History Association and the Business History Society of Japan. Its title was 'Economies under Occupation. The Hegemony of Nazi Germany and Imperial Japan in World War II'. Unfortunately, scholars are usually only working on one of the two fields. That is why the section, as well as this volume that derives from it, presents case studies written by experts. In the conclusion, the editors will try to conclude and make an attempt to compare the two war-based systems of exploitation.

As a framework for comparison, the editors proposed to the authors an outline for the case studies on occupied territories or on specific aspects of occupation. Each chapter on a country should provide a short presentation of the territorial impact of the occupation, the patterns and different stages of occupation and the impact of the local government or the administrative support of collaborating elites. In occupied territories, private property mostly prevailed, but the papers ought to have a closer look at what happened to the property rights. In order to control the occupied economy, institutions arranged by government organisations or semipublic corporations were introduced. They determined the entitlement of input factors such as raw materials, semifinished products or the workforce. Furthermore, a control on foreign trade was established, directing the flow of war goods to the aggressors' economies as well as checking the imports of commodities from them. By controlling money supply through erecting the quasi-central bank for an occupation area or introducing military scrip, the occupiers monetised occupation costs and procurement costs. Sometimes a price-controlling scheme was established at the same time. In the course of occupation, companies from the aggressor countries took the opportunity to advance in the occupied territories, trying to gain influence in their respective branches. Capital flows were noticed, aiming at buying out allied industries.

The armed forces, however, drove forward, pillaging and plundering the local economies, extracting raw materials and foodstuffs needed for warfare. For the character of the occupation, it was important if this exploitation was imposed by rude military force or by using money, for instance military scrip, in order to pay the damaged companies. A closer look should also be taken at the labour relations: Was there an important transfer of forced workers, for instance prisoners of war? Were wages paid to these people, or were they victims of slave labour? Finally, the chapters should estimate the outcome of the occupation, evaluating foreign trade and the war development of GDP or specific branches relevant to the war.

Brief overview of the chapters

The first two chapters give an outline on the Nazi strategy to build up a Greater Economic Sphere and the Japanese attempt to create a 'Greater East Asian Co-Prosperity Sphere'. The following overviews deliver a deeper insight into two systematic aspects of exploitation: the financing of occupation and the use of forced labour. For both regions of the world, a selection of countries had then to be made in order to reflect the varieties of occupation patterns. In Europe, France and Belgium represented the Western exploitation regime, which was quite similar to the economic control in Scandinavia, namely in Norway. The protectorate of Bohemia and Moravia was between this North- and West-European pattern and the devastation strategy which the Nazis applied for racial reasons in Eastern

Europe. For the latter type, the General Government in Poland was chosen as a striking example.

On the Asian side, first the Japanese struggle to control parts of the Chinese economy is described. Japan already occupied a substantial part of China before World War II, including the north-eastern district ('Manchuria'), and tried to develop industries to support the war economy. Besides China, Indonesia, Indochina, Burma and the Philippines are chosen for country studies, where different types of collaboration were introduced depending on the preoccupation status of the territories as European or American colonies.

The last section of the book presents the strategies of companies under the conditions of occupation. It enlarges our knowledge about the different types of occupation regimes, but at the same time, it reflects the behaviour of businessmen in a changing framework of regulations which the war economy provided.

I
The system of occupation

2 European economies under National Socialist rule

Marcel Boldorf

1. An outline of the National Socialist Greater economic sphere

During the Second World War, the German Reich as principal aggressor embarked on a continuous territorial expansion that lasted until 1942/43. The prewar diplomatic successes of the annexation of Austria and North Bohemia (*Sudetenland*) were swiftly followed by a series of military victories in the western, northern and eastern parts of the Reich. The use of the term *Blitzkrieg* to describe this first period of the war has been rejected, not only from a strategic military point of view[1] but also with regard to the economic theory that was derived from it. The ideas that the initial military successes were achieved despite an inadequate expansion of economic potential and that the German economy was not fully mobilised have been refuted.[2] Richard Overy has shown that the level of consumption in the German Reich had already been reduced in the prewar years to facilitate a military buildup. German rates of consumption were lower than those in Great Britain, but the number of people working in the war industry as well as the percentage of aggregate output spent on armaments were higher. The military buildup was given priority long before 1939. Hitler had vehemently demanded complete economic mobilisation as soon as the war broke out and not in 1942 as is often suggested. Overy's findings discredit the main premise of Alan Milward's theory that *Blitzkrieg* was used to ensure that private household consumption would not be jeopardised.[3] In addition, it has been shown that the expansion of an industrial foundation for a material-intensive war started much earlier than had been assumed. As early as 1936, more than half of industrial investment was poured into the armaments and autarky sector, and this percentage grew rapidly to more than 70 per cent immediately after the outbreak of war.[4] Investment remained at this level, and a further increase in 1942 and 1943 is not apparent. In other words, there was no radical change between 1941 and 1942, although the demands faced by the armaments industry were dramatically altered when the Soviet Union was invaded in June 1941.[5]

In the context of continuing military success and advancement into Soviet territory, the German area of control expanded to its maximum size, as shown in Table 2.1. This is based on data provided by the *Rüstungsministerium* (Ministry of Munitions and Armaments) from 6 December 1943. In line with the

8 *Marcel Boldorf*

peculiarities of NS logic, changes to the territorial borders brought about by the policy of Germanisation are included: Austria, the *Sudetenland* and the annexed Polish Reich districts (Wartheland, Danzig-West Prussia and Southern

Table 2.1 Expansion of territory under German control up to and including 1943

		Area (in square kilometres)	Population (in thousands)
TOTAL		3,203,149	267,762
Greater German Reich (*Großdeutschland*)	German Reich/*CdZ* areas	680,872	94,630
	Protectorate of Bohemia and Moravia	48,902	7,536
Western sphere of control	France (without Alsace, Moselle and Nord/Pas-de-Calais)	524,050	39,303
	Belgium and Northern France	29,280 + 12,414	8,238
	The Netherlands	40,829	9,089
Northern sphere of control	Denmark	42,931	3,903
	Norway	322,599	2,968
Southern sphere of control	Italian Social Republic	167,600	30,000
	Serbia and Montenegro	58,733 + 15,219	4,900
	Albania	27,538 + 14,924	1,106
	Greece	129,880	6,736
Eastern sphere of control	General Government	142,207	16,963
	Ostland (Baltic/Belarus)	499,871	15,230
	The Ukraine (including the Crimea)	339,274	25,840
	Wirtschaftsinspektions-Gebiete (Zones of the economic inspections)	106,026	1,320

Sources: Länderschema für die Großraumplanung des Reichsministeriums für Rüstung und Kriegsproduktion vom 6. Dezember 1943, in: H. Umbreit, 'Die deutsche Herrschaft in den besetzten Gebieten 1942–1945', in B. Kroener et al. (eds.), *Das Deutsche Reich und der Zweite Weltkrieg, vol. 5: Organisation und Mobilisierung des deutschen Machtbereichs, part 2: Kriegsverwaltung, Wirtschaft und personelle Ressourcen 1942–1944/45*, Stuttgart: DVA, 1999, p. 7. Statistisches Jahrbuch Deutsches Reich 1941/42, pp. 7–8. *Großdeutschland* had a population of 102 million compared to 166 million in the occupied territories. The total strength of the German armed forces (including the *Wehrmacht*, air force, navy and *Waffen SS*) grew during the war as a result, for example, of the forced recruitment of young men to a maximum of 6.6 million individuals. The 2.5 million-strong reserve army, consisting of command and administrative authorities as well as recruits, reservists and guard troops can be added to this number. By 1942 at the latest, almost every soldier in active service had been sent to one of the fronts existing on every side of the area under German control. These numerical observations alone make it clear that the German occupiers relied on the collaboration of selected autochthonous elites in order to administer the economies of the occupied territories.

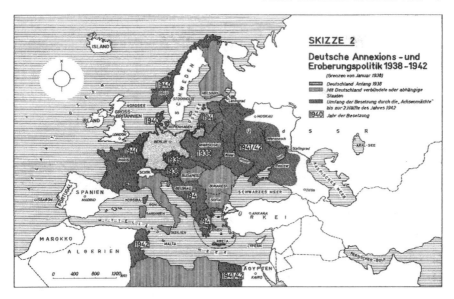

'Legend: 1940 – Year of occupation, Germany's allies: Italy (until 1943), Hungary, Rumania, Bulgaria. White: Neutrals and the Axis' opponents.'

Figure 2.1 Deutsche Annexions- und Eroberungspläne 1938–1942 (German annexations and conquests until the end of 1942).

H.A. Jacobsen, 1939–1945. Der Zweite Weltkrieg in Chronik und Dokumenten, Darmstadt: Wehr und Wissen Verlagsgesellschaft, 1959, p. 506.

East Prussia) were already regarded as German territories. For National Socialists, the Greater German Reich (*Großdeutschland*) also included areas destined for annexation such as Lorraine (Moselle Departement), Alsace, Luxembourg, former Yugoslavian territories (*Untersteiermark, Südkärnten* and *Oberkrain*) and the District of Białystok, under the control of the *Chefs der Zivilverwaltung* (Heads of the Civil Administration) referred to as *CdZ* areas.

Leaving aside the fact that the de-facto annexations of several territories, for example, did not in any way lead to a stable territorial situation, the administration of the extensive occupied territories proved to be extremely difficult. Werner Best has devised a frequently quoted typology of the NS regime which divides the administration of the occupied territories into four categories:[6] (a) *alliance administrations*, characterised by a policy of diplomatic representation, for example in Denmark. This type of administration was even practised in some of the allied satellite states such as Hungary, Croatia and Bulgaria; (b) *supervisory administrations*, where the local administrations were closely controlled by the occupier, for example in France where the French government was retained; (c) *governmental administrations*, where the key administrative activities were carried out by direct order of the occupying power, practised in the Reich Commissariats (*Reichskommissariate*), for example the Netherlands and Norway, but also in the Protectorate of Bohemia and Moravia; (d) *colonial administrations*, where the occupied territory and population were oppressed in such a way that participation in the administration is not possible. This type of administration was practised in the occupied General Government but also in other parts of Eastern Europe, such as Belarus and the Ukraine.

In accordance with the racist criteria of National Socialism, it is possible to differentiate between a western and an eastern pattern.[7] In Western and Northern Europe, autonomous forms of national sovereignty survived. Despite structural flexibility which presented the possibility of cooperation with the occupiers, the opportunities for the collaborating powers to influence basic aspects of the economic order were few and far between. However, dispensing with the implementation of an ideologically defined model of society can be interpreted as a prerequisite for successfully establishing a system of collaboration. In East-Central and Eastern Europe, the racist ideology of National Socialism did not allow the retention of independent forms of administration. The ideological will to restructure was applied to the social system as a whole. The objective of enslaving the occupied territories, as conceptualised in the different versions of the Master Plan East (*Generalplan Ost*), led to excessive levels of oppression and destruction.

2. Vague concepts of European economic integration

German military conquest led to a desire to seize the resources of Europe. Plans to exploit Europe economically, which German nationalist authors had outlined since the publication of Hitler's *Mein Kampf* in 1926, were now acted upon. However, at no time was there common agreement on the borders, structures and instruments of the Greater economic sphere (*Großraumwirtschaft*).[8] Some of the ideas that were competing with each other suggested the economic integration of Europe under German hegemony. Paul Bang came up with the idea of setting up a European economic community.[9] With regard to the restructuring of economic relations among European states, he stressed that the national economies should support each other using a properly coordinated division of labour – without the interference of England. According to Paul Bang, it was essential to retain ethnic identity ('*völkische Identität*') within the individual states. Economic coordination could be achieved by entering into long-term contracts with four main objectives emphasised: (a) an agreement on interstate production and market-regulating arrangements, (b) the expansion of bilateral clearing into a multilateral system, (c) the facilitation of payment using fixed currency exchange rates and (d) the creation of a central clearing institute in Berlin as a central accounting centre.

Some of the objectives were actually achieved during the German occupation, such as the establishment of a system of fixed exchange rates which undervalued other European currencies, Germany being the sole benefactor. These types of concept really only give us an insight into a planning scenario that was far removed from the realities of the war economy in place across much of Europe. There was, however, one organisation that has been largely ignored by researchers until now, which was based in Berlin and acted as the coordinating committee of the government department in relation to the occupied territories. A Trade Policy Board (*Handelspolitischer Ausschuss*) included representatives from the ministries of economics, finance and transport as well as from the Four Year Plan office, Reichsbank and High Command of the *Wehrmacht*. It was responsible for a number of economic and finance policy decisions affecting the interpretation of the ceasefire agreement with the occupied countries and negotiations with the respective governments. The committee also pursued concrete projects such as the creation of monetary unions with the Netherlands, Denmark and Slovakia, the expansion of the German clearing system into a European central clearing system and the setting of different levels of occupation costs for the individual occupied countries as well as the lifting of some German customs duties and import embargoes. In the case of France, for example, the Reich Ministry of Finance in Berlin realised that a realistic financial policy was essential if economic exploitation was to succeed.[10] As a consequence, officials in Berlin tried to end the extravagant spending of funds acquired through the occupation of France. In addition, commercial policy requirements were taken into account if convenience demanded it, for example the reichsmark was devalued against the Danish krone by 8 per cent in 1941 as the result of a decision made by the trade policy committee.[11]

The Central Planning Committee (*Zentrale Planung*) set up by Albert Speer in Berlin in 1941 is often referred to as a milestone in the economic control of Europe. Military historians have stressed the role played by Hitler's favourite architect in the reorganisation of the war economy to an excessive degree. He is referred to as an 'economic genius' who succeeded in carrying out a so-called armaments miracle by mobilising all available forces for the war effort.[12] It must, however, be questioned if Speer really was the all-powerful Armaments Minister in the 'Third Reich' when we consider that during the preceding period, Hermann Göring was not able to position himself as 'economic dictator' or 'economic czar'.[13] Researchers also doubt that the assumed turnaround attributed to Speer in February 1942 actually took place. The initial arguments put forward originate from an internal view of the German economy. To disprove the existence of a turnaround, it has been argued that the increase in efficiency was based on an earlier improvement in the incentive structures of the contracts agreed between the state and companies. In addition, important rationalisation measures were already in place, and the lessons learnt during the initial phases of the war were only then having a positive effect.[14] Another important argument, referred to earlier, is the structure of domestic investment, which peaked long before 1942 and did not increase from this time onwards.[15] In the light of these considerations, the question remains as to whether the establishment of the 'central planning committee' in the Ministry of Munitions and Armaments in Berlin was a turning point in the exploitation of the occupied territories.

3. Restructuring the economic system of the occupied territories

As in the German Reich itself, the legal basis for private ownership largely survived in the occupied territories. There are, however, two exceptions that represent a brutal infringement on the private ownership rights of the industrialists concerned. First, the 'aryanisation' that was carried out all over Europe, that is the ousting of Jewish company owners as part of the Nazi's racial policies. But even these confiscated factories were returned to private, however mostly German, hands. Second, the rigorous persecution of entrepreneurs in Western Poland and the General Government during which many members of the business elite were arrested by the German authorities in accordance with prepared lists, some of whom were subsequently shot.[16] These planned confiscations were placed in the hands of the Main Trustee Office for the East (*Haupttreuhandstelle Ost*) in Berlin and other subordinate trust agencies in the occupied territories of Eastern Europe.[17] The strategy of repression blended with the process of removing the local business elites. This type of massive attack against the industrial sector was rare in the West. The sequestrations carried out there were extremely selective and included, for example, the iron and steel industry in Lorraine, the aluminium and power industries in Norway and a number of companies belonging to the engineering and chemical sectors in the Netherlands.[18]

The economic mobilisation of the occupied territories started at the beginning of the occupation, even if the establishment of the necessary institutional controls took some time. In all of the occupied territories, with the exception of the Netherlands and Denmark,[19] there was an initial phase of plundering and looting that lasted almost six months and concentrated on raw materials and products that were urgently needed for the German war economy. At the same time, measures were introduced to align the occupied national economies with the war interests of Germany, with the result that an economic system based on orders and commands did not survive. The strategy was double-tracked from the very beginning, at least for Western and Northern Europe, because the systematic establishment of institutions for managing the economies went ahead before the regional German Military Command developed the idea that plundering crippled the economy and prevented a targeted exploitation of the occupied national economies.

The German occupational force adapted the control mechanisms which had already been used when establishing the war economy in the Reich to suit the requirements of the occupied territories. There were four large areas to be controlled: (a) the control of raw materials and goods through the establishment of a central exploitation apparatus under German control, (b) the supervision of finances and creation of funds by transferring excessively high occupation costs to the *Reichskreditkassen* as the occupier's banks, (c) the control of prices and wages, the other side of which was the emergence of black markets in which the *Wehrmacht* was the biggest customer and (d) the control of foreign trade through the Central Contracts Office (*Zentralauftragsstelle* or *Zast*), which was responsible for controlling the export of goods and raw materials to the German Reich.

The regulatory mechanisms were applied directly in the companies because these were seen as essential for achieving the production objectives. In some countries, such as France for example, the implementation of institutional restructuring remained in the hands of the collaborating governments, with the German supervisory bodies not allowing any fundamental deviations from their concepts.[20]

The utilisation of the occupied territories depended on the different institutions working together. The German government imposed high occupation costs on all of the occupied countries. They were justified as being payments for the administrative services which the *Wehrmacht* provided in the occupied territory and as a contribution towards the maintenance of public order. Although compliant with international law, the calculations of the Reich Ministry of Finance were arbitrary because the sums imposed were many times higher than the actual cost of maintaining the occupational armies. The German Reich and *Wehrmacht* used the large surpluses to finance the purchase of raw materials, goods and services in the occupied countries.[21] The aforementioned Central Contracts Offices, set up in several European capital cities (The Hague, Brussels, Paris, Belgrade and Prague), controlled the flow of commodities.[22] The occupied countries were obliged to prefinance exports to the German Reich, whilst the Germans themselves refused to fulfil the counterdeliveries that were partially agreed by contract. This resulted in a German clearing account debt which increased the burden caused by the occupation costs.[23] In a nutshell, the clearing account debt and inflated cost of the occupation meant that the occupied territories were financing their own exploitation.

In the face of these interlinked control mechanisms, the measures put in place to restructure the occupied national economies and even military interventions had very little impact. Neither the industrial organising committees in France nor the collaborating Belgian industrialists connected to Alexandre Galopin managed to influence the regulatory and political situation in any decisive way. At the same time, the theory of a polycracy that is often found in the literature must also be rejected. It is, however, right to say that a number of military bodies endeavoured to interfere in the economy of the occupied territories: the economic divisions of the German Military Command, the German War Economy and Armament Staff, the Todt Organisation and SS divisions as well as other military authorities with economic responsibilities. They requisitioned raw materials and commodities on the ground, interfered in the deportation of manpower and actively purchased goods on the black market. It is assumed that this led to widespread chaos and inextricable control problems.[24] Reference to the institutional restructuring of the national economies casts doubt on this assessment, because the incentives aimed at the individual companies had the intended effect regardless of the high degree of selective and local interference.

The formation of order-shifting consortiums led to a strengthening of contact at company level and a circumvention of central controlling institutions. From June 1943 onwards, representatives sent by German industrial groups monitored the formation of consortiums in which German importers were assigned a foreign trade partner.[25] These corporate consortiums set up offices themselves whose specialist personnel communicated with the resources entitlement authorities (*Warenstellen*) to ensure input allocation and control the implementation of the imposed production programme.[26] The German companies were referred to as 'companies providing support and guidance' (*Paten- und Leitfirmen*), that is they sent to their foreign partners clear production specifications and specialist staff with relevant know-how for actual production. It is often said that the system of self-administration was transferred to the occupied economies which was promoting the production of armaments.

The reorganisation of the occupied European economies displayed many features of a controlled market economy and none of an economy centrally controlled from Berlin. In light of the intrinsic logic of the management system – above all the retention of private profit as a control mechanism – the NS economic order was in a position to repress the role of individual players. It appeared necessary during the course of the war to end the political dependence of the collaborating local bureaucracies. The measures used to control the economy should be understood with this in mind. They were put in place at an early stage of the occupation and were perfected over time. However, this system harbours a clear contradiction: from 1942 at the latest, the activation of the armaments industry, which is often simplistically attributed to Armaments Minister Speer, stood face to face with the demands of the General Plenipotentiary for Labour Deployment Sauckel, who required manpower for deployment in the Reich.

4. Room for manoeuvre for industrialists?

There is an ongoing discussion in business history concerning the amount of pressure industrialists were under during National Socialism. Despite the many crimes committed by the regime, it has been shown that the use of coercion in relation to companies was minimal and the NS state preferred to use incentive-compatible methods to achieve the objectives of the war economy.[27] In the case of occupied France, research has proven that companies supporting the war effort were not subjected to permanent coercion as a result of the military occupation.[28] However, this applies specifically to armaments manufacturers and other companies that received special treatment. For this reason, it was in the interests of a company to steer its production towards armaments and the needs of the armed forces or towards the manufacture of exports for Germany. This was one way to improve the position of the company and protect it against imminent closure. With these assumptions in mind, the room for manoeuvre of companies in three areas is examined next:

(a) Allocations through the resources entitlement system

The procurement of inputs, especially manpower, raw materials and other materials, depended on decisions made by authorities. The war economy was characterised by shortages which occurred more frequently in the occupied territories. The crucial difference to the Reich was that the occupied territories were subjected to a regime that exploited their resources whilst German companies could rely on special quotas despite rationing. It can be said that the options for economic action in the German Reich were made possible by the transfer of inputs from the occupied territories. In the occupied territories, the possibilities of production were restricted by the forced removal of manpower and the shortage of raw and other materials. The term 'room for manoeuvre' is misleading because there was no real alternative to the orientation of production desired by the German occupation administration. Only those who accepted this logic could hope to be allocated inputs.

(b) Self-determination of output

The incentive system just described, which promised the companies increased profits if they exported to Germany and supplied the *Wehrmacht*, focused on output. In principle, companies could decide to accept or reject this offer. As the occupation continued, this theoretical freedom was replaced by forced decisions as a number of production bans were put in place. In addition, the Central Contracts Offices linked the allocation of inputs increasingly to the production of goods essential to the war effort. It can be shown that companies in France tried everything from 1943 onwards to be classified as *Sperrbetriebe* (specially designated factories) to prevent loss of their production permit and qualified staff.[29] These types of decisions taken by company management can only be characterised as an attempt to find a profitable way of adapting to the regime (as it was referred to in the Reich) if it is also pointed out that the existing room for manoeuvre had been reduced to a minimum.

(c) Investments of the companies

Investment is a forward-looking corporate decision. There was a real conflict between the short-term armament targets of the occupier and the long-term considerations of the industrialist who was interested in the future sustainability of his company. It can be shown that large-scale industrial producers in the occupied territories were also slow to invest, a situation which corresponds to the results of research carried out for the German Reich.[30] However, the ongoing war was certainly an incentive to invest in some situations. In Western Europe, money was initially invested in import substitutions after several categories of goods were no longer available as a result of the Allied sea blockade. The possibility of exporting to Germany was also a reason for expansion investment, for example in the textile industry. For this reason, the capital stock in the Netherlands in 1945 was even greater than in 1939.[31] In countries like France, certain sectors such as the canning industry were in a position to expand, for example for seafood products in Brittany, because the *Wehrmacht* was a solvent customer.[32] On the other hand, it was also possible for companies to refuse building contracts with the *Wehrmacht*, Organisation Todt or other authorities of the Reich without fear of major sanctions being imposed.[33] As a rule, companies kept control over their investment objectives, and attractive offers of cooperation with German companies presented themselves on occasion.[34] There is no evidence to suggest a systematic control of investment by the German occupation administration.

The amount of freedom available to do business and make autonomous decisions in the Reich postulated by some historians[35] must be substantially reduced when the conditions of the occupation are taken into account. As already described, this was largely due to the constantly growing restraints on inputs. The companies certainly had profitable fallback opportunities with regard to output, but the decision to take advantage of them was rarely taken autonomously. This was especially true in the profitable cement, construction, automotive and aviation industries: these, however, can definitely not be seen as representative of the overall economy. There were almost certainly isolated cases in the occupied territories in which autonomous objectives were pursued by some companies, but a generalisation should be avoided. There were no opportunities for branches of industry to sustain production during the period of occupation if they were not essential to the war effort.

Companies were normally spared the use of direct force, that is military intervention or sanctions by the German occupation administration as a result of behaviour that was considered unacceptable. This conclusion could be drawn if the extended periods of time in the occupied western territories during which the German armed forces did not carry out any military operations are taken as a benchmark. However, the occupied territories in Eastern Europe suffered military attack, plundering and widespread theft for the entire duration of the war. In the same way, the use of direct force in the West was not restricted to the period immediately after the German invasion of 1940. For example, the occupation of Marseilles in the winter of 1942/43 shows that company owner property rights and rights of disposal were trodden underfoot.[36] However, this type of military violence against company owners does not explain the fact that the economic system of control actually functioned. It must be stressed once again that the NS authorities used incentive-compatible methods to ensure armament production, their key concern, in an economy which was not centrally planned.

5. Results of the war economy

Raw materials and industry

The exploitation of European national economies for NS war objectives can be elucidated using statistics from the armaments industry. In foreign trade, the shift of orders was of particular importance, that is orders from German companies that were awarded to foreign exporters by the Central Contracts Office. Table 2.2 provides an overview of the annual total value of these contracts which were officially arbitrated.

Table 2.2 only includes industrial orders that were not consumed by the occupying troops in the field, that is the extensive purchases of the *Wehrmacht* on the black markets of Western European countries are not included. Two thirds of armaments and one third of the various other requirements of the armed forces were exported to Germany. Individual territories tended to specialise, for example the General Government in the production of munitions, the Netherlands in

Table 2.2 Armaments produced in and exported from the occupied territories and allied states, 1940–1944 [in millions of reichsmark]

	Western Europe	Protectorate	Italy	East-Central Europe/ Balkan States	General Government	Northern Europe	Total
1940	> 343	308	—	—	> 52	> 53	> 756
1941	2,340	1,253	152	31	272	178	4,226
1942	3,510	2,165	152	908	414	202	7,351
1943	3,401	3,231	152	1,613	628	254	9,279
1944	2,096	3,901	3,673	1,257	342	228	11,497
Total	11,690	10,858	4,129	3,809	1,708	915	33,109

Source: Jonas Scherner, 'Europas Beitrag zu Hitlers Krieg. Die Verlagerung von Industrieaufträgen der Wehrmacht in die besetzten Gebiete und ihre Bedeutung für die deutsche Rüstung im Zweiten Weltkrieg', in Christoph Buchheim and Marcel Boldorf (eds.), *Europäische Volkswirtschaften unter deutscher Hegemonie 1938–194.* Munich: Oldenbourg, 2012, p. 81.

shipbuilding and France in the production of motor vehicles and aircraft. It can be noted that contracts for parts production, in particular, and not for the final manufacturing process of armaments, were awarded to companies outside the Reich. In addition to security issues, reasons of efficiency also played a part. The *Wehrmacht* assumed that the motivation among workers to work for the occupiers in the final manufacturing process would be very low. The frequency of type changes also meant that close cooperation between the client and manufacturer was essential. In the course of the Allied aerial war, armament-related production was consciously transferred to the Protectorate and also to the Polish General Government. According to figures provided by Jonas Scherner, the foreign percentage of the armaments index peaked at 28 per cent in 1941 and fell to 24 per cent in 1942 and 17 per cent in 1943 and 1944. This proves that the occupied territories played an important role in armaments production prior to Speer's appointment.[37]

The dependency of German armaments production on the annexed and occupied territories is also clear from the data in Table 2.3. Crude steel is the most important basic product used in the manufacture of weapons.

The German Reich used its policy of expansion to take control of the Austrian and North Bohemian steel industries and, in the summer of 1940, to occupy Poland, France, Luxembourg and Belgium. Germany had an initial manufacturing capacity of 23 million tonnes, which the annexations increased to 39 million by 1940: the occupation of Meurthe-et-Moselle, Nord/Pas-de-Calais and Belgium increased capacity once again to more than 53 million tonnes. Production in the territories controlled by Germany remained up to a third below overall capacity utilisation.[38] Nevertheless, the territories conquered in 1941 provided 35 per cent of overall crude steel production within the territory controlled by Germany; these statistics provide no evidence of an eventual turnaround resulting from the appointment of Speer.

Table 2.3 Crude steel production in the territories under German control [in millions of tonnes]

	The 'Greater German Reich' plus annexed and occupied territories	Share of annexed and occupied territories
1939	23.9	9.6%
1940	23.1	16.9%
1941	32	35.0%
1942	31	33.9%
1943	34.6	40.2%
1944	28.5	35.7%

Source: Dietrich Eichholtz, *Geschichte der deutschen Kriegswirtschaft 1939–1945*, vol. 2.2: *1941–1943*, Munich: Saur 1999, p. 495.

Metals and materials that were in short supply in the German Reich and had to be imported were of particular importance to the war economy. The German war economy obtained chrome ore from the occupied South-Eastern European countries, bauxite for the production of aluminium from France and the lion's share of its manganese ore from the occupied parts of the Soviet Union from the middle of 1941 onwards.[39] The Serbian copper mines in Bor were one of the rare cases of a change in ownership. Against the wishes of the French Vichy government, the German Four Year Plan authorities bought shares in the French operating company.[40] The necessary funds were taken from the occupier's account, into which the French state treasury paid millions on a daily basis. The operating rights were transferred to a consortium made up of a Yugoslavian company and the German mining company *Mansfeld AG and Preußische Bergwerks- und Hütten AG (Preussag)*. This takeover was one of a number of similar activities that German companies, supported by major banks, were involved in, particularly in Central and Eastern European territories.[41]

Food supplies

Food imports were a significant factor in German supplies during the war. Foreign net deliveries between 1939 and 1944 covered on average 12 per cent of German civil and military needs – in some categories of goods, for example meat, up to 20 per cent.[42] Despite this substantial contribution from occupied Europe, it is somewhat exaggerated to suggest that the needs of the Reich's population were completely met up to the autumn of 1944 or to put forward the proposition that the majority of the German people never had it so good as during the Second World War.[43] It is, however, correct that the German people were for a long time receiving more calories per person than people in other parts of Europe because the allocation for the normal consumer between 1941 and 1944 was 1910 calories on average. But even this number of calories, the highest in Europe, did not reach the physiological subsistence level of 2,400 calories which the League of Nations specified in 1936 and the United Nations in 1946.[44]

The large volume of exports to Germany and other economic interventions by the occupying forces had a major negative impact on agricultural production in the occupied countries. The average daily intake of calories in the Nordic countries from 1941 to 1944 was considerably lower than in the German Reich (e.g. 1,480 calories in Norway), and large discrepancies existed in Western Europe (the Netherlands 1,800 calories, Belgium 1,400 calories, France 1,170 calories). Despite France playing a relatively minor role in German agronomic considerations in the 1930s, it became one of the main suppliers to the Reich during the Second World War. The figures for Eastern Europe were a lot worse: people living in the General Government received an average of approx. 990 calories, with the lowest value below 600 calories at times. The situation in the occupied Soviet territories was not much better. A daily food ration of 840 calories, the lowest level, was set in 1943.[45]

When the levels of malnutrition in Europe are considered, the question of how the occupiers managed to squeeze supplies from the occupied territories has to be asked. In accordance with the conduct of the war and the nature of the occupying regime, it is again possible to identify western and eastern patterns. In countries such as Denmark, the policies of the German occupiers were aimed at stimulating the willingness of the local farmers to produce and supply goods.[46] This was guaranteed using the incentive of a pricing policy that increased producer prices at a faster rate than domestic consumer prices. The Danish farmers' association cooperated closely with the German authorities. It was interested in getting higher prices for exports, for example the price of butter doubled during the first year of the occupation. In the same way, the agricultural pricing policy was used as a control instrument in the western occupied countries.[47]

The exploitation of the *Reichskommissariate* Ukraine and *Ostland* stands in stark contrast to the policy of control through pricing practised in Northern and Western Europe.[48] The units of the *Wehrmacht* that passed through on many different occasions during the eastern campaign found food on farms. Although these spoils of war were limited in quantity, they had a devastating psychological effect. The requisition vouchers that were issued could not be redeemed at the subarea headquarters, so the *Wehrmacht* did not bother to issue them or paid off the farmers using their own roubles. Agricultural production was not spared, and so-called zones eaten bare (*Kahlfraßzonen*) developed in the occupied territories.[49] The cities could no longer be supplied, and in the winter/spring of 1941/42, there was widespread mortality as a result of malnutrition and illness. This reckless strategy of plunder brought few economic gains because the Western and Northern European occupied territories provided more in the way of supplying the German Reich.

6. Conclusions

The 'Central Planning Committee' set up in the Ministry of Munitions and Armaments in Berlin was not able to coordinate business activities in occupied Europe or the overall planning of individual industrial sectors after February 1942.[50] It restricted itself to specific tasks that were important for the war effort, for example the provision of natural resources, measures for maintaining the supply of energy and the upkeep of transport and traffic routes.[51] An examination of production and trade statistics for the occupied territories reveals no turning point at the start of 1942. Recent research on the German 'armaments miracle' shows that not only the theory of a *Blitzkrieg* economy must be rejected, but also those theories which suggest that significant inefficiencies were only removed after Speer was appointed.[52] On the other hand, it should be stressed that Speer himself used his own propaganda to create the legend of the 'armaments miracle' in order to strengthen the resolve of the German people and consolidate his own position within the hierarchy of the NS state. In this respect, the increase in armaments production can also be interpreted as a phenomenon that did not result from a conscious policy of war pursued by the National Socialist leadership.

It is indisputable that the index of German armaments production that includes all military equipment manufactured in the territory controlled by Germany between February 1942 and July 1944 grew threefold, even though the reference month was chosen because of its relatively low output.[53] This expansion took place despite Allied aerial attacks and with a massive contribution from the occupied territories. However, the example of the steel industry shows that the increase in capacities did not lead to a maximum possible increase in production in all sectors of the economy. In contrast, the aviation industry achieved extraordinarily high growth rates with the support of the occupied territories. *Junkers*, *Siebel* and *Mitteldeutsche Motorenwerke* were companies whose labour productivity rose dramatically. This branch of industry also possessed the largest percentage of the growing armaments index.[54]

If a break can be perceived in 1942 as a result of the call for 'total war', then this is related to extra-economic coercion. Inhumane measures were applied in particular when recruiting manpower and are dealt with in a separate chapter on forced labour. This book also contains a chapter dealing with another specific feature of exploitation: the occupied territories financing their own exploitation through occupation costs.

Finally, the role of the institutional changes that affected the companies that were important to the war effort should once again be emphasised. The modification of the institutional structures in most of the occupied countries during the war ensured that goods were steered towards the *Wehrmacht* and German importers. In the process, the actions of interventionist intermediate bodies, be it German military authorities or collaborating local authorities, were increasingly marginalised. The relatively good production results achieved in the armaments-related industry can be explained, despite the overlapping administrative competencies, by the stimulation of the corporate desire to make profit. However, with the national economies of the occupied countries in mind, these individual results do not affect the overall evaluation of the war economy. Almost everywhere, the occupation had a negative effect on the long-term welfare of the citizens of the affected European countries.

Notes

1 K.H. Frieser, *Blitzkrieg-Legende. Der Westfeldzug 1940*, 3rd ed., Munich: Oldenbourg, 2005.
2 C. Buchheim, 'Der Mythos vom "Wohlleben". Der Lebensstandard der deutschen Zivilbevölkerung im Zweiten Weltkrieg', *Vierteljahrshefte für Zeitgeschichte*, 2010, vol. 58, pp. 299–328.
3 R. Overy, ' "Blitzkriegswirtschaft?" Finanzpolitik, Lebensstandard und Arbeitseinsatz in Deutschland 1939–1942', *Vierteljahrshefte für Zeitgeschichte*, 1988, vol. 36, pp. 379–435.
4 J. Scherner, 'Nazi Germany's Preparation for War: Evidence from Revised Industrial Investment Series', *European Review of Economic History*, 2010, vol. 14, p. 442.
5 J. Scherner/J. Streb, 'Das Ende eines Mythos? Albert Speer und das so genannte Rüstungswunder', *Vierteljahrschrift für Sozial- und Wirtschaftsgeschichte*, 2006, vol. 93, pp. 172–96.
6 C.J. Child, 'The Concept of the New Order', in A. & V. Toynbee (eds.), *Hitler's Europe*. London: Oxford UP, 1954, p. 53. W. Best, 'Großraumordnung und Großraumverwaltung', *Zeitschrift für Politik*, 1942, vol. 32, pp. 406–12.
7 J. Bähr/R. Banken, 'Ausbeutung durch Recht? Einleitende Bemerkungen zum Einsatz des Wirtschaftsrechts in der deutschen Besatzungspolitik 1939–1945', in idem (eds.), *Das Europa des 'Dritten Reichs'. Recht, Wirtschaft, Besatzung*, Frankfurt am Main: Klostermann, 2005, pp. 5–6.
8 H.G. Schröter, 'Thesen und Desiderata zur ökonomischen Besatzungsherrschaft. Skandinavien und die NS-Großraumwirtschaft', in J. Lund (ed.), *Working for the New Order. European Business under German Domination 1939–1945*, Copenhagen: University Press of Southern Denmark, 2006, p. 33.
9 J. Elvert, *Mitteleuropa! Deutsche Pläne zur europäischen Neuordnung (1918–1945)*, Stuttgart: Steiner 1999, p. 344. With reference to: P. Bang, 'Europäische Wirtschaftsgemeinschaft', *Das Neue Europa*, 1942, vol. 2, pp. 5–6 (15 November 1942 issue).
10 M. Boldorf/J. Scherner, 'France's Occupation Costs and the War in the East: The Contribution to the German War Economy, 1940–1944', *Journal of Contemporary History*, 2012, vol. 47, pp. 299–314.
11 See Jonas Scherner's chapter in this book (endnote 7).
12 R.-D. Müller, 'Die Mobilisierung der Wirtschaft für den Krieg – eine Aufgabe der Armee? Wehrmacht und Wirtschaft 1933–1942', in W. Michalka (ed.), *Der Zweite Weltkrieg. Analysen, Grundzüge, Forschungsbilanz*, Munich: Piper, 1989, pp. 349–50.
13 Idem, 'Die Mobilisierung der deutschen Wirtschaft für Hitlers Kriegsführung', in B. Kroener et al. (eds.), *Das Deutsche Reich und der Zweite Weltkrieg, vol. 5: Organisation und Mobilisierung des deutschen Machtbereichs, part 1: Kriegsverwaltung, Wirtschaft und personelle Ressourcen*, Stuttgart: DVA, 1988, p. 610. H.-U. Wehler, *Deutsche Gesellschaftsgeschichte, vol. 4: Vom Beginn des Ersten Weltkriegs bis zur Gründung der beiden deutschen Staaten*, 3rd edition, Munich: Beck, 2008, p. 916.
14 Scherner/Streb, 'Das Ende eines Mythos', pp. 172–96. R. Overy, *War and Economy in the Third Reich*, Oxford: Clarendon Press, 1994, p. 357.
15 Scherner, 'Nazi Germany's Preparation for War', p. 442.
16 M.G. Esch, *'Gesunde Verhältnisse'. Deutsche und polnische Bevölkerungspolitik in Ostmitteleuropa 1939–1950*, Marburg: Herder 1998, p. 26.

17 I. Loose, *Kredite für NS-Verbrechen. Die deutschen Kreditinstitute in Polen und die Ausraubung der polnischen und jüdischen Bevölkerung 1939–1945*, Munich: Oldenbourg, 2007, p. 323. Cf. also B. Musial, 'Recht und Wirtschaft im besetzten Polen (1939–1945)', in Bähr/Banken, *Europa des 'Dritten Reichs'*, pp. 41–2.
18 A. Tooze, *Ökonomie der Zerstörung. Die Geschichte der Wirtschaft im Nationalsozialismus*, Munich: Pantheon, 2008, pp. 452–3.
19 H. Klemann/S. Kudryashov, *Occupied Economies. An Economic History of Nazi-Occupied Europe, 1939–1945*, London: Berg, 2012, pp. 56–7. Schröter, 'Thesen und Desiderata', p. 36.
20 See, on the example of France and the effects of the institutions, Boldorf's chapter in this volume Chapter 8.
21 See Jonas Scherner's chapter in this volume Chapter 4.
22 D. Kahn, *Die Steuerung der Wirtschaft durch Recht im nationalsozialistischen Deutschland. Das Beispiel der Reichsgruppe Industrie*, Frankfurt am Main: Klostermann, 2006, p. 400.
23 P. Liberman, *Does Conquest Pay? The Exploitation of Occupied Industrial Societies*, Princeton: Princeton UP, 1996, pp. 36–68.
24 Müller, 'Mobilisierung der deutschen Wirtschaft', pp. 525, 596.
25 A. Radtke-Delacor, 'Produire pour le Reich. Les commandes allemandes à l'industrie française (1940–1944)', *Vingtième siècle. Revue d'histoire*, 2001, vol. 70, p. 109.
26 M. Margairaz, *L'état, les finances et l'économie. Histoire d'une conversion 1932–1952*, vol. 1, Paris: Comité pour l'histoire économique et financière de la France, 1991, p. 703.
27 C. Buchheim/J. Scherner, 'The Role of Private Property in the Nazi Economy: The Case of Industry', *Journal of Economic History*, 2006, vol. 66, pp. 390–416.
28 H. Rousso, *Le régime de Vichy*, Paris: Presses Universitaires de France, 2007, p. 54.
29 C. Buchheim, 'Unternehmen in Deutschland und NS-Regime: Versuch einer Synthese', *Historische Zeitschrift*, 2006, vol. 282, p. 359.
30 J. Balcar/J. Kučera, 'Nationalsozialistische Wirtschaftslenkung und unternehmerische Handlungsspielräume im Protektorat Böhmen und Mähren (1939–1945). Staatlicher Druck, Zwangslagen und betriebswirtschaftliches Kalkül', in: C. Buchheim/M. Boldorf (eds.), *Europäische Volkswirtschaften unter deutscher Hegemonie 1938–1945*, Munich: Oldenburg, 2012, pp. 165–8. For the Reich, see: J. Scherner, *Die Logik der Industriepolitik im Dritten Reich. Die Investitionen in die Autarkie- und Rüstungsindustrie und ihre staatliche Förderung*, Stuttgart: Steiner, 2008.
31 Klemann/Kudryashov, Occupied Economies, pp. 306, 423–5.
32 J.-C. Fichou, 'Les conserveries de poisson: une activité hors la guerre', in: S. Effosse/M. de Ferrière le Vayer/H. Joly (eds.), *Les entreprises de biens de consommation sous l'Occupation*, Tours: Presses Universitaires François-Rabelais, 2010, pp. 111–28.
33 F. Lemmes, 'Collaboration in Wartime France 1940–1944', *European Review of History – Revue européenne d'histoire*, 2008, vol. 15, p. 171.
34 H. Joly, 'The Economy of Occupied and Vichy France: Constraints and Opportunities', in: Lund, *Working for the New Order*, pp. 98–100.
35 Buchheim, 'Unternehmen in Deutschland und NS-Regime', p. 358.
36 M. Boldorf, 'Grenzen des nationalsozialistischen Zugriffs auf Frankreichs Kolonialimporte (1940–1942)', *Vierteljahrschrift für Sozial- und Wirtschaftsgeschichte*, 2010, vol. 97, p. 154.
37 Scherner, 'Europas Beitrag zu Hitlers Krieg', p. 80–8.
38 D. Eichholtz, *Geschichte der deutschen Kriegswirtschaft 1939–1945*, vol. 2.2: *1941–1943*, Munich: Saur, 1999, p. 494.
39 Ibid, pp. 496–7.

40 K.-H. Schlarp, 'Ausbeutung der Kleinen. Serbien in der deutschen Kriegswirtschaft 1941-1944', in: Bähr/Banken, *Das Europa des 'Dritten Reichs'*, pp. 199-201.
41 Cf. the contributions from Ralf Ahrens and Harald Wixforth in this volume.
42 Buchheim, 'Mythos vom "Wohlleben"', p. 310.
43 Wehler, *Deutsche Gesellschaftsgeschichte, vol. 4*, p. 706. G. Aly, *Hitlers Volksstaat. Raub, Rassenkrieg und nationaler Sozialismus*, Frankfurt am Main: Fischer, 2005, pp. 360-1.
44 M. Boldorf, *Sozialfürsorge in der SBZ/DDR 1945-1953. Ursachen, Ausmaß und Bewältigung der Nachkriegsarmut*, Stuttgart: Steiner, 1998, p. 73.
45 H.-E. Volkmann, *Ökonomie und Expansion. Grundzüge der NS-Wirtschaftspolitik*, Munich: Oldenbourg, 2003, pp. 393-411.
46 S. Andersen, 'Living Conditions and the Business Environment in Denmark, 1940-1945', in: Buchheim/Boldorf, *Europäische Volkswirtschaften*, pp. 27-52.
47 M. Boldorf, 'Les effets de la politique des prix sur la consommation', in: Effosse/De Ferrière le Vayer/Joly, *Les entreprises de biens de consommation*, pp. 17-28.
48 S. Kudryashov, 'Living Conditions in the Occupied Territories of the USSR, 1941-1944', in: Buchheim/Boldorf, *Europäische Volkswirtschaften*, pp. 53-68.
49 D. Pohl, *Die Herrschaft der Wehrmacht. Deutsche Militärbesatzung und einheimische Bevölkerung in der Sowjetunion 1941-1944*, Munich, 2008, p. 188.
50 Klemann/Kudryashov, *Occupied Economies*, p. 367.
51 Bundesarchiv R 3, Records of the Overall Planning Department of the Ministry of Munitions and Armaments.
52 In addition to the articles referred to, see also: A. Tooze, 'No Room for Miracles. German Industrial Output in World War II Reassessed', *Geschichte und Gesellschaft*, 2005, vol. 31, pp. 437-64.
53 Scherner/Streb, *Mythos*, pp. 173-4.
54 L. Budrass/J. Scherner/J. Streb, 'Fixed-price Contracts, Learning and Outsourcing: Explaining the Continuous Growth of Output and Labour Productivity in the German Aircraft Industry during World War II', *Economic History Review*, 2010, vol. 63, pp. 107-36.

3 Strategies and organizations for managing the 'Greater East Asia Co-Prosperity Sphere'

Tetsuji Okazaki

1. Introduction

During World War II, Japan occupied a large part of East and South East Asia. This territory, called 'Greater East Asia Co-Prosperity Sphere' (*Daitoa Kyoei Ken*), was 7,954 thousand square km in area, which is around twenty times larger than the mainland of Japan[1] (Table 3.1). As Japan had been consuming huge amounts of resources for the military activities in China since the early 1930s and was faced with increasing economic sanctions by the hostile countries including the United States at the same time, the Japanese military authorities and the government were keen on developing natural resources and industries in the occupied areas. This chapter overviews what the Japanese military authorities and the government did to develop the occupied areas in the 1930s and the early 1940s as an introduction to the chapters on individual occupied areas.

On the Greater East Asia Co-Prosperity Sphere, there are a number of studies, a seminal work of which is an article by Akira Hara in 1976.[2] This article is remarkable in that it highlighted differences in the strategies and organizations for development across occupied areas, specifically in Manchuria, China Proper and South East Asia. Also, it clearly described the economic relationships between Japan and these occupied areas, focusing on trade and financial transactions. It is not too much to say that the research on the Greater East Asia Co-Prosperity Sphere since the late 1970s has progressed following and elaborating Hara's article. This chapter briefly summarizes the development policies and the consequences in Manchuria, China Proper and South East Asia, relying on the literature.[3]

2. Manchuria[4]

Manchuria is a north east part of China where Japan obtained the railways (South Manchuria Railways) and the authorities to station army forces (Kwangtung Army) to defend it as a result of the Russo-Japanese War. In September 1931, the Kwangtung Army invaded Manchuria and founded a puppet state, Manchukuo. In Manchukuo, the Kwangtung Army, the Manchukuo government and the Japanese government tried to develop munitions and related industries in a systematic way.

The development policy in the early stage was characterized by 'special corporations' and so-called 'one-industry, one-corporation' policy. A 'special corporation'

Table 3.1 Geographical area of the Greater East Asia Co-Prosperity Sphere

			Area (thousand km²)	Population (thousand persons)
Total			7,954	485,870
Japan Empire			681	103,531
	Mainland		383	71,420
	Colonies		298	32,111
China			2,871	243,661
	Manchuria		1,303	43,203
	Mongolia		615	5,508
	North China		603	116,306
	Middle China		350	78,644
South East Asia			4,402	138,678
	Region (A)		3,152	99,106
		Malay	136	5,330
		Borneo	211	931
		Burma	605	16,119
		Dutch East Indies	1,904	60,726
		Philippines	296	16,000
	Region(B)		1,250	40,822
		Thailand	620	15,718
		Indochina	630	23,854

Source: Y. Yamamoto, *'Daotoa Kyoeiken' Keizaishi Kenkyu (Economic History of 'Greater East Asia Co-Prosperity Sphere')*, Nagoya: Nagoya University Press, 2011, p. 18.

referred to a corporation that was founded according to a special law or a treaty between Manchukuo and Japan and was regulated by the Manchukuo government. Meanwhile, 'one-industry, one-corporation policy' refers to the policy that only one special corporation should be allowed in each of the strategic industries. In many cases, the Manchukuo government invested tangible assets requisitioned from the military clique regime in Manchuria in kind. Another major investor in special corporations was the South Manchuria Railways Co., which had been working as a channel of capital investment from Japan to Manchuria since the early twentieth century. Table 3.2 shows the stock of corporate capital by industry in Manchuria in 1940 and the positions of special corporations. In total, special corporations accounted for 35.2 per cent of the corporate capital, and their shares were especially high in the infrastructure sectors, such as electricity and gas, and warehouse, insurance and telecommunication.

The Kwangtung Army and the Manchukuo government intended to construct a 'planned economy' based on the special corporations, each of which monopolized a certain industry. In 1937, they drew up 'Five Years Plan of Manchuria Industrial Development', collaborating with the Imperial Army and the Japanese government. To implement this plan, a unique measure was taken. That is, they invited influential Japanese entrepreneurs to Manchuria and requested their opinions on the plan. One of these entrepreneurs, Yoshisuke Ayukawa, the president of *Nissan Zaibatsu*, frankly criticized its flaws. As Ayukawa commented, the

Table 3.2 Incorporated firms in Manchuria and special corporations, 1940

Industry	Capital thousand yen	Capital of special corporations (included)	%	Major special corporations	Capital thousand yen
Total	7,230,792	2,543,500	35.2		
Bank	119,350	60,000	50.3	Manchuria Central Bank	30,000
Exchange	10,685	0	0.0		
Nonbank finance	2,430	0	0.0		
Securities	44,382	0	0.0		
Trade	581,801	150,500	25.9	Manchuria Necessities of Life	50,000
Market	2,560	0	0.0		
Textile	166,295	0	0.0		
Chemical	613,690	250,000	40.7	Jilin Synthetic Petroleum	100,000
Metal	533,470	280,000	52.5	Showa Steel	200,000
Machinery	547,419	263,000	48.0	Manchuria Automobile	100,000
Lumber	51,209	0	0.0		
Food	152,470	0	0.0		
Printing	15,935	8,000	50.2	Manchuria Publishing	8,000
Other manufacturing	137,742	0	0.0		
Ceramics	120,008	0	0.0		
Mining	1,006,875	445,000	44.2	Manchuria Coal Mining	20,000
Electricity and gas	400,000	370,000	92.5	Manchuria Electricity	320,000
Transportation	1,600,319	0	0.0		
Warehouse, insurance and telecommunication	114,750	103,000	89.8	Manchuria Telecommunication and Telephone	100,000
Real estate	136,338	50,000	36.7	Manchuria Building	30,000
Development	212,441	105,000	49.4	Manchuria Development	50,000
Personnel service	95,968	0	0.0		
Newspaper	5,371	0	0.0		

(*Continued*)

Table 3.2 (Continued)

Industry	Capital thousand yen	Capital of special corporations (included)	%	Major special corporations	Capital thousand yen
Hotel and amusement	19,773	9,000	45.5	Manchuria Movie Association	9,000
Holding company	530,455	450,000	84.8	Manchuria Heavy Industries Development	450,000
Miscellaneous	9,058	0	0.0		

Source: Yokohama Species Bank, *Manshukoku Tokushu Gaisha Seido ni tsuite (On the Special Corporation System in Manchuria)*, 1942; Dalian Chamber of Commerce and Industry, *Manshu Ginko Kaisha Nenkan (Yearbook of Banks and Companies in Manchuria)*, 1941 issue, Dalian: Dalian Chamber of Commerce and Industry, 1941.

Note: Special corporations are classified by industry according to the classification of Dalian Chamber of Commerce and Industry, *Manshu*, op cit.

production targets in the plan were not carefully coordinated. It is notable that this flaw reflected the situation of the Manchurian economy itself at that time. That is, although many special corporations were founded and each of them was regulated by the government, they were not well coordinated.

Accepting Ayukawa's comments, the Kwangtung Army invited him to Manchuria to entrust him with the implementation of the Five Years Plan. On the request, Ayukawa moved the whole *Nissan Zaibatsu* to Manchuria to reorganize it to be a special corporation, the *Manchuria Heavy Industries Development Co. (MHID)*, in 1937. *MHID* was a huge conglomerate that governed and managed special corporations in the heavy industries in Manchuria, as well as the existing companies affiliated to *Nissan Zaibatsu*. *MHID* is remarkable because it embodied a new mode of coordination in which a major part of economic activities in a national economy were coordinated within one private organization.

However, coordination by *MHID* was soon taken over by another mode of coordination, namely an orthodox state-led system of planning and control. When the system of planning and control started to work in Japan in 1938, it had a serious impact on the Manchurian economy through reduction of imports from Japan and requests to increase exports to Japan. In this situation, the Kwangtung Army and the Manchukuo government decided to introduce the system of planning and control from Japan. From 1939, coordination of the Manchurian economy and special corporations came to be carried out according to planning and control by the government. Indeed, 'Material Mobilization Plan' a la Japan was drawn up and implemented every quarter year.

Under this system, the development strategy of the Manchurian economy shifted its focus. Whereas the original Five Years Plan in 1937 aimed at developing a full line of munitions and related industries in Manchuria, including the automobile and aircraft industries, from 1939, the Manchukuo government

28 *Tetsuji Okazaki*

Table 3.3 International trade of Japan by area

		million yen					
		1938			1943		
		Export	Import	Export-import	Export	Import	Export-import
Total		2,690	2,663	27	1,627	1,924	(297)
Greater East Asia Co-Prosperity Sphere		1,384	998	386	1,607	1,785	(178)
	Manchuria	852	399	453	797	400	397
	China Proper	313	165	148	502	922	(419)
	South East Asia	219	434	(215)	308	464	(156)
	Region (A)	177	409	(232)	123	282	(159)
	Region (B)	42	25	17	185	182	3
The other countries		1,306	1,665	(359)	20	139	(119)

Source: Y. Yamamoto, *Daitoa*, op cit, pp. 110–3.

came to narrowly focus on production of natural resources and basic materials. In other words, a clear structure of vertical division of works between Japan and Manchuria was intended.

To see the implication of Manchurian development for the Japanese economy, Table 3.3 shows imports to and exports from Japan by area as of 1938 and 1943. First of all, trade with the countries outside the Greater East Asia Co-Prosperity Sphere declined drastically, although here we measure the volume in nominal value. Greater East Asia Co-Prosperity Sphere was, so to speak, an autarky sphere forced to be isolated from the other part of the world. Under this condition, the relative position of Manchuria in the Japanese trade went up. However, at the same time, it is notable that exports to Manchuria from Japan were substantially larger than imports to Japan from Manchuria, even in 1943. Given the general shortage of supplies in this period, this implies that development of Manchuria did not contribute to mitigating the shortage, at least from the standpoint of the macroeconomy. Of course, concerning individual commodities, the contribution of Manchuria to the Japanese economy was substantial. Table 3.4 presents imports to Japan by area and by commodity category. From 1936 to 1943, Manchuria increased export of minerals and manufactures thereof and ores and metals. The former includes coal, while the latter include iron ore and pig iron.

3. China proper

In July 1937, the Imperial Army invaded China Proper. Formally, this event was called an 'incident' in Japan, because it broke out without any formal proclamation of war. In reality, however, it was a start of the full-scale Sino-Japanese War for around eight years. By the end of 1937, the Imperial Army and Navy occupied major cities, trunk railways and surrounding areas, including Beijing, Tianjin, Nanjing and Shanghai. In each of the occupied areas, Menngu, North China and Middle China, a puppet Chinese regime was established in 1938.[5] Then finally in March 1940, a new government headed by Wang Chao-ming was founded in Nanjing, supported by a sect of the Chinese Nationalist Party and Japan.[6]

When the Sino-Japanese War broke out, the Japanese government set up the Third Committee under the Cabinet to examine economic issues related to the Sino-Japanese War, and in December 1937, the Cabinet formally decided the policy to develop the North China economy as a part of the Outline of Measures to Deal with the Incident. According to the decision, the purpose of developing the North China economy was to complement the bloc economy of Japan and Manchuria, and the decision stressed combination of Chinese capital with Japanese capital and technology. Specifically, it was pointed out that a statutory holding company should be founded to manage important industries such as transportation, telecommunication, electricity, mining and salt making and processing. This policy had a common feature with the policy on the *MHID* in Manchuria drawn up in this period, but the function of the statutory holding company in North China was relatively limited.[7]

Based on this policy, in November 1938, North China Development Co. (NCD, *Kita Shina Kaihatsu Kabushiki Gaisha*) was founded according to the special law. Out of the capital 350 million yen, half was invested by the Japanese government, 150 million yen of which, in turn, was investment in kind.[8] In this sense, at least at the starting point, the NCD substantially relied on requisitioned tangible assets. Table 3.5 shows the paid-in capital of the NCD's affiliated companies by industry in March 1944. The share of transportation was the highest, and those of electricity and coal mining were the next highest. It is confirmed that the distribution of affiliated companies basically reflects the policy in the Outline of Measures to Deal with the Incident in December 1937.

The counterpart of the NCD in Middle China was the Middle China Promotion Co. (MCP, *Nakashina Shinko Kabushiki Gaisha*). It was founded also in November 1938. The initial paid-in capital was 31.4 million yen, 18.9 million yen of which was invested by the Japanese government. Of the government's investment, 7.6 million yen, in turn, was investment in kind.[9] Table 3.6 shows the paid-in capital of the affiliated companies of MCP by industry in March 1945. Compared with NCD, the shares of electricity and textile were higher. Large investments in the electricity industry reflected the condition that the electricity equipment in Middle China was damaged by the war. Meanwhile, Shanghai was a center of the silk industry.

Table 3.7 summarizes the direct investment to China Proper from Japan and the positions of the NCD and the MCP. Direct investment in North China and Middle China from Japan increased sharply from the late 1930s, partly due to inflation. It is remarkable that the shares of the NCD and the MCP were really high in the whole capital flow. Indeed, these two companies were the main channels of direct investment to China Proper from Japan during the war.

Table 3.4 Import of Japan by area and by category

thousand yen		Total	'Greater East Asia Co-Prosperity Sphere'						The other countries
			Total	Manchuria	China Proper	South East Asia Total	Region (A)	Region (B)	
1936	Total	2,763,682	672,309	239,415	154,526	278,368	249,459	28,908	2,091,373
	Plants and animals	2,238	109	68	8	33	30	3	2,129
	Grains, flours, starches and seeds	201,176	145,796	107,417	21,834	16,546	11,279	5,267	55,379
	Beverages, comestibles and tobacco	74,602	40,741	6,048	12,024	22,668	21,514	1,155	33,861
	Skins, hairs, bones etc.	47,321	23,280	2,204	17,121	3,955	2,920	1,035	24,041
	Oils, fats, waxes and manufactures thereof	197,509	61,432	4,367	2,179	54,886	54,844	42	136,078
	Drugs, chemicals, medicines etc.	196,350	89,811	12,312	1,349	76,150	71,209	4,942	106,539
	Dyes, pigments, coatings and filling matters	23,462	3,283	64	2,104	1,114	12	1,103	20,179
	Yarns, threads, twines, cordages, materials thereof	1,109,520	67,038	4,254	38,698	24,086	23,720	367	1,042,482
	Tissues and manufactures thereof	16,745	750	133	602	15	15	0	15,995
	Clothing and accessories thereof	1,275	27	2	25	0	0	0	1,249
	Pulp for paper making, papers, paper manufactures, books and pictures	88,541	359	52	238	69	67	2	88,182
	Minerals and manufactures thereof	100,377	62,739	33,008	13,510	16,221	3,596	12,626	37,638
	Potteries, glass and glass manufactures	4,505	926	911	15	0	0	0	3,579
	Ores and metals	374,892	92,243	28,314	23,223	40,706	40,255	451	282,649
	Metal manufactures	10,598	26	6	19	1	1	0	10,572
	Clocks, watches, scientific instruments, fire-arms, vehicles, vessels and machinery	153,087	69	32	33	4	4	0	153,018
	Others	161,483	83,680	40,224	21,545	21,911	19,994	1,917	77,803

(*Continued*)

Table 3.4 (Continued)

1943									
	Total	1,924,350	1,785,264	400,122	921,896	463,246	281,817	181,429	139,086
	Plants and animals	142	142	0	141	0	0	0	0
	Grains, flours, starches and seeds	396,577	396,576	97,196	163,394	135,986	3,612	132,374	1
	Beverages, comestibles and tobacco	97,433	97,379	19,185	73,693	4,501	4,474	28	54
	Skins, hairs, bones etc.	28,061	28,028	1,494	15,538	10,996	4,971	6,025	33
	Oils, fats, waxes and manufactures thereof	155,932	155,515	15,598	43,434	96,484	95,641	843	417
	Drugs, chemicals, medicines etc.	135,665	117,578	10,690	12,898	93,991	72,766	21,224	18,086
	Dyes, pigments, coatings and filling matters	15,617	864	38	9	818	0	818	14,753
	Yarns, threads, twines, cordages, materials thereof	331,558	331,333	17,365	294,391	19,578	18,319	1,258	225
	Tissues and manufactures thereof	2,740	2,076	124	1,268	685	45	640	664
	Clothing and accessories thereof	68	31	3	26	2	1	1	37
	Pulp for paper making, papers, paper manufactures, books and pictures	1,172	1,148	999	122	27	1	26	24
	Minerals and manufactures thereof	217,841	217,641	46,421	163,957	7,263	348	6,915	200
	Potteries, glass and glass manufactures	4,820	2,725	2,677	47	2	0	2	2,095
	Ores and metals	330,034	310,879	113,766	112,452	84,661	74,065	10,596	19,155
	Metal manufactures	2,141	320	152	166	2	0	2	1,821
	Clocks, watches, scientific instruments, fire-arms, vehicles, vessels and machinery	84,667	5,569	187	5,261	121	120	1	79,098
	Others	119,883	117,459	74,228	35,101	8,130	7,454	676	2,424

Source: Ministry of Finance, 'Dainihon Gaikoku Boeki Nenpyo' ('Annual Return on the Foreign Trade of Japan') 1936 and 1943 issues, Tokyo: Ministry of Finance.

There are some documents indicating that long-term production plans and the short-term Material Mobilization Plan were drawn up for China Proper as for Japan and Manchuria.[10] However, it is questionable that those plans were strictly implemented, because the Imperial Army occupied only small areas around major cities and trunk railways, and the economies of these areas heavily depended upon the economies in the huge areas administered by the Chinese Communist Party and the Chinese Nationalist Party[11]. As a result, what Japan could do in China Proper was to develop strategic resources such as coal and iron ore using the affiliated companies of the NCD and the MCP in the occupied areas and to export the resources to Japan as much as possible.

Table 3.5 Companies and cooperatives affiliated with the North China Development Co., March 1944

Industry	Number of firms and cooperatives	Paid-in capital (thousand yen)	%
Total	40	1,454,738	100.0
Transportation	4	438,854	30.2
Telecommunication	1	51,250	3.5
Electricity	2	265,010	18.2
Coal mining	13	228,389	15.7
Other mining	5	71,200	4.9
Iron and steel	3	141,335	9.7
Chemical	6	83,200	5.7
Salt	2	30,500	2.1
Textile	1	60,000	4.1
Others	3	85,000	5.8

Source: 'Business report of the North China Development Co.', March 1944 issue.

Table 3.6 Companies affiliated with the Middle China Promotion Co., March 1945

Industry	Number of firms	Paid-in capital (thousand yen)	%
Total	16	416,406	100.0
Transportation	4	97,594	23.4
Electricity	1	109,440	26.3
Telecommunication	1	40,000	9.6
Coal mining	1	15,000	3.6
Other mining	1	20,000	4.8
Chemical	2	40,000	9.6
Textile	1	60,000	14.4
Others	5	34,372	8.3

Committee for Liquidation of Closed Organizations ed., Heisa Kikan to sono Tokushu Seisan (Closed Organizations and their Special Liquidation), Tokyo: Office for Liquidation of Closed Organizations regarding Overseas Activities, 1954, pp. 314–15.

Table 3.7 Direct investment to China proper from Japan

	North China	North China Development (included) (thousand yen)		Middle China (thousand yen)	Middle China Promotion (included)		South China (thousand yen)	Others
1938	159,644	75,484	(47.3)	71,861	32,914	(45.8)	0	123,107
1939	262,032	165,372	(63.1)	68,673	29,726	(43.3)	0	135,607
1940	308,075	270,390	(87.8)	74,976	54,999	(73.4)	5,982	63,644
1941	373,449	310,254	(83.1)	94,860	55,450	(58.5)	25,600	125,205
1942	434,702	371,733	(85.5)	101,207	60,231	(59.5)	72,063	176,008
1943	737,416	682,304	(92.5)	247,402	65,699	(26.6)	138,595	375,410
1944	871,358	788,357	(90.5)	341,443	201,443	(59.0)	65,000	288,001
1945	180,100	180,100	(100.0)	46,600	46,600	(100.0)	0	0
Total	3,326,776	2,843,994	(85.5)	1,044,022	547,062	(52.4)	307,240	1,286,982

Source: Y. Shibata, *Chugoku Senryochi Nikkei Kigyo no Katsudo (Activities of Japanese Firms in the Occupied Area in China)*, Tokyo: Nihonkeizai Hyoronsha, 2008, p. 72.

We can see the aggregated result of the development policy in China Proper in Table 3.3. While the total amount of the Japanese trade declined from 1936 to 1943, trade with China Proper substantially increased. Indeed, the share of China Proper in the imports went up to be as high as 48 per cent. In addition, imports to Japan from China were much larger than exports to China from Japan, which implies trade with China Proper substantially contributed to mitigating the shortage of commodities in Japan. This implies that Japan exploited China Proper through trade at the same time. Imports from China increased with respect to variety of commodities, such as grains, flours, starches and seeds, tissues and manufactures thereof and minerals and manufactures thereof (Table 3.4).

4. South East Asia

As the Sino-Japanese War reached a deadlock, the Imperial Army and the Japanese government came to have an idea to invade into South East Asia. First, they thought the United States and the UK materially supported the Chinese Nationalist Party regime from Indochina, and it was necessary to shut the route for support. Second, they thought that South East Asia was richly endowed with natural resources that were lacked in Japan, Manchuria and China Proper, such as petroleum and rubber. 'Outline of the Strategy to Deal with the Current State of Affairs Given the Changes in the Global Situation', decided at the Liaison Conference between the Government and Imperial General Headquarters on 26 July 1940, prescribed that they would use armed force in South East Asia, capturing a good opportunity. They considered that this was for constructing a new order in 'Greater East Asia' (*Daitoa*).[12]

Based on this policy, the Imperial Army invaded north Indochina in September 1940 and then south Indochina in July 1941. These actions, together with the

Tripartite Pact among Japan, Germany and Italy in October 1940, invoked strong repulsion from the United States. The United States embargoed steel scrap, which the Japanese steel industry heavily depended on at that time, in September 1940, and furthermore froze all the Japanese assets in the United States in July 1941. This implied that the capacity of the Imperial Army and Navy would gradually decline unless they found alternative sources of natural resources, particularly petroleum. Indeed, it was the freezing of the Japanese assets in the United States that made the Japanese military authorities and government determine the strategy to open hostilities with the United States and the UK.[13]

Before opening hostilities, the Liaison Conference decided the three principles for administering the occupied areas in South East Asia in November 1941: (a) restoration of security, (b) swift acquisition of important munitions resources and (c) self-sufficiency of the dispatched military forces. Also, the Imperial Army and Navy made an agreement on the jurisdiction of each occupied area.[14]

In the Pacific War, which broke out on 8 December 1941, the Imperial Army and Navy were superior until the middle of 1942, and they occupied a huge area in South East Asia, which was enough for the Japanese people to believe the Greater East Asia Co-Prosperity Sphere was being realized. Just after the attack of Pearl Harbor, the Liaison Conference decided on the Outline of Economic Policies in the South East Asia (12 December 1941). It classified the occupied areas into Region (A), which comprised the occupied areas in the narrow sense, and Region (B), where formally the independent regimes survived, namely Thailand and Indochina. Concerning Region (B), it was intended to purchase natural resources and food through raising local currencies according to the agreements between Japan and the local regimes, as before the Pacific War.[15]

In Region (A), a new development policy was formed. In this region, neither a special corporation, a conglomerate nor an investment company was founded, unlike in Manchuria and China Proper. For each development project utilizing the requisitioned assets at each site, an existing Japanese company was selected and designated as the firm in charge of development.[16] The firms in charge were selected and designated by the Sixth Committee under the Cabinet. In May 1945, 280 firms were designated as the firms in charge of development in the part of Region (A) administered by the Army, while in 1944, 102 firms were designated in the part of Region (A) administered by the Navy. They include medium-sized firms as well as large firms affiliated with major zaibatsu.[17] It implies that in the occupied areas in South East Asia, a policy to develop the local economies in a systematic way was not made, and the Japanese authorities gave priority to obtaining resources as much as possible in the short run.

The aggregate result of the development policy in South East Asia can be seen in Table 3.3. In spite of the efforts of the Imperial Army and Navy, imports to Japan from South East Asia did not increase substantially. Furthermore, imports to Japan from Region (A) declined. The basic reason for this is decline of marine shipping capacity that started just after the occupation. The capacity of marine shipping for civil use reached the peak of 2,466 thousand tons in October 1942 and declined to be 1,546 tons in December 1943 (Figure 3.1). The natural

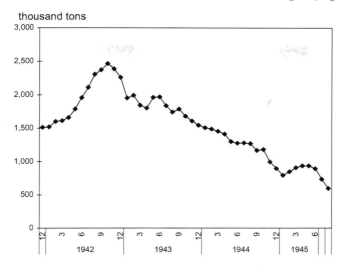

Figure 3.1 Capacity of marine shipping for civil use
Source: A. Oi, *Kaijo Goei Sen (Convoy Battle)*, Tokyo: Asahi Sonorama, 1983, pp. 382–5.

resources obtained in the occupied areas could not be utilized for the war and munitions production in Japan due to the declining limit of marine shipping capacity.

5. Concluding remarks

In the early 1930s, concern for the fragility of the economic foundation of the armed forces prevailed in the Japanese military authorities. This concern became a basic motivation of the Imperial Army to invade Manchuria and engage in the project for developing munitions and related industries there. However, the occupation of Manchuria generated in the Japanese military authorities a new ambition to obtain North China, which caused the prolonged Sino-Japanese War in 1937. Consumption of resources for the war and increasing economic sanctions by the Western countries further drove the Japanese military authorities to construct the autarky economy. The consequences were the Pacific War and the Greater East Asia Co-Prosperity Sphere.

At least for a short period during the Pacific War, Japan occupied a huge area in East and South East Asia, which was called Greater East Asia Co-Prosperity Sphere. It is remarkable that different development policies and organizations were applied across occupied areas. In Manchuria, which Japan occupied earlier, after trial and error, a system of planning and control was introduced. By this system, more or less systematic development of industries was undertaken. Meanwhile, in China Proper, the Japanese military authorities and the government prepared the statutory holding companies as channels for investment from Japan, but industrial development was basically entrusted to those holding companies and individual companies affiliated with them. Finally, in South East Asia, development was almost totally entrusted to existing Japanese firms.

Notes

1 Y. Yamamoto, *Daitoa Kyoeiken Keizaishi Kenkyu (Economic History of 'Greater East Asia Co-Prosperity Sphere')*, Nagoya: Nagoya University Press, 2011, p. 18.
2 A. Hara, 'Daitoa Kyoeiken' no Keizaiteki Jittai' (Economic Reality of the 'Great East Asia Co-prosperity Sphere'), *Tochi Seido Shigaku (Journal of Agrarian History)*, 1976, pp. 1–28.
3 They include the following studies: Y. Hikita, *'Nanpo Kyoeiken': Senji Nihon no Tounan Ajia Keizai Shihai ('South East Co-Prosperity Sphere': Administration of South East Asia Economy by Japan during the War)*, Tokyo: Nihon Keizai Hyoronsha, 1995; T. Iwatake, *Nanpo Gunsei kano Keizai Shisaku (Economic Policies under the Military Regimes in the South East Asia)*, Tokyo: T. Iwatake, 1981; T. Iwatake, *Kindai Chugoku Tsuka Toitsu Shi: Jugonen Senso niokeru Tsuka Toso (History of Currency Unification in Modern China: Currency Battle during the 15 Years War)*, Tokyo: Misuzu Shobo, 1990; H. Kobayashi, *Daitoa Kyoeiken no Keisei to Hokai (Formation and Collapse of 'Great East Asia Co-prosperity Sphere')*, Tokyo: Ochanomizu Shobo, 1975; T. Nakamura, *Senji Nihon no Kahoku Keizai Shihai (Administration of North China Economy by Japan during the War)*, Tokyo: Yamakawa Shuppansha, 1983; Y. Shibata, *Senryochi Tsuka Kin'yu Seisaku no Tenkai (Development of Monetary Policies in the Occupied Areas)*, Tokyo: Nihon Keizai Hyoronsha, 1999; Y. Shibata, *Chugoku Senryochi Nikkei Kigyo no Katsudo (Activities of Japanese Firms in the Occupied Areas in China)*, Tokyo: Nihon Keizai Hyoronsha, 2008; Y. Yamamoto, *'Manshukoku' Kerizaishi Kenkyu (Economic History of 'Manchukuo')*, Nagoya: Nagoya University Press, 2003; Y. Yamamoto, *Daitoa*.
4 This section relies on T. Okazaki, "Development and management of the Manchurian economy under Japan's Empire" in this volume.
5 T. Nakamura, *Senji Nihon no Kahoku Kieizai Shihai (Administration of the North China Economy by Japan during the War)*, Tokyo: Yamakawa Shuppansha, 1983, pp. 106–9.
6 T. Nakamura, *Senji*, pp. 89–110.
7 Ibid, pp. 115–46.
8 Y. Shibata, *Chugoku*, pp. 202–3.
9 Ibid, p. 225.
10 T. Nakamura, *Senji*, pp. 240–66, 287–300.
11 Ibid, pp. 204–9.
12 A. Hara, 'Daitoa', p. 9; Y. Yamamoto, *'Daitoa'*, pp. 17–9.
13 Y. Yamamoto, *'Daitoa'*, pp. 18–9.
14 H. Kobayashi, *'Daitoa'*, pp. 377–8.
15 A. Hara, 'Daitoa,', p. 9; Y. Yamamoto, *'Daitoa,'*, pp. 18–9.
16 A. Hara, 'Daitoa', p. 9; Y. Hikita and K. Suzuki, 'Kigyo Shinshutsu no Gaiyo' (Overview of Direct Investment) in Y. Hikita, *Nanpo*, pp. 354–8.
17 Ibid, pp. 358–62.

II
War financing

4 The German system of financing occupation

Jonas Scherner

Introduction

During World War II, Germany extracted a considerable amount of resources from occupied Europe, which normally led to a severe reduction of consumption in the respective countries.[1] For example, about one third to half of French and Dutch industrial output served to satisfy the German demand.[2] And about 14 million foreigners worked – in most cases not voluntarily – in Greater Germany during the war.[3] No doubt, without these additional resources, Germany would not have been able to fight a war for so many years against a coalition which in all relevant aspects such as access to natural resources, manpower, and industrial capacities was far superior.

For the largest part of the resources extracted from occupied Europe, the Germans paid. Given that the export earnings stemming from trade with occupied countries were low, alternative ways of financing had to be found. Indeed, most of the financial means which made these payments possible were provided by the occupied countries, especially as credits and as occupation tributes. The latter should, according to international law cover the expenses necessary for maintaining occupation troops. In order to raise all these funds, the occupied countries to varying degrees increased taxation, issued state bonds, and printed money. Each alternative presented a major problem for the occupied countries. Higher taxes drastically reduced already miserable living standards. Accordingly, borrowing or money creation were preferred but created problems for the postwar future, which could be solved either by raising taxes, by defaulting on the wartime debt, or by inflationary practices.

This chapter describes first the methods and sources which Germany employed and tapped to extract financial resources from the occupied countries and shows, as far as possible, the quantitative dimension of these different sources. In particular, it tries to shed light on an aspect of the financial exploitation which has so far eluded detailed treatment: the quantitative use the Germans made of these funds.[4] It is unclear, for example, what share was spent on the upkeep of troops stationed abroad or for the transfer of salaries of those labourers working in Germany. As a consequence, it is also unclear in how far occupation tributes were used for purposes other than maintaining occupation troops stationed in the respective countries. That the Germans misused occupation tributes for other purposes than those fixed by international law is quite clear. Yet our information about the dimensions of this misuse is only fragmentary and often contradictory. Did the spending structure change over time, and if so, why? To what extent did country-specific factors play a role, and in how far can we speak of a pan-European policy of financial exploitation? To what extent did occupation tributes constitute a net surplus of exploitation for active warfare *beyond* financing the maintenance of the respective occupation troops? These questions will be addressed, relying mostly on sources which have so far remained unused or unknown and focusing on those four occupied countries which together provided almost 80 per cent of all occupation tributes.

Sources of financial exploitation and their use

During World II, Nazi Germany extracted significant financial means from the occupied countries. The two major sources – occupation tributes and foreign credits – amounted to more than 100 billion reichsmarks, with the annual extraction steadily increasing between 1940 and 1944.[5] This was a huge sum if we consider that total German military spending between September 1939 and September 1944 amounted to about 350 billion reichsmarks.[6] Roughly a quarter of all financial means the Nazis extracted from occupied countries stemmed from credits these countries had to grant to Germany. Most of these credits were clearing credits. The clearing system was originally implemented in the early 1930s, but Nazi Germany perverted it to an exploitation tool during the war by employing two devices. First, Germany fixed the exchange rates in a way that the German currency normally was revalued compared to the currencies of the occupied countries, thus cheapening imports for Germany, and second, the Nazis forced the occupied countries to grant clearing credits.[7] A second source of foreign credit – besides clearing – stemmed from Reich treasury bonds occupied countries had to buy. This applies for some countries that were de facto part of the Reich, such as the Protectorate of Bohemia and Moravia, or those that were envisioned to become part of it, such as the Netherlands. In spite of the fact that all these funds de jure were credits foreign countries granted to Germany, there can be no doubt that they were an important exploitation device. This is not only evident by the fact that Germany dictated the terms and the amount of these loans, as mentioned, but also by the German plans that future reparations by the occupied countries would offset these commercial debts.

For which purposes were these funds stemming from foreign credits used? During the war, the German propaganda argued that these clearing deficits were caused especially by the transfer of wage payments of the foreign workforce employed in Germany.[8] This seemed to be implicitly confirmed by Germany's official trade balance figures. Between 1940 and 1944, accumulated German trade deficits amounted to only 5 billion reichsmarks – far less than the increase of Germany's foreign debts totalling about 29 billion, of which 19 billion were made up by clearing debts. Yet archival sources show that only a small fraction of these debts can be explained by wage transfers: less than 3 billion reichsmarks were spent via clearing for this purpose in spite of the huge inflow of foreign workforce from occupied countries.[9] This was caused by the fact that only a comparatively small part of the civilian workers' wage transfer was financed via clearing. Rather, alternative financial sources were employed to a much larger extent. For example, in the case of Italian civilian labourers after the German occupation of Italy, the Italian state budget had to finance the wage transfer.[10] Instead, the major purpose of foreign credits was to finance German trade deficits. As a recent paper shows, German imports were dramatically underreported in the official statistics, mainly because the customs officers for several reasons did not collect data for all import categories.[11] For example, most goods imported for the *Wehrmacht*, such as armaments, were not included in the official import statistics.

Occupation tributes offered by far the biggest source of financial exploitation. Immediately after the invasions, and when the fighting was still ongoing, the financial needs of German troops in the respective countries were met through the occupation currency of the *Wehrmacht*, the RKK vouchers (*Reichskreditkassenscheine*).[12] Yet usually, briefly after the end of fighting, the occupying forces would begin to receive funds in the country's currency – so-called occupation tributes – via special accounts for the German occupation forces, which were set up at the occupied nation's central bank – as the *Banque de France*, the *Nederlandsche Bank*, the National Bank of Belgium, the *Norges Bank*, or in Eastern Europe, at new co-opted central banks, as the *Emissionsbank in Polen*.[13] These occupation tributes were in some countries formally – totally or partially – credits granted by the respective central banks to Germany. In some countries, RKK vouchers ceased to be a legal payment instrument after a regular basis for occupation tributes was settled, such as in Norway.[14] Yet in most of the other countries, they continued to be valid, even if the Germans did no longer issue them. International law served as the basis of the imposition of occupation tributes for the support of the respective occupation troops. According to the Hague Convention, occupation tribute was only to be used to finance the needs of the occupation troops.[15] The amount of the occupation tribute each country had to pay was fixed by the Supreme Command of the German Armed Forces (*Oberkommando der Wehrmacht*, abbreviated OKW) as the payee of these means and the Reich finance ministry (RFM) due to its financial expertise. Over time, the amount of occupation tributes occupied countries had to pay for a given period changed – increasing in some countries, more or less stagnating in other countries, but even decreasing in some cases.[16] The reasons for these different developments will be discussed in more detail in what follows.

Before discussing the appropriation structure of these occupation costs on the basis of country data, some additional expenses and sources of financial exploitation besides forced foreign credits and occupation credits should be briefly mentioned to complete the picture. These include the accommodation benefits, which were far smaller than the occupation tributes, the confiscation of Jewish property, and what might be termed indirect occupation costs.[17] Of these additional expenses, the indirect occupation costs were probably the most important;

yet quantification on a country basis is still lacking. What we know is that they could differ substantially from country to country with regard to the purposes to be financed.[18] In the case of some countries such as Italy, they included, as mentioned, the wage transfer of civilian workers in Germany, in others, such as Norway, the financing of railway services used by the *Wehrmacht*.[19]

The question for which purposes the Germans used the occupation tributes is still more complicated than providing an overview about the use of the foreign debts. This can be explained first by the fact that the Germans themselves had no clear idea during the first war years to what extent the occupation tributes were used for the different spending categories, such as military pay or construction. At the beginning, when the German authorities fixed the occupation tributes, they assessed this amount rather roughly on the basis of the actual troop number in the respective county.[20] Yet troop numbers fluctuated; and especially early on, occupation expenditures were, with few exceptions, not subject to control with the effect that each unit took its current assets at its own convenience and need from the occupation account.[21] Very often, expenses were for purposes other than genuine occupation tasks, such as the purchase of huge amounts of champagne or the construction of hunting lodges for local commanders.

Over time, some control measures and checks could be implemented, which provides us with better information about the spending structure. The implementation of these control measures was, however, a slow and incremental process that did not take place simultaneously in all occupied countries. One motive for this changing attitude of German authorities towards spending control was caused by the fear of inflation in occupied countries.[22] Especially the RFM feared that noncontrollable inflation in these countries could result in an economic collapse which would hinder a policy of long-term exploitation and reparation transfer after the war.[23] In addition, rising prices abroad endangered in a system of fixed exchange rates Germany's attempts to contain inflation at home by way of imports. The alternative – especially applied in the case of goods imported for private households – the price-adjustment process (*Preisausgleich*), which covered the difference between the higher import price and the lower price of sale in Germany through subsidies, increased the German budget deficits.[24] Moreover, the *Reichsbank* recognized the dire consequences for Germany if it were surrounded by nations with collapsed currencies.[25]

As one important factor responsible for price increases in occupied countries, the RFM identified – besides measures to combat the monetary causes of inflation – the excessive German demand.[26] In the eyes of the RFM, the restriction of German demand was imperative and necessitated the planning and control of the expenditures. A first source of German demand, which the RFM at least partially was able to restrict early on, concerned the personal expenditures of the soldiers stationed in occupied countries. Personal expenditures included the military pay and *Feldpostüberweisungen*. In the case of the latter, the soldier would deposit a certain amount of reichsmarks in a German state account and, once abroad, draw it out in foreign currency from the occupation cost account. These personal expenditures amounted to a considerable share – around one quarter of all occupation costs expenditures – in many countries. Immediately after the victory in the West, the supreme command of the *Wehrmacht* had planned to increase the military pay of the occupation troops.[27] The occupation administration in some countries, for example in the Netherlands, in Belgium, and in Norway, even offered special exchange rates for soldiers which were more favourable than the official one.[28] Yet the RFM, assisted by the *Reichsbank* and the Reich Ministry of economics, opposed this policy and was in some instances able to block the attempts to increase the amount of money available for personal expenditures. Emphasizing the threat of inflation such a policy would produce, the RFM pushed through the creation of an intradepartmental committee, consisting of representatives of the Reich chancellery, the OKW, and the RFM, in late 1940.[29] From this point in time onwards, changes of the regular military pay in occupied countries were based on suggestions of this committee, which periodically evaluated the price structure and the purchase power of the reichsmark in the different countries. Military pay was only increased when the purchase power noticeably decreased in the respective country.

Still more complicated was the restriction of impersonal *Wehrmacht* expenditures. It seems that before 1942, tighter planning and rationing of expenditures had been introduced only in the Netherlands.[30] This situation changed in 1942, after the occupation authorities in some occupied countries and the RFM had started to pressure the *Wehrmacht* to introduce a certain discipline with regard to their expenditures.[31] Behind this insistence stood the danger of imminent inflation and the perception that this was to a significant extent caused by the generous spending of occupation tributes. This perception was correct given that the monthly expenditures in 1941, in the case of most of the countries occupied during the early period of the war, were significantly higher than in 1940, even necessitating the increase of the monthly occupation tributes in some countries, such as Belgium.[32] Finally, the joint forces of the RFM and the occupation authorities, especially those in France, succeeded insofar as the supreme command of the *Wehrmacht* responded with ordinances at the turn of the year 1941/1942 which introduced rationing and permit-based allocation of financial means in the occupied areas. In addition, the occupation forces now had to control ex post whether funds had actually been used for their designated purposes. Yet it seems that this system was implemented rather slowly. It also gave neither occupation administrations nor the respective military offices comprehensive veto rights with regard to expenses they considered useless for occupation purposes. The final decision rested with the OKW. Only slowly were the veto rights of the local military administration widened with regard to some expense classes. For this reason, the OKW announced in fall 1942 that so-called steering directives (*Steuerungserlasse*) would be sent out briefly to set down a uniform regulatory system for the allocation of occupation costs. This regulatory system applied to all, including civilian, offices that drew on occupation tributes in the occupied territories. This change, however slow, in the attitude with regard to the occupation costs expenditure owed to the OKW's increasing awareness the steady rise of occupation cost expenses contributed to the inflationary pressure which in turn increasingly endangered the financing of the essential needs of the occupation forces.[33] Mainly because of this new regulatory framework do we have information that allows us to make, often by using additional information, some rough estimates about the spending structure of occupation tributes for some countries under German rule.

The first example we are going to discuss is France, which contributed roughly 40 per cent of all occupation tributes Germany received.[34] The use of the French occupation tribute has only recently been identified.[35] The central question was to identify the share of expenses, which did not serve occupation purposes at all, and to determine whether and why this share changed over time.

Table 4.1 presents some of the results of these estimates. It shows that during 1941 and 1944, the majority of the occupation tributes were not used for genuine occupation purposes. Notice that the term 'genuine occupation purposes' is narrower than what the Germans themselves defined as such. According to the German definition, only purchases of goods transported to the Reich, which were financed by drawing on the occupation account, were defined as 'nonoccupation costs', that is as expenditures not necessary for occupation purposes. Such expenditures were made in France in order to finance armament purchases and all of so-called official black-market purchases by German authorities, which especially in 1942 and 1943 bought considerable amounts of textiles and raw materials first of all in Western Europe.[36] In France, such ways of import financing made up about 8 billions reichsmarks or more than a quarter of all occupation tributes.[37] Yet the German definition of expenditures for genuine occupation purposes included further expenses which in a strict sense cannot be considered 'normal' occupation expenses. Such expenses included the very substantial expenditures for fortifications, especially the Atlantic wall, which increased significantly from 1942 on.[38] A further important expenditure for nonoccupation purposes stemmed from the fact that not all soldiers stationed in France were, in the strict sense, occupation troops. This applies not only to the navy and air force units which were involved in attacks against Britain but also to units that in the course of the war in the East were continuously being newly formed or refreshed in France, and who, before being (re-)deployed, were almost completely outfitted there. For instance, 30 divisions consisting of 540,000 soldiers were sporadically stationed in France during the first six months of 1943 and afterwards sent to the Eastern front.

Table 4.1 Occupation tribute's spending structure in France, 1941–1944 (% of total occupation tributes)

Expenses for actual occupation purposes		45
Nonoccupation expenditures	Waging war outside of France	30
	Construction	20
	Purchases for German consumers	5

Source: Boldorf/Scherner, 'France's occupation costs', pp. 303–5.

In addition, genuine nonoccupation expenditures which were part of occupation-related purposes according to the German definition were made via the RKK. As mentioned, the RKK vouchers had ceased to be a legal payment instrument in some countries after a regular basis for occupation tributes was settled, such as in Norway.[39] Yet in most of the other countries where regular occupation tributes were settled, they continued to be valid, even once the Germans no longer issued them in these countries. RKK were only issued in newly occupied countries and especially in Eastern Europe in the case of the front troops in order to provide the troops with means of payment. Yet in some of countries where RKK were no longer issued, such as Belgium, the National banks were obliged to accept them, implying that the more RKK had to be redeemed, the more occupation funds additional to the regular occupation tribute amount had to be financed by the occupied country.[40] In France it was fixed that RKK vouchers had to be redeemed via the occupation account, in which the French state had to pay in an *ex ante* fixed sum for a given time period.[41] The more RKK vouchers were redeemed in this country, the smaller grew the funds available for other purposes. After the implementation of the rationing of occupation funds in 1942, RKK especially from the Eastern theatre flowed into all occupied countries in which RKK were still valid. For example, troop units who were sent for refreshment from the Eastern front to Western Europe transferred these RKK vouchers in order to purchase goods which could not be bought in the depleted East. In addition, soldiers transferred RKK vouchers to be spent for their private consumption needs or in order to buy goods for their relatives.[42] The transfer of RKK from one country to another was illegal, yet the German authorities were not willing to combat this behaviour by means of stronger controls and firmer punishment.[43] The dimension of these purchases became significant: in France, these expenses made with RKK vouchers, which had nothing to do with genuine occupation needs, amounted to up to 17 per cent of all occupation expenses in the second half of 1943.[44]

Finally, a further source of non-occupation–related expenses resulted from the fact that the amount of money available for a German soldier stationed in occupied countries was rather generous. Background of this was that the OKW and the Four Year Plan authority desired a policy that did not only allow a soldier to 'live well' in the occupied areas but also to buy goods in occupied countries to be shipped to his family at home.[45] This 'live well' policy contributed also to the fact that the OKW and the Four Year Plan authority remained at first reluctant to control and to punish the illegal influx of RKK more strictly.[46] In addition, this policy led to the creation of a second legal source of access to the currency of the respective country besides their regular military pay, the abovementioned *Feldpostüberweisungen*, a transfer of reichsmarks which could be exchanged via the occupation account into Franc. Shortly after the victory in the West, these transfer allowances were raised from an initial 50 reichsmarks monthly to 100 reichsmarks in all occupied countries.[47] This was a huge amount given that the average gross salary of a German blue-collar worker in the metalworking industry, that is an industry, which paid clearly higher wages than in the industrial-sector average, amounted to about 200 reichsmarks per month, and given that the regular military pay for a private first class (*Gefreiter*) amounted to 36 reichsmarks per month.[48] And one can assume that many soldiers at least partially exploited these official transfer possibilities since the accumulated excess purchase power in the Reich – income that could not be spent due to rationing – amounted to 23 billion reichsmarks in 1940.[49] This is also shown by the fact that besides *Feldpostüberweisungen*, additional reichsmark transfers occurred (which were exchanged on black markets), which were officially forbidden but tolerated in practice.[50] Given this attitude, it is also not surprising that attempts of the occupation authorities in some countries to restrict occupation forces in their spending of their military pay in this country were blocked by the *Reichsbank*, which explicitly stated that such a measure would foster the inflation pressure in Germany herself.[51] Unfortunately, we do not have exact information on how much of the personal expenditures were used for purchases shipped to Germany. However, from the considerations made earlier, it follows that the share of the nonoccupation expenditures on total occupation tribute expenditure (in the following abbreviated as NO/OT) reported in Table 4.1 show only a lower limit of the actual NO/OT because these soldiers' purchases are not included.

In sum, Germany clearly violated international law in France by spending occupation funds for purposes which had nothing to do with occupation purposes. Interestingly, the German spending behaviour violated also – at least to a certain extent – a principle the Germans themselves had set at the beginning of the war: the principle that payments of occupied territories for *Wehrmacht* units outside of the occupied areas, so-called nonoccupation costs, should not be settled through occupation tributes but through clearing or other forms of foreign credits to Germany.[52] There are several explanations why the Germans ignored their own principle. One explanation is that the Germans tried to avoid too sharp an increase of their clearing debts.[53] The RFM was the institution which was especially eager to shift expenses from the clearing system to the occupation costs in order to restrict the increase of Germany's foreign debt, which at least theoretically would have to have been repaid later on.[54] The OKW first did not protest because it took time before the occupying forces realized that the real exploitation of any country had its limits and could not be augmented at will by increasing occupation tributes. In the early years of the war, the belief that 'costs do not play a role' dominated the attitude of the military. A further important reason for violating the principle was the 'live well' policy pursued by the OKW and the Four Year Plan authority.[55]

The NO/OT ratio changed in France, however, over time, as Table 4.2 illustrates with a peak in 1942 and 1943. This was – from a point of view of the funds available – only possible because up to the end of 1941, the French paid more occupation tribute than the Germans were able to spend, implying a huge surplus on the occupation account, and later, by the end of 1942, by the increase of the occupation costs from 15 to 25 million reichsmarks per day.[56] Yet the NO/OT-ratio decreased slightly during the last period of the occupation of France. This occurred because the OKW became more aware that the use of occupation funds for other than occupation purposes, financing German imports

Table 4.2 Troop size, nonoccupation expenditures, and total occupation costs expenditures in France, 1941–1944

	(I) NO/OT	(II) Troops stationed in France	(III) Total average daily expenses (m. RM)
1941	~ 40%	~ 600,000	14
1942	~ 60%	~ 500,000	21.5
1943	~ 60%	~ 670,000	26.5
1944	< 60%	~ 800,000	27.7

Source: Boldorf/Scherner, 'France's occupation costs', pp. 302–5.

for example, threatened the fulfilment of occupation troops' demands in France, especially in the light of an expected invasion which entailed an increased number of troops and huge construction efforts, especially in order to build the Atlantic wall. As a consequence, the armed forces became more restrictive regarding the access of other German authorities and troops not stationed in France to the occupation funds.[57] This led to a stop of the official black market purchases by German agencies in spring 1943. By the end of the year, the use of the RKK, which had to a certain extent offset the elimination of official black-market purchases via the allocation of occupation funds, was forbidden in France. The military administration in France had already tried to push this measure through earlier on, following the example of Belgium, where the same misuse of the RKK had occurred and where they had been invalidated in summer 1942; yet, probably because France due to her size was far more important, these attempts were blocked by several central German authorities for different reasons and remained unsuccessful for more than one and a half years.[58]

France was not the only country in which the Germans clearly violated international law with regard to the use of the occupation costs. We are able to roughly estimate the NO/OT ratios in the case of two further countries, namely Norway and the Netherlands, for which more or less precise information about the structure of occupation expenditures is available. By far the best data with regard to time coverage and expenditure categories are available in the case of Norway. As in France, no control of the *Wehrmacht* expenditures took place in Norway during the first two years of the occupation.[59] This changed with the decision discussed earlier to ration the occupation costs funds. In addition, because of the exaggerated spending of the *Wehrmacht*, a committee had been appointed in 1941 which had to survey the expenditures between October 1940 and May 1941. By using these data and relying on further considerations, the former head of the finance department of the German occupation administration in Norway, Hans Claussen Korff, was able to break down the structure of the occupation expenditures in Norway.[60] Relying on the results of these estimates and calculations, we can assess the structure of the occupation expenditures, as shown in Table 4.3. Notice that as in France, we have to assume that not all troops stationed in Norway were necessary for the occupation. In Norway,

48 *Jonas Scherner*

Table 4.3 Occupation tributes' spending structure in Norway (%), 1940–1944

Expenses for genuine occupation purposes[a]		27
Nonoccupation expenditures	Waging war[b]	16–24
	Construction[c]	46
	Purchases for German consumers[d]	3–11

Sources and notes:

[a]Expenditures for genuine occupation purposes are estimated to be 50 per cent of the residuum between total expenditure minus construction. For the figures in current prices, see Riksarkivet Olso, Privatarkivet 951, box 2, Hans Claussen Korff, Norwegens Wirtschaft im Mahlstrom der Okkupation (unpublished manuscript), II, p. 251. For a justification of this procedure, see text.
[b]Waging war purposes include the expenditures of the *Wehrmacht* exceeding a force of 200,000 men minus the purchases soldiers made for their relatives, and excluding construction expenditures. For the figures in current prices, see ibid, p. 251.
[c]Ibid, p. 251.
[d]For purchases soldiers made for their relatives, only a lower limit and an upper limit can be estimated. These estimates rely on the information provided by Korff, according to whom only one third of military pay plus transfer possibilities was used for soldiers' own consumption during the first two years of the occupation (Ibid, p. 321), and the annual figures for personal expenditures (Ibid, pp. 244, 249, 251). Applying this share for the whole occupation period implies calculating an upper limit, because purchase possibilities were reduced during the second half of the war, and the transfer of reichsmarks from Germany was suspended. The lower limit estimate assumes that the soldiers were only able to make purchases for their relatives during the first to occupation years.

too, troops were stationed for offensive military operations because the country served as submarine bases for operations against the Allies. In contrast to France, no significant amount of troops was sent to Norway for refreshment purposes. Yet, in contrast to France, a significant amount of troops was stationed in Norway for defensive military operations from the beginning: their sheer presence was to deter the Allies from an invasion.[61] And by the end of the war, troops were involved in the fighting against Russia in Northern Norway. The dimension of troops of a defensive operational character is shown by the evolution of the numbers of soldiers stationed in Norway: whereas the number of troops amounted to about 200,000 in late 1940, it had been increased to about 400,000 to 450,000 one year later, that is the point in time when Hitler made the decision to heavily invest in fortifications and increase the number of soldiers in order to be prepared for a potential Allied invasion.[62] One could thus assume that the 200,000 soldiers stationed in Norway before Hitler feared an invasion were sufficient for genuine occupation purposes. If we consider this, we have to conclude that roughly half of the *Wehrmacht* expenditures for maintaining troops (as military pay and feeding) have to be considered nonoccupation expenditures. The lion's share of these nonoccupation expenses, however, were not due to these operational troops but to the gigantic construction projects carried out in the country, most of which stemmed from infrastructure projects whose purpose was the long-term incorporation of Norway in a Germanic empire and from fortifications. The significance of purchases made for German consumers, made exclusively by German soldiers, and which were financed via *Feldpostüberweisungen* and military pay, remained comparatively low. From all these considerations and estimates follows that the total share of the nonoccupation expenditures on total occupation costs expenditure was even bigger in Norway than it was in France as shown in Table 4.3.

Notice that these percentages refer – as in the case of France – to values expressed in current prices. Yet price increases during the war were uneven with regard to the single spending categories as shown in Table 4.3. Soldiers had to buy predominantly on black markets, implying that the share of consumer purchases in real prices on the real value of occupation costs would probably have been significantly lower. Moreover, the prices the *Wehrmacht* had to pay increased more significantly than the price index in the Norwegian economy as a whole.[63]

The next country for which the NO/OT ratio can be roughly estimated is the Netherlands. The Netherlands had to pay two different types of occupation tributes: a 'normal' occupation tribute from 1940 on and, from the second year of occupation on, as the only one of all occupied countries, a so-called external occupation tribute, which was defined as a tribute which should allegedly cover occupation-caused expenditures occurring outside occupied countries, such as the benefits for families of soldiers stationed abroad.[64] Yet these external occupation payments, which comprised up to one quarter of all Dutch occupation payments, were used for nonoccupation purposes such as imports and especially the financing of the 'official' black-market purchases by German agencies.[65] A significant share of the internal occupation tributes, too, was used for nonoccupation purposes. The lower limit of this share can be estimated by drawing on the information that about a quarter of these expenses was used for personal expenditures.[66] If we combine this information with an early *ex ante* calculation made by the *Wehrmacht* about the structure of the expenditures for occupation troops which stated that 40 per cent of all expenses necessary for occupation troops consisted of personal expenditures, we have to conclude that about 36 per cent of the internal occupation tribute paid by the Netherlands must have been used for nonoccupation purposes.[67] From this it follows, taking into account the use of the external occupation tribute, that roughly 50 per cent of the total Dutch occupation tributes were nonoccupation costs. It is clear that this is a lower limit of the actual value: first, it is evident that not all soldiers stationed in the Netherlands served occupation purposes. Second, military pay and transfer of money to soldiers from Germany which together constitute personal expenditures, had – as described – partly the function of enabling the soldiers to purchase goods for their families in Germany in order to relax the German consumption supply. Hence it seems plausible to assume that a similar share as in Norway and in France was also used in the Netherlands for nonoccupation purposes.[68] The same, too, may have been applied in the case of Italy. One third of all occupation tribute alone in 1944 was spent on financing German imports.[69] In addition, we know that most troops in Italy were involved in defensive military operations and that huge construction efforts – financed with occupation tributes – were carried out in Italy.

However, it would be misleading to assume that similar high NO/OT ratios always applied in the case of other occupied countries for which information regarding the use for nonoccupation purposes is scattered. In the case of Poland, for example, *Wehrmacht* expenditures far exceeded the occupation tributes the Germans received.[70] This implies that the additional expenses had to be financed via credits. For 1943, information about the structure of *Wehrmacht* expenditure in Poland is available for the first half of the year, showing that 35 per cent was spent for financing purchases which were shipped abroad.[71] Yet only half of the *Wehrmacht* expenditures in this year were financed with the help of occupation tributes. Even assuming, what seems to be plausible seeing that Poland was a backward area of the Eastern front, that not all soldiers stationed in Poland had genuine occupation tasks, it does not seem probable that the Polish NO/OT ratio reached a level similar to those in the countries mentioned, if it was positive at all. The Belgian case, to give a further example, reveals, too, that a generalization of the French, Italian, Dutch and Norwegian case results may be misleading, because in Belgium, more and more expenditures were shifted from 1942 on to clearing credits, with the effects that annual occupation tributes were decreasing.[72] By the end of the occupation, the amount of money extracted from Belgium via clearing credits amounted to 75 per cent of the occupation tributes – a share far higher than in France, where the respective ratio amounted to 25 per cent. No doubt, from the perspective of the occupied country, it made no difference with which tool it was financially exploited. Yet in order to assess the net contribution of the exploitation beyond financing genuine occupation tasks, this difference matters.

Finally, even if it is misleading to generalize the experiences of the Netherlands, Norway, France, and Italy, we are able to assess a lower limit of the occupation tributes' net effect on the German war effort. This assessment takes into account that the absolute contribution of these four countries had a share of almost 80 per cent of all occupation tributes Germany received.[73] If we assume that the occupation costs in all remaining countries at least sufficed to finance the genuine occupation tasks in these countries, we have to conclude that at least roughly half of all occupation tributes contributed to the German war effort in a strict sense, an amount even exceeding the contribution from foreign credits.

Conclusion

The chapter has shown that Germany applied similar measures to financially exploit the occupied countries. The aim was, not surprisingly, to shift the burden of waging war as far as possible from Germany to the countries under German rule. Nevertheless, the effects of this financial exploitation differed from country to country. This does not only apply to the ratio between occupation tributes and credits these countries had to grant but also with regard to other characteristics such as the per-capita burden of these countries.[74] In addition, the use of the financial funds Germany extracted differed significantly between the occupied countries and over time. This was partially caused by the strategic location of the countries and by a learning process as well as by political considerations, as the changing access to occupation funds in France has demonstrated. In sum, we can see that there was no coherent financial exploitation policy regarding the occupied countries in the sense that the same principles were applied at the same point in time or in a similar situation. Still, what was coherent in most countries is that the Germans clearly and consciously violated international law regarding the use of occupation tributes and tried to extract as much as possible.

Notes

1 For an estimate about the size of external resources in percentage of Germany's national income, see M. Harrison, 'Resource Mobilization for World War II: the U.S.A., U.K., U.S.S.R., and Germany, 1938–1944', *Economic History Review*, 1988, vol. 41, pp. 189. For the effects on the consumption within the occupied countries, see H. Klemann/S. Kudryashow, *Occupied Economies. An Economic History of Nazi Occupied Europe, 1939–1945*, London: Berg, 2012, pp. 373–405.
2 Klemann/Kudryashow, *Occupied Economies*, p. 92; M. Mazower, *Hitler's Empire. Nazi Rule in Occupied Europe*, London: Allen Lane, 2008, p. 267.
3 M. Spoerer/J. Fleischhacker, 'Forced Labourers in Nazi Germany: Categories, Numbers, and Survivors', *The Journal of Interdisciplinary History*, 2002, vol. 33, pp. 169–204.
4 R.J. Overy, 'The Economy of the German "New Order"', in: Idem/G. Otto/J. Houwink ten Cate (eds.), *Die 'Neuordnung' Europas. NS-Wirtschaftspolitik in den besetzten Gebieten*, Berlin: Metropol, 1997, p. 17.
5 For the data and the following, see J. Scherner, The Institutional Architecture of Financing German Exploitation: Principles, Conflicts and Results, in: J. Scherner/E. White (eds.), *Paying for Hitler's War: The Consequences of Nazi Hegemony for Europe*, Cambridge University Press (forthcoming).
6 BArch R 2/24250, Overview on the financing of the last five years of war, 6 October 1944.
7 The revaluation of the reichsmark was, however, not always the case. In the case of Denmark, the currency was even devalued by 8 per cent in 1941; see BArch R 901/68939, Meetings of the *Handelspolitischer Ausschuss*, 7 March, 6 and 14 November 1941, fol. 198–9, 267, 270–1.
8 For the following, see J. Scherner, 'Der deutsche Importboom während des Zweiten Weltkriegs. Neue Ergebnisse zur Struktur der Ausbeutung des besetzten Europas auf der Grundlage einer Neuschätzung der deutschen Handelsbilanz', *Historische Zeitschrift*, 2012, vol. 294, pp. 80–2.
9 BArch R 184/186, file note, 20 December 1946, pp. 8–9.
10 For further examples, see Scherner, 'The Institutional Architecture'.
11 For the following and for details, see Scherner, 'Importboom'.
12 For details about the RKK vouchers, see G. Aly, *Hitlers Volksstaat. Raub, Rassenkrieg und nationaler Sozialismus*, Frankfurt am Main: Fischer, 2005, pp. 103–7; R. Lemkin, *Axis Rule in Occupied Europe*, Washington: Carnegie Endowment for International Peace, 1944, pp. 51–2.
13 For details on occupation tributes in the respective countries, see C. Buchheim, 'Die besetzten Länder, Die besetzten Länder im Dienste der deutschen Kriegswirtschaft während des Zweiten Weltkriegs. Ein Bericht der Forschungsstelle für Wehrwirtschaft', *Vierteljahrshefte für Zeitgeschichte*, 1986, vol. 34, pp. 117–45.
14 Riksarkivet Olso, Privatarkivet 951, box 2, Hans Claussen Korff, Norwegens Wirtschaft im Mahlstrom der Okkupation (unpublished manuscript), II, pp. 198–9.

15 Scherner, 'The Institutional Architecture'.
16 Buchheim, 'Die besetzten Länder'.
17 On confiscation of Jewish property, see Aly, *Hitlers Volksstaat*, pp. 212–6, 252, 281–97, 311–4. For data on accommodation benefits in the case of France and Belgium, see BArch R 3101/32287, Sixth and Final Report of the German Economic Delegation Wiesbaden and the Reich Delegate to the French Government for Economic and Financial Questions for the period 1 July 1943–17 August 1944, Salzburg, 15 December 1944; BArch R 29/3, Belgian *Militärbefehlshaber* to Military High Command (*Oberkommando des Heeres*), 1 December 1941, fol. 39–55.
18 For further information on indirect occupation costs, see Scherner, 'The Institutional Architecture'.
19 Riksarkivet Olso, Privatarkivet 951, box 2, Hans Claussen Korff, Norwegens Wirtschaft im Mahlstrom der Okkupation (unpublished manuscript), II, p., 247–8. For further examples, see Scherner, 'The Institutional Architecture'.
20 M. Boldorf/J. Scherner, 'France's Occupation Costs and the War in the East: The Contribution to the German War Economy, 1940–1944', *Journal of Contemporary History*, 2012, vol. 47, p. 296.
21 See, for the following, ibid, pp. 307–8; Scherner, 'The Institutional Architecture'.
22 Early warnings, for instance in BArch R 2/14555, RFM, note to the files, 19 December 1940, fol. 152–7.
23 BArch R 2/24944, note for the Reich finance minister, 15.7.1942. Also Aly is critical with regard to Schwerin von Krosigk's role. Aly, *Hitlers Volksstaat*, pp. 346–7.
24 For details about the *Preisausgleich*, see e.g. J. Scherner, 'Europas Beitrag zu Hitlers Krieg. Die Verlagerung von Industrieaufträgen der Wehrmacht in die besetzten Gebiete und ihre Bedeutung für die deutsche Rüstung im Zweiten Weltkrieg', in: C. Buchheim/M. Boldorf (eds.), *Europäische Volkswirtschaften unter deutscher Hegemonie*, Munich: Oldenbourg Verlag, 2012, pp. 77–8.
25 Scherner, 'The Institutional Architecture'.
26 Ibid. In order to combat the monetary causes of inflation, the RFM forced the national administrations to reform their tax systems. See, for example, Boldorf/Scherner, France's occupation costs, pp. 311–12; so-called Currency commissioners at the National Banks were appointed, which should foster the use of the capital markets for financing the needs of the occupant and implemented the confiscation of so-called Jewish property. Aly, *Hitlers Volksstaat*, pp. 212–6, 252, 281–97, 311–4, 331.
27 BArch R 2/14555, RFM, note to the files, 30 August 1940, fol. 17–8.
28 BArch R 2/14555, RFM, note to the files, 4 September 1940, fol. 34–6.
29 For the following, see Scherner, 'The Institutional Architecture'.
30 BArch R 29/2, note, 3.9.1941, fol. 84.
31 For the following, see Scherner, 'The Institutional Architecture'.
32 About the increase of occupation tributes in Belgium (1941), see PA AA R 105284, note, 11.3.1942.
33 BArch R 2/14522, OKW to RFM, 25.9.1942, fol. 14.
34 For data on total occupation tributes, see Scherner, 'Importboom', p. 80; for the amount paid by France, see BArch R 3101/32287, Sixth and Final Report of the German Economic Delegation Wiesbaden and the Reich Delegate to the French Government for Economic and Financial Questions for the period July 1, 1943–August 17, 1944, Salzburg, 15 December 1944.
35 For the following, see Boldorf/Scherner, France's occupation cost, pp. 303–5.
36 For an estimate about armament purchases in occupied countries, see Scherner, 'Europas Beitrag', p. 81.

37 Calculated on the basis of the revised import data; data about armament imports from France, and black market purchases given in Scherner, 'Importboom', p. 112; Scherner, 'Europas Beitrag', p. 81; Buchheim, 'Die besetzten Länder', p. 130.
38 For the following, see Boldorf/Scherner, 'France's occupation costs', pp. 303–5.
39 Riksarkivet Olso, Privatarkivet 951, box 2, Hans Claussen Korff, Norwegens Wirtschaft im Mahlstrom der Okkupation (unpublished manuscript), II, pp. 198–9.
40 H. van der Wee/M. Verbreyt, *A Small Nation in the Turmoil of the Second World War. Money, Finance and Occupation (Belgium, its Enemies, its Friends, 1939–1945)*, Leuven: Leuven University Press, 2009, pp. 141–2.
41 See e.g. Boldorf/Scherner, 'France's Occupation Costs', p. 295.
42 For France: Boldorf/Scherner, 'France's Occupation Costs', p. 306; for Greece: BArch R 2/14569, RFM, note, 29 August 1941, fol. 64–5; for the Netherlands: BArch R 29/3, Report of the Administration Council of the Occupation Banks (*Reichskreditkassen*), 22 June 1942, fol. 217–9, for Belgium: Van der Wee/Verbreyt, *A Small Nation*, p. 290.
43 Scherner, 'The Institutional Architecture'.
44 Calculated on the basis of the information given by Boldorf/Scherner, 'France's Occupation Costs', pp. 302, 310.
45 For further motives, see Scherner, 'The Institutional Architecture'.
46 For further motives, see Boldorf/Scherner, 'France's Occupation Costs', p. 311.
47 Scherner, 'The Institutional Architecture'.
48 *Statistisches Jahrbuch für das Deutsche Reich 1941/42*, Berlin 1943, p. 382; BArch R 2 Anh./84, fol. 189.
49 J. Scherner, 'Bericht zur deutschen Wirtschaftslage 1943/44. Eine Bilanz des Reichsministeriums für Rüstung und Kriegsproduktion über die Entwicklung der deutschen Kriegswirtschaft bis Sommer 1944', *Vierteljahrshefte für Zeitgeschichte*, 2007, vol. 55, pp. 499–546, here p. 544.
50 Scherner, 'The Institutional Architecture'.
51 For the case of occupied Poland, see BArch R 2/14578, Deutsche Reichsbank 14.12.1940, fol. 110–2.
52 On this principle, see Scherner, 'The Institutional Architecture'.
53 For details see Scherner, 'Importboom', p. 98.
54 See, for the General Government, BArch-MA, RW 7/1710a, note, 22 February 1944, fol. 211–3.
55 For further motives, see Scherner, 'The Institutional Architecture'.
56 For details, see Boldorf/Scherner, 'France's Occupation Costs'.
57 For the following, see Boldorf/Scherner, 'France's occupation costs'.
58 Van der Wee/Verbreyt, *A Small Nation*, p. 290.
59 Riksarkivet Olso, Privatarkivet 951, box 2, Hans Claussen Korff, Norwegens Wirtschaft im Mahlstrom der Okkupation (unpublished manuscript), II, p. 246.
60 Ibid, pp. 244–51.
61 About Hitler's deep-seated concern that the Allied forces might invade Norway following the British commando raids on the Norwegian coast in 1941, see e.g. H. Espeli, 'Economic Consequences of the German Occupation of Norway, 1940–1945', *Scandinavian Journal of History*, 2013, vol. 38, p. 507.
62 For data about troop size in Norway, see Riksarkivet Olso, Privatarkivet 951, box 2, Hans Claussen Korff, Norwegens Wirtschaft im Mahlstrom der Okkupation (unpublished manuscript), II, p. 227.
63 Ibid, pp. 253–64.
64 Buchheim, 'Die besetzten Länder', p. 134. For the distinction between internal and external occupation costs, see for example Boldorf/Scherner, 'France's occupation costs', p. 296.

65 Buchheim, 'Die besetzten Länder', pp. 135–6.
66 Ibid.
67 About this *Wehrmacht* estimate, see BArch R 2/14566, Note of the files, 16 August 1940, fol. 117.
68 Götz Aly states that the respective share amounted to 60 per cent, however, without revealing his estimate; see Aly, *Hitlers Volksstaat*, p. 167.
69 BArch R 3/3026, Overview on the monthly payments for the Wehrmacht orders (in millions Lt.), 10 December 1944, fol. 118.
70 In the three budget years starting from April 1941 on, the Germans received 2,500 millions Zloty of occupation tributes. Buchheim, 'Die besetzten Länder', p. 127. Yet the *Wehrmacht* expenditure in this period was roughly three times higher, BArch-MA RW 7/1710a, Frank to *Allgemeines Wehrmachtsamt*, 13 January 1944, fol. 61.
71 BArch-MA RW 7/1710a, Frank to *Allgemeines Wehrmachtsamt*, 13 January 1944, fol. 61.
72 Buchheim, 'Die besetzten Länder', p. 127.
73 Calculated on the basis of the information provided in Scherner, 'Importboom', p. 80, table 1, footnote c.
74 For data about the financial extraction on a country level, see for example Buchheim, 'Die besetzten Länder'; P. Liberman, *Does Conquest Pay? The Exploitation of Occupied Industrial Societies*, Princeton: Princeton UP, 1996, pp. 42, 51, 65.

5 Paying for war, 1941–1945

How Japan financed Southeast Asia's occupation

Gregg Huff and Shinobu Majima[1]

Even before the outbreak of war, Japanese financial policy was clear: Southeast Asians would have to provide much of the finance for war in the region. This chapter explores Japanese financial policies and their implications in three main respects. One is to identify wartime, 'market-purchased,' resource transfers from Southeast Asians to the Japanese. Excluded from these transfers are resources that the Japanese directly confiscated and labour extraction. Although Japanese exploitation through transfers fell short of Nazi levels, it was nevertheless substantial. In Indochina, transfers reached as much as more than a third of GDP.

Second, the chapter analyses how Japan financed resource extraction. Its financial techniques of occupation costs (the expenses of occupying troops paid by the occupier), military scrip (unbacked military notes), and bilateral clearing arrangements were similar to those of Nazi Germany. Money creation was, however, substantially more important in occupied Southeast Asia than in occupied Europe.

Third, the chapter quantifies the monetary and inflationary consequences of Japanese financial policies for Southeast Asia. Even though transfers to Japan were chiefly financed by printing money, Southeast Asian inflation was limited because of Japanese legal restrictions on currency and the usefulness of money as a medium of exchange. Legal requirements to use domestic rather than a foreign currency have been advocated as a way for governments to capture seigniorage, defined as the difference between the cost of printing money and what it will buy.[2] A reason for legal requirements is that government's ability to exploit a monetary monopoly and finance expenditure through seigniorage depends on avoiding too much inflation. That, in turn, relies on the public being willing to hold, being successfully forced to hold, or being fooled into holding currency issued by the government. Money, like any commodity, can be taxed. Seigniorage is the revenue from the tax, money holdings are the tax base, and inflation is the tax rate. As money holdings tend to zero, so too does seigniorage. A danger for governments reliant on seigniorage is that high inflation may turn into hyperinflation, because when this occurs, the public is unlikely to continue to hold money for any length of time, if at all. In Southeast Asia, the avoidance of hyperinflation except for brief episodes was crucial to Japan's ability to continue to finance the war by printing money.

Financial technologies and transfers

While Japan relied heavily on money creation as a means of finance, war can also be financed by selling bonds and through taxation. Southeast Asia, however, afforded little scope for these methods. Neither the Thai and Indochinese governments nor Japanese military administrations could borrow abroad. Bonds could not be sold to Southeast Asia's banks nor through stock markets. The latter were either miniscule or nonexistent in Southeast Asian countries. European banking dominated in prewar Southeast Asia. However, these banks, including the three great British banks – the Hongkong and Shanghai, the Chartered Bank of India, Australia and China, and the Mercantile Bank of India – were closed and then liquidated by the Japanese. Some local Chinese banks were allowed to reopen, but they were small and did little business during the war. In World War II China, the nationalist government forced large corporations to buy its bonds, but that was not an option in Southeast Asia.[3] Almost all corporations had been European and no longer operated, because they had either closed or been taken over by the Japanese.

Before the war, Southeast Asian countries were highly internationally oriented export economies. Once cut off from global, chiefly Western markets, Southeast Asia's economies collapsed and so did their tax bases. Japanese administrators tried to initiate savings campaigns to raise resources from Southeast Asians and introduce new taxes as a means of finance, but to little avail. Taxation efforts included 'voluntary' gifts from Chinese businessmen, lotteries, and taxes on gambling, amusement parks, cockpits, bicycles, hand carts, dance hostesses (taxi dancers), female visitors to dance halls, restaurants, and coffee shops, the last four all associated with the great wartime upsurge in prostitution.

Monetary creation in wartime Southeast Asia proceeded along two routes. In Malaya, Indonesia, the Philippines, and Burma, which were administered by military governments, the Japanese transferred resources to themselves simply by printing as military scrip the required amount of currency. Scrip, literally campaign money given to Japan's invading forces, was legal tender only in the country where it was issued and, as before the war, denominated in rupees, dollars, guilders, and pesos for Burma, Malaya, Indonesia, and the Philippines, respectively. With 'appropriate' pictures – banana plants for Malaya and Indonesia, pagodas for Burma – scrip looked quite different from prewar notes.

In Thailand and Indochina, prewar administrations of a Thai government and the French colonial regime remained in place. Japan exercised control through these governments and used baht (Thailand) and piastres (Indochina) to buy goods it exported and to meet local military and administrative (occupation) costs. The use of prewar currencies made acquiring money to spend somewhat more complicated than in the militarily administered countries. However, in these countries, the Japanese could effectively dictate currency requirements.[4] The mechanics of supply were that, first, the *Yokohama Specie Bank* credited at the Bank of Japan in Tokyo the accounts of the *Bank of Siam* (established in December 1942) or *Banque de l'Indochine* with the yen equivalent of baht or piastres to be given to Japan. These Southeast Asian 'central banks' then credited the Yokohama Specie Bank in Bangkok or Saigon with local currency for military use.[5] Yen credited to Thailand and Indochina were 'special'. In reality, this meant that these yen were merely paper credits without practical use, since they could not be spent in Japan or used to purchase imports from Japan. Thailand did, however, negotiate an agreement for some 10 per cent of its yen credits to be converted into gold held in Tokyo.

Payments to Japan

Thailand, Indochina, and Indonesia provided the most resources to the Japanese, and we can use wartime national income estimates to evaluate transfers as a share of GDP (Table 5.1). For all three countries, exploitation was substantial at arbitrary, wartime exchange rates. It was even larger at prewar (1937 market) exchange rates, since after occupying Southeast Asia, Japan greatly revalued the yen by setting it equal to one unit of each of the region's currencies. Between 1942 and 1945, Thailand's payments averaged 6 per cent of GDP at wartime rates and a little more than 9 per cent at 1937 rates. Payments made by Indochina at Japanese wartime rates rose from 9.1 per cent of GDP in 1942 to 25.4 per cent by 1945. At 1937 exchange rates, payments in 1945 were more than a third of GDP. Indochina made such large payments, probably the biggest in Southeast Asia, because it was Japan's chief military and logistical base in Southeast Asia; because it was the second-most-important source (just behind Korea) of rice imports; and because the pro-Vichy colonial government was in no position to resist demands from Tokyo.[6]

After reaching 11.2 per cent of GDP in 1943, or nearly twice that at prewar rates, payments from Indonesia fell sharply. Japan's chief demand on Indonesia was for petroleum, but by 1944, systematic American submarine and air attacks had decimated the Japanese tanker fleet. Allied destruction of Japanese oil tankerage and merchant shipping cut Japan off from Southeast Asia by the end of 1944, and so Indonesian oil fields no longer had much value.[7]

During the war, the composition of Thai and Indochinese payments to Japan changed radically. Indeed, at the same time as Japan lost control of Pacific shipping lanes, it had to increase military expenditure in Southeast Asia to deal with probable Allied invasion. Initially, the chief component of payments was exports (mainly rice) to Japan (see Table 5.2). By the last two years of the war, however, occupation costs comprised more than 90 per cent of payments as Japan's focus shifted to defending Southeast Asia against apparently almost certain Allied invasion.

Payments in Table 5.1 constitute a lower bound for total resource transfers to Japan, because they exclude the seizure of goods, unpaid or low-paid Southeast Asian labour, artificially low prices for the requisitioned delivery of rice and so forth. Nevertheless, transfers seem unlikely anywhere in Southeast Asia to have approached the 1943 high point of the more than 50 per cent of GDP that Nazi Germany extracted from France.[8] Even in Indochina, Japan was unable to achieve

Table 5.1 Southeast Asia payments to Japan, 1941–1945

a) Thailand baht 000

	GDP current prices	Yen credits	Yen credits as a % of GDP at wartime exchange rates	Yen credits as a % of GDP at 1937 exchange rates
1942	2,531,956	61,000	2.4	3.8
1943	4,218,629	176,050	4.2	6.5
1944	7,119,363	520,840	7.3	11.4
1945	12,505,066	800,910	6.4	10.0

b) Indochina piastres 000

	GDP current prices	Occupation costs and trade surplus	Occupation costs and trade surplus as a % of GDP at wartime exchange rates	Occupation costs and trade surplus as a % of GDP at 1937 exchange rates
1941	1,919,810	183,503	9.6	13.1
1942	2,267,014	205,213	9.1	12.4
1943	2,829,739	191,014	6.8	9.2
1944	3,423,568	405,377	11.8	16.2
1945	3,710,565	943,948	25.4	34.8

c) Indonesia NI fl 000

	GDP current prices	Change in money supply	Change in money supply as a % of GDP at wartime exchange rates	money supply as a % of GDP at 1937 exchange rates
1942	4,330,250			
1943	8,849,400	990,097	11.2	21.4
1944	23,517,900	1,302,015	5.5	10.6
1945	145,778,780	1,176,991	0.8	1.5

Source: Huff and Majima, 'Financing Japan's World War II Occupation'.

exploitation on such a scale.[9] There were four main reasons for the comparatively smaller payments from Southeast Asia to Japan than France to Germany, none of them financial. One was that in Southeast Asia, a low standard of living limited available surpluses that could be appropriated. Second, Southeast Asia was a collection of highly specialized monoeconomies. They produced, among all six countries, just four main commodities: rice, rubber, tin, and sugar. Because prewar production was geared to the global (chiefly Western) market, output of these commodities was in far greater quantities than a relatively small economy

Table 5.2 Thailand and Indochina composition of payments to Japan, 1941–1945

	Payments to Japan	Occupation costs %	Trade surplus %
a) Thailand, baht 000			
1942	61,000	14.8	85.2
1943	176,050	93.0	7.0
1944	520,840	87.2	12.8
1945	800,910	96.8	3.2
b) Indochina, piastres 000			
1941	183,503	31.2	68.8
1942	205,213	41.7	58.3
1943	191,014	61.4	38.6
1944	405,377	88.8	11.2
1945	943,948	99.1	0.9

Source: Huff and Majima, 'Financing Japan's World War II Occupation'.

like Japan's could use. Third, as indicated, by 1944, Japan found it difficult to ship home those commodities it wanted because of severe shortages of merchant shipping. Fourth, Japan's rapid initial conquests boxed it into diverting resources to try to maintain a vast Pacific defensive perimeter. Until September 1943, this included not only Burma but stretched to western New Guinea in the south, encompassed the Gilbert Islands in the east, and extended northwards to the Aleutian Islands.

Financing payments

The heavy Japanese reliance on printing money to finance occupation in Southeast Asia should come as no surprise. Money creation is, as Keynes remarked, what governments and military administrations do to finance themselves if no other methods exist.[10] Although that was not strictly true in Southeast Asia, for much of the war, printing money was an effective, as well as a near costless, way for Japan to tax the mass of the population.

Table 5.3 shows the heavy Japanese reliance on money creation for Thailand and Indochina. Although data are not available for other Southeast Asian countries, the dependence on money creation in these was, if anything, probably even greater than in Thailand and Indochina since these two countries' prewar administrations and tax structures remained more intact than elsewhere in Southeast Asia. During the war in both Thailand and Indochina, government revenue growth lagged well behind inflation. Conventional government expenditure alone gave rise to modest budget deficits. These combined with occupation costs and trade surpluses with Japan to create large deficits. Currency issues, measured in Table 5.3 by the annual change in money supply, largely filled the gap. From 1943, money financed half to three quarters of total government spending in each country.

Table 5.3 Thailand and Indochina methods of financing government expenditure and payments to Japan, 1941–1945

a) Thailand baht m

	Conventional government expenditure	Yen credits	Total government expenditure	Government revenue % of expenditure	Money % of expenditure	Gold from Japan % of expenditure
1941	198.9		198.9	80.9	31.5	
1942	200.0	61.0	261.0	56.5	36.5	5.7
1943	261.1	176.1	437.1	48.4	60.6	6.6
1944	390.7	520.8	911.6	31.4	56.7	6.6
1945	425.2	800.9	1,226.1	25.7	75.7	2.0

b) Indochina piastres m

	Conventional government expenditure	Occupation costs and trade surplus	Total government expenditure	Government revenue % of expenditure	Money % of expenditure
1941	151	183.5	334.5	45.1	19.8
1942	181	205.2	386.2	46.1	65.7
1943	171.6	91.0	362.7	42.9	78.6
1944	219.1	405.4	624.5	31.1	51.5
1945	299.7	943.9	1,243.7	19.3	75.8

Notes: Money is the change in money supply from official statistics. This change as a percentage of total government expenditure and government revenue as a percentage of total government expenditure does not add to 100% in any one calendar year. However, for both Thailand and Indochina, over the five years 1941–1945, the totals for government expenditure plus money add up to close to 500%. There were also small sales of bonds in the two countries but data for these sales are not available. Source: Huff and Majima, 'Financing Japan's World War II Occupation'.

Inflation, hyperinflation and the demand for money

Although Japan had little leeway to finance occupation in Southeast Asia except through monetary expansion, that is well known, as indicated, to be a choice best avoided because it runs the risk that high inflation will quickly escalate to become hyperinflation. If this transpires, prices quickly spiral out of control, whether one defines hyperinflation according to the commonly accepted Philip Cagan criterion of price increases of 50 per cent a month or Carmen Reinhart-Kenneth Rogoff threshold of 40 per cent monthly rises.[11] Importantly, in all Southeast Asian countries, Japan could finance occupation by printing money so long as the demand for it held up sufficiently well that hyperinflation was largely avoided and confidence in money, or at least its continued use for many purposes, was not destroyed. Although the Japanese instituted numerous and detailed price controls to try to control inflation, these were ineffective.

Money supply and inflation in Southeast Asia

Money supply data derive from Japan's Ministry of Finance records and from Thailand's and Indochina's government accounts.[12] These data are reliable until sometime in 1945, when Japanese record keeping deteriorated or ceased. Then Allied reconstructions of Japanese policy provide some additional information.[13] Statistics are typically monthly for the four military-administered countries and annual for Thailand and Indochina. Data for the Philippines exist through January 1945, for Indonesia until July 1945, and for Malaya and Burma until 12 and 15 August 1945, respectively. Rapid money supply expansion during the war's last two months, and especially its final two weeks in August when surrender was inevitable, renders Malayan and Burmese data only partially comparable with those for Indonesia and the Philippines.

As Table 5.4 shows, the money creation and inflation time series are quite contrasted between Thailand and Indochina and the four military-administered Southeast Asian countries, both in the magnitude of inflation (lines 1, 4, 7, and 9) and the quantity of currency issued (lines 2 and 5). Between 1942 and 1945, inflation and money supply relationships in Thailand and southern Indochina (Cochinchina and the lower part of Annam, together represented by Saigon) appear to satisfy even the naïve quantity theory of money that prices rise at the same rate as money supply increases. The price level in Thailand at the end of occupation, at 7.1 times December 1941 prices, compares to a 6.9-fold increase in money. Inflation data may somewhat understate actual price rises.[14] However, in both countries, measures to decrease money supply helped to limit inflation. In February 1945, Thailand reduced the money supply by some 30 per cent after demonetizing the 1,000 baht note and exchanging it for bonds at 1 per cent interest, while in March 1945, Indochina limited withdrawals from banks for individual depositors to 2,000 piastres per month.[15] A separate price index exists for Hanoi (northern Indochina) but not separate money supply figures. The Hanoi index (and other data) indicates a 15-fold increase in wartime prices.[16]

Table 5.4 Southeast Asia Characteristics of inflation and money during the Japanese occupation, 1942–1945

	Burma	Malaya	Thailand	Indonesia	Indochina Saigon	Philippines
1. Ratio of prices at the end of occupation to prices at its beginning	1,856.5	11,226.5	6.9	32.0	3.6	889.3
2. Ratio of quantity of currency at the end	16.4	25.1	7.1	11.0	5.7	28.0
3. Ratio of (1) to (2)	11.3	447.3	1.0	2.9	0.6	31.8
4. Average rate of rise in prices (% per month)	16.9	16.3	4.0	7.9	2.7	18.4
5. Average rate of rise in quantity of currency (% per month)	6.3	7.4	4.1	5.6	4.1	9.0
6. Ratio of (4) to (5)	2.7	2.2	1.0	1.4	0.7	2.0
7. Average rate of rise in prices during last year of occupation (% per month)	27.1	30.5	5.4	7.6	2.8	32.3
8. Ratio of (7) to (4)	1.6	1.9	1.4	1.0	1.0	1.8
9. Average rate of rise in prices during last two months of occupation (% per month)	72.1	86.8		14.0		37.2
10. Ratio of (9) to (4)	4.3	5.3		1.8		2.0
11. Real balances at end of occupation as a % of real balances at its beginning	9.0	2.0	102.7	34.3	171.8	3.2

Source: Huff and Majima, 'Financing Japan's World War II Occupation'.

Since a main focus of the present chapter is the holding of money in rice-surplus areas, and northern Indochina around Hanoi was a rice-deficit area and one without its own money supply data, the remainder of the chapter concentrates on southern Indochina.

Among the military-administered countries, Burma was comparable to Thailand and Indochina. Data for Burma are for Rangoon, and so, like Thailand and southern Indochina, indicative of the demand for money in a rice-surplus area. Unlike Thailand and Indochina, however, Burma was subject to instability associated with political uncertainty and some of the most intense fighting in the Southeast Asian theatre. Although a lack of data for 1942 and 1943 hampers analysis, from Japan's initial bombing of Rangoon on 22 December 1941 through the city's fall on 8 March 1942 and possibly until March 1943, prices appear to have risen much faster than money supply. However, during the next twenty-one months, until December 1944, when money supply increased by about a factor of 10, prices rose only slightly faster. This changed between January and August 1945, which encompassed Rangoon's fall in May: Burma's money supply less than doubled but prices rose 21.4 times, so that by the war's end, Burmese prices had increased by a factor of 1,856.5.

In Malaya, the Philippines, and Indonesia, price rises far outdistanced monetary expansion. Malaya appears the extreme example: by the end of the war, money supply had multiplied 25.1 times, while prices were 11,000 times higher. However, the Philippines and Indonesia might well show similar money supply and price histories if data were available for the final weeks of the war when the Japanese issued particularly great quantities of currency.

Earlier work on Southeast Asia almost universally refers to wartime hyperinflation. But by either the Cagan (prices rising 50 per cent a month) or Reinhart-Rogoff (40 per cent) criteria, hyperinflation was not typical until late in the war. Only the Philippines had a 40 per cent or more monthly price rise before 1945. Even there, inflation did not reach 40 per cent until August 1943. Between November 1943 and January 1945, monthly Philippine inflation exceeded 50 per cent on three occasions but then fell back to a lower level in the next month. Malaya never approached 40 per cent monthly inflation until the final days of the war in August 1945. Burma became hyperinflationary only in the last two months of the war as retreating Japanese troops desperately drew on their monetary stocks to obtain food and supplies.

Inflation and money demand

Despite obviously high inflation, the demand for money in Southeast Asia held up sufficiently well that hyperinflation was largely avoided. But why did Southeast Asians continue to hold money to the extent they did when its value was being comprehensively debauched? While inflation judged by the public as 'not too high' or 'acceptable' is one part of persuading (or fooling) people into holding government-issued currency, it need not be the whole story.

Comparative war finance

One possible inducement, despite a history of high inflation, for people to hold the paper money of an occupying power is periodically to back it with some tangible asset. In Greece, Nazi Germany repeatedly did this by releasing a certain amount of gold to shore up confidence in the drachma and so be able to continue to finance occupation through money creation. Three programmes of gold sales and four cosmic fiscal stabilizations 'sufficed periodically to restore enough short-run public confidence in the drachma to maintain the seigniorage maximisation policy. Without these interventions, the pace of inflation would have reached such heights as to have led to public refusal to accept newly printed currency notes in return for goods and services rendered'.[17]

Similarly, in World War II Nationalist China, the Americans, at intervals, released gold for local sale to support the fapi as a viable currency. At the end of December 1944, Finance Minister H. H. Kung telegraphed United States Treasury Secretary Henry Morgenthau that 'the recent gold shipment is one of the outstanding factors contributing to the strengthening of fapi, because people believe that the arrival of gold has increased the much needed reserve of our currency'.[18] In Nationalist China, helped by American gold shipments, 'inflation did not become hyperinflation in 1937–1945 [so that China] was able to use inflationary finance to meet a large part of the government's needs all through the war, and thereafter until 1947 before hyperinflation set in'.[19] The Japanese, however, hardly wanted to ship gold to Southeast Asia.

Less subtle than the policies of the Germans in Greece or the Americans in China were the coercive powers used during the Terror in revolutionary France to boost demand for the assignat. It has been described as a 'guillotine-backed currency', which is to say one underpinned by the sanction of the execution of anyone refusing to use the currency. That sanction proved sufficient to persuade people to hold the assignat and enable France to finance the war with the German Empire and Austria that began in April 1792 by printing assignats.[20]

Japanese policies and peasants

Whether wartime Japanese administrators for Southeast Asia were aware of this French precedent can only be guessed, but they must have known of the evolution of Japan's policy in China where ultimately 'all circulation of Chinese national currency was prohibited in certain specified areas and any person bearing or using such outlawed currency in those areas was subject to punishment, often death'.[21] In Southeast Asia, military decrees, backed up by coercion, provided similarly strong incentives to hold currency. After the first year of occupation, Japanese administrations outlawed the use of prewar currencies. Their mere possession was deemed criminal and punishable with arrest, often torture, or even death.[22]

Clearly, the incentive in Southeast Asia to use government-issued money was considerable when, as a wartime Burmese government official recalled, it was the only legal currency and an unwillingness to accept it 'meant imprisonment, torture or death'.[23] There were, however, four further reasons for a continuing demand in Southeast Asia for Japanese money. They helped Japan to protect seigniorage by avoiding having to issue as much new money as would have been required if the demand for money had been less and therefore the rise in prices greater.

One reason was that good money substitutes for scrip were not available. Japan forced the Southeast Asian countries into autarky, which supported its monetary monopoly by cutting off access to substitute currencies. Indeed, all that was left was the clandestine use of prewar monies and various guerrilla-issued currencies in the Philippines.

Second, economies so highly economically specialized as Southeast Asia's greatly restricted barter as a substitute for money. The lack of scope for barter enhanced scrip's already considerable transactional benefits which, furthermore, also arose from the way Japan organized Southeast Asia's wartime economies. The Japanese instituted monopoly buying and distributing organizations. Beginning in late 1943, nominally independent governments in Burma and the Philippines favoured similar buying arrangements. Monopoly organizations dominated prewar export staples like rubber and tin in Malaya and sugar and abaca in the Philippines. Not only had prewar export markets disappeared, but there was little or no local (barter) demand for these goods. Similarly, the surfeit of rice in areas specialized in producing it told against barter demand. Malayan and Philippine staple producers could, with few exceptions, only obtain wage goods of food and other basic necessities by selling their output to Japanese buyers who paid in scrip. Likewise, labourers and others employed by the Japanese were paid in scrip. Furthermore, nearly everyone in the military-administered countries needed scrip for the many taxes levied by the Japanese, to obtain rationed goods including food and clothing, and for any other market transaction.

Third, although confidence in scrip fell because the Allies announced that it would become worthless after Japan surrendered, not all Southeast Asians believed this propaganda.[24] Almost certainly, a number of people continued to hold scrip in the expectation that, even if Japan lost the war, it would still have some value. A rational basis for this belief is confirmed by actual Bank of England strategy. Elliptically set out in a telegram, it was that: we 'have to redeem Japanese occupation currency most important that the impression should be created that we do not (repeat not) contemplate such redemption'.[25]

The fourth factor in the holding of money derives from its usefulness in everyday transactions and its function as a store of value available to command goods at a later date. This factor requires some discussion because the reasons Southeast Asians held money, and thus their propensity to do so, differed among Malaya, Indonesia, and the Philippines on the one hand and Thailand, Indochina, and Burma on the other. The transactional reasons, including severe sanctions, to hold money have already been discussed and applied throughout Southeast Asia. But in Malaya, Indonesia, and the Philippines, the usefulness of money as a store of value was increasingly doubted.

In these countries, as the war went on, scrip was more and more shunned as a store of value. By the war's latter stages in Malaya, for example, 'only the most stupid were lulled into a sense of wealth' by holding large quantities of Japanese notes. Others 'who had amassed "fortunes" quickly changed the paper money into commodities, and substantial investments'.[26] Apparently, given the opportunity, even the clerks in Japanese banks changed their pocket money into British currency.[27] Axis reversals eroded scrip as a store of value. In Malaya, 'Every time there was an Axis defeat, particularly Japanese defeats, prices of goods jumped up. Every Allied victory . . . and every visit of B-29s over Malaya, caused spurts of prices in foodstuffs. Saipan, Iwojima, Manila, Rangoon, and Okinawa were inflation spring-boards'.[28] In the Philippines, prices rose each time air-raid precautions and defence drills were held in Manila.[29] Insofar as money, as opposed to jewels or durable goods, remained a store of value, these were largely prewar currencies exchanged among those considered trustworthy.

By contrast, in Thailand and Indochina, the willingness to hold money remained impressively persistent. Holdings of money in these countries rose at about the same rate as prices. In other words, so-called real balances (the nominal value of money divided by the price level and so adjusted for inflation) remained approximately constant.

Thailand, Indochina, and Burma had transactional motives for holding money similar to those of Malaya and the Philippines. Burmese transactions were 'largely (if not entirely) based on Japanese-issued rupees'.[30] The Thai and Indochinese governments helped to sustain this demand for money through policies to support producers by buying their output.[31]

The unchanged physical appearance of the Indochinese piaster and nearly identical appearance of the Thai baht may seem to bolster a store of value motive for high real balances. But the principal explanation lies elsewhere. High real balances in Thailand, Indochina, and, for part of the war, in Burma are explained mainly by the fact that all three economies were dominated by numerous small peasant rice growers. Unlike producers in the rice-deficit areas, they could easily achieve food (if not necessarily nutritional) self-sufficiency, since rice and many other basic foodstuffs could be obtained through household production or barter. Such small rural cultivators tend to hoard money, even in the face of inflation. Under inflationary conditions, Keynes observed, as 'more money flows into the pockets of the peasants, it tends to stick there'.[32] For Thailand, it was observed that only 20 per cent or 25 per cent of notes in circulation were in Bangkok; 'The rest are in the provinces, where they largely disappear into farmers' hoards: and the demand of the provinces for fresh supplies of notes is a never ceasing one'.[33] In Burma, villagers in rice-producing districts insisted on payment in Japanese currency: 'They thought it was better than British and enjoyed the feeling of wealth which they got by carrying away large wads of brand new Jap notes'.[34] Even when brought to the cities, rural dwellers like Indochina's Cao Dài religious sect apparently had consumption patterns little affected by inflation. In Saigon, the Japanese relied heavily for their workforce on the Cao Dài, who, being vegetarians, 'ate simple food with lots of vegetables, rice, and seeds. Any extra money they earned was channelled back to their families or to their temples'.[35]

Peasant money illusion (mistaking nominal for real values) may not, however, fully account for the holding of money in rice-surplus areas. Producers in these areas had limited spending opportunities because local production generally provided no more than small quantities of inferior substitutes for prewar imported manufactures and because Japan sent few basic consumer goods like cloth, footwear, soap, matches, and batteries to Southeast Asia. Given this absence of goods, and so long as a postwar redemption of wartime notes could be anticipated, as seemed especially likely in Indochina, Thailand, and Burma, it was rational to hold money. Probably peasants realized that manufactured goods would become more abundant after the war and prices would decline dramatically.

Concluding remarks

After deciding on war to pursue empire and the creation of a Co-Prosperity Sphere, Japan had little alternative to inflation as the main way to finance occupation in Southeast Asia. Japanese war planners probably also saw that inflation had other advantages. Although in the longer term, high inflation might well reorder Southeast Asian societies, this was not inconsistent with the aim of replacing the prewar order with Japanese empire. At the same time, inflation offered an efficient means of wartime finance. It avoided the enforcement problems of overt taxation in a big geographical area with a predominantly rural population and over which Japanese officials were thinly spread. The feasibility of obtaining large tax revenues was, moreover, unlikely because of the lack of any obvious tax base in Southeast Asian countries after the wartime collapse of the region's export economies.

To fund the war effort, Japan required Southeast Asian governments to issue large amounts of currency, and, in Thailand and Indochina, enacted a yen bloc of bilateral trading arrangements. The combined effect was to create large international debts in Southeast Asia but eliminate any mechanism that forced Japan to reduce these. Although Japan appeared to 'pay' for occupation in Southeast Asia and goods from the region, the financial technologies used involved no real payment.

The striking feature of Japanese finance in World War II Southeast Asia was not a reliance on seigniorage to finance occupation. It was, rather, in ensuring that this policy worked through shoring up, through a strong element of coercion, the demand for real balances. That avoided Japan having to issue as much new money as a lower demand for real balances and so a greater rise in prices would imply. Additional, somewhat unusual aspects of Japanese finance were the help it received from a Southeast Asian pattern of highly specialized production for export, which greatly limited the scope for barter, and from peasant behaviour. Southeast Asia's wartime inflation experience, and the avoidance of hyperinflation for much of the war, is testament to a combination of strict Japanese controls and the transactions benefits of holding money despite its rapidly depreciating real value.

Scrip, occupation costs, clearing arrangements, and seigniorage afforded Japan a low-cost and relatively efficient way to finance occupation and gain control of Southeast Asian resources. In the end, however, major Japanese military miscalculations and strategic failures occurred. These prevented realization of the full exploitative potential of the financial measures analysed in this chapter.

Notes

1 An earlier version of this chapter was presented at the European Business History Society Conference in Paris in 2012. The authors thank conference participants and Andrew Bain and Hugh Rockoff for valuable comments. We also thank Shingo Kakino and Sarah Womack who provided outstanding research assistance. Huff gratefully acknowledges support and funding from ESRC grant (RES-062-23-1392) which made this article possible.
2 S. Fischer, 'Seigniorage and the Case for a National Money', *Journal of Political Economy*, 1982, vol. 90, p. 306.
3 W. C. Kirby, 'The Chinese War Economy' in J. C. Hsiung/S. I. Levine (eds.), *China's Bitter Victory: the War with Japan 1937–1945*, Armonk, NY: M. E. Sharpe, 1992, p. 193.
4 See, for example, France, Centre des Archives d'Outre-Mer, Aix-en-Provence [hereafter AOM] 1Affeco/289, 'Frais d'entretien des troupes japonaises stationnées en Indochine: Besoins en Piastres' 1er semestre, 1944, pp. 6–11.
5 United Kingdom, Bank of England [hereafter BE] OV25/9, Extract from *Bangkok Times*: 'Japan-Thailand Economic Co-operation. New Agreement Now Signed: the System of Settlement' 4 May 1942; Thailand, *Report of the Financial Adviser Covering the Years 1941 to 1950* (Bangkok, 1951), p. 55; AOM 1Affeco/289, Franco-Japanese Accords: 'Modalitiés d'application de l'échange de lettres, 1942' and 'Note: Négociation d'un nouvel accord financier entre l'Indochine et le Japon', Vichy, 23 December 1942.
6 C. Robequain, *The Economic Development of French Indo-China*, London: Oxford University Press, 1944, pp. 367–73.
7 Fuel Forum, *Nihon Kaigun Nenryo Shi (The History of Japan's Naval Fuel)* Part One, Tokyo: Hara Shobo, 1972, p. 664; United States Strategic Bombing Survey, *The Effects of Strategic Bombing on Japan's War Economy*, Washington, DC: U.S. Government Printing Office, 1946, pp. 41–4.
8 F. Occhino/K. Oosterlinck/E. N. White, 'How Much Can a Victor Force the Vanquished to Pay? France under the Nazi Boot', *Journal of Economic History*, 2008, vol. 68, p. 7; idem, 'How Occupied France Financed Its Own Exploitation during World War II', *American Economic Review*, 2007, vol. 97, pp. 295–9.
9 For discussion of this, see United Kingdom, Liddell Hart Centre for Military Archives, King's College, London [hereafter LHC], MAGIC, 'Economic Value of Indochina to Japan' 5 July 1944, pp. 13–6. MAGIC are wartime Japanese diplomatic messages intercepted and decoded by the Allies.
10 J. M. Keynes, 'A Tract on Monetary Reform' in *The Collected Writings of John Maynard Keynes*, vol. 4, London: Macmillan for the Royal Economic Society, 1971, p. 37.
11 P. Cagan, 'The Monetary Dynamics of Hyperinflation' in M. Friedman (ed.), *Studies in the Quantity Theory of Money*, Chicago: University of Chicago Press, 1956, p. 25; C. M. Reinhart/K. S. Rogoff, *This Time Is Different: Eight Centuries of Financial Folly*, Princeton: Princeton University Press, 2009, p. 5. European hyperinflations were all far more extreme than price rises in wartime Southeast Asia. See T. J. Sargent, 'The Ends of Four Big Inflations' in R. E. Hall (ed.), *Inflation: Causes and Effects*, Chicago: University of Chicago Press, 1982, pp. 41–97.

12 For a discussion of sources, see Gregg Huff and Shinobu Majima, 'Financing Japan's World War II Occupation of Southeast Asia', *Journal of Economic History*, vol. 73, no. 4, 2013, 938–78.
13 NA, T236/108, 'Report on Japanese Financial Manipulations' by Lt. Col. Sweeny; WO203/419 'Notes on the Southern Regions Development Bank', p. 24; M. Longmuir, *The Money Trail: Burmese Currencies in Crisis, 1937–1947*, DeKalb, IL: Northern Illinois University Center for Southeast Asian Studies, 2002, pp. 42–3, 100; W.L. Swan, 'Thai-Japan Monetary Relations at the Start of the Pacific War', *Modern Asian Studies*, 1989, vol. 23, pp. 317–20; P.H. Kratoska, 'Banana Money: Consequences of the Demonetization of Wartime Japanese Currency in British Malaya', *Journal of Southeast Asian Studies*, 1992, vol. 23, pp. 322–45; K. Kurusu Nitz, 'Japanese Military Policy towards French Indochina during the Second World War: the Road to the *Meigo Sakusen* (9 March 1945)', *Journal of Southeast Asian Studies*, 1983, vol. 14, pp. 336–7.
14 P. Ungphakorn/R. Suvarnsit, 'Fiscal and Other Measures for Combating Inflation in Thailand' in United Nations, Economic Commission for Asia and the Far East, *Mobilization of Domestic Capital: Report and Documents of the First Working Party of Experts*, Bangkok: Department of Economic Affairs, ECAFE, 1952, p. 70.
15 AOM, Conseiller Politique 226: Memoires d'Yokoyoma, section 7; Thailand, *Report 1941–1950*, p. 53.
16 United Kingdom, National Archives, Kew [hereafter NA], T236/108, telegram from SACSEA to War Office, 1 September 1945.
17 M. Palairet, *The Four Ends of the Greek Hyperinflation of 1941–1946*, Copenhagen: Museum Tusculanum Press, 2000, p. 102, and see the discussion pp. 96–109.
18 Quoted in A.N. Young, *China's Wartime Finance and Inflation, 1937–1945*, Cambridge: Harvard University Press, 1965, p. 284, and see the discussion pp. 281–98 on the use of gold shipments to gain leverage over the Nationalist government. See also Chou Shun-Hsin, *The Chinese Inflation 1937–1949*, New York: Columbia University Press, 1963, pp. 224–32.
19 Young, *China's Wartime Finance*, pp. 309–10.
20 T.J. Sargent and F.R. Velde, 'Macroeconomic Features of the French Revolution', *Journal of Political Economy*, 1995, vol. 103, pp. 503–7.
21 R.A. Lester, *International Aspects of Wartime Monetary Experience*, Princeton Essays in International Finance, no. 3, Princeton: International Finance Section, Department of Economics, 1944, p. 4.
22 United States, National Archives and Records Administration, 226 16 208, 'Economic Conditions in the Philippines', 13 October 1942, p. 7; Japan, National Institute for Defense Studies, Military Archives Collection [hereafter NIDS], Nansei Gunsei-17, Southern Area Military Administration: *So Cho Shi 23: Zairai Tsūka Kaishū Mondai ni tsuite (Withdrawal of Local Money from Circulation)* (by Higuchi Gorō), Singapore, Dec. 1943, p. 17; NA, CO852/510/24, C.D. Adhearne: 'The Malayan Currency Problem no. 2', p. 1; WO203/390, telegram BMA to SACSEA November 1945; Chin, 1946, 123–4.
23 U Hla Pe, *Narrative of the Japanese Occupation of Burma*, Ithaca, NY: Southeast Asia Program, Cornell University, 1961, p. 93.
24 NIDS, Nansei Gunsei-17, Southern Area Military Administration: *Zairai Tsūka Kaishū (Withdrawal of Local Money)*, p. 4.
25 BE, OV79/16, Draft telegram in reply to telegram of 20 Feb. 1943 from C.-C. – India.
26 Chin Kee Onn, *Malaya Upside Down*, Singapore: Jitts & Co., 1946, p. 45.
27 NIDS, Nansei Gunsei-17, Southern Area Military Administration: *Zairai Tsūka Kaishū* (Withdrawal of Local Money), p. 6.
28 Chin, *Malaya Upside Down*, p. 45.

29 R. T. Jose, 'The Rice Shortage and Countermeasures during the Japanese Occupation' in I. Setsuho and R. Trota Jose (eds.), *The Philippines under Japanese Occupation*, Manila: Manila University Press, 1999, p. 211.
30 BE, OV79/16, 'Burma – Reoccupation, 27 April 1944'. And for the same point, see 'A False Step in Burma', *The Times*, 22 May 1945.
31 U.S. Office of Strategic Services, *Indochina's Wartime Government and Main Aspects of French Rule*, Washington, 10 July 1945, pp. 33–4, *The Status of the Chinese in Thailand*, Washington, 13 March 1945, p. 26; *The Rubber Industry of Southeast Asia: an Estimate of Present Conditions and Anticipated Capabilities*, Washington, 16 December 1944, p. 7.
32 Keynes, *Tract*, p. 66.
33 Thailand, *Report 1941–1950*, p. 55. The same hoarding behaviour was repeated in Thailand's 1949–1951 inflation. Despite a large increase in money supply, prices did not rise to any comparable extent. Apparently, 'a large volume of notes were simply hoarded, mainly by up-country producers': Prince Wiwat, *Wiwatthanachaiyanuson* (Prince Wiwat memorial volume), Bangkok, 1961, p. 268.
34 United Kingdom, India Office Records, M4/306, A. K. Potter, 'Currency Policy, Burma', 31 May 1945.
35 Tran My-Van, 'Working for the Japanese: Working for Vietnamese Independence, 1941–45' in P. H. Kratoska (ed.), *Asian Labor in the Wartime Japanese Empire*, Armonk, NY: M. E. Sharpe, 2005, p. 291.

III
Exploiting the foreign labour force

6 Forced labour in Nazi-occupied Europe, 1939–1945

Mark Spoerer

Introduction

When Nazi Germany forced Europe again into a World War, the belligerent states had little experience with large-scale deployment of forced labourers. During World War I, most of them had deployed prisoners of war in their economies, usually in agriculture or mining. France had put most of her approximately 0.4 million German prisoners of war into work, Austria-Hungary roughly a million Russian POW, while Russia deployed 1.6 million POWs. Yet the largest use of forced labour during World War I took place in the German economy, in which not only 2.5 million prisoners of war were forced to work, but also civilian workers. In Belgium and Northern France, at least 70,000 civilians were coerced by the German army to work for them. Moreover, another 60,000 Belgian men were deported to Germany, where they joined some 400,000 ethnic Poles with Russian passports.[1] The Poles had been working in Germany, mostly in East-Elbian agriculture, and were hindered from returning home after the outbreak of the war. In the occupied parts of Poland and Russia, the German occupation forces coerced many thousands of locals to work against their will.[2] Only Germany used forced labour of civilians on a large scale during World War I.

During World War II, Germany made again (and by far) the largest use of forced labour, much more than the Soviet Union or Japan. This chapter will describe the type and scope of the German forced-labour program and discuss the – often conflicting – motives of the German administration. It will focus on the occupied territories and only very briefly sketch the much-better-researched *Arbeitseinsatz* (labour program) within the German *Reich*.

As forced labour was a politically much-debated issue in the 1990s, there is a large literature on forced labour in Germany. The classic account is the pioneering study of Ulrich Herbert, which was published in 1985 and translated into English a dozen years later.[3] For many years, there were only few studies dealing with forced labour in German-occupied territories.[4] In the last years, however, a number of studies on the German occupation policies which also deal with the issue of forced labour have been published.[5] Not much of this research is available in English, however.[6]

Foreign labour in the German *Reich*

In terms of occupied territory, the heyday of the German hegemony in Europe was in late autumn 1942. At that time, more than 6 million non-German men and women were forced to work in the German war economy. Moreover, many millions more were working outside the *Reich* for the German occupation forces against their will. Many of them were deployed outside their homes, so that they had to endure the stress of living in a camp.

For those who were sent or deported to the German *Reich*, the files of the German armaments bureaucracy allow some quantification.

The German hunger for labour becomes clear if one considers the first three columns of Table 6.1. An ever-growing number of German men was drafted to the armed forces and thus withdrawn from the German economy. The number of women in the workforce was already high in 1939 and could not be expanded without risk of social unrest. Hence Germany started to attract and recruit foreign workers already in the late 1930s and quickly started deporting Polish and Soviet citizens from the occupied territories of Central Eastern and Eastern Europe.

The non-German workers in Germany fell into three categories, which are also useful to group forced labourers outside Germany. In contrast to World War I, civilian foreign workers soon formed the backbone of the non-German labour force. Several hundred thousand came voluntarily to Germany. Those who originated from a neutral country or a German vassal state were free to return home. But many of those who came voluntarily from occupied countries were coerced to stay in Germany, where they were soon joined by hundred thousands of Poles, mainly in 1940 and 1941. In addition, in summer 1940, the German administration started to deploy prisoners of war on large scale in the German war economy, mostly French. In line with the war events, they were joined by Soviet (1941–42) and Italian (1943) prisoners of war. Starting in late spring 1942, masses of Soviet civilian workers, among them many women and teenagers, were deported to Germany.[7]

Table 6.1 Labour force in the Third Reich (including Austria, Sudetenland and Memel-Gebiet) in millions

Date	Drafted (cumulated)	German workers men	German workers women	foreign civilians	prisoners of war	conc. camp inmates	total workforce
May 1939	1.4	24.5	14.6	0.3			39.4
May 1940	5.7	19.7	13.7	2.6	0.0		36.0
May 1941	7.4	18.3	13.4	2.9	1.4		36.0
May 1942	9.4	16.2	13.7	4.0	1.5		35.4
May 1943	11.2	14.8	14.1	6.1	1.6		36.6
May 1944	12.4	13.5	14.1	7.0	1.9		36.5
Sep 1944	13.0	12.8	14.2	7.4	1.5	c. 0.5	c. 36.4

Source: M. Spoerer/J. Streb, *Neue deutsche Wirtschaftsgeschichte des 20. Jahrhunderts*. Munich: Oldenbourg, 2013, p. 202

The third group in Table 6.1 is inmates, mostly from concentration camps. It took the German SS years to realize that concentration camp inmates were the last large source for manpower in the German war economy. Their systematic deployment started in late summer 1942.[8]

Forced labour in the occupied territories

Whenever the German *Wehrmacht* extended the sphere of power of the German *Reich*, the Labour Deployment Administration was installed very soon and began manpower recruitment shortly afterwards. Official recruitment of workers for deployment in the *Reich* took place in all occupied territories apart from North Africa and Norway, which was itself a net importer of manpower owing to the tremendous German economic activity in that country. Moreover, there was recruitment in all allied and some neutral states, including the nonoccupied countries of Bulgaria and Spain, though not in Finland, Portugal, Sweden, or Switzerland.[9]

With regard to the recruitment of foreign civilian workers both for deployment in the *Reich* and in the occupied areas, four methods can be distinguished throughout occupied Europe: (1) recruitment of 'volunteers,'[10] (2) recruitment with decisive influence on living conditions, (3) conscription, that is the levying of whole year-groups with the help of the native administrations, and (4) forcible deportation by the security forces of Germany or its allied states. These four ideal categories, which of course in practice overlapped or existed side by side for some time, were found, according to the severity of the occupation regime, in almost all the territories in the German sphere of hegemony, which was designated euphemistically as the Greater Europe Economic Sphere (see also Table 6.2).

The German occupants began everywhere by recruiting volunteers and proceeded in a very similar fashion in the occupied regions of Western and Eastern Europe, except that in the case of direct German control, the stringent need for intergovernmental agreement was absent. Because the foreign civilian workers, with the exception of the East Europeans, were assured of the same wages and working conditions as their German colleagues, and the unemployment rate was steadily rising in most of the occupied countries after the conquest, the German labour deployment authorities believed they would have an easy job of it.

In the allied, officially sovereign countries of Southern and Southeastern Europe, the German recruiters could not apply direct pressure to the population. These countries were – in order of the recruitment figures actually recorded – Italy (until its capitulation in 1943), Croatia, Slovakia, Hungary, Bulgaria, and Romania. In order to engage in recruitment in these countries, the German *Reich* had to conclude bilateral agreements involving primarily the regulation of legal issues related to foreign exchange and social insurance. Both in those countries and in the occupied territories, the basic principle was that recruitment should remain the exclusive preserve of the local labour authorities, advised or led by Germans, if need be.

In Western Europe, however, where there were large numbers of highly trained skilled workers, the big German enterprises conducted recruitment activities of their own. As the labour authorities claimed a monopoly in the matter, from 1940, they repeatedly prohibited firms from recruiting on their own initiative, though without lasting success. The problem did not resolve itself until 1943 when, after the German defeat at Stalingrad, scarcely any volunteers could be found for work in Germany, which was increasingly under threat of attack from the air.

The recruitment of industrial workers in Southeastern European towns was fairly straightforward. An applicant presented himself at a German recruitment office, where he was examined medically and technically. If both sides agreed on terms, the applicant signed a standard contract, received the necessary exit documents from his own state authorities, and travelled to Germany on a fixed date in a special train together with hundreds of other volunteers. Recruiting agricultural workers proved considerably more troublesome. Since the potential applicants were dispersed through the countryside and congregated in large numbers only to attend church, recruitment usually took place in the villages on Sundays. As in the Middle Ages, the recruiters used drummers to gather a crowd. A person persuaded by the (often exaggerated) promises signed the standard contract and was required to report on a fixed date at an assembly point, usually a railway station or Danube port.[11]

Throughout Europe, the Germans also recruited workers for activities in the occupied territories themselves. Apart from the construction of military infrastructure such as defence installations, roads and railways, bridges, viaducts and tunnels, airfields, and U-boat bunkers, manpower was needed to build and operate strategically important mines and industrial plants for the raw materials industry: aluminium works in Norway, ore mines in Norway, Serbia, and Greece, petrochemical plants in Galicia, coal mines in the Ukraine. Finally, the *Wehrmacht* and the civil occupation authorities also needed workers in transport and administration, and, towards the end of the occupation, for building trenches and fortifications. The nature and extent of forced labour for the German occupants are unknown and have yet to be researched in detail.[12]

At the end of 1941, when it was clear that the Soviet Union could not be defeated by *Blitzkrieg*, a war of attrition and a corresponding reorientation of the war economy became inevitable. The *Wehrmacht* was taking in more and more German men (see Table 6.1), acutely aggravating the shortage of manpower in the *Reich* and making the employment of foreigners increasingly urgent. In March 1942, Hitler sought to step up recruitment in the occupied territories and better coordinate deployment in the *Reich* by appointing Fritz Sauckel General Plenipotentiary for Labour Deployment, thereby making him one of the most powerful men in Germany.

Born in Lower Franconia in 1894, Sauckel enlisted in the navy and spent the whole of World War I in a French internment camp. He joined the SA (quasi-military organisation of the Nazi party) and the NSDAP (Nazi party) in 1923 and made his career in the party in Thuringia, where he became *Gauleiter* (regional party leader) in 1927, chief minister and minister of the interior in 1932, and *Reich* governor in 1933. As General Plenipotentiary for Labour Deployment,

Sauckel was very successful in 1942 and 1943, systematically transforming manpower recruitment into compulsory enlistment of forced labourers. While his methods in the occupied territories showed scant regard for the population, in the *Reich*, he pleaded repeatedly for 'strict but fair' treatment of foreign workers: the reports of ill treatment of foreigners in the *Reich* made his main task more difficult. In view of the context in which it was made, his much-quoted statement of March 1944 – 'of the 5 million foreign workers who arrived in Germany, less than 200,000 came voluntarily' – should not be taken literally.[13] It is nevertheless indicative of his thought and action. Quite simply, Sauckel was a loyal follower of Hitler to the end. The International Military Tribunal in Nuremberg found him jointly responsible for the use of forced labour and sentenced him to death as a war criminal. He was hanged in October 1946.[14]

Sauckel's main adversary was just a few streets afar. The year 1942 is usually not only seen as a turning point of the German labour recruitment policy but of the armaments policy as well. Arms production had largely been made the responsibility of the Reich Minister for Armaments and Munitions, Fritz Todt, and after his death in February 1942, Albert Speer, from November 1943 with the title of Reich Minister for Armaments and War Production. Todt and Speer (who managed to get the credentials) pushed through a massive rationalization program that managed to bring about an impressive increase in the figures for finished production of armaments.[15]

Speer's production statistics concealed that a considerable part of the increase in armaments production was due to shifting production contracts abroad. The French industry in particular contributed much to the German war effort.[16] As the firms producing for Germany needed labour, both skilled and unskilled, the organizations of Speer and Sauckel competed for the same resource.

Especially since 1942, two main fields of tension shaped the German administration responsible for labour issues in the occupied areas: ideology versus economic pragmatism and the question of labour deployment on the spot (Speer) or in Germany (Sauckel).

Having obtained a monopoly on recruitment from Hitler, Sauckel installed his own agents in the occupied territories or delegated powers to other military or civil labour administrations. At the high point of expansion in 1942–43, the German Labour Deployment Administration maintained a staff of around 4,000 outside the borders of the *Reich*, of whom at least 1,500 were employed in the General Government (central Poland) and the 'occupied eastern territories' (the Soviet Union), another 1,000 in France, and more than 400 in Belgium and the Netherlands. Their task was twofold: on the one hand, to coordinate the recruitment of manpower for deployment in the *Reich*; on the other, to ensure that the decisions of the German occupation authorities in regard to economic and labour market policy created a climate favourable to recruitment, for example by establishing or maintaining a considerable pay differential in comparison with the *Reich*.

At first the German occupation authorities had no interest in forced recruitment. Apart from the fact that it required considerably greater personnel resources than the recruitment of volunteers, the use of force necessarily aggravated relations with the local population, thereby endangering the lives of the occupying forces and making their task more difficult. Finding workers for local building work and large industrial projects was difficult enough anyway, despite high unemployment in most of the occupied territories. It was not just that qualified craftsmen were in short supply; even more serious was the dwindling purchasing power of wages, caused by the inflation, to which, for various reasons, the German occupation gave rise almost everywhere. People preferred to look for work on the land, where it was easier to get hold of food. If, in response, the German occupation authorities adopted a harsher recruitment policy, the main result was to drive men into the arms of the partisans, who for their part were fighting hard against the labour deployment policy. German labour deployment officials working abroad wore uniforms and were naturally prime targets for attacks. It must have been in the interest of those German officials who were not in the Labour Deployment Administration to play the role of the good cop who shelters the local population from the demands of the bad cop – Sauckel and his men.[17]

In no region, however, did the German recruiters succeed in meeting Berlin's and especially Sauckel's ambitious expectations. Only a small percentage of the Western European industrial workforce could be induced to go to Germany by high wages and the actual or alleged accomplishments of National Socialist social policy (health care, occupational safety, supposed overcoming of the antithesis between capital and labour). It soon became apparent that voluntary applications remained far below the hoped-for order of magnitude. Whereas in the beginning, the policy had been that German recruitment officials should make no false promises, Sauckel now built up a staff of agents whose task, in France and Italy, was to 'capture people by beguiling them with alcohol and persuasive talk, just as sailors used to be shanghaied'.[18]

In the occupied territories, therefore, the German Labour Deployment Administration changed its tactics and began to use pressure and force. As the German occupiers had the right to issue directives to the authorities, they had many ways of applying pressure to the working population. In Poland, as was also the case later in the occupied territories of Western Europe and the Soviet Union, the occupation authorities' refusal to allocate essential preliminary products or issuance of direct orders to close down contributed to the crippling of businesses and the rise in the unemployment rate. If potential workers failed to register with the Labour Office (and thus risked being sent to Germany for compulsory service), the food stamps or social benefits for their families could be reduced or even denied altogether. This combination of reduction of local jobs, comprehensive administrative registration, and financial pressure on families prompted many younger, usually single, members of households to sign up for labour deployment, if need be, even for work in Germany. This demonstrates how problematic the notion of voluntariness is.

As these measures, too, failed to have the desired effect, the German occupiers finally proceeded to use overt forcible recruitment (conscription or deportation) in all the occupied territories, with the exception of Denmark. Assuming the Germans decided to leave the local authorities in office and only place them under their command or under that of a puppet government, on the one hand, this had an advantage: there was less resistance to be reckoned with. On the other hand, certain considerations had to be granted in order to induce the local authorities or their government to collaborate.

The classic example is the *Service du travail obligatoire* (STO), which was established in France in February 1943. Sauckel, who wanted to gain more and more French workers, especially skilled workers, for the German war economy, had increased the pressure on the Vichy regime to such a degree that it saw itself compelled to introduce a service obligation in September 1942, and this subsequently was institutionalized in the form of the STO. Even so, the blow of the Germans' demands could be cushioned by the STO – depending on the circumstances – in a socially acceptable way: entire age groups were called up, but exemptions (as of 1943, limited once again) were granted, for example, to married couples and family men or farmers and policemen. In total, more than 600,000 French workers went to Germany through the STO.[19]

This of course sparked conflict with Armaments Minister Albert Speer. Since spring 1943 at the latest, Speer and his officials withdrew their support for Sauckel's ambitious labour recruitment program. Speer planned to shift consumer goods production from Germany to France. This enabled German firms to intensify their armaments production and French firms to resume production and use idle capacity. In addition, the production of consumer goods was less prone to sabotage by the French *résistance* than that of armaments goods. Naturally, the Vichy government supported Speer's plans because this could have stopped or at least slowed down the forced recruitment of French workers destined to Germany. Speer and the French Production Minister Bichelonne agreed that all firms working on behalf of Germany were declared '*S-Betrieb*' or '*Sperr-Betrieb*' (blocked factory) and their workers thus protected from Sauckel's draft actions. As early as December 1943, 3,301 firms had the *S-Betrieb* status and protected 723,134 French workers. The rivalry between Sauckel and Speer became so intense that Hitler had to decide. While he first had the illusion that both ministers should go ahead with their (incompatible) programs, he decided basically in favour of Sauckel in early January 1944. Five months later, the Allied invasion in Normandy made any plans to have French firms produce for Germany illusionary. But Sauckel could not take advantage of the situation, as passive and active French resistance practically stopped all further labour recruitment for German industry.[20]

In contrast to Western Europe, the Germans did not have to negotiate with local governments in (Central) Eastern Europe. Without trying to give even the appearance of quasi-legal administrative acts, the German Labour Deployment Administration in Poland and the occupied territories of the Soviet Union proceeded to engage in deportations, almost from the very outset. As early as September 1939, isolated raids and deportations took place. In the annexed Polish regions, the norm was conscription: the local administration summoned specific individuals for labour deployment, while the German Labour Deployment

Administration in the General Government banked at first on recruitment of volunteers and then, after the failure of this approach, switched to a ruthless policy of deportation.

These methods were employed in the occupied territories of the Soviet Union as well. The lower-key variant consisted of imposing certain quotas for 'volunteers' on regional or local administrative bodies. If the quota was not met, German security forces simply seized the required number of people in the villages in question or on farms. The even more ruthless variant consisted of raids in places such as villages, residential neighbourhoods of towns, cafés, or movie theatres. Anyone unable to present papers proving that he or she was employed was simply picked up and taken to the nearest collecting point. Before the individual's departure in a transport, family members, if any, still had an opportunity to bring their children or siblings some food for the journey, clothing, and personal-hygiene articles.[21]

Table 6.2 summarizes the measures of the German Labour Deployment Administration in the occupied territories to get the local population at work.

Transport of Polish and Soviet forced labourers normally took place in closed freight cars, with a bucket in the corner where they could relieve themselves. In certain transit camps, especially Cracow, Lublin, Częstochowa, and Warsaw, the

Table 6.2 Measures of the German Labour Deployment Administration in the occupied territories

		Obligation to work		*Recruitment of civilian workers*		
Country or region	Under German control since	For Jews	For non-Jews	Voluntary to Germany	Forced at home	Forced to Germany
Remaining Czech lands	Mar 1939	yes	yes	yes	yes	yes
Poland	Sep 1939	yes	yes	yes	yes	yes
Denmark	Apr 1940	no	no	yes	no	no
Norway	Apr 1940	no	yes	generally no	yes	no
Netherlands	May 1940	yes	yes	yes	yes	yes
Belgium	May 1940	yes	yes	yes	yes	yes
France	Jun 1940	yes	yes	yes	yes	yes
Serbia	Apr 1941	yes	yes	yes	yes	yes
Greece	May 1941	yes	yes	yes	yes	few
Soviet Union	Jun 1941	no (murdered)	yes	yes	yes	yes
Tunisia	Nov 1942	yes	no	no	no	no
Italy	Sep 1943	no (deported)	yes	yes	yes	yes
Hungary	Oct 1944	yes	no	yes	no	no

Sources: Literature quoted in footnotes 4 to 6.

deportees were deloused and medically examined to determine their degree of fitness. Upon arrival in German transit camps, there generally was another round of delousing, followed by departure on foot or further transport to the respective German *Einsatzträger* (contractors): private entities ranging from an individual farmer to a major corporation, public enterprises, municipalities, church facilities, and the like.

The transfer of captured enemy soldiers was handled in a similar way. After capture, they were brought behind the front lines to transit camps, where they were deloused and then transported to POW camps for noncommissioned personnel (*Stalag, Stammlager*) or for officers (*Oflag, Offizierslager*), located in occupied areas or the *Reich*. If they were deemed fit for work, the prisoners of the Stalags were hired out in the form of labour battalions to the various contractors, with arrangements handled by the Labour Offices.

A different fate was destined for the Soviet POWs at first. The *Wehrmacht*, which had experienced no problems in the Western theatre in 1940 when transporting more than 2 million French and Belgian POWs (the Dutch prisoners were directly released) into the *Reich*, allowed 2 million of the 3.35 million Soviet POWs to starve to death in the first few months of the Eastern Campaign. Not until late October 1941, when the German advance had bogged down, did Hitler decide to deploy Soviet POWs for labour within the *Reich*. Hitler was not the only one to whom this decision must have presented some difficulty: the German security agencies, too, were not happy that, in addition to the Poles, other Slavic *Untermenschen* (subhumans), possibly 'infected' with Bolshevism, now were to find their way into the *Reich*.[22] These ideological and racial misgivings were accommodated by ensuring correspondingly inhumane conditions of deployment. This also held for other European regions where Soviet POWs were put to work by the Germans, such as France. Their conditions of life and work were especially harsh in Norway, where the *Wehrmacht* deployed nearly 100,000 Soviet POWs since September 1941. The mortality rate of the Soviet POWs far exceeded that of all other groups of forced labourers, with the exception of the concentration camp inmates.[23]

The fate of the concentration camp inmates who were deployed as labourers was in most cases inconceivably terrible. Anyone who was placed in a German concentration camp was subjected at the very least to months of harassment and torment. Starting in 1941, Jews, who until then had been crowded together in ghettos or interned in forced labour camps similar to concentration camps, were transported to specially built extermination camps, all of which, with the exception of Chełmno, were situated within the General Government. Anyone who came to Chełmno, Lublin-Majdanek, Sobibór, or Treblinka was, as a rule, murdered immediately. Auschwitz occupied a special position in the German concentration camp system. While the other camps listed above were pure extermination camps, Auschwitz used the infamous method of selections. Anyone whom the Germans deemed unfit for work went to the gas chamber. The others were either hired out through one of the Auschwitz camp's external detachments to employers in Upper Silesia or Moravia or sent farther into the *Reich*, where they were assigned to one of the concentration camps there and then hired out. Thus there now were not only Slavs but Jews again inside the *Reich*: for the National Socialist ideologues, another painful concession to the pragmatists in the armaments sector of the economy.

The most notorious case of the use of concentration camp inmates in production is that of *I.G. Farbenindustrie AG*. *I.G. Farben*, then one of the leading chemical producers worldwide, was a giant corporation created by merger in 1925 and became the very symbol of the entanglement of private industrial firms with the National Socialist regime. Even before the war, owing to its significance for the synthesis of fuel and rubber (Buna), *I.G. Farben* had been tightly woven into Germany's rearmament efforts, especially since the (second) Four Year Plan of 1936. In 1940, when *I.G. Farben* was planning a site for a new plant to produce Buna and synthetic fuel, it decided on Auschwitz. A crucial factor in this decision was the concentration camp then under construction, which from then on made prisoners available as construction workers. The pilot project of deploying concentration camp inmates started in March 1941 at the construction site of *I.G. Farben* in Auschwitz-Monowitz. At the beginning, the firm still lodged protests against the poor health situation of the prisoners, but a process of inurement quickly came into play. In mid-1942, the Auschwitz main camp even set up a subcamp of its own in Auschwitz-Monowitz, right next to the plant grounds. Of the total of around 35,000 prisoners made to work for *I.G. Farben* in Auschwitz-Monowitz between October 1942 and January 1945, between 23,000 and 30,000 died. In the nearby subsidiaries of the plant, *I.G. Farben* deployed 6,000 additional concentration camp prisoners, most of whom perished. Another 11,000 concentration camp prisoners worked at the Leuna, Wolfen, and Munich plants of the firm. Overall, at its numerous plants, *I.G. Farben* used at least 60,000 foreign civilian workers, 10,000 POWs, and 52,000 concentration camp prisoners.[24]

Conclusion

The deployment of forced workers in the German-occupied territories took place in a field of conflict between economic and ideological motives. Economic motives prevailed when it came to the question *who* was to work for the German occupation forces. The answer was more or less that everyone capable should do so – even Slavic 'subhumans' – except Jews. Ideological motives came to the fore when it came to the question of *how* the forced workers should be treated. In Western Europe, the German occupation forces were reluctant to use sheer power. They rather favoured a hybrid of carrots and sticks, with the stick becoming more important over time. In Eastern Europe, the Germans used brute force right from the start. Poles and 'Russians' (i.e. citizens of the Soviet Union) were not only regarded as subhumans but also as peoples who should cede their countries to German settlers. Their role inside the German sphere of influence was either that of humble servants or of useless eaters. In contrast, the right to exist (under German hegemony) was not denied to peoples in Western and Southern Europe. An immediate consequence of these ideological and geopolitical ideas was that, on average, Western workers were treated much less badly than those from Eastern Europe, both legally and in everyday practice.

It is often argued that Nazi Germany underwent a process of ideological radicalization in the course of the war. This is not the case for the production factor labour, as becomes most obvious in the case of European Jewry. Since 1941, Jews were systematically murdered. Those working in ghettos or Jewish labour camps were exploited until lethal exhaustion or until they were sent to an extermination camp. Yet the ever-increasing demand for human labour came into conflict with the aim of murdering the whole European Jewry. As a consequence, rather than murdering them all and at once, those who were seen as fit to work were spared immediate extermination, especially since spring 1944, when it was the turn of the Hungarian Jews to be deported to the extermination camps. The increasing dominance of economic over ideological reasons is best illustrated by the notorious ramp at the Auschwitz camp at which the newly arriving (mostly Hungarian) Jews were separated into 'fit to work' and 'immediate extermination'.

Notes

1 Cf. A. Rachamimov, *POWs and the Great War: Captivity on the Eastern Front*. Oxford, New York: Berg, 2002, pp. 39–42, 107–15; J. Thiel, 'Forced Labour, Deportation and Recruitment. The German Reich and Belgian Labourers During the First World War', in S. Jaumain et al. (eds.), *Une Guerre totale? La Belgique dans la Première Guerre Mondiale. Nouvelles tendances de la recherche historique*. Brussels: Archives Générales du Royaume, 2005, pp. 235–45; M. Spoerer, The mortality of Allied prisoners of war and Belgian civilian deportees in German custody during World War I: A reappraisal of the effects of forced labour, *Population Studies*, 2006, vol. 60, pp. 121–36, here pp. 122–5; J.F. Vance, 'World War I, Western Front', in idem (ed.): *Encyclopedia of Prisoners of War and Internment*. 2nd ed. Millerton, NY: Grey House, 2006, pp. 326–9.
2 Cf. C. Westerhoff, *Zwangsarbeit im Ersten Weltkrieg. Deutsche Arbeitskräftepolitik im besetzten Polen und Litauen 1914–1918*. Paderborn: Schöningh, 2011.
3 See U. Herbert, *Fremdarbeiter. Politik und Praxis des 'Ausländer-Einsatzes' in der Kriegswirtschaft des Dritten Reiches*. Bonn: Dietz, 1985, second and extended edition 1999; idem, *Hitler's Foreign Workers: Enforced Foreign Labor in Germany Under the Third Reich*. Cambridge: Cambridge University Press, 1997.
4 M. Spoerer, *Zwangsarbeit unter dem Hakenkreuz. Ausländische Zivilarbeiter, Kriegsgefangene und Häftlinge im Dritten Reich und im besetzten Europa 1939–1945*. Stuttgart/Munich: DVA, 2001, pp. 35–88; F. Lemmes, 'Zwangsarbeit im besetzten Europa: Die Organisation Todt in Frankreich und Italien, 1940–1945', in A. Heusler/M. Spoerer/H. Trischler (eds.), *Rüstung, Kriegswirtschaft und Zwangsarbeit*. Munich: Oldenbourg, 2010, pp. 219–52; K. Linne/F. Dierl, *Arbeitskräfte als Kriegsbeute: der Fall Ost- und Südosteuropa 1939–1945*. Berlin: Metropol, 2011; F. Dierl/Z. Janjetovic/K. Linne (eds.), *Pflicht, Zwang und Gewalt: Arbeitsverwaltungen und Arbeitskräftepolitik im deutsch besetzten Polen und Serbien 1939–1944*. Essen: Klartext, 2013; D. Pohl/T. Sebta (eds.), *Zwangsarbeit in Hitlers Europa. Besatzung, Arbeit, Folgen*. Berlin: Metropol, 2013; M. Spoerer, 'Travail forcé dans l'Europe occupée', in J.-P. Cahn/S. Martens/B. Wegner (eds.), *Le 'Troisième Reich' dans l'historiographie allemande. Lieux de pouvoir – rivalités de pouvoir*. Villeneuve d'Ascq: Presses Universitaires du Septentrion, 2013, pp. 351–74.

5 C. Gerlach, *Kalkulierte Morde. Die deutsche Wirtschafts- und Vernichtungspolitik in Weißrußland 1941–1944.* Hamburg: Hamburger Edition, 1999; S. Hodzic/T. Penter, 'Zwangsarbeit – Arbeit für den Feind. Der Donbass unter deutscher Okkupation (1941–1943)', *Geschichte und Gesellschaft*, 2005, vol. 31, pp. 68–100; C. Schölzel, *Zwangsarbeit im "Unabhängigen Staat Kroatien" 1941–1945.* Münster: LIT, 2012; S. Rutar, *Arbeit und Überleben in Jugoslawien. Regionale Bergbaugesellschaften unter NS Besatzung (1941–1944/45).* Essen: Klartext, 2013.
6 A. S. Milward, 'French Labour and the German Economy, 1942–1945. An Essay on the Nature of the Fascist New Order', *Economic History Review*, 1970, vol. 23, pp. 336–51; A. Dallin, *German Rule in Russia 1941–1945. A Study of Occupation Policies.* 2nd ed. London et al.: Macmillan, 1981; Z. Erez, 'Jews for Copper: Jewish-Hungarian Labor Service Companies in Bor', in *Yad Vashem Studies*, 2000, vol. 28, S. 243–86; K. Berkhoff, *Harvest of Despair: Life and Death in Ukraine under Nazi Rule.* Cambridge: Harvard University Press, 2004; M. Soleim, *Prisoners of War and Forced Labour: Histories of War and Occupation.* Newcastle: Cambridge Scholars Publ., 2010; H. Klemann/S. Kudryashov, *Occupied Economies. An Economic History of Nazi-Occupied Europe, 1939–1945.* London: Berg, 2012, pp. 119–73.
7 Cf. for an overview M. Spoerer/J. Fleischhacker, 'Forced Laborers in Nazi Germany: Categories, Numbers, and Survivors', *Journal of Interdisciplinary History*, 2002, vol. 33, pp. 169–204.
8 U. Herbert, 'Labour and Extermination. Economic Interest and the Primacy of Weltanschauung in National Socialism', *Past and Present*, 1993, vol. 138, pp. 144–95; M. T. Allen, *The Business of Genocide: The SS, Slave Labor, and the Concentration Camps.* Chapel Hill: University of North Carolina Press, 2002.
9 D. G. Maier, 'Arbeitseinsatzverwaltung und NS-Zwangsarbeit', in U. Winkler (ed.), *Stiften gehen: NS-Zwangsarbeit und Entschädigungsdebatte.* Cologne: PapyRossa, 2000, p. 73; M. Weißbecker, ' "So einen Arbeitseinsatz wie in Deutschland gibt es nicht noch einmal auf der Welt!". Fritz Sauckel – Generalbevollmächtigter für den Arbeitseinsatz', in ibid, pp. 54–5; Spoerer, *Zwangsarbeit unter dem Hakenkreuz*, p. 37.
10 The notion of voluntariness is of course problematic in the context of a war economy, cf. Herbert, *Hitler's Foreign Workers*, pp. 79–80; Spoerer/Fleischhacker, 'Forced Laborers in Nazi Germany', pp. 173–6.
11 J.H.E. Fried, *The Exploitation of Foreign Labor by Germany.* Montreal: International Labour Office, 1945, pp. 256–63, Spoerer, *Zwangsarbeit unter dem Hakenkreuz*, p. 37.
12 For an overview, cf. Spoerer, *Zwangsarbeit unter dem Hakenkreuz*, pp. 40–86, and for the Soviet Union; idem, 'Der Faktor Arbeit in den besetzten Ostgebieten im Widerstreit ökonomischer und ideologischer Interessen', *Mitteilungen der Gemeinsamen Kommission für die Erforschung der jüngeren Geschichte der deutsch-russischen Beziehungen*, 2006, vol. 2, pp. 68–93.
13 Herbert, *Hitler's Foreign Workers*, pp. 277–8.
14 P. W. Becker, 'Fritz Sauckel – Generalbevollmächtigter für den Arbeitseinsatz', in R. Smelser/E. Syring/R. Zitelmann (eds.), *Die braune Elite. 22 biographische Skizzen.* 2nd ed., Darmstadt: Wiss. Buchgesellschaft, 1990, pp. 236–45; Weißbecker, 'So einen Arbeitseinsatz wie in Deutschland'; S. Raßloff, *Fritz Sauckel: Hitlers 'Muster-Gauleiter' und 'Sklavenhalter'.* Erfurt: Landeszentrale für Politische Bildung, 2007.
15 J. Scherner/J. Streb, Das Ende eines Mythos? Albert Speer und das so genannte Rüstungswunder, *Vierteljahrschrift für Sozial- und Wirtschaftsgeschichte*, 2006, vol. 93, pp. 172–96.
16 O. Dard/H. Joly/P. Verheyde, Philippe (eds.), *Les entreprises françaises, l'occupation et le second XXe siècle.* Metz: Centre de Recherche Univ. Lorraine

d'Histoire, 2011; M. Boldorf/J. Scherner, 'France's Occupation Costs and the War in the East: The Contribution to the German War Economy, 1940–1944', *Journal of Contemporary History*, 2012, vol. 47, pp. 291–316.
17 Maier, 'Arbeitseinsatzverwaltung und NS-Zwangsarbeit', p. 74.
18 Sauckel at a meeting of the Central Planning Board on 1 March 1944, in *International Military Tribunal* (1947–1949): *Trial of the Major War Criminals before the International Military Tribunal: Nuremberg, 14 November 1945–1 October 1946*, vol. 38, document 124-R, p. 351.
19 Y. Durand, 'Vichy und der "Reichseinsatz"', in Ulrich Herbert (ed.): *Europa und der 'Reichseinsatz'. Ausländische Zivilarbeiter, Kriegsgefangene und KZ-Häftlinge in Deutschland 1938–1945*. Essen: Klartext, 1991, pp. 184–99; H. Bories-Sawala, *Franzosen im 'Reichseinsatz'. Deportation, Zwangsarbeit, Alltag. Erfahrungen und Erinnerungen von Kriegsgefangenen und Zivilarbeitern*. Frankfurt am Main: Lang, 1996, vol. 1, p. 248; B. Zielinski, 'Die deutsche Arbeitseinsatzpolitik in Frankreich 1940–1944', in R. J. Overy/G. Otto/J. Houwink ten Cate (eds.), *Die 'Neuordnung' Europas. NS-Wirtschaftspolitik in den besetzten Gebieten*. Berlin: Metropol, 1997, p. 123.
20 Milward, 'French Labour and the German Economy', pp. 344–50; Herbert, *Hitler's Foreign Workers*, pp. 275–8.
21 On Poland, cf. C. Łuczak, 'Polnische Arbeiter im nationalsozialistischen Deutschland während des Zweiten Weltkriegs. Entwicklung und Aufgaben der polnischen Forschung', in Herbert, *Europa und der 'Reichseinsatz'*, pp. 94–9; on the Soviet Union, R.-D. Müller, 'Die Rekrutierung sowjetischer Zwangsarbeiter für die deutsche Kriegswirtschaft' in idem, pp. 234–50; on Belorussia, C. Gerlach, German Economic Interests, Occupation Policy, and the Murder of the Jews in Belorussia, 1941/43. In: U. Herbert (ed.), *National Socialist Extermination Policies. Contemporary German Perspectives and Controversies*. New York et al.: Berghahn, 2000, pp. 210–39; on the Baltic states, T. Plath, *Zwischen Schonung und Menschenjagden. Arbeitseinsatzpolitik in den baltischen Generalbezirken des Reichskommissariats Ostland 1941–1944*. Essen: Klartext, 2012.
22 On the National Socialist racial hierarchy and anti-Slavism in particular, cf. Herbert, Hitler's Foreign Workers, pp. 44–5, 100–6, and on its popularity among the German population, M. Spoerer, 'Die soziale Differenzierung der ausländischen Zivilarbeiter, Kriegsgefangenen und Häftlinge im Deutschen Reich', in B. Chiari/J. Echternkamp (eds.), *Das Deutsche Reich und der Zweite Weltkrieg. Vol. 9/2: Die deutsche Kriegsgesellschaft 1939–1945: Ausbeutung, Deutungen, Ausgrenzung*. Munich: DVA, 2005, pp. 569–76 (English translation published in 2014).
23 Fundamental on this topic is C. Streit, *Keine Kameraden. Die Wehrmacht und die sowjetischen Kriegsgefangenen 1941–1945*. Bonn: Dietz, 1997 (first edition 1978); M. N. Soleim, 'Introduction', in idem, *Prisoners of War and Forced Labour. Histories of War and Occupation*. Newcastle: Cambridge Scholars Publ., 2010, p. 9; on the mortality rate, cf. M. Spoerer, 'Zwangsarbeitsregimes im Vergleich: Deutschland und Japan im Ersten und Zweiten Weltkrieg', in K. Tenfelde/H.-C. Seidel (eds.): *Zwangsarbeit im Europa des 20. Jahrhunderts. Vergleichende Aspekte und gesellschaftliche Auseinandersetzung*. Essen: Klartext, 2007, p. 215.
24 Erwin Schulhof (former clerk in the Labor Deployment Department at the Buna/Monowitz concentration camp), affidavit, June 21, 1947, NI-7967. Archives of the Fritz Bauer Institut, Nürnberger Nachfolgeprozess Fall VI, PDB 74 (g), p. 130; Spoerer, *Zwangsarbeit unter dem Hakenkreuz*, p. 110. For *I. G. Farben* in general and the various estimates of the number of prisoners murdered in particular, cf. P. Hayes, *Industry and Ideology. IG Farben in the Nazi Era*, Cambridge: Cambridge UP, p. 359.

7 Development of labour policy in 'Manchukuo' and its limit, 1933–1943[*]

Toshio Kojima

The labour control policy in 'Manchukuo' started from the policy for the public security, which was an urgent issue in the early stage of that country. The Manchukuo government was concerned that the spies of the Chinese Communist Party entered the country with Chinese workers. The full-scale labour control policy was implemented based on the 'Outline of the Labour Policy in Manchukuo' (March 1933),[1] which planned to introduce skilled workers from Japan and unskilled workers from North China. After that, the Labour Control Committee was established in the Special Operations Department of the Kwantung Army of Japan to play the central role in drawing up the labour policy. The Committee focused on restricting Chinese workers to enter Manchukuo. For this purpose, a special company, *Daito Konsu*, was established in Tianjin to control visas.[2]

These policies for immigration control succeeded in restricting the number of immigrated workers below the target in 1935 and 1936. After that, the direction of the labour control policy changed drastically because of the start of 'Five Years Plan for Industrial Development' (April 1937) and the break out of the Sino-Japanese War (July 1937). In 1937, immigration of Chinese workers sharply declined, while it became difficult to introduce skilled workers from Japan. Thus, the focus of the labour policy came to be securing a labour force.

For this purpose, the Manchuria Labour Association (*Manshu Roko Kyokai*, MLA) was established in January 1938. In addition, the National Mobilization Law (*Kokka Sodoin Ho*, February 1938) and the Labour Control Law (*Rodo Tosei Ho*, December 1938) enabled the government to mobilize people forcefully thorough government agencies and the MLA in case of emergency.

However, in the early 1940s, it became difficult to obtain labour from North China and Middle China under the prolonged occupation of these areas by the Japanese Army. Faced with this situation, the Manchukuo government moved to the New Labour System (*Romu Shintaisei*), which aimed at self-sufficiency of the labour force, in 1941. To establish this system, in October 1941, the Labour Control Law was amended for the government to control the labour force directly, while the MLA was reorganized into the Manchuria Labour Association for the Prosperous Country (*Manshu Romu Kokokukai*, MLAPC). Meanwhile, concrete measures for compulsory labour mobilization were implemented, including the emergent employment system, the public-duty labour system and the recruitment territory system.

Nevertheless, the New Labour System was not successful in the end. Although compulsory labour mobilization was further strengthened, the government and major companies, including the South Manchuria Railways, suffered from qualitative and quantitative shortages of labour force, and they were obliged to take additional measures, such as revision of work organization, intensification of work and distribution of necessary goods.[3] Furthermore, the people resisted forced work under the control of Japan Empire. This chapter describes the development of the labour policy and its limit, focusing on the period after the outbreak of the Sino-Japanese War, when the labour shortage became serious.

1. Development of wartime labour control policy

1.1 Start of the policy to adopt Chinese workers

1.1.1 The 'Outline of Labour Control' and establishment of the Manchuria Labour Association

The start of the 'Five Years Plan for Industrial Development' (April 1937) and the outbreak of the Sino-Japanese War (July 1937) caused a shortage of labour. As the immigration of workers from China declined and adoption of skilled workers from Japan became difficult, the labour policy of the Manchukuo government, which had focused on restricting immigration of Chinese workers, had to be changed. Since July 1937, when the Guidance Division of the Civil Affairs Department was established in the Manchukuo government, the government agencies were pressed by coping with the labour shortage.

From 1937 to 1940, the basic framework for the wartime labour policy in Manchukuo was established. In this period, while as the government agency in charge of drawing up the labour policy, the Labour Committee was established in the State Council of the Manchukuo government, the fundamental laws for labour control, namely the National Mobilization Law and the Labour Control Law, were legislated. Meanwhile, as the government agency in charge of implementation of the labour policy, the Guidance Division was established in the Civil Affairs Department in July 1937. It took charge of such issues as labour mobilization, worker registration and adjustment of labour demand and supply, which were related to the security policy.

In August 1937, the Manchukuo government drew up the 'Outline of Manchukuo Labour Control' and the 'Outline of Establishment of Manchuria Labour Association', cooperating with the Special Operations Department of the Kwantung Army.[4] The 'Outline of Manchukuo Labour Control' made clear that the focus of the labour policy shifted from restriction of immigration to securing and controlling labour. In addition, the policy that aimed at introducing skilled workers from Japan was withdrawn. Meanwhile, the 'Outline of Establishment of Manchuria Worker Association' proposed to found the Manchuria Labour Association (MLA) in order to distribute, register, protect and train workers in Manchuria. The MLA was given the role of adjusting demand and supply of labour in Manchuria. Given this role, the Manchukuo government controlled the MLA through controlling its personnel affairs, including appointment of the chairman. It is remarkable that the purposes of the MLA included maintaining security through registering workers and issuing certificates to them.[5]

In accordance with this policy change, the Kwantung Army raised the target for immigration of Chinese workers from 380,000 to 500,000 in January 1938. Moreover, to cope with the revision of the Five Years Plan for Industrial Development and the increase of labour demand for developing the northern part of Manchukuo according to 'Plan for Developing the Northern Periphery', the target was raised again to be 910,000.

1.1.2 Emergent recruitment of workers and start of compulsory recruitment

Meanwhile, concrete measures to recruit a labour force were taken. In October 1937, the 'Ordinance on the Temporary Measures on Adjusting Labour Demand and Supply' was issued, which included some important measures that were succeeded by the later policies.

The ordinance specified the procedure to recruit workers. First, the relevant government agencies should investigate the capacity of labour supply. The first-tier potential workers included refugees, released prisoners, the people who lost jobs and those who could be supplied as workers through special training. The second-tier potential workers included those who could be invited to be workers, such as unemployed people and dependents. Finally, as the third-tier potential workers, the government agencies should investigate the maximum number of the people who could be recruited compulsorily, taking account of the situation of the industries in the jurisdictional areas. The idea to mobilize refugees and unemployed people was related to the policy of mobilizing urban vagabonds implemented later in 1942.

The ordinance also specified the method for recruiting workers. The standard unit of worker supply was an organization like a traditional Chinese organization that supplied coolies. Using those units, village chiefs (in case of voluntary recruitment) or heads of police stations (in case of compulsory recruitment) recruited workers. The role of the police station chiefs implies that the compulsory recruitment was labour mobilization by the administrative authorities. Also, they were asked to tame nationalism of workers in cases of compulsory recruitment, which indicates that uneasiness and repellence of workers were recognized as a serious problem. After sending out the workers, the police should monitor them, communicating with the chief of the worker supply units, to protect them and control their unjustified requests.

In addition, concerning the case of recruiting workers from North China, the workers should be recruited through *Daito Konsu* with mediation by the

Kwantung Army, in principle. Also, the workers from North China were requested to remain in Manchukuo, and their emigration should be prohibited, if necessary.

The ordinance of October 1937 is characterized by harsh measures for recruitment and employment, such as (a) thorough investigation of potential labour force, (b) thorough recruitment including urban vagabonds, (c) compulsory recruitment using government agencies and (d) strict labour management. It was the germ of the policy taken under the New Labour System later on.

1.1.3 National Mobilization Law and Labour Control Law

Meanwhile, as the legal foundation of labour control, the National Mobilization Law (February 1938) and the Labour Control Law (December 1938) were legislated. The aim of the National Mobilization Law was to control personnel, material and financial resources during war or incident. For this purpose, the government could make people engage in the designated works by ordinances in case it was necessary for national mobilization. Also, the government was given the authority to issue orders concerning the labour condition, dismissal, registration and training of skilled workers. Given this broad authority of the government, a new organization, the Labour Committee, was established in the National Council of the Manchukuo government. This committee took over the role of labour policy making from the Labour Control Committee, the Special Operations Department of the Kwantung Army.

In December 1938, the Labour Control Law was legislated, which prescribed the concrete procedure for implementing labour control.[6] A characteristic of this law is that it gave broad authority to the Minister of Civil Affairs. Only the labour suppliers that were licensed by the Minister of Civil Affairs could conclude the agreement on recruitment, wage and labour conditions and so forth of workers. Revision of the agreement should be approved by the Minister of Civil Affairs. Also, the minister had the authority to issue commands to labour suppliers on recruitment, supply, protection and guidance of workers.

These authority of the Minister of Civil Affairs could be entrusted to the heads of provinces. Also, in emergency, the Minister of Civil Affairs could compulsorily recruit workers through government agencies and the MLA. The articles on the compulsory recruitment in the Labour Control Law expanded the emergent compulsory recruitment, which the National Mobilization Law prescribed for the period of war or incident, to peacetime. For example, the MLA could apply for recruitment of workers necessary for public works to the head of the province, and on the application, the head of the province mediated recruitment of workers. This was de facto compulsory employment in peacetime.

Also, according to the articles of the control agreement, dismissal, hiring and labour conditions could be controlled through agreements between private firms. The government intended to suppress wage and labour transfers by this measure. For this purpose, the Civil Affairs Department drew up the 'Outline on the Control Agreements' and based on it, in April 1939, the 'National Agreement on Hire and Employment of Workers' was concluded, by the mediation of the MLA.[7]

According to the Labour Control Law, the Manchukuo government obtained the authority to recruit labour as needed through government agencies and the MLA. The MLA, acquiring *Daito Konsu* in July 1939, became the organization which took charge of labour control implementation in an integrated fashion.

1.2 Transition to compulsory labour mobilization

In spite of the measures described, labour shortage and disorder of labour control became still more serious in 1940. In particular, due to the restriction of money order remittance to North China in July 1940, Chinese workers became unable to send sufficient money to their hometowns. In addition, exchange of the Manchurian currency to the notes of the China Union Reserve Bank, the Central Bank of the Republic of China, was restricted up to a certain amount. Hence, Chinese workers began to return to their hometowns.[8]

In this circumstance, the Labour Control Law was amended in August 1940, and the Civil Affairs Department of the Manchukuo government determined the 'Outline of the Measures on Labour Issues', which aimed at the stability of workers and strengthening their labour. In June 1941, the 'Outline of the Emergent Measures for Worker Recruitment' was determined, and after that, labour mobilization by government agencies was expanded. Meanwhile, mobilization of 'special workers', namely war prisoners, was also strengthened. In sum, the labour mobilization policy came to have more compulsory characteristics in 1940 and 1941.

1.2.1 Partial amendment of the Labour Control Law

The amendment of the Labour Control Law in August 1940 enabled the government to monitor private establishments directly, whereas the original law prescribed just the authority to order private establishments to report the conditions of workers.[9] This amendment was introduced because the labour control was not so effective as expected. For example, although the 'National Agreement on Hire and Employment of Workers' was concluded in April 1939, as stated, this was ineffective. Given that, the agreement on the fair wage was concluded in each province in May 1940, and the additional agreements on the fair wage were concluded in Hsinkin City and six provinces in August 1940. The amendment of the Labour Control Law in August 1940 aimed at making these new agreements effective, but these measures did not improve the situation.

1.2.2 'Outline of the Measures on Labour Issues' by the Civil Affairs Department

At the end of 1940, it became clear that the indirect control through the MLA could not resolve the labour shortage in Manchukuo. Furthermore, the prolonged occupation of North China and Middle China increased labour demand in those areas, which implied that Manchukuo should recruit necessary labour forces in its territory. This situation was the background for the 'New Labour System'. The basic idea of the 'New Labour System' was described in the 'Outline of the Measures on Labour Issues', determined by the Civil Affairs Department in January 1941.

In the 'Outline of the Measures on Labour Issues', which was composed of seven chapters and fifty articles, the Civil Affairs Department made clear the new aim of the labour policy. It declared that the aim of the labour policy was securing the labour force and expanding the munitions industry, in particular establishing self-sufficiency of labour in Manchukuo.[10] Given this aim, the 'Outline' specified various concrete measures for that. Here, we summarize the measures for securing the labour force and those for labour management.

SECURING THE LABOUR FORCE

For securing the labour force, utilization of agricultural workers, utilization of female workers, mobilization of labour force of the younger generation through volunteer labour service, training of workers, strengthening of government control, introduction of Chinese workers, strengthening the relationship of firms with the areas where they recruited workers, emergency measures, utilization of 'special workers' (war prisoners) and so forth. were listed as the measures.

The main point of the government control was that the government should grasp the vocational capacity of each worker through registration of each worker and his/her vocational capacity. It was regarded as the key for labour mobilization. The stress of training reflected the decline in immigration of skilled workers from Japan. By strengthening the relationship of firms with their recruitment areas, increasing stability of workers was intended. Concerning utilization of war prisoners, necessity of training and monitoring were stressed. Finally, the fact that introduction of Chinese workers was included in the measures indicates that the principle of labour self-sufficiency was difficult to maintain.

LABOUR MANAGEMENT

With respect to labour management, the chapter on 'protection and guidance of workers' listed the measures. Basically, this chapter stressed the measures to secure the life condition and labour condition of workers to enhance the quality of workers, such as excluding intermediate exploitation and improving the distribution of necessities. In this context, it was stressed that the advantages of the traditional indirect labour management system should be promoted, while its disadvantages should be excluded. It is remarkable that the Manchukuo government was willing to utilize the traditional Chinese labour management system. They should depend upon it for securing labour force.

1.2.3 'Outline of the Emergent Measures for Recruiting Domestic Workers' and utilization of 'special workers'

In June 1941, the 'Outline of the Emergent Measures for Recruiting Domestic Workers' was determined. This 'Outline' clearly stated that administrative agencies should be utilized for recruiting workers.[11] According to this policy, it was prescribed that based on the Labour Mobilization Plan at the national level, necessary labour supply should be allotted to each province, which in turn should allot labour supply to each prefecture and county. Then, each prefecture and county should recruit workers through a branch of the MLA. This outline was implemented by the ordinance 'On the Emergent Measures for Recruiting Domestic Workers' in July 1941.

Another important case of expansion of compulsory labour in this period was mobilization of war prisoners. As stated, there was an idea of utilizing war prisoners from the early stage of Manchukuo's labour policy. This idea was put into practice after the outbreak of the Sino-Japanese War as utilization of 'special workers'. For example, war prisoners were employed to construct the Fengman Dam in Jilin Sheng Province in 1937, and war prisoners from the northern part of Manchuria were employed at the Fushun Coal Mine and the Benxihu Coal Mine.[12] The 'Rules on Treatment of Submitting Enemy' by the North China Area Army (April 1939) prescribed that the demilitarized soldiers should be introduced into Manchukuo as workers or be employed for works of the provisional government in North China.[13] Furthermore, mobilization of civil prisoners to private firms started in 1941. Those civil prisoners were employed with approval of the Legal Department of the Manchukuo government, but the mobilization of civil prisoners lacked a legal foundation.[14]

3. Start and development of the New Labour System

The Manchukuo government was obliged to take drastic measures, faced with increasing labour shortages under the condition that they could not expect introduction of workers from abroad. Especially the start of the Second Five Years Plan for Industrial Development in 1942 urged the government to take a further step. In this situation, the New Labour System was established, in which the government directly controlled the recruitment and distribution of labour. The structure of the new system was drawn up in the 'Outline of Establishing the New Labour System', determined in September 1941. Given that, the Labour Control Law was substantially amended in October 1941, and a new organization for implementing labour control, the Manchuria Labour Association for Prosperous Country (MLAPC), was established, replacing the MLA.

3.1 The New Labour System: The system for universal compulsory employment

'The Outline of Establishing the New Labour System' aimed at securing labour for constructing the military state. According to the outline, the labour policy, which had been at least nominally based on the voluntary cooperation of private organizations, came to be implemented directly by the government. According to the commentary by the Agency of General Affairs of the Manchukuo government,[15] the aim of the New Labour System was (a) expanding labour mobilization toward universal employment, (b) allocation of labour by the administrative authorities and (c) improvement of labour productivity.

3.1.1 Full-scale amendment of the Labour Control Law

In order to establish the New Labour System, the Labour Control Law was fully amended in October 1941. First, the rules on the control agreement that private labour suppliers concluded with each other were completely deleted. This revision reflected the idea that indirect control through the agreement of private suppliers was ineffective and that direct control by the government was necessary. Meanwhile, the authority of the Minister of Civil Affairs was substantially expanded. According to the amended law, the Minister of Civil Affairs had the authority to give commands on every aspect of labour issues, including recruitment, labour condition and transfer, which reflected the basic idea of the New Labour System that the government should directly control the labour.

Second, the amended law gave legal ground to 'emergent employment'. Article 8 of the amended Labour Control Law prescribed that the Minister of Civil Affairs could make people work for important public works or national policy works in case they were urgently needed. This implies that the government could force people to work if necessary. It is true that the original Labour Control Law had the articles on recruitment of workers for public works, but these articles just prescribed that the MLA could request local governments to mediate worker recruitment. Indeed, the commentary by the Agency of General Affairs stressed that the most distinctive feature of the amended law was in the articles on the delivery of labour by the administrative power, namely the delivery of labour by compulsory power in peacetime.[16]

Third, the MLA was dissolved and its function was taken over by a new organization, the Manchuria Worker Association for Prosperous Country (MLAPC). As stated in what follows, the new organization had much larger authority than the MLA.

Besides these main points, there were several amendments reflecting the basic idea of the New Labour System, including expansion of the objects to employees in commerce, adding the rule on temporary shift of workers to other firms and strengthening of punishment.

3.1.2 Foundation of the Manchuria Worker Association for Prosperous Country

The MLAPC was founded in October 1941. It succeeded the MLA in roles such as mediation of workers, protection of workers and improvement of labour management, but in addition, it was strengthened as the organization for implementing labour control. The MLAPC was the national-level organization, which was composed of Provincial Labour Associations for Prosperous Country (PLAPC) at province level and other organizations designated by the Minister of Civil Affairs. Each of the PLAPCs, in turn, was composed of firms employing more than nine workers in forestry, fishery, mining, manufacturing, construction and transportation industries, as well as worker suppliers who supplied workers to those firms. The MLAPC and the PLAPCs were supervised by the Minister of Civil Affairs and the heads of local governments, respectively.

The MLAPC and the PLAPCs were de facto a part of the government organization for labour control. For example, in founding the PLAPC, the Minister of Civil Affairs appointed the founding committee, which drew up the statute and the member list to be approved by the Minister. Also, the chairman, board members and auditors were appointed by the Prime Minister. The chairman had wide-ranging authority in executing the affairs. The decision making was led by the chairman, not by majority of the board.[17]

In addition, according to the amended Labour Control Law, the MLAPC and PLAPCs were entrusted with the authority to implement labour control. That is, if the Minister of Civil Affairs or the head of local governments approved, the those associations could make rules on recruitment, hiring, supply, employment, dismissal, transfer, labour condition, protection, labour management, training or guidance. These rules made by the associations were applied not only to the member firms but also to the other firms in the relevant area. In other words, the MLAPC and the PLAPCs could determine the conditions which had been determined by the agreements between firms and enforce them on behalf of the Minister of Civil Affairs. In this sense, the MLAPC and PLAPCs had much stronger power than the Manchuria Worker Association.

3.1.3 Expansion of compulsory labour control

What characterized the labour policy in this period was the compulsory measures for securing labour. First, 'emergent employment' was prescribed by the Rule for Emergent Employment of Workers in February 1942. According to it, in case it was necessary for public works or emergent national policy works, those in charge of these works could declare the place of work, the sort of work, number of workers needed by type, period, labour conditions and so on to the Minister of Civil Affairs, who, in turn, ordered the local governments to deliver the workers. At the lowest level of the local government, the prefecture, city or county appointed people to be employed. In this sense, this was a system of compulsory labour mobilization.

Second, the 'public-duty labour system' was introduced by the National Public Duty Labour Law in October 1942. In December, the object was expanded to students. The students of universities, colleges and the special schools designated by the Minister of Civil Affairs should engage in construction work for national defence and railways.

Third, the recruitment territory system, which had been partially implemented at limited firms, was expanded after late 1941. The 'Outline of the Measures for Forming the Foundation of Domestic Worker Recruitment' of April 1943 requested firms to select some persons to be the leaders of the workers from the same hometown so that firms could establish worker organizations based on community relationships.

Meanwhile, the security policy was strengthened. As a part of it, in December 1941, the Peace Preservation Law was legislated, which assigned capital punishment to those who organized or participated in the organizations that aimed at transforming the structure of the state.

Concluding remarks

This chapter described the labour policy in Manchuria from the start of the 'Five Years Plan for Industrial Development' to the establishment of the New Labour System. Mobilization of labour by the powers of administrative agencies, the police and the army, the Kwantung Army and the Manchurian government intended to resolve the conflict between the industrial and natural resource development and the full-scale war with China. However, this effort was unsuccessful in the end. Moreover, it should be noted that numerous Chinese workers, farmers and citizens lost their lives in this process. Industrial development in Manchuria was accompanied by huge sacrifice due to executions by military forces and harsh labour mobilization, and in this sense it was not comparable to the ordinary industrial development.

Notes

* This chapter is based on T. Kojima, 'Manshukoku no Rodo Tosei Saku' (Labour Control Policy in Manchukuo) in T. Matsumura (ed.), *Mantetsu Rodo Shi no Kenkyu* (Research on the History of Labour at the South Manchuria Railways Co.), Tokyo: Nihon Keizai Hyoronsha, 2002.
1 Mantetsu Keizai Chosakai, 'Kantogun Rodo Tosei Iinnkai Hokokusho' (Report of the Labour Control Committee, the Kwantung Army), 18 February 1935.
2 *Daito Konsu* was a partnership company with capital of 100 thousand yen, established by the Special Operations Agency in Tianjin.
3 The article that addressed this issue in the same period is M. Sumiya, 'Manshu Rodo Mondai Josetsu' (Introduction to the Labour Problem in Manchuria), *Showa Seikojo Chosa Iho*, 1942, vol. 2 (2.3).
4 M. K. Chosakai, 'Manshukoku Rodo Tosei Yoko Shingi Hokoku' (Report on the Discussion on the 'Outline of Manchukuo Labour Control') in idem (ed.), *Manshu Gokanen Keikaku Gaiyo (Outline of the Five Years Plan)*, reprinted, Tokyo: Ryukei Shobo, 1980.
5 See T. Matsumura, 'Manshukoku Seiritsu Iko niokeru Imin Rodo Seisaku no Keisei to Tenkai' (Formation and Development of Immigration and Labour Policy after the Foundation of Manchukuo) in M. S. Kenkyukai (ed.), *Nihon Teikokuhsugi kano Manshu (Manchuria under the Japan Empire)*, Tokyo: Ochanomizu Shobo, 1972.
6 The Labour Control Law was enacted in February 1939. T. Suzuki, *Nihon Teikokushugi to Manshu, 1900–1945* (Japan Empire and Manchuria, 1900–1945), Tokyo: Hanawa Shobo, 1992, p. 330.
7 See Matsumura, *Mantestu Rodo Shi no Kenkyu*, pp. 275–6.
8 See Kojima, 'Manshukoku no Rodo Tosei Saku', pp. 67–8.
9 *Manshukoku Seifu Koho (Official Bulletin of the Manchukuo Government)*, 1 August 1940.
10 Public Relations Division, Agency of General Affairs, *Junpo (Ten-days Report)*, 11 May 1941.
11 Xue shi Xie (ed.), *Mantetsu Shi Shiryo* (Materials on the History of the South Manchuria Railways), vol. 4–2, pp. 496–7; *Manshukoku Seifu Koho*, 7 July 1941.
12 Y. Oida, '"Tokushu Kojin" to Mannin Ko' ('Special Workers' and Wanrekeng), *Yoseba*, vol. 11, 1998; Xue shi Xie, 'Manshukoku Makki no Kyosei Rodo' (Compulsory Labour in the Last Stage of Manchukuo), in Matsumura, *Mantestu Rodo Shi no Kenkyu*.
13 War History Department of the Agency of Defense (ed.), *Shina Jihen Rikugun Sakusen (Army Operations in the Sino-Japanese Incident)* 2, Tokyo: Asagumo Shuppannsha, 1976, pp. 397–9.

14 Xue shi Xie/Ke Liang Zhang (eds.), *An Gang Shi (History of An Gang Iron Works)*, Beijing, 1984, p. 343.
15 'Romu Shintaisei to Kaisei Rodo Tosei Ho' (The New Labour System and the Amended Labour Control Law), *Junpo*, 1 December 1941.
16 Ibid.
17 Norisada Tamura, *Romu Kokokukai no Igi to Shimei (Significance and Mission of the MLAPC)*, MLAPC, 1942, p. 39.

IV
Incorporation of territories in the war economy

8 The French economy under German occupation, 1940–1944

Marcel Boldorf

Introduction

In no other country occupied by Germany during the Second World War – with the exception of Denmark – was the numerical relationship between the occupier and the occupied as low as in France.[1] Because of a chronic shortage of staff, Werner Best, who was initially stationed in Denmark prior to becoming Head of the Civil Administration of the Military Command in France (*Militärbefehlshaber in Frankreich, MBF*), considered it necessary that the *Wehrmacht* control the occupied territory, but without replacing the local authorities.[2] This raises questions about the enforceability of German directives for controlling the economy. Because coercion and surveillance could not be ubiquitous due to the lack of personnel, the cooperation of the French administration appeared to be essential if German armament requirements were to be met. This chapter takes a look at direct measures of economic exploitation and at the institutional arrangements that facilitated German economic control of the occupied territory. The labour situation and the failure of French collaborationist policies will be examined in the conclusion.

After the armistice of June 1940, French national territory was divided into the occupied north zone and the south zone, which was not occupied until November 1942. For strategic reasons, three additional zones were established: (a) the forbidden zone of the heavy industrial Nord and Pas-de-Calais departments under the control of the Brussels Command, (b) the closed zone of German settlement and (c) the de facto annexed Alsace-Lorraine. The occupied north zone included two thirds of national territory and an equally large share of the country's inhabitants. It produced the lion's share of industrial and agricultural products.[3] Paris remained not only its economic centre but also the place of collaboration, because the actual negotiations between the Economic Division of the Military Command in France and representatives of French industry and the Ministry of Finance took place here.[4] In September 1941, the Economic Departments of the 38 administrative HQs in the occupied territory (*Feldkommandanturen*) and 142 local administrative HQs (*Kreiskommandanturen*) could not guarantee blanket control of the occupied zone.[5] Only a handful of military personnel was present in many locations, and the arms inspections at best sporadically controlled some of the factories that were relevant to the manufacture of weapons. The initially unoccupied southern part of France was even more difficult to control by military means. The German arms inspections in Bourges, Clermont-Ferrand, Lyon, Avignon and Toulouse supervised the disarming of the French but were hardly in a position to extend their influence to include the economy.[6]

1. The failed introduction of a corporate New Economic Order

The requisitions carried out by the *Wehrmacht* informed the first six months of the occupation. The property of the French Army was confiscated without compensation as spoils of war.[7] In breach of international law, the *Wehrmacht* also transported goods to the German Reich that were scarce in the war economy, for example by removing cotton that was stored in French ports or the inventories of textile manufacturers.[8] The demand for metals that had run out in the Reich was particularly high, such as copper, 135,000 tons of which had already been shipped to Germany as 1940 drew to a close.[9] During the ceasefire negotiations, the German and French parties could not reach agreement with regard to the financing of the requisitions. As long as the property did not belong to the French state, settlement according to the principles of private enterprise was envisaged.[10] The *Wirtschaftliche Forschungsgesellschaft* (Economic Research Company), a front company with responsibility for procuring raw materials vital to the war effort, acted formally as the buyer, that is the accounting office or intermediary. It passed on the goods acquired in France to German authorities and companies. The injured parties, if they received acknowledgement of receipt, could turn to the local French authorities for compensation.[11] The High Command of the *Wehrmacht* recognised as early as November 1940 that the reckless application of right of plunder in place was robbing France of the resources necessary to run its administration properly and especially to pay the demanded cost of occupation.[12] It was only when the German occupation administration was financially better off as a result of its ongoing earnings from occupation costs that it paid the French authorities compensation of 540 million francs for the requisitions up to the end of October 1942.[13]

There were selective and grievous interventions in the right of ownership, most notably the 'Aryanisation' of Jewish-owned companies. In 175 cases examined that mostly affected the retail sector and consumer goods industry, the plans of German entrepreneurs to be given shares of the confiscated and dispossessed companies were only successful in exceptional cases.[14] At the same time, case studies from the unoccupied zone indicate that the attack on Jewish property did not necessitate the invasion of German troops.[15] It can be concluded that there was no massive expansion of German control of French property or nationalisation of any significance. The capital almost invariably remained in private French hands, including the small amount generated by the 'Aryanisation' of dispossessed companies. Some companies had, from 1936 onwards, already been nationalised by the Popular Front government, for example the transformation of several private railways into the state-owned railway company, the *Société des*

Chemins de Fer Français (SNCF), as well as companies that were vital for the manufacture of munitions and aircraft.[16]

One of the earliest measures taken to create a New Economic Order was the formation of organisation committees (*comités d'organisation*). Like the economic groups (*Wirtschaftsgruppen*) in the Reich, these committees were normally responsible for companies in a particular branch of industry. The first organisation committee was established in the automotive industry at the end of September 1940; the number had grown to 110 by the start of 1942 and had exceeded 200 by 1944.[17] These corporatist institutions implemented economic ideas that had been developed by French right-wing parties in the 1920s. In effect, the Ministry of Industry run by René Belin was responsible for drafting them.

Economic historical research from the 1980s on the economic system of occupied France strongly emphasises the role played by the organisation committees because they were dominated by managers of large French industrial companies.[18] However, they only had far-reaching competence on paper. At no time were they able to carry out the tasks assigned to them, including the establishment of production programmes, the organisation of raw material procurement and distribution and the creation of an allocation formula. A plan by the Minister of Industrial Production, François Lehideux, to increase their power failed in the spring of 1941. The German War Economy and Armament Staff (*Wehrwirtschafts- und Rüstungsstab*) forbade the unauthorised involvement of French organisations in the shifting of *Wehrmacht* orders to occupied France.[19] In addition, the Economic Division of the Military Command in France instructed Jean Bichelonne, Head of the French Central Office for Allocating Industrial Products (*Office central de répartition des produits industriels*), emphatically that manufacturing and processing contracts as well as supply contracts were to be negotiated directly between the German and French companies involved.[20] The French authorities responsible for allocation were thus the most important regulators. The occupation authorities were looking for ways to reduce French administrative control as much as possible.

2. Institutions of economic control

The Central Office for Allocating Industrial Products came about as the result of legislation passed on 10 September 1940, at a relatively early stage of the occupation. Despite a certain degree of scepticism within the French Ministry of Industry, the authority was created with an initial 10 sections with responsibility for various raw materials and product groups such as textiles, iron, coal, industrial greases and crude oil. From the end of 1940 onwards, the sections were superordinated by German representatives who monitored the French management and became involved themselves as they saw fit.[21] Jean Bichelonne prepared quarterly plans from January 1941 in which he allocated raw material quotas for the French economy.[22] To improve the situation with regard to data availability, the Economic Division of the Military Command in France ordered a new statistical assessment of the companies. This task was first given to the prefects, then to the organising committees.[23] Allocation by the organisation committees failed, as did the French idea for a compulsory allocation programme across the whole of industry. There were enquiries from the heads of the committees but also from individual companies protesting time and time again about allocations that were inadequate.[24] Small and medium-sized companies, in particular, complained of inequalities. At the same time, symptoms typical of a shortage economy appeared: certificates of entitlement were traded, and hoarding was a widespread problem.[25] The equilibrium between the maintenance of a balanced basic supply to the French economic sectors and the implementation of short-term German armament production goals was regularly shifted in favour of the latter.

Production bans were put into effect at an early stage. In September 1940, the Economic Division of the Military Command in France demanded that the metal-processing industry bring its product range into line with the current manufacturing bans in the Reich. Lists of goods were prepared whose production was not permitted if iron was used during the process.[26] The statutory order for the reorganisation of the economy from 17 December 1941 was an important event used by the occupying power to close a number of companies.[27] In May 1942, under pressure from the Germans, the French Ministry of Industry presented a list of almost 2,000 companies for closure.[28] At the top of the agenda was the preservation of coal and nonferrous metals, resulting in the closure of sixteen glaziers, forty tin-making factories and fifty foundries. Job losses became an increasingly important concern during this period, as can be seen from the closure of many companies that manufactured consumer goods, including 300 pharmaceutical companies, 154 textile factories, 135 soap manufacturers and about 100 factories in the areas of paint, crafts and toy manufacture. This closure of factories made it clear to the collaborating French administration that the Germans were concentrating on a war economy and did not have any long-term development plans for the French economy.

The allocation of raw materials and materials was shaped by the Central Contracts Office (*Zentralauftragsstelle*), which was established in September 1940 by order of Göring. Its main function was to steer French production towards export to Germany. It directed orders from German companies that were worth 5,000 reichsmark or more to French exporters.[29] A voucher issued by the Central Contracts Office ensured the French company priority allocation of the necessary raw materials. Given the shortages, the preferential allocation of raw materials was an incentive to take the export order, safeguarding production at the factory. In addition, the business offered promised additional profit because the exporting company procured the raw materials at French domestic prices. The invoice was issued for a cost price that included a reasonable profit margin. This meant that the quoted price was considerably above French domestic prices and close to German domestic prices. Thus, the shift of German orders led to a stimulation of the French economy.[30] Over time, this sort of positive incentive was increasingly linked to a dilemma: the labour required to produce goods for export to Germany meant the workers were protected to a certain degree against deportation to Germany. This became increasingly significant as the occupation wore on.

The Central Contacts Office concentrated on armament-relevant production from the very start: from autumn 1941 onwards, it was only permitted to authorise orders for factories producing armaments or *Vorzugsbetriebe* (factories to receive preferential treatment). These *V-Betriebe*, as they were usually called, included utility service providers of gas, water and electricity and primary production companies involved in activities such as coal and ore mining. To ensure that the steering institutions were closely linked, the German committees and pools created by Armaments Minister Speer appointed agents to work in France who had to follow directions.[31] From June 1943 onwards, they monitored the creation of direct links between German suppliers and their French trading partners.[32] These corporate mergers set up offices themselves whose specialist personnel communicated with the authorities for allocation to ensure input allocation and control the implementation of the imposed production programme.[33] With the consent of Bichelonne, the system of direct links between companies was expanded to include southern France.

Despite the intention to treat the economy of the French national territory equally, the integration of the unoccupied zone was less comprehensive at first, with the result that the Vichy government was in a position to ward off German delivery requirements.[34] It was only after the invasion in November 1942 and the measures of 1943 that the system for shifting industrial orders was effectively introduced to Southern France. Random samples for two months show how strongly the deliveries affected the whole of France grew: 250 million reichsmarks in March 1941 compared with 430 million reichsmarks in April 1943.[35] According to the figures of the Central Contracts Office, 62 per cent of German orders were completed during the occupation.[36] A comparison between the official *Wehrmacht* orders shifted to occupied France (2.6 billion reichsmarks up to 1 October 1943) and the Clearing Bank debt of about 5 billion reichsmarks at this time, suggests that almost half of the deliveries were not used to cover the immediate needs of the *Wehrmacht*.[37] The goods delivered to the Reich as part of bilateral contracts included raw materials as well as investment and consumer goods. For example, the French delivered 1.2 million pairs of children's shoes and 2.2 million pairs of ladies' shoes to the Reich in 1941 to meet their contractual obligations.[38] France was among the European countries with the highest volume of industrial orders shifted from Germany, but it supplied less than half of the needs of the *Wehrmacht*, as is evident from various statistical sources.[39]

Bilateral trade was carried out using a Clearing Bank account in which a German debt of 8 billion reichsmarks had accumulated by June 1944. The third crucial mainstay of the German policy of control was the generation of funds for financing the wartime economic exploitation. Funds were generated by the imposition of disproportionately high occupation costs of 20 million reichsmarks per day.[40] The devaluation of the French currency against the reichsmark from 17:1 immediately before the war to 20:1 at the beginning of the occupation resulted in 400 million francs flowing into the account of the occupiers on a daily basis.

The extent of the occupation costs was a contentious issue during the negotiations between the German and French Armistice Commissions in Wiesbaden from 1940 to 1941. During the negotiations, the French delegation eventually managed to reduce the cost to 300 million francs per day.[41] The Germans linked this concession to an overall deal: in return, the French government had to agree to the appointment of three commissioners: one to the National Bank of France and two others for supervising foreign-exchange transactions and foreign trade. The German concessions are understandable considering that in May 1941, 2.9 billion reichsmarks had accumulated in the account for occupation payments; only about 55 per cent of the total amount received from France in the first eleven months of the occupation had actually been spent.[42] This financial cushion slowly decreased, and the German occupiers used the occupation of the unoccupied zone in November 1942 as an opportunity to increase the occupation costs to 25 million reichsmarks or 500 million francs.

Even earlier than the other control bodies, the *Reichskreditkasse* (RKK) set itself up as occupation bank in the French capital in June 1940.[43] This occupation bank issued so-called RKK vouchers (*Reichskreditkassenscheine*) that were mostly used by the *Wehrmacht* as currency when paying for purchases from French companies. In this way, armaments and equipment could be paid for without the need to carry out requisitions that might slow down the economy. The French supplier could then exchange the RKK voucher for francs at a local bank. Banks had to accept the vouchers, and they in turn exchanged the vouchers at the central bank. The amounts spent were then debited to the account for occupation payments. This system was maintained until the end of 1943 even though RKK vouchers from other occupied territories in Europe flowed into France.[44] To meet the financial demands, the French government had to increase taxes and switch on the money-printing press. The increase in the amount of French currency in circulation inevitably led to inflation.[45]

Because of this system, there was no shortage of resources available to meet German needs at the start of the occupation. It was only when resources became scarce that the occupiers pressed for price stability, which seemed to accommodate the original interests of the French collaborators to stabilise the currency. Galloping inflation threatened to diminish the performance incentives in occupied France. Prices at the start of the occupation, converted into reichsmarks, were considerably lower than in the German Reich because France had already devalued its currency in 1936. The more recent devaluation of the franc by 15 per cent demanded by the occupiers had further deteriorated the French position in relation to Germany.[46]

The German interest in preserving this differential can be attributed to three factors: (a) It encouraged exports to the German Reich. The difference in prices meant that French companies could make more profit if they exported their goods to Germany rather than selling them in the domestic market.[47] (b) A pull of imports into the occupied territory was avoided. If prices in France had overtaken prices in Germany, this might have resulted in an outward flow of consumer goods from Germany. (c) There were also pricing policy reasons that corresponded to those in the German Reich. The prevention of inflationary tendencies served to keep the level of consumption as stable as possible whilst maintaining the level of wages.[48]

In 1940, the German occupiers endeavoured to optimise the price control which had been put in place four years previously. The French system of price control was divided into a national committee (*Comité National*) and subordinated authorities at department level. The latter lost their authority to set prices and were given a purely monitoring function. The national committee was replaced by a subdivision (*Sous-direction des prix*) set up in the Ministry of Finance that subsequently served as the supreme price authority for the occupied and unoccupied zones. It prepared general guidelines for regulations governing the price of materials. In order to improve the prosecution of pricing violations, the German Military Command ordered that customs officers who were no longer needed on the external borders should be used for surveillance purposes.[49]

The reasons for increasing prices in France broadly corresponded to the reasons in the German Reich. The increasing disconnection from developments in the international market, that is the compulsory economic autarky, led to a shortage of imports, particularly in view of the fact that Germany was not fulfilling its contractual obligations. The led immediately to a decrease in production. Asset erosion resulted from requisitions and subsequently from ongoing deliveries to the *Wehrmacht* and other German authorities without the promise of goods in exchange. The production and supply shortages during the winter of 1940/41, in particular, increased costs, with the result that the French requested exceptions from the rigid price structure.[50]

Price increases were meant to act as an incentive to boost the poor agricultural and industrial output. However, the German price agency accepted French demands with greater frequency from the middle of 1941 onwards when increases in the wages of industrial workers were sanctioned.[51] To prevent an increase in the cost of living, the Economic Division of the Military Command insisted that the French authorities increase their subsidisation of basic consumption. Due to the stubbornness of the German price agency, there was, for example, no increase in the retail cost of bread prior to November 1941. However, during the winter of 1941/42, there were two increases in rapid succession before the price stagnated again until 1944. The French and German delegations had lengthy negotiations concerning the price of bread because the topic was also politically controversial. Eventually, the French exchequer had to subsidise the price of bread to the tune of 2.5 billion francs in 1941, or 125 million reichsmarks, and with 3.2 billion francs (160 million reichsmarks) in 1942.[52] The French state directly contributed to the financing of the war in other ways, for example by subsidising the cost of coal and iron production with large sums of money.

3. Results of the exploitation

Comprehensive statistical data on French production during the war is still not available, as there was, for instance, clandestine production for the black market.[53]

106 *Marcel Boldorf*

After the war, Alfred Sauvy, who was also a functionary in the Vichy regime, produced the following much-quoted index series on industrial production in strategic areas:

The overall index sank to the lowest point that French production had ever reached in the twentieth century. This reflects not only wartime shortages but also the fact that the successive closure of whole branches of industry led to an increasingly troubled economic equilibrium. Despite this general finding, some sectors managed to maintain production at a remarkable level, that is the sectors that the German occupational force most valued. Coal production remained at a relatively high level, and the same was true of cement production. Production in the steel industry fell steeply in 1940 before recovering in the three years that followed. In areas of shortage such as aluminium production, the primacy of exploitation of all available resources led to an actual increase in output. The overall picture was extremely negative because no attempts were made to get the economy moving in the long term: the emphasis was on increasing production in a selective way with a view to supporting the war effort. The identification of a middle phase of the economy during the occupation from the end of 1940 until 1943 as a search for long-term exploitation of the French economy would appear to be misguided.[54]

The argument for 'long-term exploitation' is based on the idea that for a period of time, a war economy of European dimensions existed that had been reconstructed in accordance with NS stipulations. It fails to recognise that decisions were made during the middle period referred to that were purely exploitative, including the closure of factories that were essential to the normal economic cycle as well as the beginning of recruitment of forced labour in the spring of 1942 under Fritz Sauckel, the General Plenipotentiary for Labour Deployment. In France, the occupying authorities moved to outright requisition of manpower during four so-called Sauckel Actions from the middle of 1942 onwards. From February 1943, the Obligatory Labour Service (*Service du Travail Obligatoire*) led to the forced recruitment of entire birth cohorts.[55] The deportation of labour was in sharp contrast with the policy simultaneously pursued by the Armaments Minister Albert Speer to activate French armaments production.

The French policy of collaboration manoeuvred itself into a cul-de-sac, as the meeting in Berlin in September 1943 between Minister of Industrial Production Bichelonne and Armaments Minister Speer showed.[56] The single item on the

Table 8.1 Indices of French industrial production (1939 = 100)

	Overall index	Coal	Raw steel	Aluminium	Cement
1941	65	94	69	147	83
1942	59	94	72	100	58
1943	54	89	82	102	73
1944	41	55	50	58	36

Source: A. Sauvy, *La vie économique des Français de 1939 à 1945*, Paris: Flammarion, 1978, p. 155.

agenda was the increased integration of France into the German war economy. The negotiating parties agreed, among other things, on the definition of *Sperrbetriebe* or *S-Betriebe*, specially designated factories that were important for the war effort and whose workers would be excluded from the labour draft.[57] The efforts of the French government were now directed at making the manpower remaining in France indispensable. Accordingly, the French Ministry of Industry tried to ensure that (a) armament manufacturers achieved good production results to avoid the threat of closure, (b) other factories expanded their range of products to include goods essential to the war effort so that they were added to the list of *S-Betriebe* and (c) the *S-Betriebe* retained their work forces.[58] There was a shift in the logic of collaboration in the way that the French technocrats became defenders of Speer's plans to stave off the demands of Sauckel. The figures for French forced labour read as follows: 200,000 'volunteers' and 650,000 draftees worked in the German Reich; about 1 million prisoners of war drafted into forced labour can be added.[59] German *Wehrmacht* figures at the end of the occupation show that it was only in agriculture that a substantial number of French male labourers worked for the benefit of the French people.

4. Conclusions

The National Socialist economic order is often referred to as a planned economy. Starting with the Four Year Plan adopted in 1936, a series of separate plans that included the occupied territories have been identified. Plans such as the so-called Kehrl-Plan[60] to reorganise European textile production were, however, nothing more than mutual agreements on the amount of a product to be delivered for different categories of goods. They were really only an annex to the controls of foreign trade that were already in place. However, the German authorities did not meet their contractual obligations in the vast majority of cases, with the result that the plans – especially in Europe – had no practical outcome. The economy was without doubt controlled, but there was a general lack of strategic economic planning in most areas. As a result, it does not make sense to speak of a 'National Socialist planned economy' as some research suggests, sometimes even with references to centrally planned socialist economies.[61]

Alan Milward argues that the increased exploitation of the occupied territories only started after 1941 when the Ministry of Munitions and Armaments under Albert Speer was given greater powers.[62] This does not apply to France, where the phase of requisitions and removals started immediately after the occupation of the country in 1940 and where an institutionalised arrangement for targeted exploitation was established at a relatively early stage. It is difficult to follow the argument put forward by Richard Overy that the war was not expected to start so early and confusion ensued when it did. Rolf-Dieter Müller expanded this view into his polycracy thesis, postulating that the competing structures of the Nazi Reich led to massive inefficiencies. It is assumed that there was a high level of mismanagement in the occupied territories prior to Speer taking office.[63] Time and time again, orders that were given affected economic processes negatively, and there were even conflicting strategies, such as the conflict mentioned earlier between Sauckel and Speer. This thesis of polycratic chaos is contradicted by the incentive scheme for industries that were important to the war effort; it was put in place at an early stage and was fully functional after a very short time. There is, however, a quite different interpretation that is based on stronger evidence: there was no radical break between the time before and after the end of 1941 with regard to the activation of the German war economy or, as a result, with regard to the mobilisation of other European economies.[64]

Following this reasoning, the occupation economy of France should be characterised as a command economy (*Befehlswirtschaft*) with incentive-based elements that were put in place deliberately. The main features of the wartime economy control system include (a) the establishment of institutions for controlling input, in particular, the central authorities for allocation and the Central Contracts Office; (b) the preservation of disparate trade conditions through shifting of contracts which was increasingly linked to the allocation of raw materials. The intention to exploit is shown by the continuous negative German Clearing Bank account balance; (c) the generation of funds through excessive demands for occupation costs and the realisation of resources for the *Wehrmacht* and occupation administration by issuing RKK vouchers, among other things; (d) the shifting of the cost of unavoidable inflation to the French state. From raw materials to food production, the state treasury had to provide subsidies to keep retail prices low; and (e) the minimum use of force vis-a-vis companies. While companies supporting the war effort could expect to receive special treatment as armament companies, *Vorzugs-* or *Sperrbetriebe*, factories producing consumer goods, were shut down and their work forces transported to Germany to carry out forced labour. It can be concluded that the German war economy exploited France in a subtle way by strategically placing incentives for companies instead of using anti-incentive military force to govern.

Notes

1 U. Herbert, *Best. Biographische Studien über Radikalismus, Weltanschauung und Vernunft 1903–1989*, Bonn: Dietz, 1996, p. 290.
2 W. Best, 'Großraumordnung und Großraumverwaltung', *Zeitschrift für Politik*, 1942, vol. 32, pp. 406–12.
3 H. Joly, 'Introduction', in idem (ed.), *L'économie de la zone non occupée 1940–1942*, Paris: Éditions du CTHS, 2007, p. 16.
4 Cf. the minutes of the negotiations in: Archives Nationales de Paris (ANP), F 37/3 and F 37/4.
5 Bundesarchiv-Militärabteilung (BArch-MA), RW 35/8. Militärbefehlshaber in Frankreich (MBF), Staff of Command. Status report August/September 1941, 30 September 1941. BArch Berlin R 3101/32261. Report of the German Ministry of Economics on German economic policy in France, 10 July 1943.
6 Joly, 'Introduction', pp. 21–2.
7 H. Umbreit, Les politiques économiques allemandes en France, in: Dard, Olivier/ Daumas, Jean-Claude/Marcot, François (eds.), *L'occupation, l'Etat français et les entreprises*, Paris, 2000, pp. 25–8.

8 M. Margairaz, *L'état, les finances et l'économie. Histoire d'une conversion 1932–1952*, vol. 1, Paris: Comité pour l'histoire économique et financière de la France, 1991, p. 609.
9 A. S. Milward, *The New Order and the French Economy*, Oxford: Clarendon Press, 1970, p. 80.
10 BArch-MA, RW 35/10. MBF Staff of Command. Status report for August 1940, 2 September 1940.
11 H. Umbreit, *Der Militärbefehlshaber in Frankreich 1940–1944*, Boppard: Boldt, 1968, pp. 213–4.
12 ANP, AJ 40/443. MBF Staff of Command. Status report for November 1940, 3 December 1940. H. Klemann/S. Kudryashov, *Occupied Economies. An Economic History of Nazi-Occupied Europe, 1939–1945*, London: Berg, 2012, p. 79.
13 Umbreit, *Militärbefehlshaber in Frankreich*, p. 214.
14 P. Verheyde, 'Vichy, die deutsche Besatzungsmacht und ihre wirtschaftlichen Beziehungen im Rahmen der "Arisierung" der großen jüdischen Unternehmen', *Zeitschrift für Unternehmensgeschichte*, 2005, vol. 50, pp. 218–31.
15 Cf. the case studies in the chapter '*Aryanisation des entreprises en ZNO*', in: Joly, *Économie de la zone non occupée*, pp. 301–63.
16 G. Ribeill, 'Y a-t-il eu des nationalisations avant la guerre?' In C. Andrieu et al. (eds.), *Les Nationalisations de la libération. De l'utopie au compromis*, Paris: Presses de la Fondation nationale des sciences politiques, 1987, pp. 40–52.
17 Margairaz, *L'état, les finances et l'économie*, vol. 1, p. 522.
18 H. Rousso, 'L'organisation industrielle de Vichy', *Revue d'histoire de la deuxième guerre mondiale*, 1979, vol. 116, pp. 27–44.
19 ANP, AJ 40/776. Letter to the MBF Paris, 11 March 1941.
20 ANP, AJ 40/776. Letter from the Economic Division of the MBF to Bichelonne, General Secretary of the Ministry of Industry.
21 ANP, AJ 37/2. Draft for the allocation of goods in compliance with German interests, memorandum of Jacques Barnaud, 5 September 1940. ANP, AJ 40/408. Economic Division of the MBF. Economic decree regarding the allocation of raw materials in France, 20 December 1940.
22 Margairaz, *L'état, les finances et l'économie*, vol. 1, p. 517.
23 ANP, AJ 40/408. Special economic decree of the MBF regarding the statistical survey, 15 October 1940. ANP, AJ 40/444. MBF, Head of Administration, Status report for October 1940, 1 November 1940. Cf. also: A. Tooze, 'Die Erfassung der wirtschaftlichen Tätigkeit: Zur Geschichte der Wirtschaftsstatistik in Frankreich und Deutschland 1914–1950', in: P. Wagner/C. Didry/B. Zimmermann (eds.), *Arbeit und Nationalstaat. Frankreich und Deutschland in europäischer Perspektive*, Frankfurt/Main: Campus, 2000, pp. 75–99.
24 Margairaz, *L'état, les finances et l'économie*, vol. 1, p. 578.
25 R. Vinen, *The Politics of French Business 1936–1945*, Cambridge: CUP 1991, p. 142.
26 ANP, AJ 40/444. MBF, Head of Administration. Status report for November 1940, 3 December 1940. ANP, AJ 40/408. Economic Division of the MBF. Special economic decree on the allocation of iron and steel, 22 July 1941.
27 See *Journal Officiel* from 23 December 1941, p. 5500. Loi du 17 décembre 1941 relative à l'établissement d'un plan d'aménagement de la production.
28 ANP, AJ 37/4. French Ministry of Industrial Production. First list of factory closures in accordance with the decree from 17 December 1941, established 21 May 1942.
29 ANP, AN AJ 40/444. Head of Administration, status report for October 1940, 1 November 1940.
30 Klemann/Kudryashov, *Occupied Economies*, p. 85.

31 BArch Berlin R 3101/32261. Letter from Armaments Minister Speer to the German *Ringe* regarding the utilisation of the French economy for the war effort, 1 June 1943.
32 ANP, AJ 72/1929. Minister for Armaments and Munitions/General Plenipotentiary for Armaments in the Four Year Plan, Decree on the shifting of industrial orders to the occupied western areas, 3 December 1943.
33 Margairaz, *L'état, les finances et l'économie*, vol. 1, p. 703.
34 ANP, F 37/4. Minutes of the negotiations between Jacques Barnaud and Elmar Michel, Head of the Economic Division of the MBF, 29 January 1942.
35 ANP, AJ 40/443. MBF Staff of Command. Status report for March 1941, 31 May 1941. ANP, AJ 40/444. Central Division of the MBF. Status report on the administration and economy for April–June 1943, 21 July 1943.
36 A. Radtke-Delacor, 'Produire pour le Reich. Les commandes allemandes à l'industrie française (1940–1944)', *Vingtième siècle. Revue d'histoire*, 2001, vol. 70, p. 114–5.
37 H. Umbreit, 'Die deutsche Herrschaft in den besetzten Gebieten 1942–1945', in B. Kroener et al. (ed.), *Das Deutsche Reich und der Zweite Weltkrieg, vol. 5: Organisation und Mobilisierung des deutschen Machtbereichs, part 2: Kriegsverwaltung, Wirtschaft und personelle Ressourcen 1942–1944/45*, Stuttgart: DVA 1999, p. 186. ANP, AJ 40/444. Central Division of the MBF. Status report on the administration and economy for October–December 1943, 27 January 1944.
38 Margairaz, *L'état, les finances et l'économie*, vol. 1, p. 613.
39 J. Scherner, 'Europas Beitrag zu Hitlers Krieg. Die Verlagerung von Industrieaufträgen der Wehrmacht in die besetzten Gebiete und ihre Bedeutung für die deutsche Rüstung im Zweiten Weltkrieg', in: C. Buchheim/M. Boldorf (eds.), *Europäische Volkswirtschaften unter deutscher Hegemonie 1938–1945*, Munich: Oldenbourg 2012, p. 81; as opposed to Umbreit, 'Die deutsche Herrschaft in den besetzten Gebieten', pp. 186–7. Umbreit's position on 1 October 1943 ignores Italy and the Protectorate of Bohemia and Moravia.
40 M. Boldorf/J. Scherner, 'France's Occupation Costs and the War in the East. The Contribution to the German War Economy, 1940–1944', *Journal of Contemporary History*, 2012, vol. 47, pp. 291–316.
41 ANP, F 37/3. Protocol of the meeting between the German and French delegations, 9 May 1941.
42 ANP, AJ 40/443. MBF Staff of Command. Status report for April/May 1941, 31 May 1941.
43 ANP, AJ 40/578. MBF Division of Economic Organisation. Sixth daily report to the High Command of the Wehrmacht after the occupation of France, 24 June 1940.
44 Umbreit, *Militärbefehlshaber in Frankreich*, p. 216.
45 M. Margairaz, 'La Banque de France et l'occupation', in idem (ed.), *Banques, Banque de France et Seconde Guerre mondiale*, Paris: Albin Michel, 2002, pp. 38–41.
46 Margairaz, *L'état, les finances et l'économie*, vol. 1, pp. 543–7.
47 H. Joly, 'The Economy of Occupied and Vichy France: Constraints and Opportunities', in: J. Lund (ed.), *Working for the New Order. European Business under German Domination 1939–1945*, Copenhagen: University Press of Southern Denmark, 2006, p. 99.
48 M. Boldorf, 'Die gelenkte Kriegswirtschaft im besetzten Frankreich (1940–1944)', in: Buchheim/Boldorf, *Europäische Volkswirtschaften*, p. 125.
49 ANP, AJ 40/443. MBF Staff of Command. Status report for October/November 1941, 30 November 1941.
50 Margairaz, *L'état, les finances et l'économie*, vol. 1, p. 551.
51 Boldorf, 'Die gelenkte Kriegswirtschaft', pp. 125–6.

52 ANP, AJ 40/443. MBF Staff of Command. Status report for October/November 1941, 30 November 1941.
53 Klemann/Kudryashov, *Occupied Economies*, pp. 324–5.
54 Margairaz, *L'état, les finances et l'économie*, vol. 1, p. 593. Radtke-Delacor, 'Produire pour le Reich', p. 103. H. Umbreit, 'Die Verlockung der französischen Ressourcen: Pläne und Methoden zur Ausbeutung Frankreichs für die kriegsbedingten Bedürfnisse und die langfristigen Ziele des Reichs', in C. Carlier/S. Martens (eds.), *La France et l'Allemagne en guerre. Septembre 1939–Novembre 1942*, Paris: IHAP, 1990, p. 437.
55 For an in-depth look at the Sauckel actions: B. Zielinski, *Staatskollaboration. Vichy und der Arbeitseinsatz im Dritten Reich*, Münster: Westfälisches Dampfboot, 1995, pp. 106–75.
56 ANP, AJ 72/1926. Delegation of the French Ministry of Industry (Bichelonne, Cosmi, etc.). Protocol of the meeting with Albert Speer and staff, 20 September 1943.
57 ANP, AJ 40/444. Central Division of the MBF. Status report on the administration and economy for October–December 1943, 27 January 1944. See also: Milward, New Order, pp. 157–9.
58 ANP, AJ 72/1929. Head of Cabinet of the French Ministry of the Economy Pierre Cosmi. Minutes of the negotiations on 2 February and 28 March 1944 with Sauckel's representative for France, SS Brigadier General Alfons Glatzel. Cf. also Umbreit, *Militärbefehlshaber in Frankreich*, p. 328.
59 H. Rousso, *Le régime de Vichy*, Paris: PUF, 2007, p. 98.
60 Margairaz, *L'état, les finances et l'économie*, vol. 1, pp. 612–3.
61 J. Schneider, 'Von der nationalsozialistischen Kriegswirtschaftsordnung zur sozialistischen Zentralplanung in der SBZ/DDR', in: Id./W. Harbrecht (eds.), *Wirtschaftsordnung und Wirtschaftspolitik in Deutschland (1933–1993)*, Stuttgart: Steiner 1996, pp. 1–50. In contrast to: Klemann/Kudryashov, *Occupied Economies*, pp. 57, 259.
62 Milward, *The New Order*, pp. 41–2; R. Overy, 'The Economy of the German "New Order"', in idem./G. Otto/J. Houwink ten Cate (eds.), *Die 'Neuordnung' Europas. NS-Wirtschaftspolitik in den besetzten Gebieten*, Berlin: Metropol, 1997, p. 17.
63 P. Liberman, *Does Conquest Pay? The Exploitation of Occupied Industrial Societies*, Princeton: Princeton University Press, 1996, p. 39.
64 J. Scherner/J. Streb, 'Das Ende eines Mythos? Albert Speer und das so genannte Rüstungswunder', *Vierteljahrschrift für Sozial- und Wirtschaftsgeschichte*, 2006, vol. 93, pp. 172–96.

9 German economic rule in occupied Belgium, 1940–1944

Dirk Luyten

One of the goals of German occupation policy in the Second World War was economic exploitation, with the occupied territories having to contribute to the German war effort. Looked at from this perspective, Belgium was of great interest for Nazi Germany, being a highly industrialized country with long-established sectors of great value for the war economy such as coal mining, steel, engineering, textiles and diamonds. This industry was located mainly in Wallonia, the southern French-speaking part of the country, while Flanders in the north, where the language was Dutch, was less industrialized and more dependent on agriculture. Holding companies, especially the *Société Générale* headed by Alexandre Galopin, who played a key role during the war as the leader of an economic shadow government, controlled the key sectors of the economy.

Until 1942, exploitation mainly involved industrial production for Germany. This changed in 1942, with Belgians becoming liable to be sent to Germany as forced labour, though industry continued producing for the *Reich*. Looking at the occupation period as a whole, however, having Belgian industry work for Germany, often via German companies placing direct orders with Belgian companies, was the main form of exploitation. It was also the form preferred by the German military command, the body governing Belgium for the whole occupation period with the exception of the last two months before the Liberation in September 1944. The German military command succeeded in extracting 10.3 billion reichsmarks from the Belgian economy, 11 per cent of the total for occupied Europe and 13.6 per cent of the total for Western Europe.[1] Two hundred sixty-five thousand Belgians worked in Germany as prisoners of war (only Walloons, as Flemish soldiers were allowed to return home in 1940) as voluntary or forced labourers.[2]

This chapter discusses the German policies used to exploit the Belgian economy. The focus is on institutions. Ideologically and politically, the German occupation brought a radical breach with economic liberalism, involving structural changes in the way the economy was organized, in line with the Nazi model. Putting such changes into practice turned out to be a complicated task since the understaffed German military command had to rely on domestic entrepreneurs, elites, organizations and institutions, making them cooperate with newly created economic institutions. One of the strategies used to gain cooperation was to support competing (secondary) elites challenging the dominant elite. The institutional changes also had the purpose of harnessing the economy for the German war effort. To what extent these institutional changes promoted economic exploitation and how Belgian business reacted to these changes are the main questions this chapter wants to answer. Alongside this indirect exploitation, the Germans also used direct forms of control and exploitation. These will be discussed in relation to the institutional changes.

Forms of economic control

To control the Belgian economy, liberalism was replaced by a corporatist command economy following the Nazi model, with four basic components. In industry, commodity offices *(Warenstellen)* and economic groups were introduced. The commodity offices, agencies organized on a product basis (e.g. steel, textiles), steered production by allocating raw materials. In 1941, a corporatist system of statutory trade organizations was established, the so-called economic groups, in line with the German *Wirtschaftsgruppen*.[3] In the finance sector, a new Central Bank of Issue was founded, also responsible for the clearing between Belgium and Germany that replaced free trade.[4] A new state institution, the Commission for Prices and Wages, determined price and wage levels.[5]

These institutional changes were an opportunity for economic and political elites to challenge the Belgian economic establishment, which was French speaking. Economic power in Belgium was in the hands of the Brussels financial world, while Belgian industry was dominated by holding companies of which the *Société Générale*, controlling 40 per cent of Belgian industry, was the most important one. The close link between banks and industry in Wallonia went back to the First Industrial Revolution. The holding companies had also started investing in Flanders in the late nineteenth century, targeting such sectors as the non-ferrous industry (processing raw materials from the Belgian Congo), diamonds and the Limburg coal mines. The *Comité Central Industriel* (CCI), the central employers' and trade organization established in 1895, represented the social and economic interests of Belgian industry. With the introduction of sector-level collective bargaining in the interwar period, the CCI had obtained the representational monopoly of Belgian business. The organization was closely linked to the Francophone business elite.[6]

At the end of the nineteenth century, part of the Flemish Movement, a movement going back to the 1840s, shifted its focus from language and culture to the economy and made the economic backwardness of Flanders a political issue. Though neglected in the context of the Belgian state, Flanders had its own economic assets and needs. An autonomous Flemish economic elite was needed to carry out the industrialization and economic development of Flanders. In 1926, those in favour of the economic emancipation of Flanders founded their own business organization, the *Vlaams Economisch Verbond (VEV)* (Flemish Economic League). This league became the mouthpiece of the Flemish business elite striving for the economic autonomy of Flanders. Initially, the VEV was not a purely economic institution or employers' organization, with its cultural and political activities (promoting the use of the Dutch language in Flemish business life; developing a 'Flemish economic science' looking at the particular problems of the economy in Flanders) on a par with the defence of the specific interest of employers in the 1920s.[7]

During the economic crisis of the 1930s, state intervention in social and economic life increased, albeit in a specific way, mediated through social and economic organizations. A typical example was the tripartite (government-employers-trade unions) national labour conference, convened to put an end to the 1936 General Strike. Social dialogue was introduced in all economic sectors and plans were made to create a full corporatist structure to regulate the economy. Taking into account the political impact of these institutions, the VEV tried to question the representational monopoly of the CCI. Though the VEV had the ambition to be recognized as the unique representative of the Flemish business community, the CCI succeeded in maintaining its position.[8]

The new organization of the economy during the war opened up new perspectives for the VEV. As already pointed out, the German military command based its rule on involving domestic administrations and organizations. A central element of this policy was to favour Flanders and the Flemish Movement. This resulted in the VEV and CCI being put on the same footing. Questioning the CCI's representational monopoly was part of this German policy of favouring Flanders.

German support for the Flemish business elite began in the summer of 1940 when the commodity offices started their work. As the Germans did not want to create those institutions from scratch, they appealed to Belgian business via the employers' organizations, primarily the CCI and its federations, but also the VEV. The idea here was that involving the VEV would encourage the Belgian Francophone economic elite to cooperate in reorganizing the economy. Competition with the VEV was one of the factors behind the CCI accepting a role in the new economic organizations. Losing control over these organizations would put the VEV in a position to challenge the power of the CCI and its federations, with the VEV having at its disposal an official organizational network that paralleled the CCI and its federations and compensated the VEV's organizational and representative weakness vis-à-vis the CCI.[9]

Competition between the VEV and CCI was most prevalent in the textile sector, an industry common to the whole of Belgium, with centres in Verviers (Wallonia) and in the Flemish city of Ghent since the First Industrial Revolution, though in both cases, the entrepreneurs were Francophone. The second half of the nineteenth century saw the textile industry developing further in the provinces of East and West Flanders, with the new companies smaller and not directly linked to the Brussels financial groups. Moreover, many Flemish textile industrialists represented a local bourgeoisie striving for Flemish autonomy and distancing themselves from the Belgian Francophone economic elite. In contrast to the coal mining, steel and engineering sectors, the textile industry lacked a united federation. Different organizations worked alongside each other and were often rivals. Some of those organizations supported the ideas of the VEV or were affiliated.[10] The CCI, in competition with the VEV, tried to create a united federation for the textile industry in the summer of 1940 but could not prevent Flemings, not linked with the traditional Francophone economic elite, being appointed as heads of the commodity office for textile. The first was F. Donkerwolcke, a textile engineer and member of the extreme-right Flemish Verdinaso party. In 1941, he was replaced by the Flemish Nationalist Willem Van Hee, an advocate of close collaboration with Germany. The latter made no effort to defend Belgian economic interests and the needs of the Belgian consumers.[11]

The textile industry contrasted with the other key sectors of the economy, where the heads of the commodity offices were leading industrialists enabling the traditionalist Belgian economic elite to keep control over the new institutions.[12] The persisting domination of this elite had economic as well as political reasons. From an economic perspective, the Flemish economic elite lagged behind the Belgian economic elite, who, via the holdings, controlled those sectors of the economy – coal mining, steel and engineering – vital for the German war effort. The Germans were not willing to initiate a takeover by a Flemish economic elite in those economic sectors, needing the cooperation of the elites in power to exploit the Belgian economy. There are no indications that the Germans wanted to get rid of the prewar leaders of the Belgian economy. Neither the CCI nor its federations were disbanded, as had been the case with the trade unions or the organizations of the self-employed.[13] Though not an alternative on a par with the CCI, the VEV had the potential to weaken the CCI's position. However, the internally divided VEV (not all its leaders followed the collaboration strategy of its president and secretary – general) was not a reliable partner from a German perspective.[14] German support for the VEV did not solve the latter's problem of a lack of representativeness, as not all entrepreneurs in Flanders rejected the Belgian state and some were closely linked to the Belgian Francophone economic elite. This was the case with a prominent producer of (barbed) wire, the Catholic Leon Bekaert, who headed the engineering group.[15]

Informal decision making

The final explanation for the VEV's lack of success lay with the CCI strategy. The organization avoided direct confrontation with its Flemish competitor without giving it too much influence. This policy was in line with the policy of the Galopin Committee, an informal group of leaders of holdings, banks and industry acting as a shadow government for economic policy. The Committee developed a code of conduct for economic policy under German occupation (the Galopin doctrine) and took a Belgian patriotic stance. One of the elements of this policy was to insert as far as possible 'reliable' Belgian industrialists at the top of the newly created economic institutions, even if they were organized according to Nazi principles, incompatible with the liberalism traditionally advocated by these businessmen. This policy was motivated by the will to be present in the new decision-making centres in order to be in a position to put into practice the economic policy advocated by the Galopin Committee, involving limited economic collaboration with the Germans and excluding the production of weapons and ammunition but without direct integration into the German economy.

Another motive for cooperating with the new economic organization, which became more prominent from the spring of 1941 onwards, was to avoid the politicization of the economic decision-making organizations – a factor directly relating to the competition with the Flemish economic elite. There was a need to have a maximum number of business leaders belonging to the traditional Belgian economic elite in the leading positions of the corporatist economic organizations in order to avoid Flemish nationalists or members of the collaborationist political parties being appointed and gaining control of the economy. The argument was that having politically inspired people at the top of the economic organizations made it more difficult to have a technical-economic discussion. Moreover, the economic structure of the Belgian economy needed to be preserved during the war, implying that representatives of the traditional Belgian economic sectors had to be present in the economic decision-making centres. Those arguments were used in February and June 1941 to motivate the participation of businessmen from the traditional elite in the management of the groups. Presence in these new decision-making centres to defend the interests of the traditional sectors of the Belgian economy outweighed involvement in a system contradicting the Belgian constitution and legislation.[16]

The CCI did its best to have its candidates appointed at the top of the groups, and as a result, these groups were often not more than a duplication of the private federation, with the latter controlling the group. The VEV had a similar ambition. The composition of the management of the groups is therefore a good indicator of the balance of power between the traditional Francophone economic elite and its Flemish competitors. The result was comparable with the situation at the top of the commodity offices in 1940, at the beginning of the occupation. The key sectors of the Belgian economy were firmly controlled by the traditional economic elite through the CCI and its federations. Again, in the textile sector, the picture was different: the leader was a Flemish nationalist, supported by the VEV. Representatives of the Flemish economic elite could only obtain subordinate positions or become heads of sectors not dominated by the holdings, such as wood construction or the building sector.[17]

The VEV had difficulties finding candidates with a social and economic status comparable to the entrepreneurs proposed by the CCI, reflecting the difference in the economic power of the two elites. In the autumn of 1941, when the heads of commodity offices and the groups were appointed, the power of the traditional Francophone economic elite was not fundamentally questioned: the newly created institutions remained in the hands of traditional industrialists and were dominated by the federations. In practice, decisions were taken by the private employers' organizations, able to continue their activities.[18] In the negotiations on such key issues as food supplies for the workers or forced labour for Germany, the federations and the CCI were the mouthpiece of Belgian industry, not the groups. The CCI and its federations acted as the executive organizations of the

Galopin Committee, which was in turn linked by structural and personal ties to the CCI and its federations.[19]

Politics and the economy

The persistence of the position of the traditional Belgian Francophone elite may come as a surprise after the changes that had taken place since the summer of 1940 in the economic state institutions. The corporatist organization of the economy, described earlier, was only one aspect of the shift from a liberal economy to a command economy.

The Commission for Prices and Wages was headed by a Flemish nationalist. The special commissioner in charge of wage formation and industrial relations was also a Flemish nationalist and firmly determined to replace the prewar joint commissions for collective bargaining by a system inspired by what existed in Nazi Germany.[20]

Even more striking were the changes at the top of the Ministry of Economic Affairs, a department recently established in the 1930s. At the time of the invasion, a Francophone economist, J. C. Snoy et d'Oppuers, headed the department. Having followed the Belgian government in its flight from the capital of Brussels, he was subject to a German decree that gave the occupier the right to veto the continuing employment of persons who had left the country during the invasion. Victor Leemans, the candidate of the German military command, replaced him. Leemans was an outsider in the economic world[21] and without any administrative experience. He had built a political career in the 1930s in the Vlaams Nationaal Verbond (VNV), the leading Flemish nationalist party, and headed the small Flemish nationalist trade union *Arbeidsorde*. Leemans was acquainted with economic questions, but only from a theoretical perspective and as a publicist.[22]

His appointment as the secretary-general of the Ministry of Economic Affairs was part of the strategy of the German military command to get a grip on the Belgian administration. Following in Leemans' footsteps, other Flemish nationalists gained key positions in the Ministry of Economic Affairs. One of them was Albert Michielsen, a young Flemish nationalist economist, who had already worked in the Ministry of Economic Affairs in a junior position. He became Leemans's senior advisor and was closely involved in the corporatist organization of the economy. Michielsen was appointed director of the commodity office for diamonds.[23]

Initially, Leemans was an advocate of the New Order and had the ambition to contribute actively to replacing economic liberalism with an organized economy. It soon, however, became clear that he was unwilling or unable to challenge the position of the Francophone economic elite. From the spring of 1942, when the fortunes of the war were changing, Leemans served more as an intermediary for the traditional Belgian economic elite with the decision makers in Nazi Germany, upholding the interests of the traditional sectors of the Belgian economy.[24]

A good example of his changing attitude can be found in the coal mining sector. When the Germans imposed better social conditions for the miners, Leemans supported the protest of the coal mining federation, reiterating its arguments that the social cost would threaten the financial and economic position of the Belgian coal mines.[25] However, the corporatist organization of the economy had given Leemans the instruments to develop an alternative economic policy, more in line with the ambitions of the Flemish Movement. The economic performance of the Belgian coal mines was uneven, with the much older coal mines in Wallonia, for geological reasons mainly, and less productive than the mines in the Limburg basin. These differences had been highlighted by Flemish economists in the 1930s and used as an argument against the subordination of Flemish economic interests.[26] Prices paid for coal during the occupation were in general too low, and financial problems started appearing in 1941. The solution was a state subsidy for the loss-making coal mines. A special compensation fund was established as part of the group, which, under the leadership principle, would theoretically be controlled by the Ministry of Economic Affairs (the heads of the groups were accountable only to their leader, the Secretary-General of Economic Affairs). In practice, however, control of this fund was in the hands of the coal mine industry federation and thus of the holding companies. Neither the coal mines nor the holdings were prepared to reveal information on the profitability of each coal mine, meaning that the state had no real control over the use of the state subsidy. This situation frustrated Michielsen, who had hoped that the corporatist economic organization would be an instrument to reduce the federation's power.[27]

Monetary policy

Alongside the recently established Ministry of Economic Affairs, the Ministry of Finance played a key role in financial and economic affairs. This department remained in the hands of civil servants in tune with the traditional Francophone economic decision makers, even if Secretary-General Oscar Plisnier often opposed the financial and economic elite, mainly on the question of the financial burden of the occupation and economic exploitation. Alongside the imposition of an exchange rate undervaluing the Belgian franc by 5 per cent against the reichsmark, the Germans basically used two instruments of monetary exploitation: the occupation costs, paid by the Belgian state through taxes and state bonds,[28] and the clearing deficit on the account of the Central Bank of Issue, controlled by the Belgian Francophone financial elite. This situation generated conflicts, with the distribution of the occupation's financial burden increasingly becoming a political question as the war went on and the pressure of German exploitation grew.[29] The Germans began demanding occupation costs in July 1940. In February 1941, the amount was fixed at 1 billion Belgian francs per month, rising later to 1.5 billion. It was to be financed through taxes and bonds, the latter to a substantial part taken up by the big private banks.[30] In the Belgian case, clearing accounted for nearly 43 per cent, more than in France and the Netherlands.[31]

The leadership of the National Bank was not affected by the German policy of elite change, though it had to operate in the shadow of the new institution, the Central Bank of Issue established in June 1940. This institution was to take over the role of the National Bank, which had followed the government into exile in London, taking with it the material for issuing banknotes. The Germans wanted an institution to issue banknotes and to organise the Belgian–German clearing. The Galopin Committee and the big private banks were closely involved in the creation and financing of the new institute and were prepared to play an active role in the management of the new issuing house. The banks provided the founding capital for the Central Bank of Issue and were represented on the board of directors. But, as in other sectors, the German military command wanted to give representatives of Flemish economic circles a leading role, resulting in the appointment of Flemish businessmen to the board of directors. A Flemish confidant of the Germans became managing director. In practice, however, control over the bank's management remained with the powerful Brussels private bankers, with decisions being taken in close cooperation with the Brussels financial groups, first and foremost the *Société Générale*. The Central Bank of Issue proved not to be an instrument enhancing the economic power of the Flemish economic elite.[32]

The Central Bank of Issue did not play the role initially planned by the German military command. The National Bank returned to Belgium with the consent of the Belgian government and tried to regain a maximum of its competences. In practice, the National Bank resumed its issuing-house function, remaining responsible for the organisation of public and private credit and maintaining its role as state exchequer. The Central Bank of Issue was in charge of all foreign financial transactions and, most importantly, German–Belgian clearing. This clearing was essential for the exploitation of the Belgian economy. Until the spring of 1941, clearing functioned relatively normally, but as the war continued, Germany built up a deficit, amounting to 64 billion Belgian francs at the end of the war. The economic and financial transactions between Belgium and Germany were financed via the Central Bank of Issue, which had the capacity to monitor the financial flows between the two countries, one of the key indicators of the macroeconomic development of the occupied economy.[33] For the holdings with their tendency to look at the economy from a financial perspective, having control over financial institutions was also essential for implementing the economic policy outlined in the Galopin doctrine.

The political position of the different elites was not only reflected in the distribution of management functions in the different institutions but also in how financial conflicts with the Germans were resolved. The negotiation partners of the Germans were not only the leaders officially in charge of the Central Bank of Issue but also the Galopin Committee and the leaders of the private banks which had provided the capital for the Central Bank of Issue. Alongside the bank's management and Secretary-General of Finance Plisnier, these so-called founders were the people the German military command spoke to. Representatives of the Flemish elite had no say. The position of the different groups became clear in October through December 1942 in what was called the 'crisis of the Central Bank of Issue'. In the context of the constraints imposed by the war with the Soviet Union, the clearing deficit not only increased, but it appeared that a (growing) number of transactions could not be identified by the Central Bank of Issue. These so-called transactions with special mention were in reality black-market transactions, deliveries of a military character or financial support for political collaboration. This was seen as a problem of principle: the Belgian authorities wanted to stop or at least put a limit on these transactions, since they conflicted with the principles of the Galopin doctrine and could from a legal point of view be considered economic collaboration. Some of the transactions covered the sale of Belgian holdings in Central and East European companies to German companies. Negotiations with the Germans were started, in which not only the management of the Central Bank of Issue and the Ministry of Finance were involved but also representatives of the Galopin Committee and Galopin in person. The idea was to form a 'united front' of the Belgian financial, political and economic authorities against the Germans. The Germans were not prepared to make concessions and even forced the Central Bank of Issue to immediately pay a number of contested transactions. This firm position of the Germans put pressure on the Belgian unity since, in the negotiations to resolve the crisis, the suggestion had been made to have a substantial share of these contested transactions covered by the occupation cost, an idea difficult for Plisnier to accept. The crisis reflected the conflicting interests of the different Belgian actors and the decisive influence of the private bankers and Galopin, whose main concern was to avoid a monthly ceiling on the clearing deficit limiting the possibility of Belgian industry to work for Germany, keep production going and maintain employment for Belgian workers. The united front proved to be an illusion after two directors of the Central Bank of Issue resigned.[34]

Business politics

The composition of the Galopin Committee itself provides an insight into the power relations within the economic elite. The origin of the committee was a meeting convened by the government before leaving Brussels on 15 May 1940. The government wanted to guarantee the payment of civil servant salaries and social aid, since the public financial institutions had been ordered to follow the government into exile. The government invited the representatives of the Brussels banks and holdings but also the head of the *Kredietbank*, Fernand Collin. Given the bank's predominant Flemish profile, the involvement of a top manager from this bank was part of the government's policy in the late 1930s to involve representatives of the Flemish economic elite in policy making alongside representatives of the traditional Francophone economic elite. Fernand Collin remained in the Galopin Committee and was as such involved in economic policy making during the occupation. Within the committee, Collin was more a junior partner, responsible for judicial questions, as he was also a professor in penal law. Even if the *Société Générale* took the lead in the Galopin Committee, the fact that Flemish economic leaders (not just Collin but also Leon Bekaert) were members of the Galopin Committee has political significance. One of the foundations of the Galopin doctrine, the code of conduct for production for Germany, was a common policy for all of Belgian business: Belgian entrepreneurs had to follow the same policy in their relations with the Germans. This united front was intended to strengthen Belgian business under occupation but more so after the war, in the hypothesis of collaboration being punished, as had been the case after the First World War. The Galopin Committee presented itself as the mouthpiece of the Belgian economy and the group defining and upholding the interests of the Belgian economy. To be in a position to speak for the whole Belgian economy, it was necessary to include representatives from the Flemish economic elite. Moreover, from an economic perspective, it can be doubted whether the economic interests of the Flemish and Francophone entrepreneurs differed fundamentally – they were certainly less significant than the linguistic divide.

The Galopin Committee also reflects the relative impact of the new social and economic public institutions created under the occupation. The Germans dealt directly with the big industrialists and their organisations. Where goods of a (semi)military character were produced, the leaders of the holdings intervened and took any final decision. In the key sectors of the economy – coal mining, steel and engineering – dominated by the traditional elite, the Germans were more cautious and more reluctant to use coercive measures than in such sectors as textiles, where the leadership of the official organizations was more open for collaboration. Fearing an open confrontation with powerful groups,[35] the Germans allowed economic objectives to prevail over political considerations, with the ultimate goal of making Belgian industry produce for the German war effort. Officials in the economic section of the German military command were often German businessmen known to their Belgian colleagues.

Another motive for the more cautious approach towards Belgian heavy industry was the size and international character of the companies. Firms such as *Solvay* or *UCB* (chemicals) were companies of European and even international size and scale, which gave them a certain amount of protection since the Germans had to deal with them outside Belgium too. The same went for such holding companies as the *Société Générale*, which held financial participations in Central and South-Eastern Europe, which were interesting for German companies to buy. The *Société Générale* also owned important colonial assets. The *Société Générale* sold its participations in Eastern European companies to German companies primarily because they were not particularly profitable and because Germany held a leading economic position in the region.[36]

The Germans had to take into account – at least to a certain extent – the domestic division of economic power. This concerned primarily the holding companies, since they controlled the key sectors of the economy. Much more than the much weaker Flemish economic elite, they were the bodies the economic section of the German military command spoke to.[37]

This can be illustrated by the diamond sector, concentrated in the city of Antwerp and providing employment to many Jews and the surrounding countryside.

The *Société Générale* was actively involved in the sector via *Forminière*, a company owning diamond mines in the Congo. Antwerp's position was challenged by the surrounding (Catholic) countryside, whose employers had never succeeded in being integrated and accepted by their Antwerp colleagues, causing frustration and leading to anti-Semitism. A number of them took a Flemish nationalist stance in reaction to what they saw as discrimination by the often French-speaking Antwerp diamond elite and created their own employers' organisation. The occupation opened up new perspectives for this group, with the flight and later persecution of the Jews in the sector eliminating competitors. As head of the commodity office for diamonds, Michielsen promoted the ambitions of the Flemish diamond entrepreneurs. They were not, however, able to make a breakthrough, since they did not have the capacity and were not part of the relevant networks needed to replace the prewar elites and serve German interests. Michielsen himself had to cooperate closely with the *Forminière* and thus the Francophone economic elite to reach his business targets as head of the commodity office.[38]

Direct rule

The German authorities often overruled the official organisations created under their aegis. In theory, the commodity office decided over the distribution of the raw materials for the German and Belgian markets. In practice, however, decisions were taken by the German military command. This meant that the autonomy of the commodity office was limited, with the commodity office controlled by a representative of the economic section of the German military command and, from 1943 onwards, by a representative of the commodity office (*Warenstelle*) in Germany.[39] Moreover, the Germans used the black market in an organised way to obtain the goods they needed. This situation frustrated even the head of the commodity office for textiles, who complained that he had no grip over the textile market and was often simply overruled by the German authorities.[40]

The position of the newly established economic institutions was also challenged by specific structures created by the Germans to gain more efficient control over a certain important sector, such as coal mining. The German Commissioner for Mining in the Kempen region, a section of the German coal association, had stricter control over the Limburg coal mines, counterbalancing the power of the coal mine directors. The fact that this kind of structure was created for the Limburg mines was not inspired by linguistic but by economic considerations. The Limburg coal mines were the most interesting from a German perspective, being more productive and producing industrial-quality coal, in contrast to many mines in the South of Belgium, which produced coal for domestic use. Therefore, the Germans invested a lot of effort into increasing production in the Limburg mines. One of the ideas was to encourage Walloon coal miners to move to Limburg, but this only had limited success, being rejected by the coal mines and their organizations.[41] To solve the problem of the lack of miners, Soviet POWs were sent to work in the coal mines from 1942 on, most of them in Limburg. They lived in barracks next to the mines and received normal wages but had to pay all kinds of costs themselves and were fined when productivity dropped below a certain level.[42]

Besides institutional change, a form of indirect rule, the Germans used direct means of intervention to make Belgian industry work for the German needs. To gain a better insight into Belgian industry, the German military command organized audits of the production process. German experts were sent to all companies in a particular sector. In the textile sector, which was difficult to control on account of the high number of small firms, audits were already organized in 1940. In engineering, audits did not start until 1942 but were repeated several times (two to seven). The aim of the audits was to know what was produced (certain audits showed that some firms were still producing goods for which there was a production ban) and how production was organized. The audits paved the road to concentration, with production geared to the most productive firms, while the others were forced to close down. Moreover, concentration freed up workers who could be sent as forced labour to Germany.

The German military command had other ways of directly steering production. In the metalworking sector from 1943 onwards, they specified the types of products to be produced rather than prohibiting the manufacture of certain goods. This direct steering in combination with listing a specific customer in the production permit was expected to put an end to the practice of Belgian firms to give priority to their regular customers over German ones. The second way, used in the textile sector, focussed not on the orders but on the processing thereof. The system of allocating raw materials was based on three categories of customers: the Belgian market, the German civil market and the German army. Some Belgian firms used the raw materials for the German market for their Belgian customers, which were given priority in the processing over the German (military) orders. In 1942, there was a delay in the processing of the orders for the German army. The commodity office for textiles reacted by freezing all orders for the Belgian or German civil markets until all orders for the German army had been fulfilled.[43]

The direct steering of production had its limits, as the German military command was a relatively small administration, totalling at its peak 1,166 staff members. In 1941, the German armament inspectorate in Brussels, responsible for Belgium and the annexed North of France, employed no more than about 100 people. One of the means to put pressure on firms not prepared to produce what the Germans needed was to threaten putting the firm into the hands of a German trustee who would then take over the firm's management. Though this technique was used a number of times (especially in the production of weapons and munitions), the lack of the necessary personnel prevented it becoming a general policy tool.[44]

Direct investments by Germans or German companies establishing production sites in Belgium during the war was the exception rather than the rule. In 1941, the German National-Socialist Erich Reitz set up a factory for producing uniforms for the German army, soon to become the biggest factory for uniforms in Belgium. Reitz expanded his production capacity by taking over or confiscating small Belgian firms. Reitz established his factory on the outskirts of Antwerp (Merksem), away from the traditional textile centres. Within just a short time, Reitz became a serious competitor for the Belgian textile companies, not only because of his company's size and the type of products. Reitz was an outsider who had set up in Belgium with direct support from the NSDAP. He refused to become part of the organized economy in Belgium and overruled the structures of the German military command. By presenting his company as part of the German army, Reitz succeeded in obtaining the necessary manpower and systematically used the black market to obtain the materials needed to expand his production capacity.[45] The Reitz case shows that this kind of exploitation fell outside the scope of the normal methods of the German military command for exploiting the Belgian economy for the German war effort. It also shows that the German military command was subject to the rivalries and conflicts existing between the different power centres in the *Reich*.

The occupation of Belgium opened the door to cross-ownership through direct investments in Belgian firms by German companies. Interesting opportunities were to be found in firms controlled by the holding companies. As far as companies established on Belgian territory were concerned, the *Société Générale* was rather reluctant to sell, mainly for political reasons: as long as the outcome of the war was not clear, the holding was not prepared to accept investments of German capital in Belgian companies.[46] This could be considered as part of the integration of the Belgian economy into the German economy. As already explained, the situation was different for companies outside Belgium, where business considerations played a more decisive role. Other groups were more inclined to accept German capital participations, though direct investments in Belgian companies were not a key instrument of the German military command in its economic exploitation of Belgium. Direct production by Belgian firms for German needs prevailed.

Prices and wages

Though the institutional changes put a question mark over economic liberalism, they were not that far reaching. In many cases, the mechanisms of a capitalist economy remained in place, and domestic economic actors were in no way completely subject to political decisions. Sequestration and dispossession were basically limited to enemy and Jewish property and looting immediately after the invasion.[47] As a general rule, private property was left untouched. The price (and profit) mechanism was still used by the Germans to obtain products from the Belgian economy, and as a general rule, goods were purchased and not confiscated or plundered.

However, prices were no longer set in a free market.[48] As already indicated, prices were officially dictated by the Germans, especially for such essential goods as coal and steel, for which prices were set in Berlin.[49] A rationing system was introduced for consumers, covering food, clothes and other basic products.[50]

Entrepreneurs had different ways of dealing with the regulated prices, which were kept at the lowest possible level. Businessmen were not fully at the mercy of the price-control and price-setting system. The Commission for Prices and Wages cooperated with the producers to determine prices and was dependent on them for price-setting information.[52]

If the official price was too low, the black market was an alternative. According to most recent estimates, the black market accounted for up to nearly one fifth of total production.

Belgian economic actors as well as the Germans used the black market in search of goods or profits. Different sections of the occupation troops, individual soldiers and the German army had purchased all kind of products on the black market right from the start of the occupation. The use of the black market to cover the needs of the occupation army was organised by the German military command from June 1941 on, with a special office being established to coordinate black-market purchases.[53] In order to avoid inflation caused by different agencies using the black market, the Four Year Plan set up a central register in 1942 for all black-market purchases.[54] A new inspectorate was created, the *Überwachungsstelle* (UWA), that also bought products for the German civilian population. Prices offered were still high, creating opportunities for Belgian producers.[55]

Another strategy to cope with low prices was to contain the cost of wages, especially in labour-intensive sectors. The Germans froze wages after the invasion. The system of collective bargaining and wage indexation that had existed since 1919 was replaced by state-regulated wage setting. Strikes were forbidden, and the trade unions were forced to stop their activities. The wage policy of the employers went through different phases. At the beginning of the occupation, a number of employers and employer organisations tried to cut wages and social benefits but were stopped by strikes, by the German military command or by the Belgian administration. In a second phase lasting until the major strike of May 1941, employers tried to avoid (monetary) wage increases by handing out additional food in the factories and providing alternatives to the deficient rationing system, a source of social unrest. This phase came to an end in May 1941, when, as a result of the strike, all wages were increased by 8 per cent.[56]

After this period, wage formation was a matter of power relations at factory level, which were also influenced by the growth of the illegal trade union movement. Employers continued to give extra food or illegal pay rises often disguised as loans.[57] The basic principle of the wage policy was to avoid any general and official pay rise during the occupation. This was inspired by cost-reduction motives, as seen in the coal mines, where employers strongly opposed the modifications in the wage system introduced by the Germans in 1941 to reward work regularity

Table 9.1 Clandestine production as a percentage of total production[51]

1940	8%
1941	17%
1942	19%
1943	16%
1944	13%

rather than to impose fines as had been the case before the war.[58] The coal mining federation opposed all proposals to increase wages, arguing that they threatened the sector's economic viability.[59]

In the field of industrial relations, the prewar Belgian system was replaced in 1941 by 'committees of social experts', a model inspired by Nazi ideology. Workers were represented by a collaborationist single trade union, though employer organisations were reluctant to cooperate and did not come up with senior candidates for these committees, limiting themselves to proposing lower-ranking officials from their organisations. There were two reasons for this: the employers did not want to compromise with the occupier, and they wanted to continue the policy initiated after the invasion to deal with social questions at company level. As a consequence, the committees had no real function or impact, apart from drawing up a wage-classification scheme in the engineering sector. At the same time, the employers started negotiations in the autumn of 1941with the prewar unions to prepare for the postwar social system.[60]

Low prices were, on the other hand, not necessarily always seen as a problem, with the competitive strategy of Belgian industry based on price competition in the world market. One of the arguments used to participate in the groups was to avoid Belgian prices structurally rising in line with (higher) German prices,[61] as this would endanger the competitive position of the Belgian economy after the war. It also explains the wage policy of the Belgian employers.

Conclusion

Exploitation of the Belgian economy for the German war effort was primarily based on indirect exploitation, using the Belgian industrial infrastructure to produce goods that Germany needed. Since the German military command was a small administration, it had to rely on domestic elites to organize economic exploitation. This was facilitated by institutional changes putting an end to economic liberalism. Internal rivalries between economic elites in Belgium were leveraged by the Germans to obtain the cooperation of Belgian business, but the position of the Brussels financial and economic elite was never put into question since these groups were too powerful to simply be overruled.

Notes

1 H. Klemann, S. Kudryashov, *Occupied economies. An economic history of Nazi-occupied Europe, 1939–1945,* London: Berg, 2012, p. 57, 99 and own calculation. This figure includes production for Germany as well as the direct occupation costs, but without simple plundering, which was limited and occurred mainly in the first months of occupation.
2 Ibid, p. 145.
3 Dirk Luyten, *Ideologie en praktijk van het corporatisme tijdens de Tweede Wereldoorlog in België,* Brussels: VUB, 1997, pp. 111–203.

4 H. Van der Wee, M. Verbreyt, *A Small Nation in the Turmoil of the Second World War: Money, Finance and Occupation (Belgium, its Enemies, its Friends, 1939–1945)*, Leuven: Leuven University Press, 2009.
5 P. Scholliers, 'De georganiseerde verarming: prijzen, lonen en koopkracht tijdens de bezetting' in: *1940–1945. Het dagelijkse leven in België. 21 december 1984–3 maart 1985*, Brussels: ASLK, 1984, pp. 108–19.
6 G. Vanthemsche, 'De reorganisatie van het Belgisch patronaat. Van Centraal Nijverheidscomité naar Verbond der Belgische Nijverheid (1946)' in: E. Witte, J.C. Burgelman, P. Stouthuysen (eds.), *Tussen restauratie en vernieuwing. Aspecten van de naoorlogse Belgische politiek (1944–1950)*, Brussels: VUB, 1989, p. 112.
7 O. Boehme, *Greep naar de markt: de sociaal-economische agenda van de Vlaamse Beweging en haar ideologische versplintering tijdens het interbellum*, Leuven: Lannoo Campus, 2008.
8 Vanthemsche, 'De reorganisatie van het Belgisch patronaat', pp. 112–4.
9 Luyten, *Ideologie en praktijk*, pp. 123–7.
10 B. De Wilde, *Witte boorden, blauwe kielen. patroons en arbeiders in de Belgische textielnijverheid in de 19e en 20e eeuw*, Ghent: Ludion/AMSAB/Profortex, 1997, pp. 119–27.
11 P. Nefors, *Industriële 'collaboratie' in België: de Galopindoctrine, de Emissiebank en de Belgische industrie*, Leuven: Van Halewyck, 2000, p. 233.
12 Luyten, *Ideologie en praktijk*, pp. 119–21.
13 CEGESOMA Brussels, *Overtuigingsstukken gevoegd bij de procesbundels betr. gevallen van collaboratie met de bezettende overheden, 1940–1944*. AA 1314, nr. 343–9.
14 D. Luyten, *Burgers boven elke verdenking. Vervolging van economische collaboratie in België na de Tweede Wereldoorlog*, Brussels: VUB, 1996, pp. 190–3.
15 Luyten, *Ideologie en praktijk*, p. 169.
16 Note relative au comportement de l'industrie belge pendant l'occupation du Pays, Juin 1941. Algemeen Rijksarchief Brussel (ARAB), *Archief Société Générale*, Vierde storting.
17 Luyten, *Ideologie en praktijk*, pp. 166–70.
18 Ibid, pp. 172–86.
19 The twin brother of one of the members of the Galopin Committee was the head of the CCI. G. Kurgan-Van Hentenryk, *Max-Léo Gérard. Un ingénieur dans la cite (1879–1955)*, Brussels: Editions de l'ULB, 2010, p. 11.
20 Luyten, *Ideologie en praktijk*, pp. 83–5.
21 A. De Jonghe, 'De personeelspolitiek van de *Militärverwaltung* te Brussel gedurende het eerste halfjaar der bezetting (juni–december 1940). Bijdrage tot de studie van de Duitse *Flamenpolitik* in Wereldoorlog II', *Belgisch Tijdschrift voor Nieuwste Geschiedenis*, 1972, vol. 1–2, pp. 1–49.
22 'Leemans Victor L.', *Nieuwe Encyclopedie van de Vlaamse beweging*, Tielt, 1998, 3 vol. II, pp. 1812–3.
23 E. Laureys, *Meesters van het diamant. De Belgische diamantsector tijdens het nazi-bewind*, Tielt: Lannoo, 2005, pp. 209–14.
24 Nefors, *Industriële 'collaboratie'*, p. 115.
25 Luyten, *Ideologie en praktijk*, p. 170.
26 K. Pinxten, *Het Kempische steenkolenbekken. Een ekonomische studie*, Brussels/Antwerp/Ghent/Leuven, 1937.
27 Luyten, *Ideologie en praktijk*, pp. 174–5.
28 K. Oosterlinck, 'Sovereign Debts and War Finance in Belgium, France and the Netherlands' in: C. Buchheim/M. Boldorf (eds.), *Europäische Volkswirtschaften unter deutscher Hegemonie, 1938–1945*, Munich: Oldenbourg, 2012, p. 96.

29 For the first time in November 1941, Galopin feared that Oscar Plisnier would travel to Berlin to protest against the increase of the occupation costs in the context of the war against the Soviet Union, the result being a higher clearing deficit. Van der Wee/Verbreyt, *Small Nation in the Turmoil*, pp. 224–5.
30 Ibid, pp. 143–5. Oosterlinck, 'Sovereign Debt', p. 96.
31 Oosterlinck, 'Sovereign Debt', p. 97 (figures to March 1944).
32 Van der Wee/Verbreyt, *Small Nation in the Turmoil*, pp. 117–8.
33 Ibid, pp. 132, 164.
34 Nefors, *Industriële 'collaboratie' in België*, pp. 120–41. Van der Wee/Verbreyt, *A Small Nation in the Turmoil*, pp. 283–326.
35 See Nefors, *Industriële 'collaboratie' in België*, pp. 185–255 for a detailed analysis.
36 Ibid, pp. 66–8, 83.
37 This was different for the *Dienststelle Hellwig*, in charge of the trade unions and employers' organisation, which gave more room to political considerations. E.g. Aktennotiz über die Besprechung mit den Vorstandsmitgliedern der Unibel, 20 october 1941, *Archives Nationales Paris*, AJ 40–311, no. 5.
38 Laureys, *Meesters van het diamant*, pp. 178–330.
39 Nefors, *Industriële 'collaboratie'*, p. 59.
40 Luyten, *Ideologie en praktijk*, pp. 146–9.
41 G. Coppieters, 'De politiek van de minister weerstand? De Belgisch-Limbrugse mijndirecties tijdens de Tweede Wereldoorlog, in: H. Klemann, D. Luyten, P. Deloge (eds.), *Thuisfront. Oorlog en economie in de twintigste eeuw. Veertiende jaarnoek van het Nederlands Instituut voor Oorlogsdocumentatie*, Zutphen: Walburg Pers, 2003, pp. 236–7.
42 N. Piquet, *Charbon-Travail forcé-Collaboration. Der nordfranzösische und belgische Bergbau unter deutscher Besatzung, 1940 bis 1944*, Essen: Klartext, 2008, pp. 245–310. Coppieters, 'De politiek van de minste weerstand', p. 241.
43 Nefors, *Industriële 'collaboratie'*, pp. 218, 252–3.
44 Ibid, p. 29, 62, 66, 73, 105.
45 C. Van Praet, 'Erich Reitz, een koppige Einzelgänger. Historiek van een Duitse ondernemer in België tijdens de Tweede Wereldoorlog', *Belgisch Tijdschrift voor Nieuwste Geschiedenis*, 2012, vol. 62, pp. 59–102.
46 E. Verhoeyen, 'Les grands industriels belges entre collaboration et résistance: le moindre mal' in: *Cahiers-Bijdragen*, 1986, vol. 10, pp. 65–85.
47 *De bezittingen van de slachtoffers van de jodenvervolging in België: spoliatie, rechtsherstel, bevindingen van de studiecommissie: eindverslag*, Brussel: Diensten van de Eerste Minister, 2001, 2 vol. Kim Oosterlinck, 'Sovereign Debt', p. 95.
48 Klemann/Kudryashov, *Occupied economies*, p. 267.
49 Nefors, *Industriële 'collaboratie'*, p. 183.
50 Klemann/Kudryashov, *Occupied economies*, pp. 267–8.
51 Klemann/Kudryashov, *Occupied economies*, p. 330.
52 Verslag betreffende de prijsverhoogingen in de kolenindustrie januari 1943, p. 7. ARAB, *Archief Commissariaat voor Prijzen en Lonen*, Map 126.
53 J. Gillingham, *Geld maken in oorlogstijd. Economische collaboratie 1940–1945*, Leuven: Kritak, 1979, p. 91–8.
54 M. Boldorf/J. Scherner, 'France's Occupation Costs and the War in the East: The Contribution to the German War Economy, 1940–4' in: *Journal of Contemporary History*, 2012, vol. 47, p. 307.
55 Gilligham, *Geld maken in oorlogstijd*, p. 95–6.
56 D. Luyten, 'Stakingen in België en Nederland, 1940–1941', *Bijdragen tot de Eigentijdse Geschiedenis*, 2005, vol. 15, p. 149–76.
57 P. Scholliers, 'Strijd rond de koopkracht, 1939–1945' in: *België, een maatschappij in crisis en oorlog, 1940 = Belgique, une société en crise, un pays en guerre, 1940*, Brussels, 1993, pp. 245–76.

58 Coppieters, 'De politiek van de minste weerstand?', pp. 239–40.
59 Luyten, *Ideologie en praktijk,* pp. 177–8.
60 Ibid, pp. 85–9.
61 Note sur l'organisation de l'économie. Comparaison entre la realisation allemande et le projet de Mr. Leemans, 4 March 1941. ARAB *Archief Société Générale.* Vierde storting.

10 Nazi Germany's financial exploitation of Norway during the occupation, 1940–1945

Hans Otto Frøland

Nazi Germany occupied Norway for military-strategic reasons. The country's geographic location made it imperative to control the coastline. Having occupied the country, Germany would also actuate massive building schemes, mostly for military purposes but also to bring the Norwegian economy closer to the German economic sphere. Being highly import dependent in the first place overstretched German ambitions and soon brought Norway's economy to its limits. Consequently, Germany would sustain a Norwegian import surplus and supply a massive influx of people into the country.

This structural perspective is dominating the two scholarly monographs dealing with the Norwegian occupation economy at large. Whereas Alan Milward viewed Nazi economic policies from an aggregate point of view to investigate fascist policy, Robert Bohn set out to scrutinize the economic policies of the Reich Commissariat from an institutionalist angle. In spite of those differences, their conclusive perspectives are complementary. Both emphasize the discrepancy between Norway's profound dependence on foreign trade and Germany's overstretched plans to expand the economy.[1] From these predicaments followed a specific pattern of harsh exploitation through forced credits, most profoundly addressed by Harald Espeli. Like Milward and Bohn, he identifies the cash account set up in Norway's central bank, which provided unlimited overdraft facilities for the occupation authorities, as the main instrument of financial exploitation. By drawing attention to the incentive structure for Norwegian business set by German spending as well as the long-term effects of German investments, he emphasizes the level of business collaboration as well as the long-term return of investments in the postwar years. Implying that the impact of financial exploitation was less negative than assumed by Milward and Bohn, he maintained that the 'occupation was characterized by economic modernization'.[2]

This contribution sets out to elaborate the pattern of financial exploitation more in detail. It distinguishes between direct and indirect means. Among means of direct exploitation is booty and requisitions which were unpaid for, forced credits through the bilateral clearing account and forced credits through Norwegian cash accounts. Among indirect means are terms of trade changing in Germany's favour, which would allow Germany to indirectly draw value out of Norway, as well as forced subsidies from the Norwegian government to Norwegian companies exporting their products to Germany. The pattern of exploitation is analysed in a wider institutional and structural context, which takes account of Germany's strategic aims as well as institutional rivalries between the *Wehrmacht* and the Reich Commissariat. Consistent with Milward, Bohn and Espeli, I argue that the main instrument of financial exploitation was forced credits through the occupation account set up in Norway's central bank, from which the occupant covered the bulk of its costs. *Wehrmacht* spending was the main item in the balance sheet of the occupation account. Whereas booty and uncompensated requisitions certainly mattered, the clearing account did not. On the contrary, Germany provided Norway with clearing credits. As to indirect occupation tributes, admittedly more difficult to identify, I argue that they under any circumstance were modestly applied.

Structural predicaments

Norway's strategic importance grew during the occupation. First, the American supply line of war equipment to the Soviet Union passed through the waters of northern Norway. Second, Northern Norway was regarded as a bridgehead for the war effort in northern Russia. Last, after targeted British commando raids in 1941, Hitler was convinced that an Allied invasion in the west would take place in Norway. Due to the strategic importance, Germany inhabited the country. About 200,000 troops were deployed until the end of 1941. The number more than doubled during 1942–43. When including the around 25,000 civilians, the number of Germans approached 450,000 in May 1945. Hence the German population made up almost 20 per cent of the indigenous population during the last part of the occupation. They would need food, heat, clothing, transport, fuel and so forth. The *Wehrmacht* and Todt Organisation also carried out large infrastructure schemes. The Atlantic Wall fortification was extended to the Soviet border, whereas a comprehensive network of roads, railways and ports expanded logistical capacities. Therefore they also needed raw materials, intermediate goods and labour on a massive scale. Consequently, Nazi Germany would exploit the economy far beyond the ordinary maintenance of occupation troops as settled in international law.[3]

For decades before and after the occupation, Germany ran a structural trade surplus with Norway, which used a surplus with the United Kingdom to pay for her deficit with Germany. Obviously, this was rendered difficult because Norwegian export revenue from the UK disappeared. Hence the war would for structural reasons bring Norway closer to Germany. In 1940, a German Chamber of Commerce and a new clearing institute were set up in Oslo to further bilateral trade. Germany's share of Norway's customs-declared foreign trade grew from 15 to 18 per cent before the war to 75 to 80 per cent as it ended.[4] Norway sustained her import surplus with Germany, although much of the import originated from third countries controlled by Germany.[5] These customs-declared imports were accounted for on the clearing account as the bilateral clearing agreement from 1937 was sustained throughout the occupation.

Table 10.1 Norway's balance with Germany on clearing account during the German occupation [million NOK]

1940	1941	1942	1943	1944	1945	1940–1945
27	344	228	293	−23	−108	761

Source: Statistisk Sentralbyrå, NOS X 102 Nasjonalinntekten i Norge 1935–1943, Oslo 1946, p. 163.

Table 10.1 shows that the import surplus made Norway accumulate clearing debt, which however was reduced as German exports gradually disappeared from the autumn of 1944. Germany was Norway's largest creditor until 1944.[6] Norwegian clearing debt added to 761 million Norwegian krone (NOK) when the occupation ended.[7] This makes Norway an exception, as Germany would tend to run a considerable import surplus with occupied countries and exploit the credit mechanism on clearing account to finance these imports.[8]

Wehrmacht imports were not supposed to be customs declared or be accounted for on the clearing account. However, the *Wehrmacht* also imported on clearing account, partly using domestic firms as intermediaries. On the Norwegian government's demand, the Reich Commissariat in May 1941 settled the principle that *Wehrmacht* imports through clearing would be refunded.[9] Total refunds added to 287 million NOK by May 1945. Hence, Norway's net clearing credit during the occupation was about 500 million NOK.[10]

Norway was an exception in terms of labour transfer, too. *Wehrmacht* demand soon removed unemployment, and already in July 1940, it urged for regulations that would make Norwegian labour more easily accessible.[11] In July 1941, a decree enabled public employment offices to conscript civilians for work on German construction projects.[12] At that point in time, about 15 per cent, between 150,000 and 175,000 workers, of the Norwegian work force were employed on German construction projects. As conscription failed, labour remained a profound bottleneck. In February 1944, the Reich Commissariat recorded that even fewer Norwegians had been hired, though the number was still between 90,000 and 125,000.[13] From 1942, German firms were encouraged to bring their workers with them when entering into contracts in Norway. However, the Nazi solution to the labour deficit was a massive influx of foreign forced labour. An estimate indicates that around 130,000 people were forced to work in Norway during the occupation.[14] Most were Soviet POWs, but civilian forced labourers were brought in from all over Europe. The strained Norwegian labour market explains why Norway escaped Fritz Sauckel's havoc to transfer forced labour across Europe. Except for concentration camp inmates, the Nazis never applied force to bring Norwegian workers into the German industry.

Given the increasing importance of bilateral trade and the massive transfer of goods and workers to Norway, a relevant question is whether Germany fixed par value among the currencies as well as bilateral price relations to its own advantage.

Having invaded Norway with RKK vouchers (*Reichskreditkassenscheine*), whose par value was 1.67 NOK, their technical exchange in reichsmarks provided in June 1940 somewhat more German purchasing power, as the official par value of the reichsmark was set at 1.76 NOK. Other than in Denmark, whose currency was revalued in 1942, the official parity of the NOK remained fixed throughout the occupation. The essential question, therefore, is whether the occupation parity differed from preoccupation parity. Since the German attack on Poland, the par value between reichsmark and NOK had been set at 1.77 NOK, which is close to the occupation parity.[15] Consequently, Germany hardly exploited Norway indirectly through the official exchange rate mechanism. Actually, the parity of the RKKs was deliberately set to provide Norwegians purchasing power so they would more easily accept payments for the *Wehrmacht*'s requisitions during the invasion campaign.[16]

What about the development of the overall terms of trade? By the outbreak of war, Norwegian prices tended to be higher than German prices. After occupation, the Reich Commissariat for pricing in Berlin argued that the higher Norwegian price level must be brought down to the German level. The method was to reduce real purchasing power, partly by imposing taxes and duties, partly by increasing the price of goods imported from Germany.[17] While the former would transfer value from Norwegian private accounts to Norwegian government accounts, the latter would draw value from Norway to Germany. The latter was actually what annoyed the Quisling government's Minister of Trade and Supply, Eivind Blehr, when he recorded in June 1942 that 'We must buy to a high price and sell to a low price'.[18] Through 1940 and 1941, imports from Germany were getting continuously more expensive while Norwegian export prices remained stable. Hence by the start of 1942, Germany had largely succeeded in adjusting Norwegian price levels to German ones.[19] From 1942 onwards, terms of trade remained rather stable. Norwegian prices grew annually by less than 3 per cent from 1942 because regulations were more effective. To conclude, Germany's exploitation through terms of trade was limited to the years 1940 and 1941. Further, Norwegian and German prices converged much already after Germany invaded Poland. Aukrust and Bjerve have calculated clearing trade also in 1939 prices and concluded that until 1944, the terms-of-trade effect in Germany's favour was about 500 million NOK.[20] Hence, the negative terms-of-trade effect largely offsets the positive effect of German clearing credit.

Looting and requisitions

The next question to be elaborated is the extent of *Wehrmacht* looting. By looting is meant plain booty as well as requisitions which were not compensated. Estimating a minimum level of looting is possible, as the Quisling government in 1942 started a thorough investigation of war damages. Adding to 1,784 billion NOK, in current prices their value was 1,149 when deflated into 1939 prices using the official wholesale price index.[21] The estimates of Table 10.2 do not

Table 10.2 *Wehrmacht* booty and uncompensated requisitions [million NOK]

	9 April 1940–31 March 1942	1 April 1942–31 March 1943	1 April 1943–31 March 1944	1 April 1944–7 May 1945	Total
Booty	583.2				583.2
Uncompensated requisitions	268.2	315.5	317.7	300	1,201
Total	851.4	315.5	317.7	300	1,784.2

Source: NOS X102 Nasjonalinntekten i Norge 1935–1943, Oslo 1946, p. 162.

take consideration of depreciation inflicted upon real estate when used by the *Wehrmacht*.[22]

Unsurprisingly, plain booty was mainly taken in 1940 and 1941. Military equipment taken during and after the campaign in 1940 added to 352 million NOK, while radios, which added to 120 million NOK and were confiscated mostly during 1941, made up the bulk of the booty.[23]

Whereas *Wehrmacht* requisitions from private persons and companies tended to be compensated, requisitions from public institutions were often not. Among these requisitions was transport by the government's railway agency and road administration, as well as cable communication from the government's telegraph service. Services were also requisitioned from municipal port authorities as well as various administrative departments.[24] These requisitioned services, adding to 1,784 billion NOK, were compensated by the Norwegian government. Railway transport of troops and goods seems to have made up the largest part of the requisitions. Alone, the value of these transports according to the government's budget made up 451 million NOK.[25]

Expenses related to the light metal program managed by the company *Nordag AS*, which was owned by the Reich Ministry of Aviation, were also covered by Norwegian government account. By 1944, these expenses made up 200 million NOK.[26] Obviously these were supposed to be transferred to Germany's occupation account in *Norges Bank* and were not registered as requisitions.

The occupation account in *Norges Bank*

The main source of financial exploitation in Norway was forced credits from the occupation account set up in *Norges Bank* in June 1940. German authorities referred to the account as such because the *Wehrmacht*'s occupation expenditures would be settled by the occupied country's account according to the Hague convention. Yet there is no doubt that the account was applied for purposes well beyond the confines of international law. It was not exclusively used to pay for strict occupation purposes (clothing, food, accommodation and transport of troops) but also for the construction programs of the *Wehrmacht* and Todt Organisation (steel, cement, labour etc.). It also funded the operations of the Reich Commissariat and the German police in Norway.

German troops entered Norway with RKK vouchers, which were effectively applied during the campaign. Though much goods, buildings and land were requisitioned against future compensation, the *Wehrmacht* could easily pay cash with RKK vouchers, despite calls to the opposite from the fugitive Norwegian government. RKK vouchers were accepted by Norwegian banks but soon found their way into the central bank.[27] By the end of June 1940, *Norges Bank* had accumulated RKK vouchers equivalent to 250 million NOK.[28] Much more was in circulation. The Administration Council, established in Oslo as the civilian Norwegian authority to negotiate with German authorities, feared that the RKK vouchers would soon crowd out NOK and cause uncontrollable inflation. On 24 April, *Norges Bank* decided to negotiate an occupation account, from which the *Wehrmacht* could settle purchases in NOK in exchange for withdrawing the RKK vouchers from circulation.[29] As this would allow *Wehrmacht* to take advantage of the confidence in NOK German authorities endorsed the initiative.

Technically, the agreement between *Norges Bank* in Oslo and the main administration of the *Reichskreditkassen* in Berlin said that Germany would place RKK vouchers in *Norges Bank* when drawing on the occupation account. No formal repayment clause was taken into the agreement and no formal state guarantee was attached to it when *Norges Bank* accepted to set up the account. However, because the main administration of the *Reichskreditkassen* was an agency set up by the Reich to supply the *Wehrmacht* with purchasing power, the board of directors of *Norges Bank*, which formally was a private bank, implicitly assumed that, first, the Reich would rebuy the RKK vouchers after the war and second, in case of default the Norwegian state would reimburse outlays.[30]

Due to the inefficiency of continuously shipping RKK vouchers to Norway to see them stockpiled in *Norges Bank*, on German initiative, it was soon decided that the Reich would transfer the counterpart sum in reichsmarks to the main administration of the *Reichskreditkassen*, which would send a credit note of equivalent amount to *Norges Bank*. It was agreed that when sending the credit notes, 50 per cent of the sum would be noted in NOK and 50 per cent in reichsmarks. *Norges Bank* favoured this solution, as the credit note more strongly than the RKK vouchers signalled that the Reich was indebted to the bank.[31] Later, *Norges Bank* also accepted that the *Wehrmacht* wrote a debt cheque on the main administration of the *Reichskreditkassen*. The bank transferred the requested amount of NOK to the *Wehrmacht* or to the Reich Commissariat.[32] Only right before the German capitulation did *Norges Bank* reject the cheques.[33]

The agreement was to Norway's benefit insofar as the RKK vouchers disappeared from early July 1940. Judging from the wide use of RKK vouchers for German demand elsewhere in Europe, this served to avoid an uncontrolled drain of Norwegian resources. However, the negative consequence was an excessive use of the occupation account to sustain German demand. The Administration Council's expectation that *Wehrmacht* spending would calm down as the RKK vouchers disappeared proved wrong. The occupation account worked as an unlimited source of credit to which no interest rate was attached. As the account came into operation, *Wehrmacht* spending immediately increased threefold on a monthly basis as compared with RKK voucher spending.[34]

The balance of the occupation account reached 11.676 billion NOK when Germany capitulated. The net account was, however, 11.054 billion NOK because, first, as mentioned, *Wehrmacht* also imported on clearing account. This being contrary to regulations, Germany from 1941 accepted to refund these imports from the occupation account through the clearing account.[35] Total refund added to 287 million NOK. Further, in May 1945, the *Wehrmacht* had drawn 335 million NOK from the occupation account which was still on German current account deposit in *Norges Bank*.[36] Table 10.3 shows accumulated gross spending from the occupation account by the end of the year. Annual spending was quite stable at about 2.3 billion NOK but reached 2.413 billion NOK in 1941. Measured per-capita German withdrawals from the occupation account were exceptionally high.[37] When calculating the net balance of the occupation account in fixed value (1939) on the basis of the wholesale price index, the value of German spending on the occupation account was around 7 billion NOK.[38]

The excessive use of the occupation account brought Norway's economy to the limits of its performance. When *Wehrmacht* did not reach its spending targets, this was due to lack of goods more than the will to spend. Money supply increased by almost 650 per cent due to withdrawals from the occupation account.[39] As the bulk of this money remained in Norway, *Wehrmacht* spending caused a monetary overhang which had profound social consequences. Individuals, households and municipalities were able to redeem debt whereas the government, which issued bond certificates and exchequer bills to sterilize the monetary overhang, came out heavily indebted.[40] Hence, about half of expanded money supply was continuously locked up in banks.[41] This obviously saved Norway from a Greek inflationary tragedy.

As German spending subsequently found its way back to *Norges Bank*, the Norwegian Government from December 1940 started to pay off the occupation account by transferring money to the account. By May 1945, it had paid off 3.05 billion NOK.[42] The Reich Commissariat continuously called for such payments, arguing that the occupied country must pay occupation costs in accordance with international law.[43] The Quisling government paid considerable amounts in October 1942 and in June 1943, the balance at the latter point in time being 2.05 billion NOK. In February 1944, the Reich Commissar urged for another billion NOK, which prompted the Quisling government to reject further contribution. Fredrik Prytz, the Minister of Finance who had warned that the

Table 10.3 Accumulated German spending on the occupation account [billion NOK]

1940	1941	1942	1943	1944	7 May 1945
1.45	3.958	6.311	8.757	11.077	11.676

Norges Bank under okkupasjonen, Oslo: J. Chr. Gundersen Boktrykkeri, 1945, pp. 125–6, table 2.

Reich would not repay its debt even in case of a victory, argued that Germany could not demand further occupation costs from an allied government.[44] Yet in August 1944, the Government transferred another billion NOK to the account.

Wehrmacht spending

Hans Clausen Korff, a senior financial expert in the Reich Commissariat whose assignment was to keep German spending in Norway under surveillance, maintains that *Wehrmacht* spent 96 per cent of the occupation account.[45]

Fully aware of Norway's import dependence, when invading the country, the High Command of the *Wehrmacht* (OKW) emphasized that the predicament must not be solved by imports from Scandinavia or Germany but rather by constraining domestic civilian consumption.[46] Yet during the campaign from April to June 1940, *Wehrmacht*'s Commander-in-chief of Norway, General Nikolas von Falkenhorst, ordered *Wehrmacht* units to pay Norwegians well, whether for requisitioned goods or for work. The units' paymasters were far from stingy.[47] To watch over and coordinate demand, the *Wehrmacht* soon set up Military Economic Staff Norway as well as a Chief Intendant. Nevertheless, coordinated restraint turned out to be a classic collective-action problem and failed. *Wehrmacht* units soon outbid each other and built up their own stockpiles. Having expended existing stockpiles already in the autumn of 1940, *Wehrmacht* demand largely overstretched domestic supply.

For which expenses did the *Wehrmacht* spend the occupation account? Over time, *Wehrmacht*'s demand was much higher for labour and real capital than for its own maintenance.[48] This followed from its massive construction schemes. A network of airports and naval ports was constructed soon after the invasion. And from 1941, the Atlantic Wall fortification was deliberately extended up north through Norway's coastline. In harsh climatic conditions, roads, railroads and harbours were built and maintained to move troops and equipment swiftly across the country. Yet a detailed record of these heavy expenses does not exist, as archives were destroyed. According to Korff, reliable accounts existed for 1943 and 1944, but their classification was somewhat confusing. An account for 1940–41 was also reconstructed after the war. On the basis of these three accounts and drawing on circumstantial evidence, as for example the account of the spending among *Wehrmacht* branches presented in Table 10.5, Korff estimated the composition of expenses for the period 1940 to 1944, adding up to 10.6 billion NOK. The estimate is presented in Table 10.4.

With this classification, it is difficult to precisely distinguish which of the expenses were beyond legal occupation costs and consequently illegal. The amount of expenses for construction nevertheless provides an indication. As indicated in the first row, nearly half of the expenditures were construction schemes, although the share decreased as the number of troops grew from 1943.[49]

Which of the *Wehrmacht* branches were the spenders? Korff provides an estimate of the different *Wehrmacht* branches' spending for 1940 to 1944. Adding to 10.6 billion NOK, the shares are reproduced in Table 10.5.

Table 10.4 Composition of *Wehrmacht* expenses, 1940–1944

Type of expenses	NOK million	Share (%)
Building schemes	4,833.6	45.6
Wages for troops, employed and hired persons (incl. Norwegians)	2,363.8	22.3
Acquisition/procurement	1,611.2	15.2
Maintenance of weapons, vehicles, ships etc.	0,869.2	8.2
Lease and requisitions	0,466.4	4.4
Transport	0,296.8	2.8
Miscellaneous	0,159.0	1.5

Source: H. C. Korff, *Norwegens Wirtschaft im Mahlstrom der Okkupation*, part II, p. 251.

Table 10.5 shows that the army spent as much as the navy and the air force together. Considering the Todt Organisation's large field of responsibility after Hitler's Wiking order in 1942, the amount of its spending was quite moderate, only 9 per cent. Much spending on the Wiking programme was obviously entered on the book accounts of the *Wehrmacht*'s combat branches. The National Socialist Drivers Corps was integrated into Todt Organisation in 1942 and subsequently part of the transport fleet Speer, but its spending was marginal. The rather small units of the Reich Labour Service were withdrawn from Norway in 1942. It should be remembered that not all police expenses were covered by the *Wehrmacht*. The German police in Oslo were funded by the main cash desk of the Reich Commissariat.

Surely much *Wehrmacht* spending paid for commodity and labour imports (beyond the clearing account), but most obviously remained in Norway. According to Korff's estimate, pay to non-Germans directly employed by the *Wehrmacht*, by and large Norwegians, added to around 6 per cent of overall expenses in 1943 to 1944.[50] However, the bulk of spending went through Norwegian companies, including farmers and fishermen, with whom *Wehrmacht* entered into delivery contracts or requisitioned goods against compensation. In 1944, *Wehrmacht* had contracts with 4,688 Norwegian companies for which the value of the contract was worth 600 million NOK or more.[51] Entering into contracts with the *Wehrmacht* was obviously big business for the Norwegian construction industry. Yet as from 1942, the strained resource situation made it imperative to bring in construction firms from the Reich. Evidence from the Todt Organisation indicates that slightly more than 200 were present in 1943 to 1944.[52] Obviously these firms brought profits and wages back to Germany. Much of the workers' pay was deposited in reichsmarks in German banks. The potential for such transfers was however made less significant because of massive subcontracting with a variety of Norwegian firms using Norwegian labour. Consequently, in the absence of empirical research, a fair hypothesis is that only a limited amount of value was brought out of the country through corporate profits and pay.

Table 10.5 Wehrmacht branches' expenditures, 1940–44.

	1940–44 [million NOK]	Share (%)
Wehrmacht administration	324.7	3.1
German Army	4,502.4	42.5
German Navy	2,403.8	22.7
German Air Force	2,392.8	22.5
Todt Organisation	953.2	9.0
Reich Labour Service	3.8	0.2
National Socialist Drivers Corps	1.1	
German police	17.2	
Total	10,599	100

Source: H.C. Korff, *Norwegens Wirtschaft im Mahlstrom der Okkupation*, part II, p. 244.

Korff states that throughout the occupation, 1.8 billion NOK was at the disposal of individual *Wehrmacht* troops.[53] Another relevant question is how much of this income was transferred out of the country in the form of cash or goods. We know that the Norwegian Ministry of Trade was concerned about the transfer of cash and goods already in the spring of 1941 but failed to negotiate a refund scheme. Admittedly, troops were not allowed to bring NOK freely out of the country, but through the financial mechanism of field post transfers, they could let relatives at home dispose of around 20 per cent of their pay in reichsmarks at least until July 1941.[54] Korff maintains that the amount of money transferred through this mechanism was about 5 million NOK monthly. It is unclear for how long the mechanism was in operation, but if it did so for the whole occupation period, troops transferred about 300 million NOK of their pay to German accounts. The cash flow was probably much less, but we can't answer the question more precisely.

Troops might also bring goods bought in Norway with them when on vacation or transfer outside Norway. The large number of troops in Norway made this a potential mechanism for exploitation. Their purchasing power was generally good, as in November 1940, soldiers' pay was raised by 50 per cent. Thus it largely covered the domestic price increase during the first two years of the occupation, if not necessarily the growing black-market prices. Moreover, family back home were allowed to transfer a certain amount of money to their relative through field post transfers, thereby also adding to troops' purchasing power. Korff estimates that individual purchases of goods added to about 330 million NOK in 1940 and 1941.[55] If this trend continued the next two years, we must assume total individual purchases of around 660 million NOK. But how much goods was brought abroad? Götz Aly has argued that such transfers account for much of *Wehrmacht*'s exploitation in occupied countries.[56] He does not devote much attention to Norway but informs that German soldiers were allowed to monthly send home packages of 2.5 kilos in weight. He maintains that for troops in Norway, this transfer was modest in comparative terms and largely limited to fish, herring and silver fox skins.[57] Circumstantial evidence supports Ali's assertion. First, the RKK vouchers disappeared in Norway already during the summer of 1940 as legal tender. Hence troops transferred temporarily to Norway carrying RKK vouchers would not spend as much as they could, for example, in France. Second, although the black market grew during the two last years of occupation, it seems to have been comparatively small in Norway. Further, from 1942, the Reich Commissariat worked to reduce the quotas each soldier was allowed to buy because it threatened domestic civilian supply, and from 1944, the *Wehrmacht* took measures to stop illegal transfers of herring.[58] Therefore, individual purchases might well have gone down. Korff, confirming that herring and silver fox skins were the preferred goods transferred to Germany, states that the transfers reached their peak in 1942 to 1943. Although we have no full account of the transfers, there is no reason to reject Aly's assertion that these were modest.

The controversy between the *Wehrmacht* and the Reich Commissariat

Led by Josef Terboven, the Reich Commissariat was set up on Hitler's initiative to run civilian affairs according to political objectives.[59] Terboven would, first, take account of the political goals to make Norwegians accept the Nazi course, second, tend to prepare the Norwegian economy for inclusion in the postwar German-dominated greater economic sphere.[60] To achieve these long-term goals, he would continuously warn against financial collapse. He was strongly advised by a few orthodox economists, among them Hans Claussen Korff.[61] These economists certainly worked out regulations to support *Wehrmacht*'s tasks. The civilian sector was strictly rationed and heavily taxed. In December 1940, regulations also empowered government agencies to deny civilian investments. While calling for civilian regulations, they also warned that *Wehrmacht*'s impatient ambitions were perilously overheating the economy.[62] They would therefore call for Berlin to supply Norway with goods and labour. Yet they failed to convince the OKW that the construction schemes must be funded directly from Germany.[63]

Albert Speer's reforms in 1942 did not profoundly change the course of the Reich Commissariat. As the Todt Organisation settled in Norway after Hitler's Wiking order, Willi Henne was appointed leader and subsequently also General Plenipotentiary for construction works in Norway. Authorized to approve of all construction schemes, he settled in the Reich Commissariat in charge of the new main department for technology.[64] Henne surely would expand construction projects according to *Wehrmacht*'s needs but also took account of the economist's more prudent financial logic.[65] Admittedly responding to the priorities of Speer's Central Planning, his staff reduced the amount of projects to avoid a complete breakdown of the economy as the resource deficit grew.[66]

Evidence suggests that the Reich Commissariat would prefer to adapt Norway's economy to the German course with less *Wehrmacht* influence.[67] Its strategy was not to sequestrate companies but rather to influence their corporate behaviour by appointing trustees employed by the Reich Commissariat and hired from German industry.[68] Further, following Terboven, the OKW never set up an armaments inspection agency in Norway, as it did in the Netherlands, Belgium and France. It also never established a Central Contracts Office (*Zast*) to attach Norwegian industry directly to German importers through commercial contracts.[69] However, it is difficult to judge if the existence of these institutions would have influenced *Wehrmacht*'s pattern of spending differently.

As German capital interests might have drawn preposterous profits out of the country, the Reich Commissariat's strategy does not preclude that indirect financial exploitation took place. However, there is no evidence that German stakeholders took more dividend than other stakeholders. If this had been the case, they would have met obstacles when transferring their capital to Germany, as the Reich Commissariat successfully rejected calls for allowing transfers of private capital on the clearing account.[70] Therefore, it is more likely that companies transferred value through the price mechanism. Further, there is evidence that the Reich Commissariat called for the Norwegian government to subsidize Norwegian companies that exported to Germany, thereby bringing value originating from Norwegian taxpayers to Germany through the price mechanism. However, there is no such entry in the government budget and *Norges Bank*'s report on its activities during the occupation maintained that Norwegian authorities opposed such calls 'partially with good effect'.[71] Hence we can assume that transfer of government subsidies was carried into effect only modestly. Yet Bohn has shown that for some commodities, the Norwegian export price was fixed so low that it allowed Germans to sell it further to buyers in third countries with considerable profits. He does, however, not indicate the extent of such pricing.[72] Evidence from the aluminium industry supports the hypothesis that Norwegian companies were exploited through intraindustry transactions. In 1941, they would pay a relatively higher price for imported bauxite than what they would receive for exported aluminium, which worked to transfer profits to German companies. Yet the price increase of bauxite also reflected increasing supply costs among the German companies.[73] One should be careful to interpret changing price ratios as deliberate exploitation as long as there is no systematic study of to what extent Norwegian companies were exploited through the mechanism of transfer pricing.

While deliberately constraining civilian demand, the Reich Commissariat soon took action to restrain excessive *Wehrmacht* spending. Early in October 1940, Terboven met Falkenhorst to discuss the matter, but disagreements lingered until late November, when the OKW supervised an agreement. General Georg Thomas, leader of the economic armaments department of the OKW, came to Oslo to close the quarrel. He agreed that Norway's productive potential was largely exploited. He accepted Terboven's demand that *Wehrmacht* spending must be limited to 500 million NOK biannually, that *Wehrmacht* could exploit Norwegian resources for its construction projects only after agreement with the Reich Commissar and that *Wehrmacht* troops must be supplied from abroad. Further, an import program based on priority lists must be implemented from 1941.[74] As a result of this agreement, for the rest of the occupation, much food for the Wehrmacht troops was imported from Denmark and much wood from Sweden while clothing, coal and fuel came from continental Europe.

However, the agreement did not constrain *Wehrmacht* spending. Whereas the spending target for the autumn of 1941 was scheduled for 500 million NOK, *Wehrmacht* demanded 2.1 billion NOK. Terboven and Falkenhorst again clashed in 1941. Rudolf Sattler, also a member of Terboven's group of economic advisors, tabled a plan to restrict *Wehrmacht* spending to legal occupation costs.[75] In response, Falkenhorst underlined military primacy and suggested introducing reichsmarks in Norway to dispose of the Reich Commissariat's perpetual concerns about inflation. Terboven now complained to Field Marshall General Keitel, who set up the so-called Commission N, consisting of financial experts from the OKW, to investigate Norway's economic and financial limits. The commission admitted that the economy worked at its limit but concluded that the construction projects were of strategic importance. Accordingly, it accepted *Wehrmacht*'s spending target.[76] Admitting that this must be drawn from the occupation account, the commission also accepted that spending would largely exceed the *Wehrmacht*'s maintenance costs. Therefore, it suggested a scrutiny of the occupation account with the purpose of distinguishing between *Wehrmacht*'s maintenance costs and the residual credits given to Germany, furthermore to agree with *Norges Bank* on interest and terms of payment for the residual credit share.[77]

In the wake of Commission N's work, the Reich Ministry of Finance had talks with the High Military Command at the end of 1941, leading the latter to start rationing occupation account funds in 1942. Each different *Wehrmacht* unit in Norway was now obliged to report in advance planned monthly procurements above 20,000 NOK and planned construction projects above 50,000 NOK to the Chief Intendant, whose powers allowed him to endorse or reject requests.[78]

Whether unwilling or unable, the Chief Intendant did not restrain *Wehrmacht* demand. He surely would have seen a more prudent use of the occupation account but would not downgrade the military construction projects. Therefore he suggested that *Wehrmacht* abstain from providing compensations when making more use of requisitions. Targeted looting would imply a radical new policy and was rebuffed by the Reich Commissariat.[79] Hence the *Wehrmacht* continued to draw credits from the occupation account.

The Quisling government agreed with the Reich Commissariat to restrain *Wehrmacht* spending, but also the government receded for *Wehrmacht*'s power. In a memorandum to Quisling in August 1942, the Minister of Finance, Frederik Prytz, ascertained that the balance of the occupation account had reached 5 billion NOK and concluded that German withdrawals must end, yet with an exception for the fortification along the coast.[80] This shows that the Quisling government also gave in to military imperatives.

Concluding remarks

The contribution has argued that Nazi Germany's main instrument of financial exploitation was forced credits from the occupation account set up in the central bank. German spending of more than 11 billion NOK obviously went far beyond the confines of international law. Though representing considerable value, booty and uncompensated requisitions adding to 1.7 billion NOK mattered less. Thus nominal direct occupation costs in current value approached 13 billion NOK. In 1946, the Norwegian Statistical Bureau calculated direct occupation costs in current prices to be between 34 per cent and 37 per cent of the national income for the years 1940 through 1943.[81] These are reliable estimates and probably valid also for the last years of occupation. However, the net balance of 500 million NOK in Norway's favour, brought forward from the clearing account, was not included.

Whereas there is no indication that confiscated goods were brought out of the country, transfers of value through field post transfers and troops' purchases must have been marginal. Certainly value was brought out by Wehrmacht spending in exchange for commodities and labour, but it is impossible to qualify its value. Nevertheless, the bulk of spending must have found its way into Norwegian pockets. As opposed to France, the value of direct occupation costs remained in circulation within Norway.[82]

Whereas Germany provided credits through the clearing account, this was largely levelled out by indirect terms of trade effects in Germany's favour in 1940 to 1941. Other indirect forms of financial transfer through corporate channels, whether through dividend or profits subsidized by the Norwegian government, seem negligible.

The High Command of the *Wehrmacht* endorsed military spending although Norway's economy was working at its limits from 1941. From a theoretical point of view, the discrepancy between *Wehrmacht* ambitions and the structural predicaments of the Norwegian economy might easily have caused an economic and social catastrophe. This never occurred, although the general welfare loss as measured by consumption levels was estimated to be at least 25 per cent.[83] Korff argues that the economy would have crumbled into disarray already in 1941 had not the Reich Commissariat continuously worked to adjust German demand to supply.[84] The Reich Commissariat surely opposed the spending and was supported by Speer's Central Planning.

Notes

1 A. S. Milward, *The Fascist Economy in Norway*, Oxford: Clarendon Press, 1972; R. Bohn, *Reichskommissariat Norwegen. 'Nationalsozialistische Neuordnung' und Kriegswirtschaft*, Munich: Oldenbourg, 2000.
2 H. Espeli, 'The German Occupation and its Consequences on the Composition and Changes of Norwegian Business Elites', *Jahrbuch für Wirtschaftsgeschichte*, 2010/2, pp. 9–24; idem, 'Economic Consequences of the German Occupation of Norway, 1940–1945', *Scandinavian Journal of History*, 2013, vol. 38, p. 510.
3 Convention (IV) respecting the Laws and Customs of War on Land, The Hague, 18 October 1907, Section III.
4 Statistisk Sentralbyrå (ed.), *Statistisk-økonomisk utsyn over krigsårene*, Oslo: H. Aschehaug & CO., 1945, pp. 96–105.
5 Ibid, p. 115.
6 Ibid, pp. 16, 113–6.

7 Norway's government budget for 1939–40 might serve as a reference point: whereas revenue was 562 million NOK, total expenditures were 714 million NOK.
8 J. Scherner, 'Der deutsche Importboom während des Zweiten Weltkrieges. Neue Ergebnisse zur Struktur der Ausbeutung des besetzten Europas auf der Grundlage einer Neuschätzung der deutschen Handelsbilanz', *Historische Zeitschrift*, 2012, vol. 294, pp. 79–111.
9 Riksarkivet Oslo (RAO), Norge Bank, X-trykksaker, saksarkiv 1940–49, box 0001, Beretning om Norges Banks virksomhet i året 1941, pp. 28–9.
10 *Norges Bank under okkupasjonen*, Oslo: Banken, 1945, pp. 125–6 (table 2).
11 RAO, RK, FD 5325/45, Generalbericht der Gruppe Arbeitseinsatz für die Zeit vom 21.4.1940 bis 31.12.1942, established 18 February 1943.
12 Bohn, *Reichskommissariat*, p. 228.
13 Ibid, p. 240; Espeli, 'Economic Consequences', p. 506. For details, see SSB, Statistisk-økonomisk oversikt over krigen, pp. 218–23.
14 G. Hatlehol, *Forced Labour under Todt Organisation in Norway during Nazi Germany's occupation*, forthcoming PhD thesis at Norwegian University of Science and Technology, Trondheim.
15 100 NOK was 60 RKK vouchers and 56.82 reichsmark, *Norges Bank under okkupasjonen*, p. 28. RAO, Norges Bank, X-trykksaker, saksarkiv 1940–49, box 0001, Beretning om Norges Banks virksomhet i året 1940, pp. 24–5.
16 RAO, Private Archive 951, box 2. H.C. Korff, *Norwegens Wirtschaft im Mahlstrom der Okkupation*, 1949, part II, pp. 194–8 (unpublished manuscript in two parts from 1949, henceforth: Korff, *Norwegens Wirtschaft*).
17 Bohn, *Reichskommissariat*, pp. 246–7, Korff, *Norwegens Wirtschaft, part I*, pp. 59–60. German export prices increased as the export premiums were removed and transportation as well as insurance costs grew.
18 RAO, Landssvikarkivet, L-dom Oslo 4367, box 2, document 43, Letter from Blehr to Quisling, 2 June 1942.
19 Statistisk Sentralbyrå, *Statistisk-økonomisk utsyn over krigsårene*, pp. 32–5; Bohn, *Reichskommissariat*, p. 251.
20 O. Akrust/P.J. Bjerve, *Hva krigen kostet Norge*, Oslo: Dreyer, 1945, p. 32.
21 NOS X102 Nasjonalinntekten i Norge 1935–1943, Oslo 1946, pp. 164–5.
22 Aukrust/Bjerve, *Hva krigen kostet Norge*, p. 25.
23 Ibid, p. 24.
24 Ibid, p. 24.
25 Ibid, p. 68 (table 17).
26 BArch, R 2/357, Bericht über die Wehrmachtausgaben in Norwegen und ihre Auswirkung auf die Finanzlage des norwegischen Staates, 6 June 1944, quoted in Bohn, *Reichskommissariat*, p. 332.
27 *Norges Bank under okkupasjonen*, p. 26.
28 Ibid, p. 125; Korff, *Norwegens Wirtschaft, part II*, p. 217.
29 H. Espeli, ' "Det gavner ingenting å gjøre store vanskeligheter i små saker. Dette er ikke store saker". Norges Bank, Administrasjonsrådet og etableringen av okkupasjonskontoen i 1940', *Historisk Tidsskrift*, 2011, vol. 90, pp. 559–84.
30 RAO, Norge Bank, X-trykksaker, saksarkiv 1940–49, box 0001, Innstilling fra komiteen til gransking av Norges Banks virksomhet i okkupasjonstiden, p. 33a–34; Beretning om Norges Banks virksomhet i året 1940, p. 18; Bohn, *Reichskommissariat*, pp. 304sq.
31 Korff, *Norwegens Wirtschaft, part II*, p. 199; *Norges bank under okkupasjonen*, pp. 51–2.
32 Korff, *Norwegens Wirtschaft, part II*, p. 200; *Norges bank under okkupasjonen*, pp. 28–9.
33 Korff, *Norwegens Wirtschaft, part II*, p. 214.
34 Ibid, part II, p. 218.

35 *Norges Bank under okkupasjonen*, p. 50.
36 RAO, Norge Bank, X-trykksaker, saksarkiv 1940–49, box 0001, Innstilling fra komiteen til gransking av Norges banks virksomhet i okkupasjonstiden, p. 29; *Norges Bank under okkupasjonen*, pp. 125–6; Korff, *Norwegens Wirtschaft, part II*, pp. 230, 243.
37 H. Klemann/S. Kudryashov, *Occupied Economies. An Economic History of Nazi-Occupied Europe, 1939–1945*, London: Berg, 2012, p. 202.
38 NOS X102 Nasjonalinntekten i Norge 1935–1943, Oslo 1946, p. 164–5.
39 Espeli, 'Economic Consequences', p. 508.
40 Statistisk Sentralbyrå, *Statistisk-økonomisk utsyn over krigsårene*, pp. 13–5. Much was also channeled into government bank deposits through taxes.
41 Aukrust/Bjerve, *Hva krigen kostet Norge*, pp. 51–7.
42 *Norges Bank under okkupasjonen*, pp. 125–6.
43 Korff, *Norwegens Wirtschaft, part II*, p. 240.
44 Ibid, part II, pp. 240–1; *Norges bank under okkupasjonen*, p. 103; memorandum frå finansminister Prytz/Quisling, 6 March 1944.
45 Korff, *Norwegens Wirtschaft, part II*, p. 244.
46 Vorschläge der Wehrmacht für die Regelung der allgemein wirtschaftlichen und rüstungswirtschaftlichen Fragen (Norwegen), published in *Undersøkelseskommisjonen av 1945 Innstilling. Bilag 1–3*, Oslo: H. Aschehoug & CO., pp. 62–6.
47 Korff, *Norwegens Wirtschaft, part II*, pp. 207–8.
48 Aukrust/Bjerve, *Hva krigen kostet Norge*, p. 59.
49 This is also confirmed by Bohn, *Reichskommissariat*, pp. 268–9.
50 Ibid, p. 251.
51 Bohn, *Reichskommissariat*, p. 266.
52 Henne, *Die Organisation Todt*; RAO, RAFA-2188, Gla-Loo17/001, Firmenliste der Einsatzgruppe Wiking, 1 December 1943.
53 Korff, *Norwegens Wirtschaft, part II*, p. 320.
54 Ibid, p. 321.
55 Ibid.
56 G. Aly, *Hitlers Volksstaat. Raub, Rassenkrieg und nationaler Sozialismus*, Frankfurt am Main: Fischer, 2005.
57 Ibid, p. 123.
58 Ibid; Korff, *Norwegens Wirtschaft, part II*, p. 326.
59 H.-D. Loock, *Quisling, Rosenberg und Terboven. Zur Vorgeschichte und Geschichte der nationalsozialistischen Revolution in Norwegen*, Stuttgart: DVA, 1970; Bohn, *Reichskommissariat*, pp. 36–44, 193–4.
60 RA, Interrogation Carlo Otte; Bohn, *Reichskommissariat*, p. 36.
61 Bohn, *Reichskommissariat*, pp. 161–2; Korff I, p. 96.
62 This was also maintained in retrospect by L. Graf Schwerin von Krosigk, *Staatsbankrott. Die Geschichte der Finanzpolitik des Deutschen Reichs von 1920 bis 1945*, Göttingen: Messerschmidt, 1974, p. 296. The Reich Ministry of Finance continuously supported the Reich Commissariat.
63 *Norges Bank under okkupasjonen*, p. 33.
64 W. Henne, *Die Organisation Todt in Norwegen. Aufgabe, Organisation, Art der Baudurchführung mit aufgetretenen Schwierigkeiten, Leistungen, Okt./Nov. 1945*. Private property of Johan Ditlev-Simonsen, Oslo.
65 Bohn, *Reichskommissariat*, pp. 180–3.
66 Henne, *Die Organisation Todt in Norwegen*.
67 RAO, RK, FD, 5325/45, Ein Jahr Reichskommissar für die besetzten norwegischen Gebiete, April 1941.
68 Korff, *Norwegens Wirtschaft, part II*, p. 8; Bohn, *Reichskommissariat*, pp. 296–300.
69 E. Dickert, *Die Nutzbarmachung des Produktionspotentials besetzter Gebiete durch Auftragsverlagerungen im Zweiten Weltkrieg. Staatliche Regulierung und*

Verlagerungsverhalten von Maschinenbau- und Automobilunternehmen, Trondheim: PhD NTNU, 2014, pp. 31sq.
70 Korff, *Norwegens Wirtschaft, part II*, p. 8.
71 *Norges Bank under okkupasjonen*, p. 26.
72 Bohn, *Reichskommissariat*, pp. 289–91.
73 RAO, PA 0892, D, L0275, correspondence 1 May 1941–31 December 1941, Festlegung Rohmaterialpreise und der Verkaufspreise für Hüttenaluminium für das Jahr 1941, 5 May 1941.
74 RAO, RK, FD 5325/45, Besprechung über die Deckung der Wehrmachtbedarfs in Norwegen, 21.11.1940; Bohn, *Reichskommissariat*, p. 193; Korff, *Norwegens Wirtschaft, part II*, pp. 221–6.
75 *Norges bank under okkupasjonen*, p. 40–1. The plan also said that the Reich should take over some of the obligations of the central administration of the *Reichskreditkassen* and pay interest for this.
76 Korff, *Norwegens Wirtschaft, part II*, p. 229.
77 Korff, *Norwegens Wirtschaft, part II*, p. 231, *Norges Bank under okkupasjonen*, p. 41.
78 Korff, *Norwegens Wirtschaft, part II*, p. 232.
79 Ibid, p. 233.
80 Ibid, pp. 238–9.
81 Statistisk Sentralbyrå, NOS X 102 Nasjonalinntekten I Norge 1935–1943, Oslo: H. Aschehaug & Co., 1945, p. 164.
82 On France, see M. Boldorf/J. Scherner, 'France's Occupation Costs and the War in the East: The Contribution to the German war Economy, 1940–1944', *Journal of Contemporary History*, 2012, vol. 47, pp. 291–316.
83 Aukrust/Bjerve, *Hva krigen kostet Norge*, p. 48.
84 Korff, *Norwegens Wirtschaft, part II*, p. 244.

11 The incorporation of the General Government in the German war economy

Stephan Lehnstaedt

1. Organising occupation

Poland was occupied by the German armed forces in autumn 1939 following a campaign lasting only six weeks. The territory of the central European state was divided between the German *Reich* and the Soviet Union, the latter also participating in the war as an aggressor. The German National Socialists incorporated the western regions around Posen and Danzig into the territory of the *Reich*, while central Poland around the cities of Warsaw and Krakow was administered as the so-called General Government, which is the subject of the present investigation. In a deliberate attempt to make a distinction from the occupied Polish state, Krakow was chosen as the new seat of government, where Hans Frank resided from 26 October 1939 as General Governor in the former royal palace of Wawel. From there, he ruled over the four districts all named after their most important cities – Krakow, Lublin, Radom and Warsaw, to which Galicia, with its seat of government Lemberg, was added during the campaign against the Soviet Union.

The civil administration developed from the military bureaucracy. Under Hans Frank, governors reigned in each district, with municipal and regional directors also reporting to them. The occupation administration was able to operate with a minimum of German personnel, since the Polish communal administration had not been dissolved, but rather continued to exist as a recipient of commands.[1] In 1940, there were only around 7,300 members of the occupying force active within the apparatus of the General Governor, and although this number increased to 18,550 by 1944,[2] it was still small in relation to the size of the territories under its control: including Galicia, Frank ruled over 144,000 square kilometres with 17 million inhabitants[3], equalling roughly 22 per cent of both the area and population of the German *Reich* within the borders of 1938.

The administration of the conquered territories was possible only through a decentralised, personnel-intensive structure which enabled access to the entire country. The manpower for this was drawn from the *Reich* itself, from which several specialist administration bodies, such as the Ministry of Labour, for example, had delegated the appropriate employees. After the establishment of the first employment office in Siedlce on 26 October 1939,[4] the employment administration in the General Government, led by the director of the Employment

Department Max Frauendorfer,[5] had managed by February 1940 to achieve a structure which remained more or less intact until the end of the war.

The districts each had their own employment department, which themselves presided over five employment office boroughs. In the regional and municipal boards, which represented the lowest level of German administration in Poland, an employment office was also to be established. In addition, several other cities also had subsidiary offices,[6] of which the employment office in Warsaw alone had nineteen.[7] When Galicia was added to the General Government as the fifth district in 1941, further employment office boroughs were established there, producing a total of twenty-one employment offices and eighty-six subsidiaries by summer 1942.[8] The key positions were, of course, held by established employment office staff who had proved themselves both as leaders and as national socialists.[9] Below this level, however, this was no longer exclusively the case. The number of these workers increased consistently during the course of the war: 782 German nationals and ethnic Germans were active in the employment administration in 1940, with this figure, despite a constantly growing demand for soldiers in the *Wehrmacht*, rising to 1,135 by 1944, representing an increase of almost 50 per cent. There were, however, almost twice as many Polish workers employed who had been incorporated from the prewar Polish employment offices.[10]

Such an organisation structure, which allowed access to the human resources of the General Government – the employment administration was also responsible for the deportation of Polish forced labourers to the German *Reich* – could also be observed in most of the other branches of the economic administration, which was split into many different individual areas. Alongside the General Government, its subsidiary organisations and the agents of the Four Year Plan,[11] the permanent state apparatuses of a military and civil nature included the armaments inspection of the War Economy and Armaments Office under General Thomas and, from 1942, under the *Reich* Minister for Weapons and Ammunition. Additional players seeking to further their interests in the General Government included special institutions such as *Karpaten Öl*, private companies such as banks or the *Reichswerke Hermann Göring* and the SS, whose economic activities are, however, often overestimated in terms of their importance.[12] The Reich Ministry for Nutrition and Agriculture, for example, had several disagreements with Heinrich Himmler, who, as Reich Commissioner for the Consolidation of German Culture, also held jurisdiction over the agrarian sector, although this did not have any effect on the exploitation of agriculture.[13]

Hitler's plans for Poland were very general and, before the outbreak of war, did not extend much beyond the Prussian policies concerning Poland in the nineteenth century: the General Government was to function primarily as a labour reservoir.[14] Further concepts were not developed until after September 1939, with even a comprehensive planning basis not being completed until October.[15] The fundamental dictum of the entire occupation policy was expressed in very striking words by Hans Frank in 1940: 'Subsequently, the only option was an exploitation of the country through indiscriminate pillaging, extraction of all provisions, raw materials, machines, factory infrastructure etc. of importance for the Germany war economy, drawing upon the labour force for deployment within the *Reich*, a reduction of the entire Polish economy to the minimum level required for the most basic survival of the population [...]. Poland is to be treated like a colony, with the Poles becoming the slaves of the Greater German world empire'.[16]

This, however, does not reveal anything about the concrete development of the occupation, for this had to be adapted to the realities and demands of war, which indeed led to a range of different strategies being employed. It was already obvious by 1939 that policy was directed particularly against Jews, who were to be 'eliminated' from the economy, as countless confiscations of property directly following the invasion demonstrated. This process – until the commencement of the mass murder under the aegis of the SS in summer 1942 – operated on two levels, being led both by the district governors according to guidelines from Krakow and from the central administration, legitimised through the appropriate legal standardisations;[17] however, the process was far less characterised by formal legal parameters than was the case in Western Europe.[18]

The implementation speed of the anti-Jewish economic policy can be observed in the example of Warsaw. Of the roughly 500 larger firms which had 20 or more employees before the war, 193 were Jewish, with a total of around 9,400 employees. Of the 144 industrial companies among this number, only 32 were still active by April 1940, and with 60 per cent fewer employees.[19] In October of the same year, 296 custodians administered 393 Jewish firms, and from the more than 4,000 rented properties, an income of almost 5.5 million zloty was gathered within a single month (the official exchange rate was 2 zloty for 1 reichsmark).[20] In Warsaw alone, the value of the confiscated property was calculated to be 2 billion reichsmarks.[21] Statistics also show that the custodians were predominantly German nationals, followed by Poles and ethnic Germans; Germans tended to be responsible for the larger firms, while Poles and, to an extent, Ukrainians received smaller businesses.[22] At the same time, the mostly Polish large landowners were persecuted and had their lands confiscated, such that by May 1943, more than half of the 4,523 businesses with holdings of more than 50 hectares were in the hands of the occupying Germans: they had confiscated 558,900 hectares of agricultural land.[23]

2. Phases of exploitation

The period directly following the invasion was characterised primarily by plundering, which was often carried out by various competing institutions such as the *Wehrmacht* and the Four-Year Plan Authority, and which led to the extraction of around 25,000 freight carriages of goods worth several billion reichsmarks.[24] This initial phase of the occupation economy lasted until November 1939.

General Governor Frank, who wished to rule his territory legalistically and through the use of decrees,[25] demanded an end to the largely random plundering and quickly found support, which was paradoxically aided by the institutions which had previously profited the most from organised theft: both General Georg Thomas from the *Wehrmacht* High Command and Hermann Göring, as chief of the four-year plan, announced their interest in making use of Polish industry.[26]

From 15 November 1939, a new directive from Hitler thus came into force which signalled the beginning of a second period of economic policy in the

General Government lasting until roughly the middle of 1940 – or to be more precise: until the collapse of France. The deindustrialisation during this period was limited to factories producing consumer items, while the production of armaments for the western campaign was resumed and to some extent even involved rebuilding. In the district of Warsaw, where by January 1940 there were already more than 600 businesses with more than 26,000 workers deemed vital for the war effort, this number grew to 727 firms with 46,644 employees by October.[27] At the same time, the Polish economy continued to increase in importance for the goals of the German *Reich*. In a meeting with Hitler on 8 July 1940, Frank had been tasked with intensifying production in his territories, particularly of military equipment. However, this did not mean investment in the General Government, and certainly not in its industrialisation, and Hitler also rejected the use of unemployed Poles in the region.[28] In fact, the opposite was the case: Frank was to increase delivery of workers to the *Reich*.

From the middle of 1940, the aim was to make the General Government as useful as possible for the German war economy and to enable the maximum possible mobilisation of human and material resources,[29] as following the successful campaign against France, explicit preparations for a longer war against the western powers were the next goal – a war for which, in turn, a *Blitzkrieg* against Russia was to be waged in order to secure resources there as well.[30] Alongside industrial goods and manpower, as well as a direct financial contribution of no small size, the General Government was mainly charged with delivering food supplies. Poland, to a large extent an agrarian country, was known principally as a deficit area, but Berlin was willing to accept the starvation of the local population if that were to guarantee the food supply at home. At the same time, the national socialists had a long-term plan to 'Germanise' the region, in which Poles were to live only as simple labourers and Jews were to be removed completely. Large-scale investments were required to meet this goal, which was diametrically opposed to the first aim concerning the region. Ingo Loose pointed out that the Germanisation plans foresaw a continuation and adaptation of the existing economic system, while exploitation required new economic structures[31] – requirements which were mutually exclusive and would hardly have found support among the occupied population in a conquered territory.

However, the invasion of the Soviet Union and the massive losses sustained there saw the beginning of a further, fourth phase of the occupation economy, which once again demanded a reorientation of policy. Poland was now to increase its production of clothing, ammunition, weapons and transport but was also required to repair vehicles. The armaments industry was now to deliver not only quantity, but also – particularly following the start of the bombing raids – quality: the first production plants from the *Reich* moved east and attempted to establish assembly points and production techniques there. The employment authorities also put massive pressure on both Polish and German firms to employ Jews.[32] This represented a change in German policy, which in 1939 and early 1940 had insisted upon Jews being excluded from employment.[33] Now, the task was to transport as many Poles as possible into the *Reich*, and if their labour could be replaced in Poland by Jews, then it would be possible to fulfil the forced labour quotas at home. At the same time, the wages in the General Government were to be kept as low as possible.[34] This too, however, proved only to be a part of a short-term mobilisation strategy aiming for immediate profit for the war economy and the war against the Soviet Union, without any consideration of a sustainable long-term plan for the General Government. Only in the agricultural sector was the excessive exploitation to be perpetuated through sporadic investment, dung delivery and the use of machines.[35]

The methods used to gather the harvest in Poland were also extremely brutal. This was largely due to the fact that the district and municipal governors, the lowest level of German administration, were charged with the collection of quotas. The local leaders were required to meet certain quantitative standards, with the way in which this was achieved being irrelevant. In most cases, this meant excessive punishments being exacted upon farmers. These began with monetary fines for minor breaches of the delivery requirements but grew quickly to property confiscation, violence and detention in camps. The Polish farmers were, as the leadership of the General Government stated, 'not the subject of a population-oriented farming policy'[36] and could thus be brutally exploited. The Warsaw district governor, Ludwig Fischer, reported in October 1941:

> At the beginning of the harvest operation, it became clear that many farmers did not want to deliver the required goods. I therefore set up forced labour camps in several of the districts, for which we were able to use the facilities of the water management section of the Department of Nutrition and Agriculture. Every farmer who does not obey the delivery command on time is sent to these camps and must carry out soil improvement work there. Since the relatives of the farmers send plenty of food supplies, their upkeep also costs nothing.[37]

The district governors in particular not only passed on the pressure put on them but also allowed themselves to be guided by their career ambitions and their ideological convictions.[38]

For a comprehensive gathering of the harvest, however, it was necessary to establish new trade relationships, since the former, mostly Jewish traders had been systematically removed from their ancestral jobs and forced to live in ghettos and were eventually murdered. This also resulted in a drop in the number of trading businesses from 195,000 to less than 45,000. In the General Government, therefore, a Central Agricultural Office was established through Department of Nutrition and Farming in Krakow, which was responsible for the import and export of food supplies and for their storage. In order to carry out these tasks, the entire country was covered with a network of branch offices, which by 1941 already had a total of 362 German and 1,124 Polish employees. At the same time, Polish and (from 1941) Ukrainian collectives were also forced to cooperate, providing well over 6,000 local workers. Those active as traders for the Central Agricultural Office were primarily Poles who had fled from the Soviet-occupied eastern regions and the German-annexed western regions of the country and who were now looking for work.[39] As a further supervision authority, there were agronomists active at regional, district, municipal and village levels, with the more than 18,500 men on the lowest two levels being locals forced to work by the occupiers using a combination of incentives and disciplinary measures to gather the harvest as completely as possible.[40]

Despite all the efforts undertaken there, Berlin was still unhappy with the results in Poland, with the General Government losing its responsibility for gathering the harvest in 1942 to a special commissioner of the four-year plan.[41] His methods, however, were not significantly different from those used up to that point and mostly involved a further increase in the pressure applied to the locals, who were now faced with the threat of execution or collective punishments, such as the razing of entire villages.[42] Using the catchphrase a 'harvest emergency situation', renewed reductions were made to the rations of the urban population and the delivery quotas of the farmers were raised by a further 25 per cent. A change in policy in the General Government was thus not foreseen, with only the confiscations in the villages now being the responsibility of securing commandos (*Sicherungskommandos*), which were to search specifically for embezzled food supplies.[43]

During the entire period of occupation, there was no change to the quota principal. The Central Department of Nutrition and Agriculture in Krakow continued to determine the absolute amount of agrarian production which the districts were required to deliver; there, the quotas for the individual districts were decided upon, which in turn delegated to the individual villages. At the lowest level, it was left to the Poles themselves to decide which farm was to deliver what amount of goods, with harvest councils and village committees taking responsibility for the organisation. These groups, however, were the first to be held accountable by the occupying forces, even though they had no influence on the total amount produced. If a community produced more than it was required to deliver, this surplus had to be offered to the authorities as well – for a predetermined low price,[44] although the Germans primarily awarded premiums in the form of vodka and basic commodities, spending 200 million zloty for these purposes in 1943.[45]

The extent to which the occupation authorities ran a two-tier operation foreseeing greater production and smaller distributions was demonstrated by the plan of the Department of Nutrition and Agriculture in Krakow under Karl Naumann, who, in 1942, suggested allocating food ration cards – which were the only legal method of acquiring food supplies – only to those Poles who were working in the German interest. Their numbers, it must be noted, are not to be underestimated, with 107,000 people working in armaments production alone. There were also 170,000 working for the German eastern post and the eastern railway, 180,000 forestry workers, 21,000 employees of the monopoly administration, 100,000 workers in the building industry and another 108,000 people employed by the *Wehrmacht* – with the families of all these workers to be considered as well. In spring of 1943, there were thus 350,000 German and 3.5 million non-German regular consumers who needed to be supplied, 700,000 heavy labourers and 800,000 regular workers employed in German interests, with another 230,000 Jews who, at this point in time, had not yet been murdered and were being exploited in labour ghettos.[46]

However, while Higher SS and Police Chief Friedrich-Wilhelm Krüger, Himmler's representative in the General Government, supported the plan to supply only those workers employed in the direct interests of the Germans, Hans Frank was against such a policy. Cutting off two million people from food supplies seemed to him at this time to be too much of a risk – it was not moral qualms but rather the fear of strengthening the resistance which thwarted the plan.[47] As far as the Jews were concerned, however, there were no such scruples. 'Operation Reinhard', which entailed the SS deporting around two million ghetto inhabitants to the extermination camps of the General Government in the summer of 1942, where they were subsequently murdered, also had the effect of reducing the number of mouths to feed. Although the nutritional situation of the Jews had been catastrophic anyway, with at least 80,000 Jews dying from the direct and indirect results of malnutrition in Warsaw alone,[48] any contribution to improving the supply to German nationals was considered worthwhile.[49] With an absolute minimum annual supply of 250 kg bread cereals per person, the murder of one million people led to 'savings' of around 250,000 tonnes[50] – with ideology and economics thus meeting in a grotesque combination.[51] Starvation, however, also affected the non-Jewish population: only in 1944 did the official calorie allocation in Warsaw reach more than 30 percent of the necessary requirement,[52] meaning a ration of 900 calories for adults and 550 for children.

Nevertheless, the overall economic performance of the General Government did in fact suffer from the genocide. The murder of the last remaining Jews in the labour camps at the beginning of 1943 caused further disruptions, this time only affecting the armaments factories, since it was only there that Jews were still working. The *Wehrmacht* was unhappy once again with the activities of the SS, since they were detrimental to its economic interests:

> 'The sudden removal and relocation of the Jewish labourers from the armaments factories and others important for the war effort resulted in considerable disruptions to the work process, lost time and a subsequent delay in the delivery of vital war equipment. Since this entire operation must be seen for the most part from a political perspective, the intervention of the armaments commando could only take place very cautiously'.[53]

The 'intervention' in question was unsuccessful, with ideology winning out yet again over economic considerations.

At the beginning of 1943, various measures brought about the next phase[54] in the mobilisation of the General Government, representing a reaction to the shortage of labour following the completed deportation of the Jews on the one hand and, on the other hand, to the increasing success of the Polish underground state. As part of the changes, and despite the protests of the *Reich* Ministry for Nutrition, the food allocation for Polish workers was increased, which Hans Frank had labelled virtually impossible to realise as late as March 1943.[55] But at the beginning of May, the *Wehrmacht* had allowed all of its suppliers to buy additional food supplies on the black market for their employees and their families to such an extent that the allocations were raised to the level of some of the best in

Warthegau. This set a new standard, and since the government in Krakow did not want to inspire additional dissatisfaction among the population, it agreed a short time later to this level of food allocations for all workers.[56]

3. Effects and effectiveness

Since a large number of forced labourers had been deported from Poland into the *Reich* by summer 1942, with further such deportations planned, the proposition at this point was to replace Polish workers with Jews. The genocidal plans of the SS were thus met with the resistance – unsuccessful at the end of the day – of the employment administration.[57] Although there were many producers, particularly in the armaments industry, which operated using Jewish labourers, their replacements, which the SS had promised at the beginning of the deportations, came either slowly or not at all, despite the *Wehrmacht* having demanded that 'the Jews be eliminated as quickly as possible, but without restricting the work essential to the war effort'.[58]

It was thus of even greater importance now to use the remaining Polish workers not yet deported into the *Reich* as efficiently as possible. Their work capacity had hardly been satisfactory for the occupation forces up to that point, but in March 1943, the realisation had sunk in that this could not be changed significantly through further force, simply because the conditions under which the Poles were working were too poor. A heavy labourer received the same level of rations as a normal consumer in Germany. At the same time, the provisions for his family were 'so minimal, that he was dependent on purchases from the black market. For this reason, every armaments producer was forced to give its workers two free days per week', so that they could make their purchases there – which, considering the intentional inflation and astronomic prices in comparison to the low level of wages, produced additional difficulties of its own. 'For all these reasons, the armaments industry in the General Government, in order to achieve the same production as within the *Reich*, required around 230 per cent of the personnel'.[59]

However, the deportation of forced labourers into the *Reich* had remained far below expectations since it began. In April 1940, Krakow was forced to admit its first failure in this regard: instead of the 1.2 million workers originally hoped for, only 210,000 had been sent over the entire year, with the mostly peaceful means and economic incentives producing little success. Frank subsequently overlooked any remaining doubts and began to use violence, with forced recruitments in broad daylight becoming commonplace. Even these methods, though, produced little success, with the results one year later being worse in relative terms than in 1940 – despite the increased effort. When Fritz Sauckel became General Commissioner for worker deployment in March 1942, the efforts towards the recruitment of forced labour intensified once again. In September 1942, raids took place in Warsaw almost on a daily basis, while in smaller towns, businesses began to be closed down for the explicit purpose of deporting the workers. The transport of workers to Germany reached its peak in March 1943, after which it began to decrease again.[60]

This fact is particularly astounding when one considers the additional measures undertaken by the occupying forces from autumn 1942 onwards. Two operations could be observed: first, the mass closure of 'businesses not productive for the war economy'[61], which saw the shutting down of 832 industrial producers and around 13,600 handicraft enterprises.[62] Second, the issuing of food entitlements was no longer carried out through the nutrition office for all Poles but rather only through businesses working in the German interest for their employees.[63] The plan to cut off two million nonworking people from the food supply, thus indirectly forcing them as labourers into the *Reich*, was not successful, though. Paradoxically, however, a real 'achievement' was evident in precisely this field, with around 1.2 million Poles moving from the General Government into the *Reich* by 1944, which represented 7 per cent of the population – a figure which becomes even more significant when one considers that children and the elderly were not eligible for deportation.

In other areas of the occupation economy, however, the growth rates could only be achieved due to the low starting levels.[64] The delivery of armaments to the *Reich* reached a value of 86 million reichsmarks in May 1944 – by way of comparison, the Warsaw ghetto alone had produced almost 9 million in July 1942, with the Jews there being murdered regardless. Jonas Scherner recently produced a statistical overview according to which the outsourced production for the *Wehrmacht* in the General Government during the entire war reached a value of 1.7 billion reichsmarks – the total figure for German-occupied and German-allied Europe being 33.1 billion.[65] In 1943, the General Government's proportion of weapons production among all territories under German control – including the *Reich* – was 1.8 per cent, with a figure of 3.9 per cent for ammunition production.[66] The financial contribution was similarly disastrous, making up only 6.5 per cent of the total contributions from all occupied territories – roughly the same proportion as Norway and half that of the Netherlands.[67] For the agricultural sector, the failure of the occupation institutions can be seen when compared to the prewar yields: in the last complete harvest year, the General Government, in comparison to the average between 1935 and 1938, produced around 41 per cent less wheat, 20 per cent less rye and 37 per cent fewer potatoes.[68] The production in 1942/43 was approximately 6 per cent of that harvested within the *Reich*.[69]

Nevertheless, the question of whether the exploitation of the General Government contributed to postponing the end of the war, as has been established for

Table 11.1 Agricultural exports from the General Government to the *Reich*[70]

	1940/41	1941/42	1942/43	1943/44
Cereals (tons)	55,000	51,000	633,500	571,700
Potatoes (tons)	122,000	139,000	434,400	387,700
Sugar (tons)	5,000	4,500	28,700	27,500
Livestock (animals)	9,000	22,000	54,300	53,800
Fat (tons)	8,00	900	7,200	1,400

the rest of occupied Europe,[71] does not seem to be one which can be answered in any meaningful way: the occupation cost money and tied down manpower, that is soldiers. Even if the situation were to be successfully represented in a mathematical-economic model, one would still have to consider the fact that conquered territory can also serve as a launching pad for further expansion and as a buffer against attacking enemies. Waging a war against the Soviet Union would, of course, not have been possible directly from *Reich* territory; the Red Army would, of course, have reached the *Reich* more quickly had it not had to cross Poland first. Not taking these factors into consideration, however, the occupation as such was not effective: prewar Poland was much more economically productive than the territory conquered by the National Socialists, which was ravaged first by war, then by further violence, murder and pillaging. There would probably have been 'better' ways to make use of the region, but it is certainly evident that force and oppression were not particularly sensible practices when attempting to achieve maximum economic production.

In a certain sense, Hans Frank had realised this very early on, remarking in March 1940: 'The General Government cannot be bled dry economically while simultaneously running a wartime economy within the *Reich*'.[72] This realisation was more than accurate in the sense that the constantly changing priorities in Berlin prevented a goal-oriented development of the region which would have made it more useful in the long term. Dietrich Eichholtz pointed out that this economic policy geared towards immediate profit was, ironically, appropriate for the later phases of the war, since faced with the increasingly obvious prospect of defeat, it was only logical to destroy the very economic substance of the territory in order to obtain at least some use from the occupation.[73] There remained a complex situation consisting of market mechanisms and state intervention impossible to combine in a productive way – but this was, in fact, the essence of the National Socialist tactics.[74]

Ideology took on a decisive role for economic policy here, often conflicting with the policy of exploitation, with the Holocaust being just one of many examples. Sometimes the two aspects went hand in hand, though, for example when the extermination of the Jews also served the purpose of reducing the number of people needing to be supplied with food in order to transport more nutritional supplies into the *Reich*. There could, however, be no fundamental contradiction between ideology and economic policy simply for the reason that the occupying forces were not pursuing long-term goals regarding the Jews or the General Government as a whole but were rather leaping from one temporary solution to the next. The Jewish labour thus initially served to benefit the Germans and to avoid immediate costs, later also replacing the Polish forced labourers transported into the *Reich*. When Hans Frank argued in favour of the removal of Jews from the territory under his jurisdiction in spring of 1942, he was indifferent to the question of whether they would then be murdered. He was pursuing different interests to those of his employment administration, but his weak position in relation to the SS led him to search for ways to consolidate his power. He thus did that which Ian Kershaw described as 'working towards the Führer' – he

Government in the German war economy 157

radicalised the anti-Jewish policy in order to conceal his own weakness, as he knew very well that the 'final solution' was viewed favourably in Berlin.

Contrary to what Christopher Browning writes,[75] race ideology was, therefore, not any more important for the local implementation of the Holocaust than economic considerations. It was rather financial and purely opportunistic motivation on the part of the regional rulers which provided the central impetus for the dynamics of the genocide against Jews.[76] This, admittedly, does not rule out the fact that ideology provided the general framework, which can also be said of the economic policy as a whole, which, through all its stages, was determined by the phantasmagorias of living space in the east with all its related implications, including genocide and race war. A conflict or contradiction between ideology and economics, however, should not be constructed from this situation, as indeed quite the opposite is true: they were two sides of the same coin. Neither war nor occupation would have been conceivable without the national socialist ideology.

Notes

1 Structure and competences of the civil administration are explained in B. Musial, 'Recht und Wirtschaft im besetzten Polen 1939–1945', in J. Bähr/R. Banken (eds.), *Das Europa des 'Dritten Reichs'. Recht, Wirtschaft, Besatzung*, Frankfurt/Main: Klostermann 2005, pp. 31–57; see also R. Seidel, *Deutsche Besatzungspolitik in Polen. Der Distrikt Radom 1939–1945*, Paderborn: Schöningh, 2006, pp. 35–86.
2 S. Lehnstaedt, '"Ostnieten" oder Vernichtungsexperten? Die Auswahl deutscher Staatsdiener für den Einsatz im Generalgouvernement Polen 1939–1944', *Zeitschrift für Geschichtswissenschaft*, 2007, vol. 55, p. 708.
3 I. Loose, *Kredite für NS-Verbrechen. Die deutschen Kreditinstitute in Polen und die Ausraubung der polnischen und jüdischen Bevölkerung 1939–1945*, Munich: Oldenbourg, 2007, p. 78.
4 J. Adamska, 'Działalność urzędów pracy dystryktu warszawskiego w zakresie werbunku robotników przymusowych do Rzeszy', *Studia Warszawskie*, 1975, vol. 23, p. 195.
5 T. Schlemmer, 'Grenzen der Integration. Die CSU und der Umgang mit der nationalsozialistischen Vergangenheit – der Fall Dr. Max Frauendorfer', *Vierteljahrshefte für Zeitgeschichte*, 2000, vol. 48, pp. 675–742.
6 Hauptabteilung Arbeit Krakau an die Distrikte, 30 June 1940, in Archiwum Akt Nowych Warsaw (AAN), 111/1414–1.
7 See Adamska, 'Działalność', p. 196.
8 D.G. Maier, *Anfänge und Brüche der Arbeitsverwaltung bis 1952. Zugleich ein kaum bekanntes Kapitel der deutsch-jüdischen Geschichte*, Brühl: Fachhochschule des Bundes für Öffentliche Verwaltung, 2004, pp. 7–8.
9 Schlemmer, 'Grenzen', pp. 677–9.
10 See the printed budgets: 'Haushaltspläne des Generalgouvernements', 1940–44.
11 In the General Government, Hans Frank was responsible for the Four Year Plan since 4 December 1939; the corresponding office was directed by Major General Bührmann; vgl. Frank an Amt des Generalgouvernements, 9 January 1940, Bundesarchiv Berlin (BArch), R 2/5101, fol. 11–12.
12 D. Eichholtz, 'Institutionen und Praxis der deutschen Wirtschaftspolitik im NS-besetzten Europa', in R. Overy/G. Otto/J. Houwink ten Cate (eds.), *Die*

'Neuordnung' Europas. NS-Wirtschaftspolitik in den besetzten Gebieten, Berlin: Metropol, 1997, pp. 36–8.
13 Loose, *Kredite*, p. 70.
14 C. Łuczak, 'Basic assumptions of the economic policies of Nazi Germany and their implementation in the occupied Poland', *Studia Historiae Oeconomicae*, 1976, vol. 11, pp. 193–4; Eichholtz, 'Institutionen und Praxis', p. 34.
15 See 'Zusammenstellung von Wirtschaftszahlen des ehemaligen Staates Polen', 2 October 1939, BArch, R 2/23717.
16 Hans Frank's speech of 3 October 1940, quoted in G. Eisenblätter, *Grundlinien der Politik des Reichs gegenüber dem Generalgouvernement, 1939–1945*, Frankfurt: Phil. Diss., 1969, p. 112.
17 B. Musial, *Deutsche Zivilverwaltung und Judenverfolgung im Generalgouvernement. Eine Fallstudie zum Distrikt Lublin 1939–1944*, Wiesbaden: Harrasowitz, 2000, p. 147.
18 J. Bähr/R. Banken, 'Ausbeutung durch Recht? Einleitende Bemerkungen zum Einsatz des Wirtschaftsrechts in der deutschen Besatzungspolitik 1939–1945', in Bähr/Banken, *Europa*, p. 7.
19 'Statistik der Betriebe im Warschauer Ghetto, 15. April 1940', in K.-P. Friedrich (ed.), *Die Verfolgung und Ermordung der europäischen Juden durch das nationalsozialistische Deutschland 1933–1945, vol. 4: Polen, September 1939–Juli 1941*, Munich: Oldenbourg, 2011, Document 107, pp. 274–7.
20 'Bilanz der Treuhandstelle des Distrikts Warschau für Oktober 1940, 8. Nov. 1940', in Ibid, Document 194, pp. 436–41.
21 'Protokoll einer Besprechungen Hans Franks in Krakau, 19. Jan. 1942', in W. Präg/W. Jacobmeyer (eds.), *Diensttagebuch des deutschen Generalgouverneurs in Polen, 1939–1945*, Stuttgart: DVA, 1975, p. 464–5.
22 Instytut Pamięci Narodowej Warszawa (IPN), NTN/288. Fünfjahresbericht der Wirtschaftsabteilung des Distrikts Krakau, September 1944; IPN, NTN/285. Rapport of the Warsaw Governor, 15 August 1942.
23 C. Rajca, *Walka o chleb 1939–1944. Eksploatacja rolnictwa w Generalnym Gubernatorstwie*, Lublin: Państwowe Muzeum na Majdanku, 1991, p. 248.
24 C. Łuczak, Polska i Polacy w drugiej wojnie światowej, Poznań: Wydawn. Naukowe UAM, 1993, pp. 201–2.
25 A. Wrzyszcz, 'Die deutsche 'Wirtschafts'-Rechtsetzung im Generalgouvernement 1939–1945', in Bähr/Banken, *Europa*, pp. 59–79.
26 Łuczak, 'Basic assumptions', p. 194. Less convincing is the new book by P. Matusak, *Przemysł na ziemiach polskich w latach II wojny światowej*, Warsaw: Siedlce, 2009, especially pp. 290–312.
27 Rapport of the Economic Department of the General Government on the year 1940, BArch, R 52 VI/7.
28 Łuczak, 'Basic assumptions', pp. 194–7.
29 Rapport of the Economic Department of the General Government on the year 1940, BArch, R 52 VI/7.
30 J. Scherner, 'Nazi Germany's preparation for war. Evidence from revised industrial investment series', *European Review of Economic History*, 2010, vol. 14, pp. 445–6, 464; see for the paradoxon that the perspective of total war can lead to preventive campaigns to ensure urgently needed raw materials: P. Liberman, *Does Conquest Pay? The Exploitation of Occupied Industrial Societies*, Princeton: Princeton UP, 1996, pp. 153sq.
31 Loose, *Kredite*, p. 68.
32 'Monatsbericht des deutschen Arbeitsamts im Ghetto Warschau, 29 August 1941', Yad Vashem Archiv Jerusalem, O 6 (Poland Collection), No 198.
33 M. Weichert, Jüdische Soziale Selbsthilfe 1939–1945, Tel Aviv, 1962, pp. 261–2.

34 Rapport of the Economic Department of the General Government on the year 1940, BArch, R 52 VI/7.
35 Łuczak, 'Basic assumptions', pp. 196–7.
36 IPN, NTN 196/251. Internes Schreiben der Regierung des Generalgouvernements, 7 August 1942.
37 'Regierungssitzung in Warschau, 14.–16. Oct 1941', in Präg/Jacobmeyer, *Diensttagebuch*, p. 419.
38 M. Roth, *Herrenmenschen. Die deutschen Kreishauptleute im besetzten Polen. Karrierewege Herrschaftspraxis und Nachgeschichte*, Göttingen: Wallstein 2009, p. 174.
39 Musial, *Deutsche Zivilverwaltung*, pp. 150–4. See also Steding, 'Der organisatorische Aufbau der Landwirtschaftlichen Zentrale', *Die Ernährungswirtschaft*, 1943, vol. 3, pp. 33–7; AAN, 117/370. Annual Report 1940/41 of the Central Agricultural Office.
40 Roth, *Herrenmenschen*, p. 152.
41 Eisenblätter, *Grundlinien*, pp. 347–51. Göring had forced this after the nutrition crisis of August 1942.
42 Musial, 'Recht und Wirtschaft', p. 44.
43 Roth, *Herrenmenschen*, pp. 164–8.
44 Rajca, *Walka o chleb*, pp. 41–4.
45 AAN, 111/1395, p. 58. Aktenvermerk der Regierung des Generalgouvernement, 24 May 1943.
46 'Arbeitssitzung der Regierung des GG, 14 April 1943', in Präg/Jacobmeyer, *Diensttagebuch*, pp. 639–40.
47 Roth, *Herrenmenschen*, pp. 168–9.
48 R. Sakowska, *Menschen im Ghetto. Die jüdische Bevölkerung im besetzten Warschau 1939–1943*, Osnabrück: Fibre 1999, p. 40.
49 'Besprechung in Krakau, 24 August 1942', in Präg/Jacobmeyer, *Diensttagebuch*, p. 549.
50 Musial, *Deutsche Zivilverwaltung*, p. 350.
51 A. Tooze, *Ökonomie der Zerstörung. Die Geschichte der Wirtschaft im Nationalsozialismus*, Bonn: Bundeszentrale für politische Bildung, 2007, pp. 629–31.
52 See T. Szarota, *Warschau unter dem Hakenkreuz. Leben und Alltag im besetzten Warschau, 1.10.1939 bis 31.7.1944*, Paderborn: Schöningh 1985, p. 114. Calculations based on the 2,400 calories considered as a daily minimum by the League of Nations in 1936.
53 Rüstungskommando Lemberg to Wehrwirtschaftsamt, 5 January 1943, Bundesarchiv-Militärarchiv Freiburg (BArch-MA), RW 23/13, fol. 8.
54 Eisenblätter, *Grundlinien*, pp. 360–1.
55 'Besprechung in Krakau, 26 March 1943', in Präg/Jacobmeyer, *Diensttagebuch*, p. 635.
56 See Kriegstagebuch des Rüstungskommandos Krakau für das 2. Vierteljahr 1943. Überblick des Dienststellenleiters, BArch-MA, RW 23/11, fol. 11–13; Rüstungsinspektion im Generalgouvernement. Die wesentlichen Probleme, ihre Entwicklung und Lösung im 2. Vierteljahr 1943, Ibid, no. 3, fol. 40–1.
57 'Hauptabteilungsleitersitzung in Krakau, 22 June 1942', in Präg/Jacobmeyer, *Diensttagebuch*, p. 516.
58 Militärbefehlshaber im Generalgouvernement an Oberkommando der Wehrmacht, 18.9.1942, BArch-MA, RH 53–23/87, fol. 116–20.
59 'Ausführungen des Rüstungsinspektors im Generalgouvernement, General Schindler, bei einer Besprechung in Krakau, 26 March 1943', in Präg/Jacobmeyer, *Diensttagebuch*, p. 635; Schindler made similiar explanations in Krakow on 14 April 1943, in ibid, p. 638.

60 Roth, *Herrenmenschen*, pp. 127–9.
61 Kriegstagebuch des Rüstungskommandos Radom vom 1.7.1942–30.9.1942, Überblick, BArch-MA, RW 23/16, fol. 16–20.
62 Rüstungsinspektion im Generalgouvernement. Die wesentlichen Probleme, ihre Entwicklung und Lösung im 2. Vierteljahr 1943, ibid, no. 3, fol. 40–4.
63 'Besprechung in Krakau, 20 November 1942', in Präg/Jacobmeyer, *Diensttagebuch*, p. 573.
64 S. Lehnstaedt, 'Das Generalgouvernement als Mobilisierungsreserve. Anspruch und Realität nationalsozialistischer Ausbeutungspläne', in O. Werner (ed.), *Mobilisierung im Nationalsozialismus. Institutionen und Regionen in der Kriegswirtschaft und der Verwaltung des 'Dritten Reiches' 1936 bis 1945*, Paderborn: Schöningh, 2013, pp. 235–50.
65 J. Scherner, 'Europas Beitrag zu Hitlers Krieg. Die Verlagerung von Industrieaufträgen der Wehrmacht in die besetzten Gebiete und ihre Bedeutung für die deutsche Rüstung im Zweiten Weltkrieg', in C. Buchheim/M. Boldorf (eds.), *Europäische Volkswirtschaften unter deutscher Hegemonie 1938–1945*, Munich: Oldenbourg, 2012, p. 81.
66 H. Umbreit, 'Die deutsche Herrschaft in den besetzten Gebieten 1942–1945', in B. Kroener et al. (eds.), *Das Deutsche Reich und der Zweite Weltkrieg, vol. 5: Organisation und Mobilisierung des deutschen Machtbereichs, part 2: Kriegsverwaltung, Wirtschaft und personelle Ressourcen 1942–1944/45*, Stuttgart: DVA 1999, pp. 186–7.
67 C. Buchheim, 'Die besetzten Länder im Dienste der deutschen Kriegswirtschaft während des Zweiten Weltkriegs. Ein Bericht der Forschungsstelle für Wehrwirtschaft', *Vierteljahrshefte für Zeitgeschichte*, 1986, vol. 34, pp. 123–4; see also Tooze, *Ökonomie*, p. 450.
68 C. Łuczak, 'Grundlegende Probleme der Landwirtschaft und Ernährung in Ost- und Südosteuropa während des Zweiten Weltkrieges', *Studia Historiae Oeconomicae*, 1982, vol. 17, pp. 286–7.
69 J. Scherner, 'Bericht zur deutschen Wirtschaftslage 1943/44. Eine Bilanz des Reichsministeriums für Rüstung und Kriegsproduktion über die Entwicklung der deutschen Kriegswirtschaft bis Sommer 1944', *Vierteljahrshefte für Zeitgeschichte*, 2007, vol. 55, pp. 516–7.
70 Musial, 'Recht und Wirtschaft', p. 44. All statistics are probably not accurate due to (intentional) mismeasurement. In 1942, 8 per cent of the harvest got lost when transported to the Reich, corresponding to about 40,000 tons of grain: AAN, 111/1301. Aktenvermerk der Regierung des Generalgouvernements, 10 September 1942.
71 Scherner, 'Europas Beitrag zu Hitlers Krieg', p. 91; for similar results in the French case, see J. Scherner/M. Boldorf, 'France's Occupation Costs and the War in the East. The Contribution to the German War Economy, 1940–1944', *Journal of Contemporary History*, 2012, vol. 47, p. 314.
72 Sitzung des Reichsverteidigungsausschusses, 2 March 1940, in Präg/Jacobmeyer, *Diensttagebuch*, p. 129.
73 Eichholtz, 'Institutionen und Praxis', p. 35.
74 A. Tooze: 'No Room for Miracles. German Industrial Output in World War II Reassessed', *Geschichte und Gesellschaft*, 2005, vol. 31, pp. 439–64.
75 C. Browning, 'Jewish Workers in Poland. Self-Maintenance, Exploitation, Destruction', in idem (ed.), *Nazi Policy, Jewish Workers, German Killers*, Cambridge: Cambridge UP, 2000, pp. 58–88.
76 See for detailed explanations on Jewish labour: S. Lehnstaedt, 'Generalgouvernement. Ideologie und Ökonomie der Judenpolitik', in J. Hensel/S. Lehnstaedt (eds.): *Arbeit in den nationalsozialistischen Ghettos*, Osnabrück: Fibre, 2013, pp. 159–80.

12 The Protectorate of Bohemia and Moravia under German control, 1939–1944

Harald Wixforth

1. Introduction

Since the middle of the 1930s, the First Czechoslovakian Republic was the target of German influence and control. In contrast to other countries of Central and South Eastern Europe, Bohemia and Moravia enjoyed an advanced level of industrialization. In the League of Nations' rank of developed economies, Czechoslovakia was among the world's 10 largest per-capita producers of industrial goods and the seven largest suppliers of armaments. It had intensive trade relations with other European countries and was an important link to the British and American financial markets. International business considered it attractive for investments because of its very high concentration of industry and banking, its comparative low level of wages and its relatively stable political conditions as one of the prominent successor states of the former Habsburg Monarchy.[1]

Because of this economic performance, the British, the French and the German governments as well as large industrial combines from these countries tried to enlarge their influence in Czechoslovakia since the end of the 1920s. Interrupted by the Great Depression and its consequences, these attempts restarted in the middle of the 1930s. German economic penetration began under the conditions of a new political rule. Hitler and his government tried to intensify ethnic conflicts in Czechoslovakia itself in order to destabilize the political and economic situation. By financing the German minority and its political struggle with the Czechoslovakian government in Prague, the German government tried to strengthen the ties with the Sudeten area, where most of the German population in Czechoslovakia lived. In spring 1938, it became obvious that these attempts had been successful from the German point of view: ethnic and political conflicts intensified considerably, and the First Czechoslovakian Republic was faced with a severe political crisis, enforced by the collaboration of the *Sudetendeutsche Partei* and its political leader Konrad Henlein.[2]

As a result of Austria's *Anschluss* to Germany in March 1938, the threat for Czechoslovakia's independence grew considerably. Half a year later, as a result of permanent German political pressure, the Munich Agreement led to the dismemberment of the First Czechoslovakian Republic. It had to admit severe losses of industrial and agricultural capacities, especially in the northern region of the

Sudeten territory. Under these circumstances, life in the rump of the state's territory, the so-called Second Republic of Czechoslovakia, was doomed. In the short period from September 1938 and the occupation of Bohemia and Moravia on 15 March 1939, the position of the Czechoslovakian economy was weakened considerably. The aims of Hitler and his Four Year Plan administration were quite clear, as the largest parts of the iron and steel industry as well as of mechanical engineering were concentrated in Bohemia and Moravia. Moreover, a great part of a very modern consumer goods industry, such as textiles and glass, was situated in the border areas of the Sudetenland.[3] Berlin wanted to get control over these industries in order to enlarge Germany's industrial capacities. Some big German companies and banks hoped to strengthen their competitive position by incorporating Czechoslovakian industrial plants or credit institutions. The government in Prague could not withstand this pressure and had once again to accept the conditions of political surrender dictated by Hitler and his satraps.[4]

2. The occupation of the Second Republic of Czechoslovakia

Officially the invasion of the Czech lands by German troops is dated 15 March 1939, when Prague was occupied. But the real starting signal for crossing the frontier into North Moravia demonstrates the importance Nazi Germany attached to the heavy industries in this region. Already on the afternoon of 14 March, Hitler issued an order to his chief general Wilhelm Keitel to occupy immediately the largest Central European iron- and steelworks, the Vitkovice Mining and Foundry works in Ostrava, before starting the real invasion. By this measure, the Polish government should be prevented from getting control over these plants before the arrival of German troops in Prague. These measures clearly underlined Hitler's economic estimation, which led to his decision to occupy Bohemia and Moravia.[5]

The international position of the Second Republic of Czechoslovakia was very weak when Nazi Germany decided to invade Bohemia and Moravia. Nevertheless, Hitler tried to establish a smoke screen of legality over his ruthless aggression. When the invasion had already started, he began negotiations with Emil Hacha, the president of the so-called rump government of Czechoslovakia. During Hacha's humiliating visit in Berlin on 15 March 1939, Hitler guaranteed him to save the Czech nations' autonomous development according to its 'national character'.[6]

In fact, this was only a vague promise, because on the next day, Hitler decreed the establishment of the 'Protectorate Bohemia and Moravia as an integral part of the German Reich'.[7] Thus, a quasi-colonial status was preserved for the Czech lands, according to the model of the French-Tunesian agreement of 1881. Nevertheless, some scholars up to now ask the question why Hitler and his ministries chose this complicated model of occupation which should lead to problems in reorganizing Czech industry and banking for the benefit of German war production in particular and to exploit the Czech economy.[8]

The new legal arrangement persisted, except for minor changes, until 1943. It contained organizational and administrative elements of a 'dualist government', which consisted of the Czech rump government in Prague and the newly established office of the Reich Protector. If necessary, the German authorities or the great war producers could take advantage of this dualist structure. This held true during the period of German military war successes and the penetration of Central Europe. Hacha's government guaranteed social peace and order and paved the way to an intensive exploitation of the Protectorate's economy for the German war effort. In 1943, however, when Germany's military position considerably weakened after the defeat at Stalingrad and political protest and sabotage by Czech partisans arose, the rest of governmental autonomy was abolished. The protectorate was set under the brutal control of German authorities.[9] Almost 92 per cent of the former industrial production of the Second Republic of Czechoslovakia was controlled by German authorities and firms. Seventy per cent of these capacities were concentrated in the Protectorate of Bohemia and Moravia, 22 per cent were located in the border regions, especially the Sudeten area, and the remaining 8 per cent in Slovakia. The latter state declared its independence on 14 March 1939 and became a German satellite with its own government, but under the control of the Berlin ministries.[10]

3. The administrative structure of the Protectorate

From the beginning, Germany installed a Reich Protector, whose authority was practically unlimited because he was directly responsible to Hitler. Together with his administration on Hradschin of Prague, he decided about the extent of economic exploitation and the reorganization of the Czech economy. The first to be appointed was Konstantin Freiherr von Neurath, a diplomat of the old school but willing to impose the new order. Beside him, Hans Hermann Frank, an ambitious and violently anti-Czech leader of the *Sudetendeutsche Partei*, had similar importance as he was appointed State Secretary and Vice Protector, being only responsible to von Neurath.

Unlike in Germany, in Austria after the *Anschluss* and in the Sudetenland, the activities of the Nationalsozialistische Deutsche Arbeiterpartei (NSDAP) in the Protectorate were strictly kept separate from executive organisations. The economic advisers (*Gau-Wirtschaftsberater*), who had elsewhere a considerable impact on decision making in 'aryanisation' and restructuring the economy, had almost no importance in the Protectorate. More important was the economic administration of twenty district administrators (*Landräte*) – twelve in Bohemia and eight in Moravia – appointed on 22 April 1939. Subordinated to the Reich Protector and his secretary, they supervised the Czech district and communal authorities. Astonishingly enough, a considerable number of these district administrators were Germans (*Volksdeutsche*) born in Bohemia and Moravia or even Czechs. Thus, they had an intimate knowledge of the regional political and economic situation and organised the control of the Protectorate.[11] In contrast, President Hacha and his Czech government were of minor importance for the reorganization of the Czech economy. According to the promises of Hitler, Hacha had expected even after the occupation of Prague to head an autonomous Czech government, giving him the opportunity to pursue his own economic policy. However, Hacha and his administration were kept apart from decision making in economic matters. All the important posts in the new economic administration were in German hands, in some cases with close contacts to Czechs who were willing to collaborate with the new authorities. The main task of Hacha's government was to ensure law and order in the Protectorate. The Czech government, on the first glimpse, could maintain control over the police forces. In reality, however, they completely depended on the Reich Protector's orders. On the other hand, the Czech government was obliged to punish all actions of sabotage in public life as well as in economy. Conflicts with national Czech political groups should be regulated until 1942 by Hacha's government and the Czech police, whereas the German administration tried to control the other spheres of public life.[12]

The Czech government, therefore, was an efficient instrument for the German occupier. Continuing to work smoothly with the local Czech administrations, it helped the occupation regime to keep its number of civil servants low and to concentrate its personnel in the political police, the different units of the SS, the *Gestapo* and the *Sicherheitsdienst* (SD). Some hundreds of thousands of native Germans managed to establish an efficient control over the country, while millions of Czechs were degraded to second-class citizens. The German occupation cannot be classified as a classical colonial situation: it was not imposed on a backward agrarian country but on a developed society in the heart of Europe which was on the same economic level as Germany. An efficient economic policy in the Protectorate could not merely consist of plunder but of sophisticated methods of economic penetration. Indeed, only such methods were suitable to guarantee an efficient exploitation of the Protectorate, its highly developed industry and, above all, its skilled labour force, consisting of qualified technicians and workers.[13]

4. Concepts of economic policy

Generally speaking, two different concepts of economic policy prevailed in the Protectorate until Reinhard Heydrich, the main chief of police forces, became the Reich Protector on 28 September 1941 transformed the German rule into a brutal regime in almost every respect. On the one hand, Neurath's concept was largely supported by the army and the major part of the German diplomacy. It was based on traditional elements of economic penetration such as the intensive collaboration between German authorities and Czech leaders. Neurath tried to avoid useless competence conflicts with the Czech industrial elite and fostered the integration of the most important industrialists into the economic administration. On the other hand, his State Secretary Frank wanted to eliminate the Czech influence in the economy by strengthening the direct control by German authorities. This concept emanated from radical chauvinist circles in the Sudeten area who pursued the aim to establish German dominance and hegemony in every part of policy and economy in the Protectorate, if necessary even by methods of violence and terror. Frank favoured solving the 'Czech question' by a forced Germanisation, by an expulsion of large parts of the Czech population and by its physical liquidation. He wanted the total incorporation of the Czech lands as a province into the Reich and the German-controlled economic sphere.[14]

In contrast to other occupied territories, such as the Polish General Government or the Reich Commissariat Ostland, the strong industrial base of the Protectorate and its role for the German war economy prevented uncontrolled mass terror and a barbarian extermination. Neurath's administration recognized quickly that brutal oppression over the population would be an obstacle to the strategy of increasing industrial output. Moreover, the appointment of Sudeten Germans in the board of directors of great companies and thus into the industrial business class of the Protectorate also prevented a repressive regime for a long time. They were aware of the problems of Czech industry as well as of the political discussions among Czech industrialists. Their knowledge of Czech traditions became a useful instrument for economic control. Neurath's administration rapidly noticed that their knowledge could be helpful for increasing industrial output. And, indeed, the specific forms of involving Sudeten Germans and even some Czechs in the industrial and political leadership guaranteed relatively stable political and economic conditions and led to remarkable industrial growth during Neurath's administration. As his concept was successful, Hitler also privileged it as a short-term model of exploitation. However, it soon became obvious that the long-term model of occupation was different. It was closer to Frank's ideas of eliminating the Czech elite in industry and banking by a far-reaching Germanisation of Bohemia and Moravia and an expulsion of the autochthonous population.[15]

Different stages of German hegemony and economic control can be therefore identified. In the first period from occupation until the outbreak of World War II, the Czech influence in industry and the political collaboration were instrumentalised for the targets of war economy and the efficient exploitation of the industrial potential. In the second phase when the Nazi regime conquered European territories, the first attempts were made to reduce Czech influence and to strengthen the German authorities. The situation changed when Reinhard Heydrich was appointed as Reich Protector in September 1941 and the German army defeated at Moscow in the winter of 1941/42. After Heydrich's assassination on 27 May 1942, a period of brutal terror and barbarian inhumane policy started with the complete liquidation of the former dualist government of Prague in August 1942. The requirements and demands of German war production marked the starting point of almost total control of the industry by German authorities and political terror against the population. The terror led to the uprising in Slovakia in autumn 1944 as well as in Prague and the Protectorate in spring 1945.[16]

5. Establishing economic control and exploitation

On 16 March 1939, when Hitler decreed the establishment of the Protectorate, Hermann Göring as the responsible party for the Four Year Plan dispatched a note to the Berlin ministries concerned, to the Reich Protector and its administration demanding more centralized control of the Czech economy in order to improve efficiency. Simultaneously, he claimed the final decision on all important economic questions for himself. The export-oriented Czech industry should maintain its position on the European market in order to gather foreign exchange which should be used for the payment of German imports. Göring urged the Reich Ministry of Economics to evoke all suitable measures to reduce the shortage of foreign currencies. He demanded from the Prague administration to deliver its foreign currencies to the German government. Foreign contracts of Bohemian and Moravian companies should be fulfilled in time to secure the foreign exchange revenues for the German war economy. At the same time, he pronounced against a rush of German buyers to acquire Czech assets as well as against unauthorized capital transfers and 'wild aryanisations'. To ensure a correct transfer from the Protectorate to Germany and a controlled transformation of Czech industry to the aims of German war economy, he demanded strict discipline and a centralization of economic planning for the Protectorate within the Four Year Plan administration.[17]

Göring's note was typical for the Third Reich's economic policy and its so-called polycratic chaos. Conflicts among different German authorities in Berlin and the new local administration had been obvious in Austria after the *Anschluss*, but Göring had to respect the demands of Austrian corporations and interest groups to reorganise the economy. In the Protectorate, however, he wanted to achieve his aims, as he believed the Prague government and the Reich Protector's administration to be in a weak position. He claimed for his own administration the suitable instruments to exercise economic control. This intention, however, failed after a short time, because the Four Year Plan administration ignored the political and economic conditions in the Protectorate as well as the economic situation of most of the companies.[18]

Nevertheless, the Göring administration initiated without any delay a rigorous inventory of the foreign exchange and gold reserves of all Bohemian and Moravian banks and savings institutes. The Czech National Bank (*Česká Národní Bánká*) was ordered to transfer its gold reserves deposited in London to the German *Reichsbank*. On 24 March, it was confirmed by the Bank of International Settlement in Basel that an amount of more than 740 million of Kč in gold was transferred to the *Reichsbank*. At the same time, the *Reichsbank* received further remarkable amounts of gold from big firms in the Protectorate, like the *Škoda* Works from Plzen or the Czech Armaments Works in Brno, in order to purchase raw materials urgently needed in both the German and Czech armaments industries. Moreover, the *Reichsbank* asked Czech creditors to pay their liabilities in Germany only in 'hard currency' and to transfer it directly to Berlin. The British government, however, blocked Czech gold, currency and shares deposited in British banks because it quickly understood the real intentions of these transfers. Negotiations between the British government and German authorities on this subject were rapidly terminated by the outbreak of World War II.[19]

Another example for the adaption of economic policy and occupational policy is the case of the Customs Union between the German *Reich* and the Protectorate, where for a distinct time the interests of both sides coincided.

The decree of 16 March 1939 which established the Protectorate pointed out in Article 9 that the annexed territory was integrated in the German customs area and had to subordinate its customs sovereignty. The interests of both sides coincided for a while because German entrepreneurs and politicians welcomed the abolishing of customs borders, and Czech business circles expected better conditions for their trade to the Reich. However, the Czech National Bank, now transformed into the National Bank of the Protectorate, and some of the autonomous Czech ministries argued in a memorandum to the German Ministry of Economic Affairs in April 1939 to maintain the financial economic and custom autonomy of the Protectorate. They were concerned that a sudden unification with Germany might threaten the export opportunities of the Protectorate's industry and lead to a loss of traditional markets for Czech companies. Furthermore, they feared rising prices for raw materials. The National Bank and the ministries argued that a hasty introduction of the German prices and wages could harm the industry and the population's consumption. The Reich Minister of Economics Funk followed the Czech request and promised in summer 1939 to avoid the quick establishment of a customs union but announced that the project should be realized in the nearby future.[20]

Germany as well as Bohemia and Moravia took substantial advantages of the export surplus of the Czech economy while the peace lasted in Europe in summer 1939. Czech businessmen and industrialists could cooperate in an export program under the direction of the largest combines such as the *Škoda* works or the Czech Armament Works in Brno, which was initiated in May 1939 by the occupier. The German authorities rapidly recognized the advantages of the Protectorate's rising exports as well as of rising profits of the great combines which could be invested in modernizing the industry. The advantages for both sides were obvious: the Czech industry could widely enhance its production capacities, whereas Germany profited by a rising export surplus and by a substantial amount of foreign currencies.[21]

In the concept of a greater economic sphere under German hegemony, the Czech export opportunities played a significant role. The great combines of the Protectorate should directly penetrate the markets in Southeast and Eastern Europe because of their more favourable geographical transport position, whereas the German companies such as the *Vereinigte Stahlwerke* should conquer the West European markets and, if possible, those overseas. These concepts lasted only until the outbreak of World War II. Then the market position of the Czech works changed dramatically as well as the conditions for establishing a European Greater economic sphere. By then, Czech companies, even under control of German authorities, were able to penetrate the markets in South East Europe more successfully. As a result, the export structure changed dramatically. In spring 1940, half a year after the beginning of the war, 70 per cent of the total exports of the Protectorate went into countries of south-eastern Europe. The leader was Yugoslavia with nearly 30 per cent, followed by quasi-autonomous Slovakia with 22 per cent, Romania with 15 per cent and Hungary with 3 per cent. It became obvious that Czech industry was forced to intensify its trade with countries which were closely linked to the Nazi regime.[22]

Vice versa, Czech industry lost its favourite position in trade with countries with hard currencies and even with Germany. Between the end of 1937 and summer 1939, trade and the proportion of exports with these countries fell from 61.5 per cent to nearly 29 per cent. In spite of this change, the Protectorate's trade balance remained positive. By the end of 1939, the balance was still more than half a billion crowns in surplus. This situation prevailed as long as the custom border with Germany existed. But even in this period, the industry of the Protectorate could not gain any hard currency by trade surplus, which was urgently needed in Bohemia and Moravia as well as by Germany's requests. After the establishment of the custom union, Czech trade with countries with hard currencies and a still comparatively free market declined considerably. One of the most important economic targets, growing surpluses in trade and gaining hard currency by Czech industry, vanished. By the end of 1940, the Protectorate's trade with Germany had reached 80 per cent of its imports and 71 per cent of its exports. This was the immediate consequence of the custom union, which was introduced on 1 October 1940 despite all requests by the Czech government. The industry of the Protectorate had to orient its development on the German economy and the intended greater economic sphere. The previous favourable Czech position in international trade vanished completely, with big disadvantages for most of the companies and for the economic structure of the Protectorate.[23]

6. The enforcement of the war economy

When the war broke out, the most important target was to put the Czech market economy under central control and regulation. The outstanding war industries should be incorporated into the German war machine. To achieve this, already in May 1939, the Supreme Price Office (*Nejvyšší úřad cenový*) was established by an order of the Czech government but initiated by the German authorities. Its tasks were similar to those of the Reich Commissar for pricing in Berlin. At the same time, a total conscription of the workforce, similar to the procedure in the Reich, was started by the Czech ministry of Industry, Commerce and Trade. In June 1939, an order for regulating wages and the duties of the workers was issued. Finally, the order on the 'organic construction of the economy' of July 1939 adopted the German model of the reorganizing the economy by introducing the *Führerprinzip* and economic groups (*Wirtschaftsgruppen*). In August 1939, the corporative structure was completed by the establishment of new industrial associations. Every prominent entrepreneur had to join the Central Association of Industry for Bohemia and Moravia. In addition, there was a separate German association which pursued the Germanisation of the Czech economy and allowed only Germans as members. The Czech Central Association had several subdivisions, such as for trade, transport, agriculture, forestry, finance and insurances, each controlled by a Prague ministry. Furthermore, an Office for Exports and Imports was established which had to regulate the Czech industry's foreign trade. All these organisations were controlled by the Reich Protector's administration on the Hradschin: the most important were the departments for economics, armaments inspection and the central contracts office (*Zentralstelle für Kriegsaufträge*). The established institutional control, which was organised according to the Reich, pursued the only aim of reorganizing Bohemian and Moravian industry and trade for the sake of Germany's war effort.[24]

The previous freedom of manoeuvre of Czech industrialists was abolished step by step. The increasing German domination over the Czechs, who were regarded as racially inferior by German authorities, was only tempered by the crucial importance of the war contributions the Czech were able to make. Frank pointed out in a memorandum to Hitler from August 1940 that the increasing importance of the economy would prohibit considerations of Germanising the Protectorate. More important was the rapid and efficient rise of war production and the exploitation of the Czech economy. This prohibited the immediate liquidation of the Czech nationality. Frank and the German authorities in Prague and Berlin were aware that a disturbance of the new economic order had to be avoided until Germany's aim of establishing a hegemony in Central and Eastern Europe was reached.[25]

This order changed considerably when Reinhard Heydrich, the chief of the police forces, was appointed as Reich Protector on 28 September 1941. During his short time in office, the Czech lands were completely integrated into the Reich, and the authority of the Czech government ended with the incarceration of Prime Minister Alois Elias on 19 January 1942. Until Heydrich's assassination of 17 May 1942, the oppression of the Czech population increased, and after Heydrich's death, a period of brutal terror began with the execution of thousands of people who were accused of supporting the Czech national movement. In this context, the Czech government was dissolved and only a few ministries remained. The most important was the Ministry of Economics and Labour, put under control of the German official Walter Bertsch.[26] Meanwhile, the output of Czech industry increased considerably. At the same time, the persecution of persons supposed to sabotage German administration increased. Hitler issued an order on 21 May 1942 in which the Czech population was threatened with heavy penalties for false or withheld information about labour supply, material reserves, production targets and important raw materials as well as products, machines and equipment needed for the warfare.[27]

Kurt Daluege, Heydrich's successor, and Frank continued an economic policy which was based on submission and order towards the Czech population to ensure the war production.[28] Considerable changes in the structure of Czech industry followed. Output and employment, especially in metallurgy and metalworking, nearly doubled between March 1939 and May 1945, while production and employment in the consumer goods industries fell. Especially after 1942, the Czech lands were considered a safe area from Allied bombing. Therefore, industrial capacities could be transferred in order to concentrate war production in Bohemia and Moravia. As a result, the Czech lands contributed between 9 and 12 per cent to the industrial production of so-called Greater Germany. Moreover, the share of the Protectorate to the Greater German GDP increased more than that of any other German region between 1941 and 1945. This clearly demonstrates the importance of the Protectorate for the German war economy in those years characterised by an increasing repression against the Czech civil population.[29]

7. Transfer of capital and properties

The German authorities in Prague as well as the Berlin ministries tried to intensify control of the Protectorate's industry. They tried to gain the capital majority of the most prominent Czech companies and transferred a considerable part of industrial properties in the hands of German firms, governmental offices, for instance the Berlin administration for war planning. With his dispatch of 16 March 1939, Göring tried to monopolise the decisions about the economic integration of Bohemia and Moravia into his Four Year Plan administration. In addition, he demanded the transfer of values, such as large estates, industrial companies, and majority shareholdings of large industrial trusts. For this purpose, he declared that each transfer of Czech properties into German hands had to be approved by him if the transferred value exceeded 500,000 reichsmarks. Hans Kehrl was installed as his general agent on 20 March 1939, responsible for the acquisition of the most important Czech firms, such as the armaments works in Brno (*Waffenwerke Brünn*), the *Škoda* works in Plzen and above all the Vitkovice Mining and Foundry Works with all their subsidiaries.[30]

The Czech government and leading Czech industrialists and bankers had hoped for a long time that a German takeover of the armament complex in the Protectorate could be avoided. Towards the end of the Second Czechoslovak Republic, the government had even started the privatization of its shares of the *Škoda*-works and the Brno Armament Works, which stood at the head of a complicated structure of intertwined bank-industry combines. Thus an armament group with vertical and horizontal linkages to Czech heavy industry was formed, led by a syndicate incorporating the most important banks and companies of the country. On the eve of German occupation, the Prague government and prominent Czech bankers and industrialists hoped that this complex could be maintained. They hoped for a similar solution as in Austria after the *Anschluss*, where the entrepreneurs could save their properties as long as they were not Jewish. However, this was totally misleading because of Kehrl's strict order to incorporate the Czech industry into the German warfare.[31]

But it was obvious that the capital structure of most important combines was an obstacle for the transfer of properties. Since the early 1920s, British and French investors held a substantial share of Czech industry and banking capital. Until peace lasted, representatives of German private banks and the government negotiated in London and Paris in order to buy the equity owned by British or French firms in former Czechoslovakia.[32] When the war broke out, the capital shares of British and French investors were declared enemy property and could be acquired by German private and state-owned companies. The result was a total change of property rights in most of the Czechoslovak combine within a short time. At the end of 1937, Britain and

France were the first-ranked countries with investments in Czechoslovakia. British investors held a percentage of 30.8 per cent and French of 21.4 per cent, that is more than half of total foreign investments, whereas Germany was only in fifth place. At the end of 1940, the German Reich reached the leading position in this ranking, holding 47 per cent of total foreign investments in Bohemia and Moravia. The former shares of British and French investors were not confiscated but under control of a special trusteeship, mainly managed by the *Reichswerke Herman Göring*. At this time, the *Reichswerke* controlled almost eighty companies with a total workforce of 150,000 in the Protectorate's war-relevant branches.[33]

By autumn 1941, most industrial branches were dominated by the German authorities or combines. The methods to exercise control were installing German trustees, replacing members of the board of directors with Germans, acquiring capital control by purchasing shares or by 'aryanisation'. Managers like Paul Pleiger or Rudolf Delius gained considerable influence on the Protectorate's war economy, while the former Czech directors and managers were placed in subordinate positions or had to leave the companies.[34] The Germanisation of small business, however, went more slowly, compared to border regions such as the Sudetenland. Yet the policy of Germanisation was intensified since 1941 in all industrial branches, especially after the German defeats in the Soviet Union and in Africa. State-owned companies and banks played a more and more important role in establishing German control on the economy. Statistics show that the strategic aims could be reached in 1943 and 1944 when the Protectorate's war production was at its peak.[35]

8. Increase of aryanisations

Immediately after the invasion of Prague, the new Czech government under Prime Minister Rudolf Beran took the initiative to start aryanisation in the Protectorate. The reason was to secure more Czech influence than German by taking over Jewish properties. An order of 21 March 1939 empowered the Czech government to appoint trustees in order to run Jewish companies according to Czech interests. For these purpose, lists of Jewish properties and of proposed commissioners and purchasers were hastily drawn up. All these attempts, however, were soon prohibited by the German occupation authorities. They regarded the aryanisation as a strictly German affair that should be kept entirely in their hands.[36]

Anti-Jewish measures were taken until the first days of occupation mainly by German military authorities who usurped the administration of Jewish properties. The German administration on the Hradschin pursued by anti-Jewish legislation the aim of a far-reaching Germanisation of the Czech lands. Aryanisation was intended to bring as many German administrators into the Protectorate as possible and to transfer Jewish properties into the hands of German owners. The Reich Protector's order of 29 March 1939 stipulated that all aryanisation measures should be controlled by his administration. The right to appoint trustees for

Jewish properties was reserved to the Protector, who exclusively appointed Germans. Another even more important decree was issued in June 1939 which gave a broad definition for 'Jewish companies'. The expropriation should be executed if the firm owner or his partner was Jewish. A joint stock company was 'Jewish' if one of member of the board of directors was declared Jewish or if a quarter of the equity was in Jewish hands.

The appointment of suitable trustees by the Reich Protector could be also applied to Czech companies. Hacha protested against this, but the Reich Protector answered that the new decree was only confirming the Czech government's own order of 21 March. Since July 1939, all these regulations were used to follow the aim of a far-reaching Germanisation. The Nuremberg laws were applied to the Protectorate in order to extend the control of Jewish properties.[37]

Further orders and decrees regulating aryanisation followed in fast succession. In January 1940, Jews should deposit their assets and securities with banks, which they could draw only with the Ministry of Finance's permission. The centre for Jewish emigration granted them permission to emigrate after they had relinquished their property. By the end of 1940, exit visas were issued to 27,000 Jews who wanted to emigrate. German banks with their affiliations in the Protectorate were given preference in aryanisation deals. With the help and support of the German banks, concerns such as the *Reichswerke Herman Göring* could acquire large parts of Jewish property in the Czech industry, whereas the German bourgeoisie could acquire plenty of Jewish shops and workshops. The Jews in the Protectorate first lost their civil rights, then their property and finally their lives.[38] In autumn 1940, aryanisation intensified, being extended to all private limited and public limited companies employing more than 100 persons and having an annual turnover of more than 3 million crowns as well as to banks and insurances. Furthermore, a registration was ordered for the Jewish possession of bonds, gold, silver, jewels, art objects and collections of any kind valuing more than 10,000 crowns. Until the end of 1940, Jews in the Protectorate had to liquidate their bank savings accounts. When Heydrich was appointed as the new Reich Protector, the racial and anti-Jewish persecution reached its height. Mass transportations of Jews into the concentration camps started in October 1941.

The total losses of Jewish lives cannot be enumerated precisely. The value of confiscated Jewish property, however, was carefully estimated by some agents working for the German Reich Bank, especially for the so-called *Devisenschutzkommando*. Their reports estimated the amount of confiscated goods like cash, savings, foreign exchange and securities at more than 1.75 billion crowns. Another report on confiscated Jewish property from July 1942 sums up the value of the movable and immovable assets, which was taxed on more than 6 billion crowns. At the end of 1942, the German authorities declared that there was nothing left to 'aryanise'.[39] The aryanisation of Jewish property was one of the most effective methods to foster a rapid Germanisation of the Czech lands. Simultaneously, the influence of Czech business circles on the economy decreased rapidly.

9. The policy of 'Germanisation' in the agrarian sector

The economic policy encompassed aspects of terror against the population as well as measures for a total Germanisation of the Protectorate. The instruments of economic control and exploitation must be assessed in the context of the 'final solution of the Czech problem', which was intensively discussed by Nazi leaders in Berlin as well as in Prague since summer 1942. In this context, Karl Hermann Frank became the most prominent supporter for the idea to abolish Czech nationhood. This aim also manifested in the economic policy. The intensive agriculture of the Czech lands was expected by German authorities to solve the problem of food supply of the Reich, which was regarded as a threat since 1937. In March 1939, regulating measures were decreed which changed the structure of agriculture considerably. Agriculture was the part of the Czech economy which became the best-controlled sector. Agricultural workers were not allowed to leave their employment without the permission of a German authority. A decree of June 1939 empowered these authorities to force workers into agricultural labour. Another decree of September 1939 gave the Ministry of Agriculture the possibility to control the whole production chain in agriculture from sowing to consumption. A corporative system, similar to the reorganisation of the industrial sector, was introduced with compulsory membership of producers in eight state-controlled associations.[40]

Czech peasants should be chased from their farms and replaced by German settlers. The plans for this replacement were prepared and executed by the SS Race and Settlement Main Office in connection with a subordinated German Settlement Association (*Ansiedlungsgesellschaft*).[41] They draw maps of the villages with German-speaking populations in Bohemia and Moravia. Areas were designed to host ethnic Germans coming from Eastern or South Eastern Europe or Germans willing to leave the Reich to become farmers in the annexed territories. To realize these plans, the autochthonous Czech population had to be expelled, according to the policy of the 'final solution of the Czech question'. Plans for German model villages and new farms were distributed among potential German setters to encourage them to move into the Protectorate. The SS Race and Settlement Main Office as well as the German occupation authorities in Prague hoped to realize the Germanisation of the Protectorate. The Czech population should be treated in three ways: assimilation, evacuation or physical liquidation. While the war lasted, this goal could not be fully realized. Expulsions from Czech villages, however, really happened in these cases, where no Czech peasants were living. According to contemporary reports, 16,000 holdings over an area of about 550,000 hectares (1,359,000 acres) were confiscated in Bohemia and Moravia for the settlement of Germans. Czech people were evacuated from wide areas which were made available for the German army, which made plans for resettlements after a victorious end of the war. The policy of Germanisation could not come to the end that the SS wanted. It remained a patchwork without being a framework that could have been realized in a rather short period of time.[42]

10. Conclusion

The Czechoslovakian Republic had a major importance in the international economy and trade during the interwar period. Her advanced and modern industry was of special value for preparing the war. The leading principles of occupation policy developed by the German authorities derived from this strategic importance. It also paved the way for the construction of the Protectorate as a semi-autonomous state with an own government but under the control of a German Reich Protector and his administration. The initially granted freedom of manoeuvre of the Czech government lost importance, whereas the power of the Reich Protector and his administration rose considerably. The economic policy as well as the control of industry changed remarkably over the period of occupation. However, the increasing demand of the German war industry set limits to mass terror and led to a policy of 'carrots and sticks'. Specific arrangements were made with Czech industrialists aiming at the sole target of increasing industrial growth for warfare purposes. Nevertheless, the Czechs lost influence in their companies, while German authorities as well as industrialists from the Reich started attempts to purchase and control Czech industrial plants at a low price. Compulsory measures such as aryanisation or the resettlement of ethnic Germans strengthened the German influence in the Protectorate and destroyed the stronghold of the Czech nationality. The Protectorate was an occupied territory whose strong economic position prevented, at least in some respects, a brutal occupation policy like in other East European occupied territories.

Notes

1 For an overview on Czechoslovakia during the interwar period, see above all A. Teichova, *An Economic Background to Munich. International Business and Czechoslovakia 1918–1938*, London: Cambridge UP, 1974; idem, *Wirtschaftsgeschichte der Tschechoslowakei*, Vienna: Böhlau, 1988; V. Lacina, *Zlatá Léta Československehó hospodařství 1918–1929*, Prague: Hist. Ústav AV ČR, 2000, pp. 38–75. C. Boyer, *Nationale Kontrahenten oder Partner? Studien zu den Beziehungen zwischen Tschechen und Deutschen in der Wirtschaft der ČSR (1918–1938)*, Munich: Oldenbourg, 1999.
2 For the political and economic situation in the Sudetenland, see R. M. Smelser, *Das Sudetenproblem und das Dritte Reich, 1933–1938*, Munich: Oldenbourg, 1980; V. Zimmerman, *Die Sudetendeutschen im NS-Staat. Politik und Stimmung der Bevölkerung im Reichsgau Sudetenland (1938–1945)*, Essen: Klartext, 1999; D. Brandes, *Die Sudetendeutschen im Krisenjahr 1938*, Munich: Oldenbourg, 2008.
3 For the industrial structure, see RGVA Moscow, Fond 1458, Inventory 10, File 2. Reichsamt für wehrwirtschaftliche Planung: Die wehrwirtschaftliche Lage der Tschechoslowakei unter besonderer Berücksichtigung Böhmens, Berlin, October 1937; Inventory 10, File 3, Reichskreditgesellschaft: Die Wirtschaftslage der Tschechoslowakei Mitte 1938 unter besonderer Berücksichtigung der Sudetendeutschen Gebiete, Berlin 1938; Boyer, *Wirtschaftsinteressen*, pp. 3–11.
4 Ibid; W. Hummelberger, 'Die Rüstungsindustrie der Tschechoslowakei 1933 bis 1938', in F. Forstmeier/H.-E. Volkmann (eds.), *Wirtschaft und Rüstung am Vorabend des Zweiten Weltkrieges*, Düsseldorf: Droste 1975, pp. 308–30; J. Balcar/J. Kučera, 'Nationalsozialistische Wirtschaftslenkung und unternehmerische

The Protectorate of Bohemia and Moravia 175

Handlungsspielräume im Protektorat Böhmen und Mähren (1939–1945). Staatlicher Druck, Zwangslagen und betriebswirtschaftliches Kalkül', in: C. Buchheim/M. Boldorf (eds.), *Europäische Volkswirtschaften unter deutscher Hegemonie 1938–1945*, Munich: Oldenbourg, 2012, pp. 150–2.

5 RGVA Moscow, Fond 1458, Inventory 10, File 2, Reichsamt für wehrwirtschaftliche Planung: Die wehrwirtschaftliche Lage der Tschechoslowakei unter besonderer Berücksichtigung Böhmens, Berlin, October 1937; H. Radandt, 'Beteiligungen deutscher Konzerne an Unternehmungen in der Tschechoslowakei 1938 bis 1945', *Jahrbuch für Wirtschaftsgeschichte*, 1969/2, pp. 157–201.

6 Protocol of President Hacha's visit in the Reichskanzlei, in Akten zur deutschen Auswärtigen Politik, series D (1937–1945), vol. 2, Deutschland und die Tschechoslowakei, 1937/38, Baden-Baden, 1950. See also Ian Kershaw, *Hitler*, vol. 2, 1936–1945, Stuttgart: DVA, 2000, pp. 327–38.

7 Reichsgesetzblatt, 16 March 1939; Balcar/Kučera, 'Nationalsozialistische Wirtschaftslenkung', pp. 150–1.

8 See R. Overy, 'German Business and the Nazi New Order', in T. Gourvish (ed.), *Business and Politics in Europe 1900–1970. Essays in Honour of Alice Teichova*, Cambridge: Cambrigde UP, 2003, pp. 171–83.

9 K. Fremund/V. Král (eds.), *Die Vergangenheit warnt. Dokumente über die Germanisierungs- und Austilgungspolitik der Naziokkupanten in der Tschechoslowakei*, Prague: Orbis 1960, p. 59, document 6: Letter von Neurath to Hans Heinrich Lammers, 31 August 1940; H. Kaden/W. Schumann (eds.), *Nacht über Europa, vol. 1, Die faschistische Okkupationspolitik in Österreich und der Tschechoslowakei, 1938–1945*, Cologne: Pahl-Rugenstein, 1988, pp. 110–11, document 36: Anlage zum Protokoll einer Staatssekretärsbesprechung vom 25. März 1939 über die Stellung der okkupierten tschechischen Ländern im deutschen Machtbereich.

10 RGVA Moscow, Fond 1458, Inventory 10, File 2, Reichsamt für wehrwirtschaftliche Planung: Die wehrwirtschaftliche Lage der Tschechoslowakei unter besonderer Berücksichtigung Böhmens, Berlin, October 1937. See, for Slovakia, T. Tönsmeyer, *Das Dritte Reich und die Slowkei. Politischer Alltag zwischen Kooperation und Eigensinn*, Paderborn: Schöningh, 2003; J. Hoensch, 'Die Slowakische Republik 1939–1945', in H. Lemberg et al. (eds.), *Studia Slovaca. Studien zu Geschichte der Slowakei und der Slowaken. Festgabe für Jörg K. Hoensch zu seinem 65. Geburtstag*, Munich: Oldenbourg, 2000, pp. 221–47; idem, 'Grundzüge und Phasen der deutschen Slowakei-Politik im Zweiten Weltkrieg', in ibid, pp. 249–62.

11 RGVA Moscow, Fond 1458, Inventory 10, File 13, pp. 234–5, Mitteilung des Zentralverbandes der Industrie in Böhmen und Mähren an das Reichswirtschaftsministerium betr. Organisation der gewerblichen Wirtschaft im Protektorat. See also Balcar/Kučera, 'Nationalsozialistische Wirtschaftslenkung', pp. 151–2.

12 Ibid, pp. 152–3.

13 Ibid, p. 153. For statistical data, see RGVA Moscow, Fond 1458, Inventory 10, File 2, Reichsamt für wehrwirtschaftliche Planung: Die wehrwirtschaftliche Lage der Tschechoslowakei unter besonderer Berücksichtigung Böhmens, Berlin, October 1937.

14 J. Balcar/J. Kučera, 'Von der Fremdherrschaft zur kommunistischen Diktatur. Die personellen Umbrüche in der tschechoslowakischen Wirtschaft nach dem Zweiten Weltkrieg', *Jahrbuch für Wirtschaftsgeschichte*, 2010/2, pp. 71–94; K.H. Frank, 'Die Wirtschaft des Protektorats im großdeutschen und kontinentaleuropäischen Wirtschaftsraum', *Deutsche Wirtschaftszeitung*, 1940, no. 37, p. 1040; see also: RGVA Moscow, Fond 1458, Inventory 10, File 13, pp. 53–5. Minutes of the Reichswirtschaftsministerium, 11 April 1939.

15 Ibid, pp. 74–88; Frank, 'Die Wirtschaft des Protektorats', p. 1040; Appendix to the minutes of the *Staatssektetärbesprechung* on 25 March 1939 on the position

of the occupied Czech territories under German control, in Kaden/Schumann, *Nacht über Europa*, document 36, pp. 111–2.
16 Balcar/Kučera, 'Nationalsozialistische Wirtschaftslenkung', pp. 154–6; D. Brandes, 'Nationalsozialistische Tschechenpolitik im Protektorat Böhmen und Mähren', in idem/V. Kural (eds.), *Der Weg in die Katastrophe. Deutsch-Tschechische Beziehungen 1938–1947*, Essen: Klartext, 1994, pp. 46–55; idem, 'Tschechoslowakei. Vom Protektorat zur Volksdemokratie', in U. Herbert/A. Schildt (eds.), *Kriegsende in Europa. Vom Beginn des deutschen Machtzerfalls bis zur Stabilisierung der Nachkriegsordnung*, 1944–1948, Essen: Klartext 1998, pp. 263–75.
17 Balcar/Kučera, 'Nationalsozialistische Wirtschaftslenkung', p. 155; A. Teichova, The Protectorate Bohemia and Moravia, 1939–1945. The Economic Dimension, in M. Teich (ed.), *Bohemia in History*, Cambridge: Cambrigde UP, 1998, pp. 267–305.
18 Brandes, 'Tschechoslowakei', pp. 264–6; J. Balcar, *Panzer für Hitler – Traktoren für Stalin. Großunternehmen in Böhmen und Mähren 1938–1950*, Munich: Oldenbourg, 2014, pp. 49–61; Teichova, 'Protectorate Bohemia and Moravia'.
19 Teichova, 'Protectorate Bohemia and Moravia', pp. 281–5; E. Kubů, 'The Czechoslovak gold reserves and their surrender to Nazi Germany', in *Nazi Gold. The London Conference, 2–4 December 1997*, London: The Stationery Office, 1998, pp. 245–8, idem/Drahomír Jančík/Jiří Šouša, *Arisierungsgewinnler. Die Rolle der deutschen Banken bei der 'Arisierung' und Konfiskation jüdischer Vermögen im Protektorat Böhmen und Mähren, 1939–1945*, Wiesbaden: Harrassowitz 2011, pp. 29–39.
20 Teichova, 'Protectorate Bohemia and Moravia', pp. 281–6; Kubů/Jančík/Šouša, *Arisierungsgewinnler*, pp. 31–6; Brandes, 'Tschechoslowakei', pp. 265–73.
21 Teichova, 'Protectorate Bohemia and Moravia', pp. 282–6; Brandes, 'Tschechoslowakei', p. 269.
22 For these figures, see A. Teichova/R. Waller, 'Der tschechische Unternehmer am Vorabend und zu Beginn des Zweiten Weltkriegs', in: W. Długoborski (ed.), *Zweiter Weltkrieg und sozialer Wandel. Achsenmächte und besetzte Länder*, Göttingen: Vandenhoek und Ruprecht, 1981, pp. 298–9. See also Teichova, 'The Protectorate Bohemia and Moravia', pp. 281–6; M. Boldorf, 'Neue Wege zur Erforschung der Wirtschaftsgeschichte Europas unter nationalsozialistischer Hegemonie', in idem/Buchheim, *Europäische Volkswirtschaften*, pp. 5–10.
23 Teichova/Waller, 'Der tschechische Unternehmer', p. 299; V. Průcha, *Hospodářske dějiny Československa v 19. a 20. stoleti*, Praha: Svoboda, 1974, pp. 506–59; idem, 'The Integration of Czechoslovakia in the economic system of Nazi-Germany', in: M. Smith/P. Stirk (eds.), *Making the New Europe. European Unity and the Second World War*, London: Pinter, 1990, pp. 87–97; Brandes, 'Tschechoslowakei', p. 269; idem, 'Nationalsozialistische Tschechenpolitik', pp. 51–5.
24 Teichova, 'Protectorate Bohemia and Moravia', pp. 281–6; idem, 'Die Tschechen in der NS- Kriegswirtschaft', in A. Suppan/E. Vylozil (eds.), *Edvard Beneš und die tschechoslowakische Außenpolitik 1918–1948*, Frankfurt/Main: Lang, 2003, pp. 165–79; Balcar/Kučera, 'Nationalsozialistische Wirtschaftslenkung', pp. 154–6; Balcar, *Panzer für Hitler*, pp. 50–66, 102–22; P. Nemec, 'Das tschechische Volk und die nationalsozialistische Germanisierung des Raumes', *Bohemia*, 1991, vol. 32, pp. 39–59.
25 Ibid, pp. 281–6; idem, 'Die Tschechen in der NS-Kriegswirtschaft', pp. 170–8; R. Küpper, *Karl Hermann Frank (1889–1946). Eine politische Biographie eines sudetendeutschen Nationalsozialisten*, Munich: Oldenbourg, 2010.
26 M. Karný, 'Reinhard Heydrich als stellvertretender Reichsprotektor in Prag', in idem/M. Karna/J. Milotová (eds.), *Deutsche Politik im 'Protektorat Böhmen und Mähren' unter Reinhard Heydrich*, Berlin: Metropol, 1997, pp. 10–76.
27 Reichsgesetzblatt I, 1942, p. 165.

28 See, for example, the report of Daluege to Martin Bormann, Hitler's secretary, in 'Abschlussbericht über den Mordanschlag auf SS-Gruppenführer Heydrich', in: *Acta Occupationis Bohemiae et Moraviae*, Prague: Academia, 1968, document 385, pp. 486–9.
29 Teichova, 'Protectorate Bohemia and Moravia', pp. 284–5.
30 Teichova, 'Protectorate Bohemia and Moravia', pp. 281–6; Balcar, *Panzer für Hitler*, pp. 89–112.
31 Teichova, 'Die Tschechen in der NS-Kriegswirtschaft', pp. 170–8; Balcar, *Panzer für Hitler*, pp. 102–12. For the establishment of bank-industry combines during the First Czechoslovak Republic, see Teichova, *An Economic Background to Munich*.
32 Ibid; Teichova, 'Protectorate Bohemia and Moravia', pp. 281–6; H. Wixforth, *Auftakt zur Ostexpansion. Die Dresdner Bank und die Umgestaltung des Bankwesens im Sudetenland*, Dresden: Hannah-Arendt-Institut, 2001, pp. 12–34.
33 Figures according to Teichova, 'Protectorate Bohemia and Moravia', pp. 284–5. See also H. Wixforth/D. Ziegler: 'Die Expansion der "Reichswerke Hermann Göring" in Europa, *Jahrbuch für Wirtschaftsgeschichte*, 2008/1, pp. 257–81.
34 Wixforth/Ziegler, 'Expansion der Reichswerke', pp. 257–81.
35 Teichova, 'Protectorate Bohemia and Moravia', pp. 281–6; Teichova/Waller, 'Der tschechische Unternehmer', p. 299. For the role of the banks, see H. Wixforth, 'Die Banken in den abhängigen und besetzten Gebieten Europas 1928–1945. Instrumente der deutschen Hegemonie', in Buchheim/Boldorf, *Europäische Volkswirtschaften*, pp. 185–207.
36 Teichova, 'Protectorate Bohemia and Moravia', pp. 280–5.
37 M. Karný, 'Die "Judenfrage" in der nazistischen Okkupationspolitik', *Historica*, 1982, vol. 21, pp. 137–93; J. Osterloh, 'Die "Arisierung" im Protektorat Böhmen und Mähren, in: H. Wixforth, *Die Expansion der Dresdner Bank in Europa (Die Dresdner Bank im Dritten Reich, vol. 3)*, Munich: Oldenbourg, 2006, pp. 306–11.
38 Karný, 'Die Judenfrage', pp. 141–3; Osterloh, 'Die "Arisierung"', pp. 308–9.
39 Teichova, 'Protectorate Bohemia and Moravia', pp. 280–5; Karný, 'Die Judenfrage', pp. 141–51.
40 Ibid, pp. 280–5; Nemec, 'Das tschechische Volk', pp. 59–79.
41 See I. Heinemann, *'Rasse, Siedlung, deutsches Blut'. Das Rasse- und Siedlungshauptamt der SS und die rassenpolitische Neuordnung Europas*, Göttingen: Wallstein, 2003.
42 Teichova, 'Protectorate Bohemia and Moravia', pp. 280–5.

13 Development and management of the Manchurian economy under Japan's empire

Tetsuji Okazaki

1. Introduction

In September 1931, the Japanese Army, specifically the Kwangtung Army, a part of it stationed in Manchuria, the northeast part of China, to defend the South Manchuria Railways, started military movements and occupied the whole of Manchuria by the end of February 1932.[1] In the next month, foundation of a new state, Manchukuo, was declared. Formally, Manchukuo was an independent state with its own government, but in reality the Kwantung Army totally controlled the state.[2] Because the Japanese Army was keen on expanding the capacity of munitions production, and Manchuria was supposed to be richly endowed with natural resources, the Kwangtung Army and the Manchukuo government tried to develop munitions industries and basic material industries rapidly in Manchuria. In the new state, where there were few existing legal constraints, the Kwantung Army and the Manchukuo government started almost with a clean slate. However, they did not have a solid program in the first place. Indeed, as stated in what follows, the process of Manchurian development in the 1930s and 1940s was full of trial and error.

This process provides us a good opportunity to observe and compare different modes to develop an economy. In this chapter, I exploit this opportunity. To do that, a standard framework of economics of organizations is used. Namely, it is assumed that coordination and motivation are the two fundamental functions for an economy to work and that modes of coordination and motivation are diverse across economies.[3] In particular, I focus on overtime changes in the modes of coordination.

Development of the Manchurian economy under the Japan Empire has long attracted the interest of economic historians in Japan, and several detailed studies have been published.[4] This chapter relies on these studies, especially on Akira Hara's works. Hara described not only the drawing-up process but also the implementation process of the development plans in detail, using rich original documents of the Kwantung Army, the Manchuria government and the South Manchuria Railways Co.[5] In addition, in another article, Hara made clear the background and the activities of the Manchuria Heavy Industries Development Co., a special cooperation founded to implement the long-term development plan.[6]

This chapter aims at contributing to the literature in two ways. First, I introduce the standpoint of economics of organizations, as stated, which enables us to characterize different modes of coordination in the successive phases of Manchurian economic development. Second, related to the first point, this chapter tries to propose a new evaluation of the economic policies in Manchuria. In the literature, it is sometimes argued that Manchuria went ahead of Japan in planning and control of the economy and the experience in Manchuria was imported to Japan.[7] However, looking at the Manchurian economy from the standpoint given, we have a different view.

The remainder of the chapter is organized as follows. Section 2 describes the drawing up process of the 'Five Years Plan of Manchuria Industrial Development' as well as the Manchurian economic system at its early stage. Section 3 discusses the meaning of the Manchuria Heavy Industries Development Co. as a device of coordination. In Section 4, I focus on the transition to a state-led planned economy after 1939. Section 5 concludes.

2. Start of a long-term plan of industrial development

Foundation of Manchukuo and the early stage of economic construction

Just before the foundation of Manchukuo, the Kwantung Army examined how to manage the occupied area of Manchuria, collaborating with the South Manchuria Railway Co. (SMR), which not only managed the railways in south Manchuria but also governed the areas attached to the railroads since 1906. After the foundation of Manchukuo in March 1932, the Kwantung Army transmitted the draft of the policy for economic construction to the Manchukuo government to make it an official document of Manchukuo. In March 1933, the Manchukuo government announced *Manshukoku Keizai Kensetsu Koyo* (Outline of the Policy for Constructing Manchukuo Economy).[8]

This document shows the basic idea of the Kwantung Army to manage the Manchukuo economy in the early stage. It stressed that fruits of the economic construction should not be seized by a certain class and that important industries should be controlled by the government, which reflected the anticapitalism ideology of the Army. Based on this idea, that document indicated the policy that important industries should be managed by public corporations or 'special corporations'. A 'special corporation' referred to a corporation that was founded according to a special law or a treaty between Manchukuo and Japan and was regulated by the government. In many cases, Manchukuo government invested tangible assets requisitioned from the military clique government in Manchuria. There was a similar category, 'quasi-special corporation'. A quasi-special corporation referred to a company whose shares were owned by the government, that was established according to an ordinance by the government and/or that was controlled by the government according to its statutes or the law.[9] By the end of 1936, twenty-six special and quasi-special corporations were founded. They include *Manshu Denshin Denwa* (telephone and telecommunication), *Manshu Dengyo* (electricity), *Showa Seikojo* (iron and steel), Manshu Keikinzoku (aluminium), *Manshu Sekiyu* (petroleum mining and refinery), *Manshu Tanko* (coal mining), *Dowa Jidosha Kogyo* (automobile) and *Hoten Zoheisho* (munitions). Major sources of the capital of those corporations were the Manchukuo government and SMR.[10]

Concerning special and quasi-special corporations, it is remarkable that the so-called 'one industry, one corporation policy' was adopted. That is, just one special corporation was founded in each industry and no outsider company was allowed. In other words, each special or quasi-special corporation was given the authority to monopolize a certain industry by the government. This 'one industry, one corporation' policy characterized the early stage of Manchurian development.[11]

Drawing up and revision of the 'Five Years Plan of Manchuria Industrial Development'

While many special and quasi-special corporations were founded and they were regulated by the Manchukuo government, there was no systematic and quantitative plan for developing the whole Manchurian economy in the early 1930s. It was in 1935 when the Army started to draw up the plan for long-term development of the Manchurian economy as a part of a plan that included Japan and Manchuria. The motivation of the Army was to reduce the gap of munitions production capacity between Japan and the Soviet Union, a major potential enemy for the Army. Kanji Ihihara, the chief of the Strategy Section of the Army General Staff Office, requested a staff of the South Manchuria Railways, Masayoshi Miyazaki, to organize a research institute, Nichiman Zaisei Keizai Kenkyukai (Research Institute on Public Finance and Economy in Japan and Manchuria, RIPEJM), and to draw up long-term plans of industrial development in Japan and Manchuria. On the request, RIPEJM made a draft plan (Five Years Plan on Revenue and Expenditure from Showa 12 Fiscal Year, supplemented by Outline of Emergency National Policies), which was presented to the Ministry of Army and the Kwantung Army in August 1936.[12]

After it was revised by the Ministry of Army, the Manchurian part of the draft plan was examined and revised at an informal meeting of the three influential actors in Manchuria, namely the Kwantung Army, the Manchukuo government and the South Manchuria Railways, held at Tang Gang Zi close to Shenyang in October 1936. The draft plan incorporating the opinions of these three actors was transmitted to the Japanese government again. Through these procedures, 'Five Years Plan of Manchuria Industrial Development' was finally determined and launched in January 1937.[13] Table 13.1 summarizes the quantitative targets of the plan. As shown in the table, the Five Years Plan was quite ambitious. It aimed at developing varieties of heavy and chemical industries rapidly in Manchuria. They include automobile and aircraft, which would directly contribute to munitions production, as well as materials such as iron, steel and coal. Also, it is notable that

Table 13.1 Outline of the 'Five Years Plan of Manchuria Industrial Development'

		Capacity at the end of 1936	Production target for 1941 Initial plan (Jan. 1937)	Production target for 1941 Revised Plan (May 1938)
Pig iron	1,000 tons	850	2,530	4,680
Crude steel	1,000 tons	580	2,000	3,160
Iron ore	1,000 tons	3,180	7,740	15,990
Coal	1,000 tons	13,558	27,160	34,910
Alcohol	ton	15,080	56,690	56,690
Aluminium	ton	—	20,000	30,000
Magnesium	ton	0	500	3,000
Lead	ton	2,200	12,400	29,000
Zinc	ton	1,900	6,600	50,000
Salt	1,000 tons	340	974	911
Soda ash	1,000 tons	12	72	72
Chemical fertilizer	1,000 tons	—	—	454
Pulp	1,000 tons	70	120	400
Electricity	1,000 KW	459	1,405	2,571
Automobile	unit	—	4,000	50,000
Aircraft	unit	—	340	5,000

Source: Yamamoto, *Manshukoku*, pp. 38–9.

the speed of expansion was very high. That is, production of all the commodities in the plan was expected to be more than doubled in five years.

Ambitious as the 'Five Years Plan' was, it was further revised upward in May 1938. There were two major reasons for this. The first is that the long-term plan for production capacity expansion in Japan was taking shape in 1937. The origin of the plan was the draft plan by RIPEJM (Five Years Plan on Revenue and Expenditure from Showa 12 Fiscal Year, supplemented by Outline of Emergency National Policies) mentioned earlier, the Manchurian part of which was the origin of the 'Five Years Plan'. Based on the draft plan, the Ministry of Army officially determined *Juyo Sangyo Gokanen Keikaku Taiko* (Outline of the Five Years Plan of Important Industries, 'Outline') in May 1937. 'Outline' by the Ministry of Army included the production targets in Manchuria in addition to those in Japan (Table 13.2). It is notable that the production targets in Manchuria in the 'Outline' were substantially larger than those in the 'Five Years Plan'. Leaders of the political and business societies in Japan almost reached a consensus that they should accept the plan by the Army.[14]

The second reason for the upward revision was the breakout of the Sino-Japanese War in July 1937. This was the start of the full-scale war for Japan lasting until August 1945. Huge consumption of munitions for the war further strengthened the Army's request for Manchuria to expand production. Particularly, the Army requested Manchuria to supply basic materials such as coal, pig iron and crude

182 Tetsuji Okazaki

Table 13.2 Outline of the 'Five Years Plan of Important Industries'

		Production target in 1941		Production in 1936
		Japan	Manchuria	Japan
Aircraft	unit	7,000	3,000	1280.0
Automobile	10,000 units	9	1	1.2*
Machine tool	10,000 units	45	5	1.6
Steel products	10,000 tons	700	300	432.0
Pig iron	10,000 tons	750	400	222.0
Iron ore	10,000 tons	1,050	1,200	125.0
Gasoline	10,000 kl	190	140	65.3
Alcohol	10,000 kl	45	5	3.3
Benzol	10,000 kl	14	6	
Heavy oil	10,000 kl	135	100	45.7
Coal	10,000 tons	7,200	3,800	4790.0
Aluminium	10,000 tons	7	3	0.5
Magnesium	10,000 tons	6	3	0.6*
Ship	10,000 tons	86	7	24.7*
Electricity	10,000 KW	1,117	140	654.3

Source: M. Inaba, T. Kobayashi, T. Shimada and J. Tsunoda (eds.), Taiheiyo Senso eno Michi: Kaisen Gaiko Shi (Road to the Pacific War: Diplomatic History toward the Outbreak of the War), supplementary volume, Tokyo: Asahi Shinbunsha, 1963, p. 232 for the targets. Kokumin Keizai Kenkyu Kyokai, Kihon Kokuryoku Dotai Soran (Compendium of Movement of Basic National Resource), Tokyo: Kokumin Keizai Kenkyu Kyokai, and Toyo Keizai Shinposha, Showa Sangyoshi (Industrial History in Showa Era) vol. 3, Tokyo: Toyo Keizai Shinposha, for the production in 1936.

Note: The production data with '*' does not include production in the colonies. The production of alcohol is for 1937.

steel to Japan. Originally, the Kwantung Army had the idea to develop its own munitions and related industries in Manchuria, and this idea was reflected in the 'Five Years Plan', but the Japan Army came to have the strategy to utilize Manchuria as a source of raw materials and semimanufactured goods to the Japanese industries. Responding to the request, the Manchukuo government revised the 'Five Years Plan' in February 1938. The production targets were substantially raised for most of the commodities in the plan (Table 13.2). In addition, reflecting the reason for the upward revision, the 'Revised Five Years Plan' indicated the target of supply to Japan for each commodity.[15]

3. Trial of coordination by a private conglomerate: Manchuria Heavy Industries Development Co.

To implement the 'Five Years Plan of Manchuria Industrial Development', the Kwantung Army considered the possibility of utilizing the capability of private companies in Japan. For this purpose, they invited several influential Japanese entrepreneurs to have them observe the Manchurian economy in 1936. Also, the Kwantung Army presented them the draft of the 'Five Years Plan' to ask their advice. Those entrepreneurs included Yoshisuke Ayukawa (president of Nissan), Kojiro Matsukata (ex-president of Kawasaki Dockyard) and Shitagau Noguchi (president of Nippon Nitrogen).[16]

After Ayukawa came back to Japan, he gave the following comments on the draft of the 'Five Years Plan' to the Ministry of Army. First, the plan is just listing the production targets in the final year based on the military demand, and there is little consideration of the relationships between industries and timing of expansion. Second, it is necessary to coordinate related heavy industries by organizing them in a hierarchical organization, whereas special corporations had not been operated in a coordinated manner until then. These two points are closely related to the third point. That is, in order to develop the aircraft and automobile industries as the 'Five Years Plan' aimed at, it is necessary to develop the industries that supply parts to them. In summary, what Ayukawa proposed was that they should coordinate the development of related industries to implement the 'Five Years Plan' and that to do that, those industries should be organized in a hierarchical organization.

Ayukawa's first point is on the evaluation of the 'Five Years Plan' as an economic plan. A similar evaluation from the academic standpoint is seen in an article by Ishikawa.[17] Along with the fact that special and quasi-special corporations were not systematically coordinated, planning and control in the Manchurian economy was really at a rudimentary stage in 1936.

Ayukawa's second and third points can be interpreted as a development strategy similar to that known as a 'big push' in the literature of development economics. An essential element of a 'big push' is complementarity between industries. In case industries are complementary with each other, in the sense that a certain industry enhances other industries' efficiency, and other industries vice versa, concerted expansion of those related industries is necessary to have an economy to escape from a stagnating 'bad equilibrium'.[18] Ayukawa seems to understand the essence of that idea. At the same time, it is notable that as a measure for coordinating complementary industries, he proposed not a government intervention but a private hierarchical organization. This is just what major zaibatsu business groups did at the early stage of Japanese economic development in the late nineteenth century.[19]

As is well known, a 'big push' needs large amount of funds in a short period. Japan exported a substantial amount of capital to Manchuria in the early 1930s, but Japan itself was being faced with a shortage of funds due to the expansion of the military budget and production capacity expansion. Given these conditions, Ayukawa argued that it was necessary to import capital from abroad other than Japan, particularly from the United States.[20]

These comments by Ayukawa strongly impressed the Ministry of Army, and they wanted Ayukawa to participate in the implementation of 'Five Years Plan'. At first, the Army intended to have Ayukawa manage just the automobile and aircraft industries, because Nissan had one of the largest automobile companies,

Nissan Jidosha Kogyo. To the Army's proposal, Ayukawa replied that if he was entrusted with the development of all the heavy industries, he was ready to move the whole Nissan business group to Manchuria.[21] Ayukawa's response was surprising because Nissan was the fourth-largest business group in Japan in 1937.

The Kwantung Army, the Manchukuo government, the Japan Army and the Japanese government examined Ayukawa's proposal and negotiated with one another to reach the cabinet decision, 'Manshu Jukogyo Kakuritsu Yoko' (Outline of Establishing Heavy Industries in Manchuria) in October 1937.[22] The Cabinet decision presented the basic policy that in order to establish heavy industries rapidly in Manchuria, they would reform corporate firms and invite powerful entrepreneurs. The main points were as follows. First, they would found a new corporation owned half and half by the government and Nissan, and this corporation would invest in such industries as iron and steel, light metals, automobiles, aircraft and coal to have dominant shares. Second, in developing those industries, this corporation would make an effort to introduce capital from abroad. Third, the Manchukuo government would provide some special treatment for the investment in this corporation and its businesses. Fourth, management of this corporation would be entrusted to an appropriate person from the Japanese private sector, Yoshisuke Ayukawa of Nissan.

Based on this cabinet decision, Nissan moved its headquarters to Hsinking, the capital of Manchukuo, in November 1937, and in December it was reorganized to a special corporation of Manchukuo according the special law, the Law for Managing the Manchuria Heavy Industries Developing Co. At the same time, Nissan changed its name to the Manchuria Heavy Industries Developing Co. (MHID).

By April 1939, the MHID acquired four existing special corporations, *Showa Seikojo* (Showa Steel), *Manshu Tanko* (Manchuria Coal Mining), *Manshu Keikinzoku* (Manchuria Light Metals) and *Dowa Jidosha* (Dowa Automobile), from the Manchukuo government and the South Manchuria Railways Co., while it newly founded four special corporations, *Manshu Kozan* (Manchuria Mining), *Manshu Hikoki Seizo* (Manchuria Aircraft Manufacturing), *Manshu Magnesium*, and *Tohendo Kaihatsu* (Dongbiandao Development).[23] Thus, MHID constructed the huge conglomerate of heavy industries in Manchuria as Ayukawa imaged in the first place. However, at that time, the environment of conditions for the MHID to work well had been lost, as described next.

4. Transition to a state-led planned economy

Changes in the international environment

When the MHID was founded, the international environment of the Manchurian economy was changing rapidly. The fundamental condition was that the Sino-Japanese War became long and drawn out. When the Prime Minister of Japan, Fumimaro Konoe, declared that they would not negotiate with the Chinese National Government after the Japanese Army occupied Nanjing in January 1938, the possibility of early conclusion of the war was lost.

Given the prospect of a prolonged war, the Japanese government strengthened the system of wartime economic control in 1938. While the international trade and the flow of long-term funds had been already controlled since the previous year, the government began to draw up and implement the short-term plan to adjust the demand and supply of strategic commodities (Material Mobilization Plan, *Busshi Doin Keikaku* in Japanese) in January 1938. The Material Mobilization Plan was implemented by means of distribution control of each commodity. At the same time, price control was implemented for a number of commodities.[24] The Japanese economy became a planned economy in the sense that a substantial part of coordination, that is resource allocation, was carried out by the planning and control by the government instead of the market mechanism.[25]

Operation of the Material Mobilization Plan by the Japanese government had a serious impact on the Manchurian economy, as the Manchurian economy heavily depended upon the trade with Japan, in particular imports from Japan. The percentage of imports from Japan to total imports was 75.1 per cent in 1937, for instance.[26] In this situation, the Japanese government decided on the downward revision of the Material Mobilization Plan in June 1938, due to the unexpected decline of exports. As the basic constraint for the Material Mobilization Plan was the import of essential raw materials from foreign countries, decline of exports affected the scale of the plan through decline of foreign currencies. This revision obliged the Japanese government to restrict export to Manchuria, because Manchurian yuan was not convertible to US dollar or pound sterling and hence export to Manchuria did not contribute to Japan to earn foreign currencies.[27]

As stated, Ayukawa stressed importing capital from abroad, and the major reason for it was removing the constraint of foreign currencies. Restriction of imports from Japan made capital imports still more vital. Indeed, Ayukawa made great efforts to import capital, but all of these attempts were unsuccessful. This was mainly because the diplomatic relationship between Japan and the United States was deteriorating due to the prolonged Sino-Japanese War.[28]

Material Mobilization Plan and distribution controls

Given the downward revision of the Material Mobilization Plan in Japan in June 1938, the Manchukuo government decided the 'General Guideline for the Contribution of Manchuria to Japan's Material Mobilization Plan'. The 'General Guideline' stated that Manchukuo would entirely cooperate with Japan on its emergency measures determined in July 1938, following the revision of the Material Mobilization Plan. In the same month, the governments of Japan and Manchukuo held a conference on the Material Mobilization Plan to reach the following agreements. First, concerning pig iron, steel, coal and livestock feed, out of the strategic materials that Japan had imported from foreign countries, Manchukuo should meet the demand of Japan as much as possible. Second, Manchukuo should import most of the equipment for industrial development from Japan, and all the demand for the equipment in Manchuria should be concentrated on the Manchukuo government to be approved.[29]

Based on these agreements, the Manchukuo government decided to draw up the Manchurian version of the Material Mobilization Plan in August 1938. The purpose of it was to meet such needs as exporting materials to Japan, implementing the 'Revised Five Years Plan' and maintaining people's lives. Given the tight constraint on the supply side, planning and control on allocation of commodities was indispensable to meet those needs simultaneously. The Planning Committee, in particular the Commodities and Prices Committee (*Busshi Bukka Iinkai*), which was one of the four committees under the Planning Committee,[30] took charge of making the Material Mobilization Plan, collaborating with other relevant sections of the Manchukuo government and the Kwantung Army. The Commodities and Prices Committee, in turn, was composed of four subcommittees, each of which covered a specific group of commodities.[31]

In August 1938, the Commodities and Prices Committee determined the official manual to draw up the Material Mobilization Plan.[32] According to it, the plan was drawn up through the following procedure. First, for each important commodity, the domestic demand was estimated. The domestic demand was classified into (a) the military demand, (b) the public demand, (c) the demand of special corporations and (d) the private demand. Second, for each of the same commodities, the domestic supply was estimated, which was composed of (a) production and (b) stock and collection. In case the demand exceeded the supply, measures for covering the shortage were devised, such as (a) emergent production, (b) saving, substitution or collection, (c) import from Japan, (d) import from the areas of China under control of Japan and (e) import from foreign countries. Because import from Japan was restricted, which was the starting point of drawing up the Material Mobilization Plan in Manchuria as stated, and import from foreign countries was constrained by availability of foreign currencies, it was necessary that a certain part of the gap between demand and supply was covered by saving. This implies that rationing was inevitable. The Material Mobilization Plan was drawn up mainly for providing the quantitative framework for rationing.[33]

Indeed, while preparing for drawing up the Material Mobilization Plan, the Manchukuo government began to introduce the distribution control for strategic commodities. For instance, in April 1938, the Iron and Steel Control Law (*Tekko-rui Tosei Ho*) was legislated, which prescribed that Japan Manchuria Trading (JMT, *Nichiman Shoji*), a special cooperation, should take charge of all the international trade and domestic sales of iron and steel, and the sales prices by the JNT were controlled by the government. Also, with respect to cement, in September 1938, the Cement Joint Sales Corporation was founded by the JMT, cement producers and cement traders, which took charge of domestic and international trades alone, under the supervision by the government.[34]

The first Manchuria Material Mobilization Plan was for the first quarter of 1939 fiscal year, but it was determined as late as February 1939, and also it was just for four commodities: steel, cement, coal and lumber. In this sense, the first full-scale Manchuria Material Mobilization Plan was that for 1939 fiscal year (April 1939–March 1940). To implement the plan, the Planning Committee determined the 'Outline for Preparing Distribution System' (*Haikyu Kiko Seibi Yoryo*). It prescribed that besides those commodities whose distribution control systems had been already prepared, including iron and steel and cement, they should prepare the distribution control systems for all the important commodities, such as nonferrous metals, chemical products and necessities of life. By these measures, the system of planning and control by the state was almost ready to work. After that, coordination of economic activities in Manchuria was carried out mainly by this system.

Transition to the state-led system of coordination had a substantial impact on the MHID, because its major role was replaced by the new system. In the literature, conflicts between MHID and JMT on the distribution of commodities were stressed.[35] These conflicts reflected the transition from the coordination system based on a private conglomerate to the state-led one, because the JMT was an essential element of the latter system.

5. Concluding remarks

In 1933, the Manchukuo government declared implementing economic controls to develop the economy, and in January 1937, it determined the 'Five Years Plan of Industrial Development'. Given these facts, the literature stressed the view that planning and control went ahead in Manchuria to be imported to Japan from there.[36] However, as stated, when the 'Five Years Plan of Industrial Development' was determined, the coordination system substituting for the market mechanism was underdeveloped in Manchuria. It is true that there were many special corporations based on the 'one industry, one corporation policy', but they were not intentionally coordinated each other. Furthermore, the targets of 'Five Years Plan of Industrial Development' themselves were not coordinated. Indeed, this is the issue that Yoshisuke Ayukawa stressed in his comments on the Manchurian development.

Accepting Ayukawa's comments, the Kwantung Army and the Manchukuo government introduced a new mode of coordination, that is, coordination by a private conglomerate. For this purpose, the Manchurian Heavy Industries Development Co. (MHID) was founded, as a huge holding company that managed the special corporations of heavy industries in Manchuria. Whereas this system was different from a typical market economy in the sense that a substantial part of coordination was supposed to be conducted within an organization, on the other hand, this was essentially different from the system of planning and control by the state in the sense that the organization was a private conglomerate. In other words, the experience of MHID was a trial of a new system of coordination in which a major part of the national economy was coordinated within the one huge private conglomerate.

188 *Tetsuji Okazaki*

However, finally in 1939, under the condition that import from Japan was restricted and there was no prospect of capital import from foreign countries, the Kwantung Army and the Manchukuo government decided to introduce an alternative system of coordination, namely the state-led system of planning and control. This was similar to the system that had already started to work in Japan. In this sense, the system of full-scale planning and control was imported from Japan to Manchuria, not from Manchuria to Japan.

Notes

1 The northeast part of China, composed of Liaoning, Jilin and Heilungjiang provinces, was called 'Manchuria'. According to the Portsmouth Treaty and the Japan-China treaty on Manchuria after the Russo-Japanese War, Japan took over the railways in south Manchuria and the authorities related to it, including station of a garrison, which was the origin of the Kwantong Army. See T. Suzuki, *Nihon Teikokushugi to Manshu, 1900–1945 (Japan Imperialism and Manchuria)*, vol. 1, Tokyo: Hanawa Shobo, 1992, pp. 70–90.
2 T. Furuya, ' "Manshukoku" no soshutsu' (Creation of Manchukuo) in Y. Yamamoto (ed.) *'Manshukoku' no Kenkyu (Study on Manchukuo)*, Tokyo: Ryokuin Shobo, 1995; S. Yamamuro, ' "Manshukoku" tochi katei ron' (On governance of Manchukuo) in Yamamoto, *Manshukoku*'; S. Yamamuro, *Kimera: Manshukoku no Shozo (Chimera: A Portrait of Manchukuo)*, Tokyo: Chuo Koronsha, 2004, chap. 2–3.
3 P. Milgrom/J. Roberts, *Economics, Organization and Management*, Englewood Cliffs, New Jersey: Prentice-Hall, 1992.
4 A. Hara, '1930 nendai no Manshu keizai tosei seisaku' (Economic control policies in Manchuria in the 1930s) in Manshu Shi Kenskyukai (ed.), *Nihon Teikokushugi kano Manshu (Manchuria under the Japan Empire)*, Tokyo: Ochanomizu Shobo, 1972; A. Hara, ' "Daitoa Kyoeiken" no keizaiteki jittai' (Economic Reality of the 'Great East Asia Co-prosperity Sphere', *Tochi Seido Shigaku (Journal of Agrarian History)*, 1976, pp. 1–28; A. Hara, ' "Manshu" niokeru keizai tosei seisaku no tenkai: Mantesu kaiso to Mangyo setsuritsu wo megutte' (Economic control policies in Manchuria in the 1930s: On the reorganization of the South Manchuria Railways Co. and foundation of Manchuria Heavy Industries Development Co.) in Y. Ando (ed.), *Nihon Keizai Seisakushi Ron (History of Economic Policies in Japan)* vol. 2, Tokyo: University of Tokyo Press, 1976; H. Iguchi, *Ayukawa Yoshisuke to Keizaiteki Kokusaishugi (Y. Ayukawa and U.S.–Japan Relationship)*, Nagoya: Nagoya University Press, 2012; S. Ishikawa, 'Shusen ni itaru made no Manshu Keizai Kaihatsu: Sono mokuteki to seika' (Development of Manchuria economy until the end of the WWII: Its purpose and performance) in Japan Association of Diplomacy/T. Ueda (eds.), *Taiheiyo Senso Shuketsu Ron (On the Conclusion of the Pacific War)*, Tokyo: University of Tokyo Press, 1958; H. Kobayashi, '1930 nendai shokuminchi "kogyoka" no shotokucho' (Characteristics of industrialization in colonies in the 1930s), *Tochi Seido Shigaku (Journal of Agrarian History)*, 1969, pp. 29–46; H. Kobayashi, *Daitoa Kyoeiken no Keisei to Hokai (Fomation and Collapse of 'Great East Asia Co-prosperity Sphere')*, Tokyo: Ochanomizu Shobo, 1975; H. Kobayashi, '1930 nendai "Manshu kogyoka" seisaku no tenkai katei: Manshu Sangyo Gokanen Keikaku no jisshi katei wo chushin ni' (Development of 'Manchurian industrialization' policy: Focusing on 'Five Years Plan of Manchurian Industrialization'), *Tochi Seido Shigaku (Journal of Agrarian History)*, 1976, pp. 19–43; Y. Yamamoto, *'Manshukoku' Keizaishi Kenkyu (Economic History of 'Manchukuo')*, Nagoya: Nagoya University Press, 2003.
5 A. Hara, '1930 nendai'.

6 Idem, 'Manshu'.
7 C. Johnson, *MITI and the Japanese Miracle: The Growth of Industrial Policy, 1925–1975*, Stanford, California: Stanford University Press, 1982, p. 132; H. Kobayashi, *Nihon Kabushikigaisha wo Tsukutta Otoko: Miyazaki Masayoshi no Shogai (A Man who Created the Japan Inc.: The Life of Masayoshi Miyazaki)*, Tokyo: Shogakkan, 1995, chap. 11–12; T. Nakamura, *Showa Shi (History of Showa Era)*, vol. 1, Tokyo: Toyo Keizai Shinposha, 1993, p. 163.
8 A. Hara, '1930 nendai', pp. 9–19; Y. Yamamoto, *Manshukoku*, pp. 28–9.
9 Research Department of the Yokohama Species Bank, 'Manshukoku tokushu gaisha seido ni tsuite' (On the special corporation system in Manchukuo), 1942, pp. 2–3.
10 A. Hara, '1930 nendai', p. 46; H. Kobayashi, *Daitoa*, pp. 50–1; Y. Yamamoto, *Manshukoku*, p. 32.
11 A. Hara, '1930 nendai', p. 45; A. Hara, 'Manshu', pp. 2–3; Y. Yamamoto, *Manshukoku*, p. 31.
12 A. Hara, '1930 nendai', p. 62.
13 A. Hara, '1930 nendai', pp. 63–5; Y. Yamamoto, *Manshukoku*, p. 34.
14 A. Hara, '1930 nendai', pp. 72–9.
15 S. Ihikawa, 'Shusen', pp. 749–52; A. Hara, '1930 nendai', pp. 72–4.
16 A. Hara, 'Manshu', p. 229; Iguchi, *Ayukawa*, p. 38.
17 S. Ihikawa, 'Shusen', p. 745.
18 P.N. Rosenstein-Rodan, 'Problems of Industrialization in Eastern and South-Eastern Europe', *Economic Journal*, 1943, vol. 53, pp. 202–11; K.M. Murphy/A. Schleifer/R.W. Vishnny, 'Industrialization and the big push', *Journal of Political Economy*, 1989, vol. 97, pp. 1003–26.
19 T. Okazaki, *Mochikabu Gaisha no Rekishi: Zaibatsu to Kigyo Tochi (History of Holding Companies in Japan: Zaibatsu in Perspectives of Corporate Governance)*, Tokyo: Chikuma Shobo, 1999; T. Okazaki, 'The Role of Holding Companies in Pre-war Japanese Economic Development: Rethinking Zaibatsu in Perspectives of Corporate Governance', *Social Science Japan Journal*, 2001, vol. 4, pp. 243–68; R. Morck/M. Nakamura, 'Business groups and the big push; Meiji Japan's mass privatization and subsequent growth', *Enterprise and Society*, 2007, vol. 8, pp. 543–601.
20 A. Hara, 'Daitoa', pp. 2–3; A. Hara, 'Manshu', p. 269; Iguchi, *Ayukawa*, p. 35.
21 A. Hara, 'Manshu', p. 231.
22 Ibid, p. 232.
23 Manchuria Heavy Industries Development Co., *Mangyo narabini Zaiman Kankei Jigyo Gaiyo (Outline of the MHID and Its Businesses in Manchuria)*, reprint, Tokyo: Yumani Shobo, 2004, p. 7.
24 A. Hara, 'Japan: Guns before rice', in M. Harrison (ed.), *The Economics of World War II: Six Great Powers in International Comparison*, Cambridge: Cambridge UP, 1998, pp. 235–36; T. Okazaki, 'Senji keikaku keizai to kakaku tosei' (Wartime planned economy and price control) in Kindai Nihon Kenkyukai (ed.), *Nenpo Kindai Nihon Kenkyu (Yearbook of Research in Modern Japan)* vol. 9, Tokyo: Yamakawa Shuppansha, 1987.
25 T. Okazaki/M. Okuno-Fujiwara (eds.), *The Japanese Economic System and Its Historical Origins*, Oxford: Oxford University Press, 1999.
26 Manchukuo government, *Manshu Kenkoku 10 Nen Shi (10 Years History since the Foundation of Manchukuo)*, Tokyo: Hara Shobo, pp. 612, 616.
27 A. Hara, 'Japan', p. 236.
28 A. Hara, 'Manshu', pp. 269–75.
29 A. Hara, '1930 nendai', pp. 84–5.
30 The other three committees were Foreign Exchange Committee (*Kawase Iinkai*), Finance and International Trade Committee (*Kin'yu Boeki Iinkai*) and Labor Committee (*Romu Iinkai*).

31 A. Hara, '1930 nendai', p. 86.
32 'Juyo Busshi Jyukyu Keikaku Sakutei Yoryo' (Manual to Draw Up the Demand and Supply Plan for Important Commodities).
33 A. Hara, '1930 nendai', pp. 87–8.
34 A. Hara, 'Manshu', pp. 253–6; Yamamoto, *Manshukoku*, pp. 59–63.
35 A. Hara, 'Manshu', pp. 255–6.
36 Johnson, *MITI and the Japanese Miracle;* Kobayashi; Nakamura.

14 The Philippine economy during the Japanese occupation, 1941–1945

Gerardo P. Sicat[1]

Introduction

This chapter's main concern is to provide a working estimate of the aggregate economic damage on the Philippine economy of the Japanese occupation during World War II. Though economic measurement is the main focus, the chapter also summarizes the outline of events that featured the efforts of the military occupation to establish political and economic hegemony and the response of the conquered nation to these efforts.[2]

The Second World War broke out for the Philippines on December 8, 1941. At that time, it was an American colonial possession on the way toward full political independence scheduled for July 4, 1946. The US Congress had passed an independence law in 1934 that created a commonwealth government under American dominion. This transitional government was fully run by Filipinos, and it administered the country's political affairs, except foreign policy, on the way to full independence. That commonwealth was to transition into an independent republic.[3] The timeline toward full independence was broken by the Japanese occupation of the country.

By the time of the outbreak of war hostilities, Filipinos had developed a strong sense of loyalty and friendship with the United States. Four decades of American colonial policy had passed and were characterized by political and administrative tutelage that brought in an era of economic and social prosperity for the country. Also, the independence struggle had been won and was on its inevitable political course.

The attack on Pearl Harbor automatically dragged the Philippines into war. Philippine military forces which were a distinct unit being trained for independence were also introduced into the war as an integral part of the American defensive control.

Japan invaded the Philippines shortly after Pearl Harbor as part of its military offensive in Southeast Asia. The Japanese military command had an easy massive invasion of the major islands. The American defensive plan was to wage the decisive battle on the Bataan peninsula and in the island fortress of Corregidor. With the fall of Bataan in April 1942, the country was finally consolidated under Japanese military command.

Establishing military and political control[4]

The Japanese military government established political control through the appointment of civilian authorities along with the administrative framework that was already in existence. To install civilian control over government matters, the Japanese military command selected an Executive Commission of three members from cabinet members of the existing Commonwealth government to form a local government. (To avoid capture, the Commonwealth president and vice president had retreated within the defensive parameters of battle and later went into exile to the United States.)

The occupation military command issued edicts to take control of the reallocation of efforts to corner resources for the war effort for Japan. Thus, the Japanese military was able to obtain supplies for its war effort. Such moves included the procurement of food and military supplies for the occupiers. In actual terms, this often meant confiscation or forced purchases of war materiel and the consolidation and use of enemy assets for the military occupier's own objectives.

Important to this mobilization of the occupied territory for the war effort were monetary and fiscal measures. Price controls, issuance of military currency and use of scrips to take over private assets were the major tools of mobilization. The takeover of strategic industries through their acquisition by enterprises allied with the occupying power was prevalent.

The banking sector was critical in financing transactions and the issuance of money. Foreign banks that were associated with Japanese interests became important partners of the war effort. The banking powers of the state-owned *Philippine National Bank* were mobilized for the monetary function. In this way, Japanese interests were able to take a considerable role over the economy's operations. Under a war in which business activity was largely declining and where a substantial amount of state resources had been taken over to help mobilize the war effort for Japan, however, these developments could only lead to an inflationary spiral.

Political control of domestic affairs was carried out by the civilian Filipino government initially under the Executive Commission. It was easier to impose an occupier's will on a single entity – a national government – than to have an unorganized effort dealing with sundry administrative units of governance.

For about one year, the Executive Commission undertook its job of governing what it was allowed to do under a military command. Its chairman, Jorge Vargas, was formerly executive secretary in the Commonwealth government and was now the nominal head of the government with two former senior cabinet members. This commission worked toward easing the problems of political control of the invading army, working in part to get the population to cooperate with the new rulers and protecting them from harm as far as practicable. Thus, the wishes of the Japanese military were in part carried out by the civilian commission through its own civil command system. In the main, and in pursuit of the military effort and in aligning the whole economy toward the war effort, the commission was essentially a puppet government.

In early 1943, after the whole commission went to Japan, the idea of granting independence was broached. This was a palatable option that appeared politically attractive to the occupying power. The grant of Philippine independence just so soon after the military conquest appeared to show Japan's intentions under its program of the Greater Co-Prosperity Sphere within the Asian region. Progress toward discussion for independence improved after the visit of Japanese prime minister General Tojo to Manila, where he received a warm welcome.

A Preparatory Commission for Independence was therefore appointed, which proposed an independence Constitution. As the Constitution was framed, the election for a National Assembly was undertaken. These steps were similar to those taken before when the Commonwealth government was organized under the American era. Under wartime conditions of hurried political steps to be taken, the members of the National Assembly were chosen through local consultations. By October, the National Assembly convened to elect the president of the new, 'independent' republic. Jose P. Laurel, a former Justice of the Supreme Court and a member of the three-man ruling Executive Commission, was elected president.

An independent republic in name only was what the Japanese government had expected of the new leader. But Laurel was a wily politician: he avoided total subservience to Japanese wishes. He resisted a declaration of war by the Philippine government against the United States but allowed the signing of a treaty of alliance with Japan. By avoiding a declaration of war against the United States, a major demand Japan had wanted, Laurel avoided the consequence of conscripting Filipinos into the Japanese armed forces.

Under the Commission, two major institutions for social and political control were set up. One was an association of like-minded individuals that worked like a political party. The Kalibapi, as it was called (a local acronym), stood for a national association that promoted unity of purpose at the community level and up to town and national level. The Kalibapi was designed to foster community cohesiveness, yet it was also a means of monitoring political deviants at the local level. The members were activated as committed citizens for the group. In short, it served as a spy organization on citizens.

The other organization was the local police unit. An acronym for the name of a police group, the Makapili, designed to enforce domestic peace and order, was also created under the Commission government. Although under the local civilian government, it had to cooperate with the commands of the military administration in what was considered the peace-keeping operations with police powers. This was the equivalent of the national constabulary organization of the prewar days.

Both organizations and their activities carried over to the newly organized Republic. At the end of the war, those deeply associated with such organizations were brought under public scrutiny with the charge of collaboration with the enemy. During the occupation, they were instruments for keeping public order according to the wills of the occupiers.

As the years of the occupation wore on, the hold of Japan over the Philippine territory became weaker and more tenuous. As a result, its occupation policy became even harsher against the populace, especially as that related to its pursuit of the war objectives.

The decline of economic conditions[5] has been a major cause that weakened the Japanese hold on the country. For a country that was before in large part dependent on external trade to earn its wherewithal for its own needs, being cut off from international commerce made economic life more difficult. The country's means for earning exports were redirected toward meeting Japanese needs and the resupply of its war efforts.

Whatever was exported often depended on scrips for accounting the trade, and payments were not fulfilled. Scarcity and economic decline dominated the lives of the people, leading to hard domestic conditions for the population.

The weakening of Japanese control was also due to the growing strength of the guerrilla movement in the countryside. Not only was the prosecution of the war becoming more difficult for Japan, but the guerrillas were receiving strength from their own sporadic field victories and for being able to establish contact with the American military to help replenish their supplies. This happened in the major islands of Luzon and some Visayan islands where the guerrillas had built up their bases. The guerrillas were able to add to the destruction of military assets, including the operations of major businesses that had strategic values. They helped to paralyze some road networks and also mining operations.

Thus, transport routes, mining and commercial assets and other properties were damaged through wear and tear as the war progressed but also by skirmishes with the guerrillas that added to the destruction of property and infrastructure as the Japanese tried to hold ground in defensive position.

In the course of the war years of occupation, the unravelling or decline of the domestic economy was severe. Agriculture, industry and commerce declined. Facilities were destroyed. Existing productive capacities either went into neglect or were destroyed during a war. This decline of assets was aided by the scarcity of spare parts and the disappearance of supply lines for raw materials.

The extent of these efforts led to an easier war of liberation of the rural areas. Strategically, the Japanese military command decided to yield the countryside territory but not Manila. A last-ditch effort to defend Manila with their military forces would bring major destruction to urban private and government property. Manila was the second most battered city in the Second World War, next only to Warsaw, according to a postwar assessment made by the US military. The bombardment and destruction of Manila was the last stand of the Japanese military in the populated and largely modern government facilities and private residence areas of the city, especially south of the Pasig River. A collateral outcome of this was the untold human carnage inflicted upon the citizenry of a desperate army that faced almost certain death at the hands of a defending army facing destruction.

The war ended with the Philippines badly ravaged. Beyond the lives lost or changed forever, the experience of battles and conflagration added more economic damage towards the end of the war. The years of Japanese occupation brought about destruction of economic and human capital as the three years of occupation wore on.

Historians such as Teodoro Agoncillo recounted many florid anecdotes of the war. It is a challenge for historians (social, political and economic) to unravel the recorded history from extant historical records and data that could be pieced together. Such a history is yet to be written. For this occasion, what is undertaken is to provide a measure of the economic cost of the occupation seen as the damage to the productivity and output of the economy.

Wartime economic decline[6]

The output of the economic sectors and the standing capital stock of the economy – what could be measured directly – indicated how bad the situation had come to be by the end of the war.[7]

Take, first, the production of food. During the first crop year after the war, in 1946, the area under cultivation was sharply lower than the 1940 areas under cultivation, all across the food crop categories.

In fact, total areas under cultivation had not recovered even by 1949. The same story, but worse compared to food crops, was the situation of the export crops. The perennials among the export crops – coconut and abaca – did not fall in hectarage as food crops drastically. There was no replanting. And most of these plantations had been neglected to weeds and other jungle growth. Sugar cane hectarage suffered a catastrophic reduction. Nearly 90 per cent of the prewar hectarage was not planted in 1946, and recovery would not be total even by 1949.

The case of livestock and poultry indicated the reduction of meat supply during the war. The number of livestock suffered great reduction during the war. Total livestock was 37 per cent of the 1940 level. The people were forced to slaughter livestock during the war. The proportion of the diminution was worse for cattle and for hogs. But carabaos were 46 per cent of the prewar stock. By 1950, the livestock population was still 84 per cent of the prewar population.

In 1940, food produced domestically was in general insufficient for the population. Around 19 per cent of total imports represented additional food supply. Earnings from export prosperity increased the food budget for domestic consumption, supplementing the nation's diet.

During wartime, the country was reduced to self-reliance on the ever-dwindling supply of food. The per-capita figures for 1949 (when the population was 19.6 million, or already 3 million more than the prewar level of 16.6 million) showed that food production was still way below the 1940 levels, except in the case of corn.

It was not only food production that had been hit. The experience was endemic to all of agriculture. Worse, some sectors stopped production, like the mining industry.

The sectors that used to produce large surpluses for exports had all suffered enormous cuts in their earnings and in their output. Forced changes in asset ownership through confiscation of enemy property and destruction of standing assets and inventories of goods reduced much of the incentive for production at the onset of the war. Price controls – along with heavy penalties for transgressions – were in force, and these measures took a toll on the reduction of total output.

During the more than three years of occupation, the earnings of the export industries practically fell to nil. Under wartime occupation, exports of goods to Japan were undertaken mainly in the form of accounting prices, largely without hard revenues made in payment for them.

Total export trade before the war accounted for at least one quarter of total output. This trade fell precipitously by 1942 with the loss of shipping and of the markets of America that, before the war, accounted for more than 80 per cent of exports. By the last year of the war, foreign trade was inconsequential. Domestic output of all sectors fell as a result of the destruction of much capital equipment.

In 1940, total exports exceeded imports by about 36 million pesos ($18 million). During the prewar period, exports could finance all the imports with even a surplus to account for. Since all imports would be practically reduced and exports would practically disappear during the last years of the war, the economy's trading capacity was practically hobbled.

The economy's production capacity was quite low during the first full year of the postliberation period. For instance, during the 1945–1946 planting season, traditional exports of agricultural products were very low compared to the levels of 1940.

Centrifugal sugar production amounted only to 12,837 short tons from five active mills. By the next year, 1946–1947, when sixteen mills would have been rehabilitated to process sugar, output would rise only to 85,000 tons, only enough to begin to cover domestic demand for sugar. Abandoned sugar fields were made to remain idle except for the plots used to help in food production for survival.

Copra would have been plentiful, because the nuts of the huge standing trees in the islands would bear fruit unimpeded, but the sad state of the coconut mills and desiccated coconut mills would restrict output. Secondary growth and weeds ravaged the abaca plantations after their abandonment to the elements towards the end of the war. Mineral output practically stopped by the end of the occupation, as the mineral operations had stopped for want of shipping and for want of lubricating and fuel supply.

For the rest of the productive sectors of the economy, there was general decline on a massive level compared to the prewar economic activity. The state of capital equipment in existing prewar industries was very destitute, with much of the surviving equipment unable to run due to lack of lubricants and fuel.

The economy that Japan tried to transform to serve the latter's military objectives was unable to perform that task except minimally and with resistance. That all efforts were made to gear it for military production was made clear by the various efforts to take over vital industries. Confiscation and use of forced labor when necessary were instruments of undertaking economic recovery and pursuit of output objectives.

The open economy in 1940 of the Philippines enjoyed one of the highest standards of living in Southeast Asia. This economy was reduced to being dependent on its own productive capacity through the war years. It became largely a subsistence economy under complete autarky, with relatively unused or badly damaged capital stock. It was an economy forced to help sustain an occupying army and whose agriculture was inadequate to maintain the relatively large population because of the destruction or disuse of capital.

This author's reasoned guess from all this discussion is that, easily, after the first two years of war, total output had fallen by more than one half of the output before the war (1940). That was calculating up to the end of 1943. The fall in output continued as a result of additional destruction and measures undertaken by the military authorities. The year 1944 involved a further deterioration of output. With the additional destruction brought about by the war for liberation, a further decline of economic capacity took place. By the end of the war, the output by the beginning of 1945 was around 30 per cent of the level of the 1940 output. This meant a fall of output by around 70 per cent of the value measured in terms of the 1940 output level.

Wartime inflation[8]

The inflationary experience during the Japanese occupation from 1941 to 1945 was severe. No economic study, so far as is known, has been devoted to the wartime inflation of the Philippines, a topic of useful value to historians. There is a lot of anecdotal evidence, but the problem is to get a clear accounting of the inflation.

The prices of goods entering the price index before the war can be compared with the record of prices recorded on June 30, 1945. This was when price statistics began to be monitored officially again. This date was about two months after the liberation of Manila, while the war was still going on in the Pacific.

By this time, the legal tender had already been changed to the prewar money in use. Old pesos and Victory notes of the Commonwealth government, including US dollars, were already in wide circulation by then. The Japanese military peso notes had become without value.

The postwar peso was then exchanging at 2 pesos to the US dollar, the old prewar exchange parity. More important, civilian relief agencies sent by the liberating military forces from abroad had already been operating to distribute various food items to alleviate the hunger of the people. These had already caused price expectations to fall. Huge purchasing power had begun to be pumped in with the pay of the US military leading the way.

Most necessities (rice, charcoal, beef, chicken, bananas, cooking oil, salt and soap) were in the price multiples of 8 to 10 times the prewar 1940 prices. The overall basket of current household needs was 7.3 times the cost of the same prewar basket. Clothing and transportation were 10 times more.

The price inflation during the Japanese occupation was very severe. It was aggravated by the use of military notes to pay for war goods and requisitions that the Japanese military needed from the domestic economy. These military notes were decreed legal tender. Initially made equivalent nominally to the prewar peso, as the war progressed, the military peso notes practically disintegrated in value as the supply of printed money overwhelmed the available stock of goods.

Midway through the war, the military note became 30 pesos to the old peso. The Japanese military authorities used inflation as the engine of resource mobilization for the state. Inflation essentially taxes people whose incomes cannot catch up with prices. That basically causes income redistribution. Those who produced current goods with value for exchange – like food and other necessities – were able to extract higher prices for their goods. And people with limited purchasing power had to rely on their possessions by monetizing these in order to buy the goods that they needed.

Hartendorp's war account in his *History of Trade and Industry of the Philippines* of the Japanese times gave a partial indication of the levels to which prices of various necessities had risen, especially that of rice and other food items. Official prices that were decreed by the government gave an indirect clue to the adjustments made by the government as it faced the inflationary situation. As in most cases, such prices decreed by the government were unrealistic and hard to implement.

In early 1944, the government could decree that a sack of rice of 44 kilos could be sold at 80 pesos after distribution costs were taken into account. But with the disappearance of grain from the market, the government was forced almost as soon to fix the price of rice at a higher level – 200 pesos per cavan sack or 10 pesos a ganta (20 gantas to a cavan) or around 4.54 per kilo. These prices were far above the going price before the war when a ganta of rice cost 30 centavos (or 13.6 centavos per kilo).

Calculating the implied inflation rates from these data when set against the prewar base period gives a price index of 3,333 per cent for rice. At about the same time, the price for beef was 17 pesos per kilo (compared to the prewar price of 70 centavos). For sugar it was 30 pesos per kilo (compared to 12 centavos before the war). For a whole chicken, it was 18 pesos (compared to 1 peso before the war). Thus, the index price for beef at about this time was 2,429 percentage points compared to 100 in 1940; for sugar, 25,000 percentage points; and for chicken, 1,800 percentage points.

Times became even harder as greater uncertainties occurred. In the case of rice, prices further moved up to from 500 pesos per sack shortly before the bombings of Allied forces of military targets took place in Manila by six times, that is to 3,000 pesos per sack.

As Hartendorp put it (p. 139), 'The black market price of rice, which had still been 500 [pesos] a sack in May [1944] had risen to 3,000 [pesos] just before the bombing and jumped to 5,000 immediately after. Sugar, which had been selling at 30 a kilo, jumped to 70 pesos . . .'

These prices are translated into our price index calculations. The index price for rice moved to 8,333 percentage level compared to the prewar price base of 100 percentage points by the time the price of rice became 3,000 pesos per sack. This rose to 83,333 percentage points (relative to the same base) when the price of rice became 5,000 pesos per sack. For sugar, the corresponding price index was 58,333 percentage points when the price of sugar became 70 pesos per kilo.

Under these inflationary conditions, the turnover of trading transactions rose while the availability of newly produced goods fell. This is characteristic of inflationary times when output is swamped by uncertainty.

The release of the supply of food items became subject to extreme speculation on stocks kept awaiting further price increases. Few tradeables from new output were available. Instead, much of the trading came from the inventory of personal wealth accumulated by people in earlier times.

To avoid hunger, the consumption exigency of the times forced families to liquidate these assets in exchange for current goods. This consisted of personal belongings, economic assets of the rich and middle class in exchange for the opportunity to buy necessities. In such a setting, a great deal of income redistribution happened. Inflation took care of that.

Indirect information from currency that was put in circulation during the period further helps to substantiate the severity of the inflationary experience. In 1940, the amount of money in circulation was 200 million pesos. By the end of 1946 (one and a half years after June, 1945), normalcy of the postwar was being anticipated, and money in circulation was 889 million pesos.

The transaction demand at a lower level of output was nearly five times higher than in 1941. The estimate of Japanese war notes circulated in Manila during the three years of occupation was between 6,623 million and 11,148 million pesos.

The note issues were relatively moderate, at around 9 million to 10 million pesos per month during the first three months of the occupation. But these monthly issues increased to 16 million per month as prices rose and as the military authorities had to extract more output and resources from the economy.

By the end of 1942, the note issues amounted to 144 million pesos. By December 1943, note issues had cumulated to 480 million. The next year, by December 1944, the amount of notes in circulation had reached 1,000 million pesos.

The debasement of the currency continued with further note issues as inflation fed upon additional note issues. The note issue in the month of February 1945 was 1,300 million pesos. By July 1945, the total notes in circulation reached the peak of 11,148 million pesos.

This supply of currency abetted the rapid loss of value of the peso and the huge inflationary experience. Thus, taking the upper and lower range of these estimates, the amount of pesos in circulation at the height of the Japanese occupation was between 55.7 and 33.1 times the amount of money normally maintained during prewar days for monetary supply management. And yet, as this study has now made clear, the amount of output had continued to decline.

During this period, the banking sector had become less functional as people depended more and more on cash in order to transact their business on a daily basis. As a result, the demand for liquidity was very high.

Personal assets were sold for rapidly changing value in cash or were directly bartered for other useful commodities. When the currency had been debased, only actual goods become a guarantee of value. This was the valuation framework during the later months of 1944 when uncertainty was high and people were essentially awash with paper money of little value.

The world war damage in today's economic values

An important exercise to close this chapter is to assess the damage of the Philippine wartime occupation period. This is done utilizing the current values for the year 2003, the year when the estimates for the damage were constructed.[9]

To achieve this calculation, the estimates of competent bodies were first undertaken. Such numbers begin with valuation of the destruction of capital goods and loss of private and public wealth at the end of the war.

The Philippine Commonwealth government (shortly before independence in 1946) undertook a survey of the damage and arrived at an amount of 1.2 billion US dollars. Later, during the early 1950s, the Philippine government also produced another set of calculations in line with the reparations treaty negotiations with Japan that were even larger in magnitude.

The United States government, through its government-owned War Damage Corporation, sent a mission to the Philippines to assess the war damage soon after the war. It undertook many surveys, block by block, of various regions of the country from province to province and including Manila. Based on sample reports that it received, photographs, and reports from local officials, the total estimate amounted to 708 million dollars. By regions of the country, such estimated damage adds up to a total amount of US 798 million dollars.

These estimates were calculated in terms of dollar values. In 1940, the US dollar had a much higher multiple value in terms of purchasing power compared to today's US dollar. In the context of sixty years ago, such damage was staggering. The dollar of 1940 is worth at least 15 times in current terms. The US estimates of war damage are used for expediency, ignoring other estimates of war damage established as basis for negotiations of war reparations.

Converting the corresponding values to current period dollars therefore, the losses would need to be multiplied by at least a factor of 15. This would mean something like 10.6 billion US dollars of 2003. Thus converting these into current 2003 pesos at 55 pesos to the dollar (for 2003), this amounts to 584.1 billion pesos (= 708 × 15 × 55) or over half of a trillion pesos. These are staggering numbers even when viewed in terms of relatively inflated current pesos. In terms of the 4.4 trillion pesos GDP (gross domestic product) in year 2003, this economic damage accounts to around 13.2 percent of GDP in current terms.

The estimates of output that were used for 1940 were simply based on indexes of output constructed after the war by the national income accountants. These estimates were rebased for purposes of this study. Lacking the level of the GDP estimates in 1940, it is still to arrive at some rough estimates of the value of the damage on the basis of reasonable assumptions. The idea is to gear the estimates of the war damage to the total output for the year 1940, the benchmark used to compare wartime with prewar times.

The GDP of 1940 per head was definitely somewhat lower than the GDP per head of 2003. It would be easier then to make an assumption that there had been no increase in GDP per head. Not only does this lead to a conservative assumption about the initial year GDP, 1940. But it leads to simpler arithmetic. For the output of 2003 can be assumed to be a fixed scale of the population increase.

The population of 2003, which is about 80 million Filipinos, is 4.27 times the population of 1940. Then, the denominator comprising the current 2003 GDP (as used in the measure above) would be simply 4.27 times the level of GDP in 1940. Thus, GDP of 2003 would have to be divided by 4.27 to calculate the implied value of the current GDP of 1940 (in terms of 2003 values).

The result of that calculation is an estimate of total war damage being equivalent to 64.1% of GDP of 1940. This is an overestimate because of the conservative assumption of no increase in per capita output. The denominator, of GDP of 1940, would be higher than the actual GDP of 1940 when relative per capita growth of output is taken into account.

Working backwards from 2003, the GDP of 1940 would then be somewhat smaller, to take into account the additional growth in per capita output. In short, the war damage level could have been more than 64% of GDP.

Given this estimate a little further in terms of actual drop of total output resulting from the economic damage in order to extend the economic reasoning to a fuller conclusion, the more important question arises: What was the effect of the loss of capital on total output?

Making the conservative assumption that the economy's capital output ratio during the period under study was equivalent to 2 (an estimate that says that two units of capital would help produce one unit of output). This is a realistic if not conservative assumption, given the relative stage of economic development at the time.

This assumption is needed to arrive at the projection of output loss or contraction arising from the loss of capital in the economy. By taking the upper limit of 64% of economic damage ratio to the GDP of 1940, as calculated, for every year when output would have been theoretically measured, the decrease in output would be roughly equivalent to a reduction of output of 32% of GDP. (The calculation is to halve the ratio of damage to GDP as estimated.)

This result is somewhat higher than the estimate of output capacity by the end of the war. However, it should be remembered that this is a conservative assumption. A less conservative assumption would lead to higher output fall. Moreover, the cumulative level of capital destruction by the end of the war could have caused that drop of output as suggested – the level of GDP by 1945 being only around 30 per cent of that obtaining in 1940.

From the discussion of this chapter, however, it is known that the economic damage of the war was not imposed on the nation or on the capital stock in a single shot. It happened incrementally over the years of the war. The largest initial damage took place at the beginning – the first year of the war – when hostilities began. But throughout the period of the war, there was a progressive decline of output because of the continued decline of the capital stock – through wear and tear and additional destruction of capital.

Now, to summarize. By using intuitive knowledge based on the review of the estimates of damage and output, it was possible to undertake some qualitative and quantitative assessments of the economic effects of the Japanese occupation.

Using conservative assumptions about economics on capital stock and physical facilities by the end of the war (1945), the level of national output fell to about 30 per cent of the level of the prewar output. Another way of saying this was that 70 per cent of total output level of 1940 had disappeared by the end of the war in 1945.

It is now possible to estimate the war damage in current 2003 terms. It is to be emphasized that this is only the economic loss (excluding the value of human loss, of course). War always has an infinite cost when counting human loss. When the war damage is translated in terms of a percentage of GDP, the amount comes to around 13 per cent of the (current) GDP of 2003. This is not as small as it looks.

In 2003, the Philippine economy is much more developed, with a vaster accumulation of capital and physical wealth in place. By then, the country's population at more than 80 million was more than four times that of the population in 1940. Moreover, the current GDP of the country is also much larger.

Notes

1 During a vacation trip to Washington, DC, in 2002 and while reading related books on his country at the reading room of the US Library of Congress, the author made an accidental discovery of a declassified paper put out by the United States intelligence community: United States Foreign Economic Administration (FEA, 1944), *Economic Changes in the Philippines During Two Years of Japanese Occupation*, August 1944. This led the author to write a discussion paper that was widely circulated in the Philippines but not published. (The author, who was busy with other work, forgot to follow through the request of the Philippine Historical Commission to have it published.) That paper explored the economic changes during the Japanese occupation, dealing with broader issues and, in particular, estimating the impact on total output immediately after the war. See G. P. Sicat, *The Philippine Economy During the Japanese Occupation, 1941–1945* (University of the Philippines School of Economics, Discussion Paper No. 0307, November 2003). This chapter is an abridged rendition of that work.
2 Subsequent research of the author led to further research on the period of materials found in the Philippines, utilizing the resources of the Main Library of the University of the Philippines, especially its Filipiniana section, and of the UP School of Economics Library.
3 The comprehensive study of the American colonial period which is helpful in understanding the strong relationship of the Philippines and the United States at the outbreak of the war in the Pacific is F. H. Golay, *Face of Empire: United States – Philippine Relations, 1898–1946*, Quezon City: Ateneo University Press, 1997 (published in cooperation with the University of Wisconsin–Madison, Center for Southeast Asian Studies). On economic history in general, see O. D. Corpuz, *An*

Economic History of the Philippines, Quezon City, University of the Philippines Press, 1997.

4 The two-volume work of historian T.A. Agoncillo, *The Fateful Years. Japan's Adventure in the Philippines, 1941–45*, Quezon City: University of the Philippines Press, 2001, is the most widely read Philippine account of the Japanese occupation period. This book contains a discussion of the chronology of the military administration and the political events leading to the end of the occupation period. A more recent work that represents a joint effort of Japanese and Filipino scholars is I. Setsuho/R.T. Jose (eds.), *The Philippines Under Japan. Occupation Policy and Reaction*, Quezon City: Ateneo University Press, 1999. Of particular interest to this chapter are the essays of Ikehata Setsuho (introduction and chapter 4: 'Mining Industry Development and Local Anti-Japanese Resistance'), Nagano Yoshiko (chapter 5: 'Cotton Production under Japanese Rule, 1942–1945') and Ricardo Trota (chapter 6: 'The Rice Shortage and Countermeasures during the Occupation').

5 Though the economic decline was evident from the accounts of Agoncillo, *The Fateful Years*, the detailed evidence was reported in the observations derived from the document cited in footnote 1: United States, Foreign Economic Administration (FEA, 1944), Special Areas Branch, Far East Enemy Division, *Economic Changes in the Philippines During Two Years of Japanese Occupation*, August, 1944. This document tried to pull together sensitive military intelligence at the time and was monitored and centrally analysed by the US military. The report had 119 footnotes to substantiate the claims made. Most of the sources were from foreign broadcasts monitored by the US military intelligence. It is difficult today to check these sources except for those based on printed materials; for instance, the US government published *Journal of Commerce*, the *Wall Street Journal*. An independent but postwar document summarizing some of the overall and sector damage is contained in A.V. Castillo, 'Economic Reconstruction Problems in the Philippines', Philippine Council, Institute of Pacific Relations, Manila, Philippine Paper No. 1. Mimeo, 1946 [Paper presented by the Philippine Council of the Institute of Pacific Relations for the 10th Conference of the Institute of Pacific Relations held at Stratford-upon-Avon, England, September, 1947.] Castillo was then a Philippine commonwealth government employee.

6 See on the long-run economic development: R.W. Hooley, 'Long Term Growth of the Philippine Economy, 1902–1961', *Philippine Economic Journal*, 1968, vol. 7, pp. 1–24; G.P. Sicat, 'On the Measurement of Long Term Output', *Philippine Economic Journal*, 1968, vol. 7, pp. 25–41.

7 Most of the accounts of war damage and decline in output were piecemeal, but they could be deduced from the reports of the US High Commissioner, the highest government official in the Philippines just before independence. The last two years of the reports summarized many aspects of the assessment of war destruction and economic damage on property. See United States, *Seventh and Final Report of the United States High Commissioner to the Philippine Islands, covering September 14, 1945 to July 4, 1946*, Washington, DC: US Government Printing Office, 1947; and United States, *Sixth Annual Report of the United States High Commissioner to the Philippine Islands, covering FY July 1, 1941 to June 30, 1942*, Washington, DC: US Government Printing Office, 1943. Finally, another valuable report on postwar economic conditions and assessment of the development problems was contained in United States, *Report to the President of the United States by Economic Survey Mission to the Philippines (1950)*, otherwise known as the Bell Mission Report (Government Printing Office, Washington, DC). The paper by Andres V. Castillo, cited in footnote 3, summarizes a Philippine government assessment of the problems at the time of independence in 1946.

8 A.V.H. Hartendorp, *Short History of Industry and Trade of the Philippines from Pre-Spanish Times to the End of the Roxas Administration*, Manila: American Chamber of Commerce of the Philippines Inc., 1953 (this first volume became volume 1 of an extended book). Hartendorp's account is graphic and journalistic, but he reproduced many useful statistical numbers that were taken from government reports of the period. Some of the official accounts of prices after the war can be gleaned from the statistical tables reproduced in the last report of the US High Commissioner (op. cit.).

9 The author benefited from the various studies of national income estimation during the 1950s in undertaking these estimates. The most important references for such estimates come from the use of baseline statistics from the 1938 census. The Cornell studies of F. H. Golay, *Philippines: Public Policy and National Economic Development*, Ithaca, NY: Cornell University Press, 1961. Frank Golay's work relied on early statistical work undertaken under his supervision that was useful in providing statistical anchors for his assessment of income growth immediately after the war. See M. E. Goodstein, *The Pace and Pattern of Philippine Economic Growth: 1938, 1948 and 1956*, Ithaca, NY: Southeast Asia Program, Department of Asian Studies, Cornell University, 1962 (mimeographed).

15 The eclipse of the Indonesian economy under Japanese occupation

J. Thomas Lindblad

The three and a half years of Japanese occupation formed a highly traumatic experience for most if not all inhabitants of the Indonesian archipelago. Yet in Indonesian historiography, the Japanese occupation does not only stand out because of the hardship it brought but also because it accelerated decolonization and made independence inevitable. The Indonesian Revolution, four and a half years of armed struggle against the Dutch wishing to restore colonial rule, became the logical sequel to the Japanese occupation. Much has been written on the important political ramifications of the Japanese rule of the archipelago and far less so about the economic consequences, apart from the general observation that the economy took a sharp downturn during these years of acute disruption. This contribution seeks to shed some light on the economic aspect of the Japanese occupation by discussing a number of themes that may lend themselves to international comparisons.

A major bottleneck when writing on the Indonesian economy between March 1942 and August 1945 is the extreme lack of data, in particular statistics. The Dutch colonial administration was dysfunctional, an Indonesian administration had not yet been established and the information collected by the Japanese armed forces has been either lost or remains inaccessible. By necessity, this chapter therefore relies on piecemeal and incomplete evidence.[1]

The following five themes are discussed: the economic framework of occupation, appropriation of economic resources by the Japanese, economic institutions, resource transfers (including labour) and the final verdict on what the Japanese occupation meant to the Indonesian economy.

Economic framework

The Japanese had played a role in colonial Indonesia well ahead of the Pacific War. By by-passing European traders and cooperating directly with Chinese and indigenous traders, Japanese businessmen secured a strong position in imports of consumer goods into Java, in particular textiles, whilst also on occasion acting as pioneers in the forestry industry, notably in East Kalimantan.[2] In the early 1930s, the double impact of a cheap yen and reduced purchasing power among consumers bolstered imports from Japan, and in 1934, one third of all Indonesian imports had originated in Japan. The Netherlands Indies government responded with protectionist policies, discriminating against Japanese goods; by 1937, the share of Japan in total imports was down to 15 per cent.[3] In 1939, there were about 6,500 Japanese nationals living in colonial Indonesia.

Access to Indonesian oil was of crucial importance to the Japanese war effort. Tarakan and Balikpapan in Kalimantan were attacked at an early stage, on 10 and 23 January 1942, respectively; Palembang in South Sumatra followed on 14 February. On 8 March, the Dutch capitulated in the aftermath of defeat in the Battle in the Java Sea. Casualties during the invasion amounted to 2,500 Dutchmen and Indonesians and 845 Japanese soldiers, whereas more than 42,000 prisoners of war were taken into custody by the Japanese, of whom at least one fifth did not survive.[4]

The occupied archipelago was split into three parts: Sumatra under the 25th Japanese army (administered in conjunction with the Malay peninsula), Java and Madura under the 16th Japanese army and Kalimantan, Sulawesi and all islands of East Indonesia under the second southern army and the Japanese navy. A rigorous Nipponization immediately took place. The Japanese calendar was applied, with the year 1942 becoming 2602, and so on. Tokyo time was used, one and a half hours ahead. Strict reverence to the Japanese was enforced, including compulsory bows in the direction of Tokyo. The Dutch colonial administration was disbanded and all manifestations of Dutch culture, including language, were banned from public life. Some 100,000 European civilians, mostly Dutchmen, were interned, whereas another 160,000 persons of mixed European and Asian descent stayed outside the camps but met with considerable hardship because of their loyalty to the Dutch.

The Japanese authorities promulgated the change of regime as the 'Greater East Asia Co-Prosperity Sphere', a great future for Asians in the absence of European colonialism. To enlist Indonesian support, a propaganda campaign was launched labelled *Tiga A* ('Three As'), which stood for 'Asia tjahaja [light], Asia pelindoeng [protection], Asia pemimpin [leadership]'. The campaign did not catch on and was discontinued in October 1942. The entire Indonesian society was infiltrated, to the most local level of neighbourhood community (*tonarigumi*). This institution has, as it happens, survived to this very day under the designation RT (*Rukun Tangga* ['Association of Neighbours']).[5] All opposition to Japanese rule was ruthlessly crushed by the secret police, *Kempeitai*, which made liberal use of local informers in the population.[6]

Initial Indonesian reactions were mixed, to the shock and dismay of many Dutchmen. Some greeted the Japanese as liberators from Dutch colonialism, setting up 'Freedom' committees. From the start, indigenous Indonesians participated in the administration of the occupied territory.[7] In late 1942, the *Tiga A* campaign was succeeded by an organization of cooperation, called Poetera (*Poesat Tenaga Rakyat*, 'Centre of People's Power'), governed by a council consisting of an even number of Japanese and Indonesians. Leading figures in the Indonesian nationalist movement took an active part, with Sukarno serving as chairman and Hatta as vice chairman, both men intending to use the Japanese in their fight against Dutch colonialism. In January 1943, the Japanese set up an Indonesian militia, PETA (*Pembela Tanah Air*, '[Volunteer] Army for Defence of the Fatherland'), that eventually gathered 36,000 Indonesians and later was to play a prominent part in the struggle against the Dutch during the Indonesian Revolution. Numerous Indonesians were recruited as unarmed volunteer soldiers (*heiho*) and as members of the auxiliary police (*Keibodan*) or the new youth labour organization (*Seinendan*).[8]

Collaboration by indigenous Indonesians with the Japanese has traditionally been viewed in the context of the struggle for independence. Very few Indonesian organizations were involved in resistance against the Japanese. Notable exceptions to the rule were the Indonesian communists and the Sjahrir group, named after the moderate nationalist leader Soetan Sjahrir, who alienated himself from Sukarno during the war (but curiously not from Hatta) and who served as Indonesia's first prime minister after independence in 1945. Virtually all other recorded resistance was undertaken by Dutchmen and Eurasians. One of the most spectacular cases was a group under leadership of the Dutch colonel R. T. Overakker in Sumatra. The group was ruthlessly crushed by the Japanese armed forces, and Overakker himself was executed.[9]

Appropriation of resources

Outright plundering did not occur on a large scale immediately upon arrival by the Japanese armed forces, as the Japanese were eager to capitalize on the initial goodwill in large segments of Indonesian society. Dutch-controlled economic resources, however, were rapidly claimed. All Western banks, including the four Dutch ones, were taken over in the first few days of occupation. Cash worth 52 million guilders ($19.6 million) was confiscated, most of which was subsequently paid out as liquidation payments to Indonesian, Chinese and Arab creditors. Interestingly, however, all shares held by the banks were left untouched.[10] Estates with non-Indonesian owners were expropriated without compensation and placed under direct command of the Japanese armed forces. While awaiting the arrival of Japanese supervisors, the estates were managed by either senior Indonesian staff or Dutchmen, some of whom even had to be fetched from internment camps.[11] In May 1942, the Dutch leading trading concerns, which before the invasion had handled the largest slice of international imports, were forced to surrender all stocks.

Appropriation of property held by Dutchmen and Indonesians of mixed descent increased as the occupation deepened. Large amounts of cash and goods were simply stolen from government offices, business firms and private individuals. An estimate for the entire period of the occupation goes as far as to a total of 143 million guilders ($54 million), which could only be designated as 'theft on a vast scale'. In addition, the Japanese attempted to squeeze as much profit as possible from these categories of residents. Heavy taxes were levied in April as well as in July 1942, but it does not seem likely that the Japanese armed forces were capable of actually collecting much of these taxes, especially not in cases when the persons liable to payment were held in custody in camps.[12]

Some takeovers were of immediate relevance to the Japanese war effort. This includes the oil installations, the banks and arguably also the agricultural estates, especially those producing rubber. The same does not hold true for assets of small business firms or government agencies, let alone private property owned by individuals.

Economic institutions

The ulterior aim of the Japanese occupation of Southeast Asia had been secretly laid down at a cabinet meeting in Tokyo in November 1941. The aim was simply a maximal economic contribution to the Japanese war effort, regardless of consequences for the civilian population. This aim was reiterated in a document dated 14 March 1942 titled 'Principles governing the administration of occupied Southern areas'. In Java, all enemy-held property was entrusted to the *Gunseikanbu* (Military Administrator's Office), a complex of offices within the 16th Japanese army, containing separate departments for each sector of the economy.[13] These departments were closely together with private Japanese companies, the well-known *zaibatsu*, now entering occupied territory in large numbers. In total, some 600 *zaibatsu* were involved in the execution of policies formulated by the *Gunseikanbu*.[14] New types of business corporations, so-called *kumiai*, were introduced after Japanese model in order to further cooperation between private Japanese businessmen and enterprising indigenous Indonesians. Protests from Indonesian nationalists about an uneven distribution of sacrifices and benefits had little effect.

Money supply was altered as the Netherlands Indies guilder was replaced by the Japanese yen at an exchange rate highly favourable to the Japanese. In October 1942, the rate was one yen per guilder instead of the prewar one, 44 cents to the guilder. Continuous huge demands for cash prompted the Japanese authorities to expand money supply by printing money. It is estimated that the money supply rose sevenfold in the course of the occupation. This led to rapid inflation and a growing black market.[15]

After the early seizure of foreign-owned banks, the entire financial sector came under control of three Japanese banks, the Yokohama Specie Bank, the Bank of Taiwan and the Mitsui Bank. Central bank functions, in particular the issue of money, were handled at first by the Yokohama Specie Bank in Java and Sumatra and the Bank of Taiwan elsewhere. In April 1943, all such capacities were moved to the *Nanpo Kaihatsu Kinko* (Southern Development Bank), which had been created one year earlier. This institution eventually accumulated very large funds.[16] Interestingly, the major banking institution that in the colonial period had catered to the needs of small-scale indigenous clients, the AVB (*Algemeene Volkscredietbank*, People's Credit Bank), was permitted to continue operations, but under a new name, *Syomin Ginko*.

The large agricultural sector producing for world markets had been of paramount importance in the preceding colonial economy. The Netherlands Indies counted among the world's chief producers of cane sugar and natural rubber, whilst also figuring as a major supplier of tobacco, copra, coffee and tea and palm oil and even enjoying a near-monopoly in quinchona, a small-scale production line vital for the combatting of malaria.[17] Logically, the Japanese occupation forces gave much attention to control and management of the several thousand agricultural estates scattered throughout Java and Sumatra in particular. Separate organizational structures were designed for rubber, sugar and the other agricultural commodities.

Rubber was one of the essential inputs in the Japanese war economy, providing tyres for all vehicles. Estates and smallholder units in Sumatra were brought under supervision of the newly founded Singapore Rubber Association, a joint supervisory body for Sumatra and Malaya within the 25th Japanese army. Strict military control was exercised up to the end of the war.[18]

In 1942, there were eighty-five sugar factories in Central and East Java. Production was managed by a new body, *Sato Renggokai* (Java Sugar Association), whereas distribution was organized by the Surabaya Sugar Sale Union replacing the preceding Dutch-led sales organization. In November 1942, the estates were transferred to six private Japanese companies: *Dai Nippon Seito*, *Taiwan Seito*, *Meiji Seito*, *Ensuiko Seito*, *Nanyo Kobatsu* and *Okinawa Seito*, each being allotted with sugar factories that had had the same owner before the war.[19]

All other branches of export agriculture in Java were concentrated under the authority of the SKKK (*Saibai Kigyô Kanri Kôdan*, Public Corporation for Management of Cultivation Enterprises), acting as an intermediary between the 16th Japanese army and individual estates. In June 1943, the SKKK was replaced by the SKK (*Saibai Kigyô Kôdan*, Public Corporation of Cultivation Enterprises), which was set up to smooth the transition of the estates to private Japanese companies yet to arrive. One year later, the SKK in turn was replaced by a federation of Japanese estate-owning firms, which then incorporated also the six proprietors of sugar factories.[20] An attempt to cultivate cotton in Java in support of the local textile industry failed dismally.

Mining had, together with export agriculture, provided a solid basis for economic expansion in the prewar era. Indonesia was the only large-scale producer of petroleum in Southeast and East Asia and had emerged as one of the world's foremost suppliers of tin, whereas coal was produced for domestic consumption, especially in interisland shipping within the archipelago. The oil fields in East Kalimantan and South Sumatra came under direct command of the armed forces. Operations were only temporarily slowed down by the scorched-earth tactics deployed by the Dutch in the face of the approaching Japanese forces.[21] Other mining production was entrusted to renowned Japanese concerns. Mitsubishi took charge of the tin mines in Bangka and Belitung, Mitsui was responsible for coal mining in West Sumatra, Banten in West Java and East Kalimantan, Sumitomo got the nickel mining in Sulawesi and diamond cutting in South Kalimantan ended up with Nomura.[22]

Not much had been accomplished in terms of industrialization in the Netherlands Indies before the war, partly as a result of lobbying by exporters in the Netherlands not keen on competition in the colonial market. Estimates of the contribution of manufacturing towards GDP (gross domestic product) by 1940 vary between 12 and 20 per cent.[23] Priorities changed with the Japanese occupation since all manufactured goods that could not be produced domestically would have to be imported from Japan, but available shipping capacity was increasingly needed for military transport. Already in 1942, various attempts were made to set up domestic manufacturing plants in Java, but most failed for shortage of intermediary goods and components. In November 1942, a coordinating body was created in Bandung, *Balai Pengoeroes Peroesahaan Tenoen Priangan Shu* (Office for Management of Textile Companies in Priangan Region), but results remained disappointing.[24] Ambitious plans were drawn up for shipyards expected to deliver more than 900 vessels, measuring 138,000 tons, but scarcely more than 400 were actually produced.[25]

Attempts to stimulate the manufacturing sector were reinforced from 1943. This served the double purpose of reducing demand on limited shipping capacity to Japan and a means of preparation for a possible Allied landing in the archipelago.[26] Self-sufficiency at all levels of administration became top priority, but, again, results were highly disappointing. In 1944, for instance, the local textile industry in the Bandung area was deprived of much of its mechanical equipment when it was claimed by the armed forces; production came to a virtual standstill.[27]

The institutional apparatus created by the Japanese occupation authorities to manage the Indonesian economy was, in short, elaborate and ambitious, often combining coordination from above with direct participation by private Japanese firms. There was, at any rate throughout 1942 and 1943, little room for activities undertaken by enterprising Indonesians. In 1944, however, the Japanese authorities, all of a sudden, it seems, became aware of the weakness of local entrepreneurship, especially in Java. A committee was set up by the *Gunseikanbu* that in July and September 1944 presented several recommendations, such as assigning management of enemy-owned estates to qualified Indonesians or helping them set up rubber-processing plants and home industry. Nationalist Indonesian economists were invited to participate. Ali Sastroamidjojo, the later prime minister, headed the *Kantor Perekonomian Rakjat* (Office for People's Economy), established in August 1944. A selection committee targeting Indonesians aspiring to become managers of estates followed in May 1945 with Hatta as its chairman. Training facilities were envisaged.[28] But it was too late in the day for these initiatives to have much effect before the occupation was over.

Resource transfers

The leading principle of utilization of economic resources during the Japanese occupation of Indonesia was to meet military needs first, civilian needs second. The aim, laid down in a conference between cabinet ministers and the military leadership in Tokyo in November 1941 and reiterated within days of the invasion, was to 'promote acquisition and development of resources vital to national defence', with the important corollary that 'If the acquisition of resources vital to national defence and the aim of making the troops self-sufficient adversely affect the standard of living of the indigenous people, this must be accepted'.[29] The transfer of resources in response to military requirements pervaded the entire Indonesian society, including labour participation, and had far-reaching consequences for the standards of living of millions of people.

The production of petroleum, rubber and coal was strongly geared towards military use. Large quantities of petroleum were shipped to Japan: 1.6 million tons in fiscal year 1942/43, 2.1 million tons in 1943/44, but nothing at all in the final year of the Pacific War as Allied war ships controlled the routes to Japan.[30] These figures need to be compared with the estimated total need of oil for the Japanese war effort during one year, 7.9 million tons, which happened to coincide with total prewar capacity of the Indonesian oil industry. Oil deliveries to the Japanese military forces were far below expectations and requirements of the Japanese military. Rubber similarly became a bottleneck as total production declined at an alarming rate, eventually, in 1944, corresponding to only 25 per cent of the prewar level. The situation, from the point of view of the Japanese armed forces, was not much better in the supply of coal, necessary for both military and civilian shipping. Output at the chief coal mine, the Ombilin mine in West Sumatra, fell from 230,000 tons in 1942 to 73,000 tons in 1944 and even less in 1945.[31] These bottlenecks in the provision of the military inevitably resulted in serious shortages for the civilian population.

A rather curious instance of transferring resources was an attempt to convert sugar factories into distilleries of butane. It was not very successful, and again, total output in the sector dropped every year. The sugar harvest in 1943 delivered 680,000 tons, scarcely more than one half as compared to 1942. By 1945, output was down at less than 100,000 tons, with few sugar factories still in operation for their original purpose. Much sugar was requisitioned by the armed forces for delivery to units in other parts of Southeast Asia. In the course of the Japanese occupation, sugar was becoming an extremely scarce good.[32]

The most serious consequences for ordinary people of the changes in resource use occurred in food supplies, especially provisions of the main staple food, rice. In October 1943, a system of local self-sufficiency was introduced, again in preparation of guerrilla warfare in case of an Allied landing, which by that time no longer appeared entirely unrealistic. Farmers were forced to deliver paddy to the authorities at unrealistically high targets of the next harvest, rice shortage areas were not in a position to replenish supplies and rice surplus areas could not send excess quantities to other regions. Rationing of rice applied in urban areas. The result was a huge black market with rapidly rising prices and acute shortages.[33]

Total rice production had been about 8.3 million tons in 1942, which was barely sufficient to feed a population of 66 million people, inclined to eat rice three times a day. The harvest of 1943 was slightly less, 8.1 million, but a prolonged drought in 1944 caused a critical situation. Total production fell to 6.9 million tons, which under no circumstances would have been sufficient for the entire civilian population. A further drop in 1945, to 5.6 million tons, signalled the danger of famine in certain areas where local rice production was insufficient and stocks could not be replenished from elsewhere.

A key element in the Japanese restructuring of the economy concerned the mobilization of labour. The system of coolie labour was retained from the colonial period with low wages and few rights but heavy obligations for workers. In Java, wages at only 50 cents were common. Remuneration was slightly better in North Sumatra, 60 to 80 cents per day.[34] This may be compared to the standard wage of 40 to 45 cents per day paid to contract coolies at rubber and tobacco estates in Sumatra during the 1920s and 1930s.[35] However, we must not overlook that wartime inflation during the Japanese occupation reduced the purchasing power of wages at the prewar standard.

Forced labour was, it appears, first tried out in Aceh, where at an early stage of the occupation, all men between 16 and 26 years of age were requested to work two weeks per month without pay for the Japanese; no show carried a twenty-year prison sentence. Acehnese rulers were forced to act as intermediaries in mobilizing the labourers.[36] It is likely that similar schemes were applied elsewhere in the archipelago as well, but the Aceh case is the one best documented and therefore best known.

The most infamous and most thoroughly despised system of forced labour was that of *romusha* ('work soldier'). It was launched in late 1942 and early 1943 with youngsters from Java being sent to work on the construction of the Pekan Baru railway across Sumatra. Horrifying accounts are given about schoolboys of 14 or 15 years of age, virtually kidnapped in the streets of Yogyakarta and brought to work under extraordinarily harsh conditions in Sumatra.[37] The system was expanding fast, and by November 1944, it is estimated that 2.6 million Javanese were working as *romusha*, the majority remaining in Java.[38] Accounting for a relatively rapid turnover, it is likely that as many as one half of the able-bodied male population in Java and Madura was at some stage forced to work as *romusha*.[39]

The worst plight was for those Javanese who were shipped to Sumatra and other islands outside Java. Almost 300,000 Javanese left Java to work as *romusha* elsewhere in the archipelago; only 77,000 ever returned.[40] This large-scale system of brutal, forced labour in the occupied territory could not possibly have been executed without the assistance of indigenous Indonesian leaders. It is a memory of lasting embarrassment that Sukarno at one time, in September 1944, lent himself to actively making propaganda for work as *romusha*.

Most changes in the use of economic resources were planned by the Japanese authorities, but some were not. The occupation did open up possibilities for enterprising indigenous Indonesian businessmen, especially traders in Sumatra. One of the foremost examples was Agoes Moesin Dasaad, originally from Lampung, who before the war had succeeded in breaking the Chinese monopoly in the import of Japanese textiles. He had good contacts with Japanese business and was very soon after the invasion put in a position to acquire the largest textile factory in Indonesia, Kantjil Mas near Pasuruan, East Java, which had been seized by the Dutch authorities shortly before the invasion, as it had German owners. During the occupation, Dasaad quickly expanded his trading activities. He was advisor to the *Persatoean Perniagaan Indonesia* (Association for Indonesian Commerce), an organization set up in 1944 to further indigenous Indonesian entrepreneurship. In May 1944, Dasaad figured as spokesman for Javanese businessmen who allegedly were prepared to make donations for the purchase of airplanes for both the Japanese Air Force and PETA. Another example was the brothers Achmad and Abujamin Bakrie, also from Lampung and trading under the Japanese-sounding label *Yasuma Shokai*. Bakrie & Bros. was eventually to develop into one of the most successful indigenous conglomerates in Indonesia. Others include Soelaiman Djohan and Perpatih Djohor from West Sumatra (related to Hatta) and the Javanese Raden Mas Soedarmo, who began a rope and sack factory near Jakarta.[41]

Final verdict

Due to the acute shortage of data, it is very difficult to ascertain what the precise economic impact of the Japanese occupation in Indonesia was, apart from the fairly obvious observation that those three and a half years of integration into the Japanese war effort meant a profound disruption of economic life and extreme hardship for most inhabitants of the archipelago. Initial estimates by Pierre van der Eng of long-term developments of national income in Indonesia suggested that GDP during the Japanese occupation fell to less than one half of the pre war level.[42] Acknowledging that these projections were merely wild guesses, subsequently publications wisely leave blanks for the years 1942 through 1945 when portraying the development of Indonesia's GDP over time.[43]

Some inferences can be made from a comparison between GDP immediately before and immediately after the Japanese occupation. According to estimates by Van der Eng, total GDP declined by one third between 1941 and 1949. In 1941, per-capita GDP amounted to Rp 329,000 (expressed in the prices of 1983). Only in 1971 was Indonesia to return to that average level per person.[44] The years of the Indonesian Revolution (1945–1949) represented continued economic stagnation, but growth was resumed upon the transfer of sovereignty. The early and mid-1950s saw an estimated growth of per-capita GDP at about 3 per cent per year.[45]

Production figures speak plain language about the overall downward trend in the economy during the occupation. The output of oil fell from the prewar capacity of 7.9 million tons per year to 4 million in the fiscal year 1942/43, recovered to 7 million tons in 1943/44, yet dropped to 5.5 million tons in 1944/45.[46] As mentioned, a steeply declining proportion of total output ever reached Japan due to bottlenecks in shipping capacity and, towards the end of the occupation, Allied control of sea routes in the Pacific. Production of rubber, coal, sugar and rice stagnated severely, as indicated. The record was also dismal for an entire range of agricultural commodities such as maize, cassava, peanuts and soybeans (a decline of 56–66 per cent) as well as coffee and tea, with estates operating at 25 to 30 per cent below prewar capacities. Livestock was reduced by one half, the fishing fleet by 30 per cent.[47] Significantly, the output of cinchona remained intact, as the finished product, quinine, was needed to combat malaria among the Japanese.

Foreign trade was reoriented to serve Japan and other occupied territories in East and Southeast Asia. Exports consisted mainly of raw materials, in particular oil, whereas imports entering the market in Indonesia were dominated by textiles. Volumes of trade fell sharply in 1944 in response to the policies of local self-sufficiency introduced in occupied Indonesia in late 1943 and increasing Allied command of the seas. Foreign trade came to a virtual standstill in the first half of 1945.[48]

The monetary situation grew increasingly difficult as the occupation progressed. Relentless printing of money by the Japanese authorities and widespread black-market practices, especially as caused by rice shortages, fuelled inflation. According to one estimate, prices in 1942 were, generally speaking, 39 per cent above the level that had prevailed in 1938 but doubled in the course of 1943 and again in 1944. By early 1945, prices were, by this yardstick, ten times as high as in 1942.[49] It goes without saying that such an extreme inflation wiped out asset values and added to the disruption of the economy.

Rapidly falling incomes, shortages due to less production and an erosion of asset values translated as a sharp reduction in standards of living for the vast majority of the Indonesian population. It is estimated that daily calorie intake per person fell from an average of 2,000 kcal at the time of the Japanese invasion to at most 1,500 kcal in the final year of occupation.[50] Incidences of starvation were reported in traditional rice-shortage areas such as Indramayu (West Java) and Madura.[51] There was a dramatic deterioration in medical care since many hospitals were claimed for the Japanese armed forces. Many poor people flocked to the major cities, where beggars became a familiar sight in the streets. The population of Jakarta, for instance, increased by more than 40 per cent, from about 600,000 in 1940 to at least 850,000 in 1945.[52] The most humiliating experience of the Japanese occupation among Indonesians, reflecting the severe fall in standards of living, was the shortage of clothing. People on occasion had to use gunny sacks for lack of textiles.[53]

The physical damage of the occupation was very considerable. The total cost of restoring facilities to prewar levels was shortly after the war estimated at 2.2 billion guilders ($800 million).[54] The even more severe toll was the loss of human lives, victims of both starvation and diseases. The excess of deaths above births in the populations of Java and Madura amounted to 120,000 persons in 1943, 813,000 in 1944 and 1.5 million in 1945, a total net loss of population of 2,250,000 people in the main island of the archipelago and not counting those *romusha* who never returned home.[55]

Conclusion

The sudden Japanese capitulation on 15 August 1945, following the atomic bombing of Hiroshima and Nagasaki, presented a window of opportunity for the Indonesian nationalists. A committee preparing for independence with Sukarno and Hatta at the helm had been at work since May 1945, tolerated and increasingly encouraged by the Japanese authorities. Yet the time for action came earlier than anybody could have anticipated. Upon instigation by eager Indonesian youths, Sukarno hastily declared independence on 17 August 1945. It would take another four and a half years of struggle before the Netherlands was prepared to transfer sovereignty, but the clock could not be turned back. The acceleration and inevitability of independence was the chief outcome of the Japanese occupation for the Indonesian people.

The gain in terms of regime change came at a tremendously high cost, as this brief survey has made clear. Indonesian economy and society were squeezed into the framework of the Japanese war economy. Assets of great value were appropriated by the Japanese authorities, often without direct relevance to the war effort. An entire institutional apparatus was conceived, which did not signify much improvement in the efficiency of allocation, nor did it prove to be of lasting importance. Resources were forcibly transferred on a huge scale, in particular in the mobilization of labour. The final verdict, based as it is on highly incomplete statistics, was one of loss and misery.

Notes

1 This contribution draws on references cited in two earlier surveys: L. de Jong, *The Collapse of a Colonial Society. The Dutch in Indonesia during the Second World War*, Leiden: KITLV Press, 2002; J. T. Lindblad, *Bridges to New Business. The Economic Decolonization of Indonesia*, Leiden: KITLV Press, 2008, pp. 48–57. In addition, I was able to benefit from information in a then-unpublished manuscript by Pham Van Thuy for his PhD dissertation at Leiden University on the political economy of Indonesian decolonization. A very useful reference is P. Post et al.(eds.), *The Encyclopedia of Indonesia in the Pacific War*, Leiden: Brill, 2010.
2 J. T. Lindblad, *Between Dayak and Dutch. The Economic History of Southeast Kalimantan, 1880–1942*, Dordrecht/Providence, RI: Foris, 1988, pp. 104–7; P. Post, *Japanese bedrijvigheid in Indonesië, 1868–1942. Structurele elementen van Japan's economische expansie in Zuidoost-Azië*, Amsterdam: PhD Free University, 1991.
3 H. Dick/V. Houben/J. T. Lindblad/K. W. Thee, *The Emergence of a National Economy. An Economic History of Indonesia, 1800–2000*, Crows Nest, NSW: Allen & Unwin, 2002, pp. 158–9.
4 De Jong, *The Collapse of a Colonial Society*, pp. 41, 283, 419.
5 R. Cribb, *Gangsters and Revolutionaries. The Jakarta People's Militia and the Indonesia Revolution, 1945–1949*, Sydney: Allen & Unwin, 1991, pp. 40–1.
6 De Jong, *The Collapse of a Colonial Society*, p. 203.
7 S. Sato, *War, Nationalism and Peasants. Java under the Japanese Occupation, 1942–1945*, Sydney: Allen & Unwin, 1994, p. 26.
8 De Jong, *The Collapse of a Colonial Society*, p. 45.
9 Ibid, pp. 145–226; E. Zwinkels, *Het Overakker-complot. Indisch verzet tegen de Japanse bezetter op Sumatra 1942–1946*, Houten: Spectrum, 2011.
10 Y. Shibata, 'The monetary policy in the Netherlands East Indies under the Japanese administration', in P. Post/E. Touwen-Bouwsma (eds.), *Japan, Indonesia and the War. Myths and Realities*, Leiden: KITLV Press, 1997, pp. 181–2; De Jong, *The Collapse of a Colonial Society*, pp. 77–8.
11 P. Keppy, *Sporen van vernieling. Oorlogsschade, roof en rechtsherstel in Indonesië, 1940–1957*, Amsterdam: Boom, 2006, pp. 116–8.

12 De Jong, *The Collapse of a Colonial Society*, pp. 79–82.
13 Sato, *War, Nationalism and Peasants*, p. 11; Post et al. *The Encyclopedia of Indonesia*, p. 222.
14 Y. Hikita, '"Japanese companies" inroads into Indonesia under Japanese military domination', in Post/Touwen-Bouwsma, *Japan, Indonesia and the War*, pp. 160–1.
15 De Jong, *The Collapse of a Colonial Society*, p. 235.
16 M. Aziz, *Japan's Colonialism and Indonesia*, The Hague: Nijhoff, 1955, p. 191; Shibata, 'The monetary policy', pp. 187–9.
17 Dick et al., *The Emergence of a National Economy*, p. 126.
18 *Economisch Weekblad voor Nederlandsch-Indië*, 6 July 1946.
19 Ibid; Keppy, *Sporen van vernieling*, pp. 124–6.
20 T.F.H. Postma et al. 'De Javasuikerindustrie gedurende de Japanse bezetting', *Mededelingen van het department van Economische Zaken in Nederlandsch-Indië*, 1946, vol. 12, pp. 8–12; J.O. Sutter, *Indonesianisasi: A Historical Survey of the Role of Politics in the Institutions of a Changing Economy from the Second World War to the Eve of the General Election, 1940–1955*, Ithaca, NY: PhD Cornell University, 1959, pp. 219, 254–5; Aziz, *Japan's Colonialism and Indonesia*, p. 190; Keppy, *Sporen van vernieling*, pp. 139–42.
21 Lindblad, *Between Dayak and Dutch*, p. 115.
22 Hikita, 'Japanese companies', p. 141.
23 A. Booth, *The Indonesian Economy in the Nineteenth and Twentieth Centuries. A History of Missed Opportunities*, London: Macmillan, 1998, p. 88; P. van der Eng, 'Indonesia's growth performance in the twentieth century', in A. Maddison/D.S. Prasada Rao/W.F. Shepherd (eds.), *The Asian Economies in the Twentieth Century*, Cheltenham/Northampton, MA, 2002, pp. 171–2.
24 S. Sato, 'Japanization in Indonesia re-examined. The problem of self-sufficiency in clothing', in L. Narangoa/R. Cribb (eds.), *Imperial Japan and National Identities in Asia, 1895–1945*, London: Routledge, 2003, p. 279.
25 S. Miyamoto, 'Economic and military mobilization in Java, 1944–1945', in A. Reid/O. Akira (eds.), *The Japanese Experience in Indonesia, 1942–1945*, Athens, OH: Ohio University Press, 1986, p. 241.
26 Hikita, 'Japanese companies', p. 139.
27 P. Keppy, *Hidden Business: Indigenous and Ethnic Chinese Entrepreneurs in the Majalaya Textile Industry, West Java, 1928–1974*, Amsterdam: PhD Free University, 2001, pp. 87–94.
28 Sutter, *Indonesianisasi*, pp. 213, 250–4.
29 M. Nakamura, 'General Imamura and the early period of Japanese occupation', *Indonesia*, 1970, vol. 10, p. 7.
30 De Jong, *The Collapse of a Colonial Society*, p. 236.
31 Post et al. *The Encyclopedia of Indonesia*, pp. 227, 263–6.
32 De Jong, *The Collapse of a Colonial Society*, p. 254.
33 P. van der Eng, *Food Supply in Java during the War and Decolonisation, 1940–1950*, Hull: Centre of Southeast Asian Studies, 1994.
34 De Jong, *The Collapse of a Colonial Society*, pp. 237, 241.
35 E. Leenarts, 'Coolie wages in western enterprises in the Outer Islands, 1919–1938', in V.J.H. Houben/J.T. Lindblad et al. (eds.), *Coolie Labour in Colonial Indonesia. A Study of Labour Relations in the Outer Islands, c. 1900–1940*, Wiesbaden: Harrassowitz, 1999, pp. 140, 153.
36 A. Reid, *The Blood of the People. Revolution and the End of Traditional Rule in Northern Sumatra*, Kuala Lumpur: Oxford University Press, 1979, pp. 125–6.
37 H. Neumann/E. van Witsen, *De Pekanbaroe spoorweg: een documentatie van gegevens, in en direct na de oorlog verzameld*, Amstelveen: Pieter Mulier, 1982.

38 A. Kurasawa, *Mobilisasi dan kontrol. Studi tentang perubahan sosial di pedesaan Jawa, 1942–45*, Jakarta: Gramedia, 1993.
39 Sato, *War, Nationalism and Peasants*, pp. 147–9.
40 De Jong, *The Collapse of a Colonial Society*, p. 249.
41 P. Post, 'The formation of the pribumi business elite in Indonesia, 1930s–1940s', in Post/Touwen-Bouwsma, *Japan, Indonesia and the War*, pp. 87–110.
42 P. van der Eng, 'The real domestic product of Indonesia, 1880–1989', *Explorations in Economic History*, 1992, vol. 29, pp. 343–73.
43 Idem, Indonesia's growth performance', p. 172; J.L. van Zanden/D. Marks, *An Economic History of Indonesia 1800–2010*, London: Routledge, 2012, p. 152.
44 Ibid, pp. 172–3.
45 J.T. Lindblad, 'Economic growth and decolonization in Indonesia', *Itinerario. International Journal on the History of the European Expansion and Global Interaction*, 2010, vol. 34, p. 99.
46 De Jong, *The Collapse of a Colonial Society*, p. 236.
47 D.H. Burger, *Sociologisch-economische geschiedenis van Indonesia*. Wageningen: Agricultural University, Amsterdam: Royal Tropical Institute, Leiden: KITLV, 1975, II, pp. 160–1.
48 Post et al. *The Encyclopedia of Indonesia*, p. 238.
49 De Jong, *The Collapse of a Colonial Society*, p. 525.
50 Van der Eng, *Food Supply in Java during the War*, pp. 17–21; A. Kurasawa, 'Rice shortage and transportation', in Post/Touwen-Bouwsma, *Japan, Indonesia and the War*, pp. 121–4.
51 Sato, *War, Nationalism and Peasants*, pp. 122–36.
52 S. Abeyasekere, *Jakarta. A History*, Singapore: Oxford University, 1987, pp. 140–1.
53 Miyamoto, 'Economic and military mobilization in Java', p. 248.
54 A. Fruin, *Het economisch aspect van het Indonesische vraagstuk*, Amsterdam: Vrij Nederland 1947, p. 47.
55 De Jong, *The Collapse of a Colonial Society*, p. 280.

16 The Burmese economy under the Japanese occupation, 1942–1945

Michael W. Charney and Atsuko Naono

Introduction

The Japanese occupied British-ruled Burma over the course of a six-month period, from the outbreak of hostilities on 7 December 1941 until May 1942, when the British were pushed back into India. For the next three and a half years, the Imperial Japanese Army (IJA)'s Fifteenth Army, which was assigned charge of Burma, would exercise effective control over the country, although local collaborating bodies were created to mediate the IJA's relationship with the Burmese population. The collaborating bodies included the Provisional Administrative Committee (June to July 1942), the Burmese Executive Administration (BEA) also known as the Central Administrative Government (1 August 1942 to July 1943), and the nominally independent Government of Burma (1 August 1943 to May 1945), all headed by Ba Maw.[1]

Despite the rhetoric of independence, genuinely believed by the Burmese in the Government of Burma, real power was in the hands of the Japanese. By the time the Burmese ministers found that their plans were not being acted on, it was too late, and the war was rapidly coming to a close. Aside from the Burmese governments, some highland areas of Burma would remain autonomous of Burmese authority throughout the war, and the Shan areas so only until 1 August 1943, but this meant in effect direct Japanese control rather than the local rule of the colonial era. The IJA's presence in Burma was the largest concentration of Japanese troops in the region because of the preparations for the invasion of India, using Burma as a base. These preparations were also the reason for the construction of the Thai-Burma railway, across the Burma-Thai border, from 1942.

Management of the economy

The general principles by which the economies of the 'Southern occupied areas' (the Nampo) such as Burma would be managed were laid out at the Liaison Conference between the Government and the Imperial General Headquarters on 20 November 1941. It was agreed at the conference that in so far as they did not impede actual military operations, the occupation forces should mobilize and transport local resources necessary for Japan's national defence, there to be handled by the Resources Mobilization Program of the Central Government of Tokyo and also secure their own support according to the plan of distribution. The plans for resource procurement, exploitation, and management would be set up by the Central Organ of the Planning Office. The occupation forces would also control trade and exchange and make certain that no valuable resources, including tungsten, quinine, rubber, tin, or oil, would reach the enemy. Existing currencies would be used as much as possible, supplemented where necessary by the use of military scrip made out in the units of the local currency. The indigenous population would have to endure the pressures of supporting the occupation forces and the flow of resources to Japan. As imperial control strengthened, the enforcing mechanisms of the military administration would eventually be integrated or transferred to a new administration.[2] 'The General Plan of Economic Policies for the Southern Areas' submitted to the Liaison Conference on 12 December 1941, after the war had begun, repeated the main principles outlined but added that in exploiting resources, existing local enterprises should be managed in a way that encouraged their cooperation so that the occupation would not place a drain on the Japanese economy. Moreover, it was now stressed that the one goal of the occupation, vaguely stated, was the establishment of the permanency and self-sufficiency of the Greater East Asia Co-Prosperity Sphere. On 15 March 1942, a week after the IJA took Rangoon, General Shojiro Iida issued a revised plan for the areas occupied by the Hayashi Army on the basis of Burma's local conditions, including the long-term eradication of the influence of Asian immigrant minorities in the country, such as the Overseas Chinese and Indians.[3]

The Japanese Military Administration (JMA) in Burma was established in March 1942 and at first included five departments. These included a General Affairs Department, an Industry Department, a Finance Department, a Transportation Department, and a Religious Affairs Department (although this was not instituted at the time), each under a chief directly responsible to the Superintendent of the JMA, who would be, as a rule, the Deputy Chief of Staff of the Hayashi Army Group.[4] In the General Affairs Department, the Political Affairs Bureau would be responsible for mobilizing resources and manpower, managing enemy property, and other duties. The Industry Department consisted of four bureaus, those responsible for the management of mining, commerce, agriculture and forestry, and foreign trade. The Finance Department had three bureaus responsible for public finance, credit and banking, and customs. The last of the four operating departments, that of transportation, included bureaus for land transportation, marine transportation, aviation, and postal services.[5] Over the course of the next year and a half, several new departments (Political Affairs, Education, Military Administration Accounting Supervision Department, and Investigation Department) would be added and older departments reorganized to reflect changing demands. The Industry Department, for example, was expanded in January 1943 to include a General Affairs Bureau, which included amongst its many tasks the collection of scrap metal. In the last two months of the JMA, an Enemy Property Control Department was added.[6]

The JMA in Burma was initially similar to other military administrations throughout the Southern Region, as the Japanese occupation referred to Southeast Asia (although the term also included Australia and New Zealand). Nevertheless, the military administration of Burma (like that of the Philippines) soon differed from other areas in Japanese-occupied Southeast Asia because the Japanese forces began to manage the country in cooperation with an independent indigenous government.[7] The JMA was officially disbanded and these functions taken over by the Burma government on 1 August 1943, when Burma formally declared independence within the Greater East Asia Co-Prosperity Sphere. Formally, the Burma government would become self-reliant and would develop her economy through free and fair economic activities within the overall plans for the Greater East Asia Co-Prosperity Sphere, enemy property would be restored to Burma, and she would have control over transportation and communications. But her management would comply with Japan's special needs, and property necessary for the prosecution of the war would remain under Japanese control.[8]

Although Burmese were superficially in charge, in reality, a parallel shadow structure was put in place in which Burmese ministries, including those responsible for mining, agriculture, industry, and transportation, were assigned thirty Japanese civilian advisers. They were handpicked and headed, from December 1943, by Dr. Gotaro Ogawa, the 'Supreme Adviser to the Burmese Government' and the real decision-making authority in the new government. A Kyoto University professor and financial expert, the author of a major published historical study of the long-term economic impact on Japanese society of the introduction of the conscription system,[9] and a former Japanese cabinet minister in charge of commerce and railways, Ogawa was charged with mobilizing Burma effectively for the war effort.[10]

Currency and banking

Japanese policy gave the JMA a free hand in seizing anything required for 'war purposes'. The easiest way to do this was to label something 'enemy property'. As the Burmese found, the label was applied very loosely to anything that the JMA seized, from 'pins, screws, and nuts to steam rollers, locomotives and ships, no matter who owned them' as one member of Ba Maw's government remembered. The Ba Maw government, when given independence, made property rights and the recovery of this 'enemy property' a goal of its inaugural New Order Plan.[11] Nevertheless, the obligation of the new government to support the JMA seizure of necessary resources for the war effort was included in the Japan-Burma Secret Military Agreement signed on 1 August 1943 at the same time as the grant of independence. The government was to provide the IJA free of charge any lands and buildings necessary for the prosecution of the war and to aid it in commandeering and transporting anything else necessary and to either exempt or reduce the taxes on any resources used by Japanese forces.[12]

Regarding its currency, as outlined in November 1941, Japanese policy was to support existing currency in prospective occupied countries or, where not possible or insufficient, to rely on military scrip issued in the local monetary unit.[13]

In Burma, the Yokohama Specie Bank (YSB) was officially responsible for issuing the JMA's occupation currency until 1 April 1943, when this task was taken over by the *Nampo Kaihatsu Ginko* (Southern Regions Development Bank).[14] The volume of this currency in circulation in the country swelled to 560 crores by the end of the war, which was a face value sixteen times greater than amount of British Burma currency in circulation when the Japanese invaded. As inflation set in, more occupation currency had to be printed. The declining value of the currency and the fact that the JMA at all levels used the currency led to a widely held belief that Japanese military and company officials printed the currency when required using portable presses, although in fact the currency was imported from abroad, most likely printed at Kolff Printing Works in Jakarta.[15]

The declining value of the currency prompted concern amongst the leadership of the Burmese government under Ba Maw, technically made independent on 1 August 1943. The new government at first relied upon the Bank of Japan's *Nampo Kaihatsu Ginko*, which had taken over the printing of JMA currency four months earlier and which was mainly responsible for the development of Burmese government enterprises and for funding the fledgling Burmese government.[16] The Ba Maw government very soon pursued the creation of the Burma State Bank, opened on 15 January 1944 with a capital of Rs. 10,000,000, with the hopes of having it print and issue a new currency for the country that would resolve the currency situation. It was believed by at least some in the Ba Maw government that an understanding existed with the Japanese that as new Burma State Bank notes were circulated, JMA currency would be withdrawn. In any case, these plans never went very far and the new notes never appeared.[17] One postwar report estimated that at 1954 prices, the equivalent of Burmese goods and services the Japanese took in exchange for the worthless currency it circulated in the country was between 3 and 5 billion kyat.[18]

In Burma, there was not much of a banking system left to rely upon, so the YSB and other Japanese or connected banks stepped in. The JMA in Burma would mainly rely upon the YSB, closely connected to the Japanese military since the late 1930s. The YSB had been forced to close its Rangoon branch on 8 December 1941, when hostilities broke out, only to set up operations shortly after the Japanese occupation of Rangoon. It also opened up branches at Bassein, Lashio, Mandalay, Maymyo, Mergui, Moulmein, Myingyan, Prome, Tavoy, and Toungoo, giving it a countrywide presence.[19] In addition to its services to the JMA, the YSB effectively provided the functions of the now evacuated colonial exchange banks and, by the end of the occupation, it mainly served the needs of Japanese corporations operating in the country.[20] The Chosen Bank (the Central Bank of Korea), which followed the Japanese military from one occupied country to another, also began operations of a less clear nature in Rangoon, but likely to facilitate the activities of the Japanese military authorities, and Japanese businesses.[21] The Free Indian Bank (*Azad Hind*), established to support the operations of the pro-Axis Indian National Army, made up of volunteers from Indian POWs, also opened up a branch in Rangoon, and from patriotic persuasion convinced Indians in Burma to deposit their valuables to the amount of 215 million Indian rupees.[22]

For the Burmese public, there was little left in the way of useful, reliable, or safe financial institutions. Most of the colonial-era banks, along with their records and assets, had fled the country with the Japanese invasion. The YSB issued calls that it was now to receive payments on loans made by these banks before they left as well as pay 10 per cent on accounts to depositors with the previous banks, but both depositors and creditors alike were said to have ignored these requests.[23] There was some lip service paid to the need to develop financial institutions for the Burmese. The JMA permitted the reopening of the Bank of Chettinad and its forty-five branches as the People's Bank of Burma on 7 December 1942, managed by the JMA, the BEA, and the YSB, with a capital of 100,000 JMA rupees and headquartered in the old Central Bank of India building in Rangoon. Nevertheless, although the bank was supposed to revive the agricultural economy, it never really escaped military control and wound up having very little real impact on the economy.[24] With independence in 1943, Ba Maw established a Burmese Central Bank Preparatory Committee to open a state bank, directed by a Burman who had been sent to Japan for training in banking administration. The bank opened as the Burma State Bank on 1 November 1943 and two months later was assigned a 'Chief Advisor', Chuichi Shimooka, the former head of the Kyoto Branch of the Bank of Japan. Nevertheless, the rapidly declining economic picture meant that this bank could achieve little.[25]

Business and property

As outlined, in December 1941, free trade was the goal of policies regarding local businesses. The JMA would depend as much as possible on the local business systems of Overseas Chinese and indigenous merchants, although three months later, Iida admitted that he planned to use the skills of overseas Chinese and Indian merchants only in the short term, in the long term eradicating their influence in the country in favor of Japanese and Burmese merchants. In the meantime, the entrance of Japanese firms into the country to do business would be carefully monitored so that 'delinquent Japanese merchants' would not take advantage of the situation.[26] It had also been decided in 1941 that the flow of resources, both imports and exports, would be closely connected to the military during the war, with the help of Japanese intermediary businesses. Moreover, intermediary organizations would be established for the distribution of supplies in occupied areas, with the employees of those enterprises making resources necessary for Japan, such as farms producing certain crops and mining operations getting preferential treatment.[27]

Burma's internal and external trade was thus put under the control of Japanese companies through the monopolies established over commodity distribution, which did not differentiate between Burmese products for domestic sale or for export, mainly to Japan, and foreign, largely Japanese imports. At the local level, with the disappearance of British and many Indian firms, Burmese companies had quickly stepped in to fill the vacuum. Nevertheless, very soon after the occupation, they became dependent on Japanese monopolies placed over commodities, although with the transportation conditions during the war, only the Japanese companies could have transported commodities anyway.

Three main commercial unions dominated Burma's wartime economy. First, the Japan Burma Rice Union monopolized the rice trade. It was formed by a consortium of three Japanese companies, *Nihon Menka*, *Mitsui Bussan*, and *Mitsubishi Shoji*, and made a joint investment (50 per cent, 25 per cent and 25 per cent, respectively) of 5 million rupees. Its early tasks included buying up the 1940–41 and 1942 bumper paddy harvests for the use of the JMA.[28]

Second, the Japan Burma Timber Union monopolised Burmese timber.[29] Even though Burma had been a major timber exporter before the war, Burmese forestry suffered particularly from the loss of Indian labour who had run the mills, from the destruction of these mills, and because of difficulties in transportation. While some production was maintained to satisfy local demands, teak from Siam was much easier for the Japanese to import than was Burma's. Moreover, Japanese policy for the occupied Southern Regions was that Japanese entrepreneurial involvement in forestry, as in agriculture and marine exploitation, should be restricted as much as possible.[30]

Third was the giant Commodity Distribution Association of Burma, made up entirely of Japanese members, which monopolized every other commodity in Burma.[31] The Commodity Distribution Association of Burma, created in July 1942, supplied the JMA first and also controlled the wholesalers supplying Burmese retailers who sold to the Burmese public. For the latter, ration coupons were issued, government servants receiving theirs from the BEA and the general public receiving theirs from the Commodity Distribution Association.[32] The Union had five branches: (1) piecegoods and materials dominated by *Sankoka Bushike kabushiki kaisha (KK)*, (2) firewood, kerosene oil, petrol, and candles, by *Mitsubishi Shoten KK*, (3) hardware and machinery, by *Ataki Shokai*, (4) food, by Japan Cotton Company, and (5) scientific and miscellaneous, by *Mitsui Bussan KK*. The Commodity Distributing Association also distributed controlled commodities such as sugar, salt, and matches to retailers.[33]

Burmese governments intervened on occasion to control prices, except in cases where the commodity in question was needed by the JMA. In 1943, for example, the BEA controlled prices in response to noticeable fluctuations in prices of certain commodities. In response to the rapid rise in prices of both sesamum oil and groundnuts late in the 1942–43 year, the BEA put in controlled prices in the districts that produced most of these crops. Even so, the JMA had the right to control prices for cotton anywhere and to require their delivery to Japanese firms.[34] In January 1944, the Burmese government again stepped in and created a new Commodity Control Bureau that targeted profiteering and hoarding amongst the indigenous population.[35]

Resource development

From its establishment on 1 August 1943, the new Government of Burma gave first priority to war tasks, the development of war finances, war industries, war communications, war health measures, war labour, war supplies and the economy generally, and civil defence.[36] Nevertheless, the Government of Burma would also make a sincere effort to offset some of the worst excesses of the Japanese military occupation. It drafted plans and sometimes promulgated laws and policies intended to reduce Japanese dominance in the economy, although the end of the war meant these plans were never put into meaningful effect.

The JMA took under its administration all existing manufacturing factories and workshops in Burma that had been owned by those defined as the enemy, mainly the British and other Europeans. Such industries owned by Chinese, Indians, and Burmese were to be allowed to continue under their own management so long as they were not hostile and met JMA demands on their production. The JMA-managed concerns would have to conform with the synthetic industrial plan for the Southern Areas and operate within the limits of the industrial allotment decided for Burma by Tokyo.[37] The development of new industries, except those such as repair facilities necessary for the maintenance of equipment already in the field and shipbuilding, was discouraged in the economic plans drawn up in December 1941, although the further development of existing industries was to be permitted so far as they did not overtax transportation systems.[38] Thus, although Japanese firms did secure control over existing industrial plants, new Japanese-controlled industries did not emerge to a significant degree in occupied Burma, although the Burma government did encourage some enterprises of its own. Instead, the emphasis in Burma was on repair facilities and the transfer of raw materials to Japan.

It is no surprise that the JMA believed that Burma was not important to Japan because of preexisting industry but because of its natural resources, both its forestry and its mining products.[39] From the beginning of the occupation, the Japanese had exported significant amounts of resources to Japan early in the occupation, mainly in the form of scrap and stocks that had been left behind in the colonial retreat. Nevertheless, the Burmese population were also soon instructed to submit lists of the iron and zinc they possessed (as well as the cotton) to the JMA.[40] Automobiles both working and derelicts as scrap metal, cotton, timber, furniture, refrigerators, cutlery, crockery, silver heirlooms, and the like were gathered up and exported to Japan.[41]

Burma's rich mining resources were also important. In the case of Burma's most important mine, the Bawdwin Mine, operations were at first put under military control, perhaps because of its isolated position in the mountains close to the frontier with China.[42] Nevertheless, Japanese policy for the occupied Southern Regions was that after mining operations were restored, their control should be concentrated in the hands of a single company in any one locality for efficiency, but control over any single mineral or metal resource distributed among at least two companies in the occupied region as a whole, to avoid the 'evil' of a monopoly.[43] Hence, a flood of Japanese companies, permitted on the basis of their previous experience with a particular product, entered Burma to develop mining and related industries, but each was dominant in one resource in one area, explaining their range of interests and their relatively large number for the Burmese mining industry. *Kobayashi Mining KK*, for example, had opened up a branch in Burma from 10 July 1942, operating the Mawchi Wolfram Mine.[44] Amongst its many other activities in the country, *Ataka Sangyo KK*, establishing its branch in Burma on 7 April 1942, operated mines in the Yamethin area. *Mitsubishi Kogyo KK*, operating in Burma from the same date, owned mines in Tavoy and, temporarily, the Mawson mines.[45] By 1944, these Japanese mining companies were joined by additional formal mining concerns, such as *Aoyagi Steel KK*, *Iwaki Cement KK*, *Meiji Mining KK*, *Chuou Boseki Corporation*, *Gosho KK*, and *Nichinan Sangyo*, as well as companies such as *Hokuetsu Paper KK* and *Fuji Gas & Spinning KK*, whose interests in mining were secondary to other enterprises.[46]

Decisions regarding mining operations in Burma were made in the context of the general Japanese occupation in the region. Those raw materials that were seen as the local country's peculiar advantage were emphasized, while duplicate sources of some materials were not encouraged. For example, since supplies of tin from Malaya, also under Japanese control, were sufficient for Japan's wartime needs and easier to access than supplies in Burma, there was little effort made during the war to reopen the tin mines at Tavoy.[47] Despite the damage from the British 'denial' programme and Allied bombing, Burma's contribution to the flow of raw materials to Japanese industries in the home islands was said to be significant. By March 1943, for example, Japanese radio claimed Burma was exporting zinc sufficient to meet Japanese war production needs.[48]

Burma's rice production was potentially no less important than its mineral reserves, Burma having been the world's leading exporter of rice before the war. Because of the sabotage and bombing of Burma's 600 steam mills, the Japanese had to make bringing Burma's rice mills back into operation an economic priority.[49] Rice cultivation shrank anyway, partly because of labour problems but also because civilian commercial traffic always took second order of precedence to military demands and the resulting limited and unreliable nature of both rail and river transport hindered the revival of the rice export economy.[50] It was impossible to move rice even within Burma, and while rice prices fell dramatically, to levels significantly less than the worst years of the World Depression, in Upper Burma where the population was greater, rice prices shot up. Because of the various problems related to the abnormal excess in paddy and rice, due to the disappearance of former colonial export markets, the BEA set up a paddy purchase scheme. Under its terms, the government would appoint buyers in thirteen Lower Burma districts who would pay Rs. 80 per hundred baskets, and these would be sold in seven Upper Burma districts where demand was not being met.[51]

Because of Burma's position on the fronts with both India and Yunnan, and because of its distance from normal Japanese channels of supply, Burma suffered from wartime requisition especially hard. Allied bombing and the lack of available gasoline meant the Japanese depended, alongside the railways and boats, on bullock carts and other animal transport. Moreover, feeding the IJA placed a heavy demand on cattle and pig stocks, already hampered by the spread of disease due to the wartime situation. The animals and their manure were sorely needed in the agricultural sector, and the rural economy suffered as a result.[52] The Burma government responded with efforts to encourage the breeding of buffalo, goats, fowl, sheep, and pigs, rural education programs to teach cultivators how to conserve manure, and, in conjunction with JMA veterinary officers, to inoculate cattle against disease on a mass scale wherever possible.[53]

Cotton production was another crucial resource which the Japanese hoped to derive from Burma. From the beginning of the Japanese occupation in Burma, Iida had made an increase in the production of cotton a key economic policy of the JMA there.[54] Before the war, cotton had been an important Burmese export to Japan and Japan sought to expand Burma's production of cotton for the war effort. Cotton production was encouraged by several means. The BEA established an Agricultural Bureau in 1943 to encourage cultivators to 'grow deficient crops', which were in great demand within the State. These included cotton, jute, sesamum, groundnut, wheat, chillies, onions, and so on. The Bureau afforded help in the form of lectures and demonstrations to teach new and suitable methods of cultivation. Cotton Associations were also formed within each district, free cotton seeds were distributed, and in one district (Myingyan), agricultural loans were extended. In Pakkoku District, a Japanese firm made loans of Rs. 10,000 to cultivators who would grow cotton. The firm distributed 300 theikpan ploughs free of charge. It also set up a reward system whereby any cultivator who delivered no less than 300 viss. of cotton received not less than Rs. 300 in rewards.[55] After placing control over Burma's cotton cultivation under three Japanese firms, a five-year plan was put in place to increase Burma's production by 400 per cent, although acreage under cotton merely doubled from 285,720 acres to 528,000 acres in 1944–45. By January 1943, several thousand tons of Burmese cotton had reached Japan. The production of other fibre crops, such as roselle, hemp, and lady's finger, was encouraged as well.[56] By mid-1944, the cultivation of flax and different varieties of cotton was being experimented with alongside castor and vegetables with the help of both the Burma government and Japanese companies, such as the Fugigatsu Ginning Company, which helped the government open an experimental station at a village in Shwebo District in Upper Burma.[57]

The BEA and then the Burma government also attempted to introduce jute cultivation in Lower Burma. With isolation from Europe and India, however, clothing imports stopped and rice sacks were cut up for replacement clothing, leaving no cheap means to bag up rice for movement or distribution, and jute appeared to be a way to meet this demand.[58] The BEA thus cooperated with Japanese firms in early 1943 to convert 10,000 acres of paddy land in Danubyu, Yandoon, Maubin, and Henzada Townships to jute cultivation. Arrangements were made between landlords and tenants and between tenants and the Burma Asia Union. As a result of these arrangements, (1) the cultivator was given jute seeds free of charge, as well as interest-free loans for cultivation which had to be repaid only when the jute crop was delivered and sold, (2) the landlord was paid a rent of Rs. 20 per acre for one year, and (3) the jute was sold only to the JMA for military purposes at a 'reasonable price' fixed by the JMA.[59]

The special attention the JMA gave to such fibre crops, however, produced tensions with the Burmese. Burmese also tried to use the cotton for themselves, for textiles, rather than deliver it to Japanese companies for export to Japan. As a result, the JMA imposed an antihoarding ordinance to prevent cotton hoarding.[60] The Burma government also tried to develop the spinning and weaving industry under the management of the Fuji Cotton Spinning Company, with 150,000 to 300,000 'high-quality' spindles imported from Japan and a quota of cotton agreed by the Japanese authorities to be used for domestic purposes, to produce textiles within the country.[61]

No estimates of Burma's GDP during the occupation are currently available, by contrast to other occupied countries in the region. Economic historians such as (a) Huff and Majima and (b) Takahashi point only to the contrast between figures for the 'prewar level' (Takahashi) or 1938 (Huff and Majima) and 1950, the GDP being in the latter case 41 per cent (Takahashi) or 47 per cent (Huff and Majima) less than the former.[62] Part of the reason for this is the failure of the JMA or the Ba Maw government to collect accurate data, which was due in part to the country's position as a wartime front. The BEA complained in 1943 that it could not muster comparative figures on the prices of paddy and rice sales as when the 'big Nippon firms bought as much paddy as was available' at the end of 1942, 'there were no records of the purchase and sale prices at the time'.[63] The problem was also due to the impact of wartime devastation through combat and bombing throughout the period.

However, some indications of the decline in GDP are possible to reconstruct. In agriculture, where acreage under cultivation of any kind continued to slump downwards throughout the war, already by June 1943, halfway through the war, the level was lower than at any other point since 1928.[64] Indeed, the sown area of Burma had fallen from 4.99 million ha in 1941 to 2.63 million ha in 1945, a fall in acreage by nearly half.[65] Mining and oil output had completely halted, as had the export trade.

Labour

Labour was one of the JMA's most significant concerns during its occupation of Burma. Burma's prewar nonagricultural manual labour was dominated by the Indian community, and when large numbers of Indians fled Burma in 1942, there was a resulting shortage of both skilled and manual labour. Without this labour, it would be difficult to run the rice and timber mills, the mines, or the port facilities, even after they had been repaired after British sabotage. Some Indians remained, however, and others contemplating or caught trying to escape were induced to remain and work by higher wages than had been normally paid. In 1942, these wages were in the area of Rs. 1 to Rs. 1/8/ per day in Japanese currency or, for Indian coolies, 9 to 12 annas per day as well as two seers of rice.[66]

Because of the decline of cultivation in rural Burma, unemployed Burmese cultivators also began to look for nonagricultural work. Poor agricultural conditions, including flooding in some areas, failed irrigation systems in others, and a range of other problems made it difficult to return to cultivation. The breakdown in social order also provoked fear of working land anywhere beyond the vicinity of one's own village, due to the threat of 'bad characters'.[67] According to the BEA, in 1943, cultivators were undertaking nonagricultural work, such as employment as salt boilers, carting, boat plying, petty trading, fishing, weaving, manufacture of kerosene, and so on, which paid much more than work as an agricultural labourer.[68] The agricultural labour shortage eventually became so bad in some districts that prisoners were forced to work the fields in the vicinity of the prisons, such as in Tharrawaddy District in 1944.[69]

The JMA in Burma sought to mobilize Burmese manual labour through the *heiho*, a system used throughout the occupied region. Burmese between the ages of 16 and 30 were recruited to form labour groups who worked on the construction, repair, and maintenance of Japanese military installations such as aerodromes, roads, railways, and defences.[70] Although the *heiho* gained a negative reputation for the use of force and failure to live up to promised working conditions, at first, Burmese cultivators found this paid manual labour for the JMA more remunerative than working fields for uncertain income.[71] During November and December 1942, however, there were some problems between the Japanese military administration and the BEA over Burmese being forced to work on military projects during the paddy-harvesting season.[72] For the construction of the rail link from Thailand to Burma, the Japanese infamously utilized both European POWs taken from Malaya and the Dutch East Indies. But they also mobilized Burmese *heiho* labourers to build the Burmese side of the line. The BEA was formally asked to make arrangements to fill a quota of 30,000 men from 1942. After deciding terms of remuneration, rewards, and terms, the BEA made advertisements and commitments to especially good terms, high rates of pay, free medical care, and support for families at home. Even then, quotas were placed on villages, rich villagers bribing poor villagers to take their place and splitting the take with the village headman. Those who undertook the work found conditions and rewards were not those promised, and ultimately, as word spread, the JMA had to act unilaterally, forcing villagers such as those in Thaton and Moulmein Districts to the work camps. Labour officers of the BEA were not permitted to visit the camps.[73] Even after the opening of the line in 1943, the need for frequent repairs and other work in keeping the line open meant the Burmese *heiho* labourers were still at work at Thanbyuzayat through 1944.[74]

From March 1943, the JMA organized and dispatched a new labour force, 'the Labour Service Corps for the Construction of the Burma-Thailand Railway', known as the 'Labour Service Corps' for short. This was a joint effort by the JMA and the BEA, and organizers would select Burmese candidates from every district throughout the country, and these would be formed into Labour Service Corps groups numbering 2,000 workers each that would then be dispatched to Thanbyuzayat. These units would be kept separate from previously organized labour groups, would receive better treatment and pay, and would not be treated as 'common labourers' as the others had been, and there would be no use of the word 'coolie'. Their duties were clearly defined – the raising of the ground level for the railway – and clearly defined work hours would be established. Indicating the conditions prevalent at the time of their organization, the workers were promised aerial defence measures.[75]

The creation of the independent Burma state in August 1943 and the appointment of the aforementioned Japanese financial and conscription expert, Dr. Ogawa, as 'Supreme Adviser' to that government less than five months later were part of an effort to mobilize the Burmese fully for the war effort. Burmese labour was to be organized for the first time at the national level. National service was made compulsory and was to be directed into either the labour service or as a reserve for the Burma Defense Army.[76] Although a Burma Defense Army was mobilized, this force ultimately turned on the Japanese after they proceeded in the direction of the front, and with the Allied offensive beginning in 1944, the potential impact of the mobilization of the Burmese for other activities is difficult to judge.

As elsewhere among the Axis states in 1945, their declining fortunes meant that the economic controls put in place were soon compromised by advancing Allied fronts. Both the JMA and the government of Burma came to an end rather quickly in the rainy season of 1945. Several months after the opening up of the Allied counterinvasion of Burma in October 1944, the Burma Defense Army, led by officers who had formed the Anti-Fascist Peoples Freedom League, deserted Ba Maw, joined the Allies, and rose up against the Japanese, playing an important role in the Allied victory on this front. Over the course of the last eight months of the war, different parts of Burma were under three authorities, the government of Burma, the Japanese Army, and Allied Forces' South East Asia Command. Rangoon fell to Allied forces in May 1945.

Notes

1. K. Nemoto, 'Between Collaboration and Resistance: Reconsidering the Roles of Ba Maw and Aung San in Their Context Asserting Burmese Nationalism', in idem (ed.), *Reconsidering the Japanese Military Occupation in Burma (1942–45)*, Tokyo: Tokyo University of Foreign Studies Research Institute for Languages and Cultures of Asia and Africa, 2007, p. 3.
2. F.N. Trager (ed.), *Burma: Japanese Military Administration*, Selected Documents, 1941–1945, Philadelphia: University of Pennsylvania Press, 1971, pp. 36–8.
3. Ibid, pp. 38–39, 45–52.
4. Ibid, pp. 52–3.
5. Ibid, pp. 55–58.
6. Ibid, pp. 86–7.
7. Boei cho, Boei kenkyujo, Senshi bu (eds.), *Shiryoshu Nampo no Gunsei*, Tokyo: Asaguymo Shimbunsha, 1985, p. 188.
8. *Burma: Japanese Military Administration*, pp. 148–9.
9. G. Ogawa, *Conscription System in Japan*, New York: Oxford University Press, 1921.
10. *Burma During the Japanese Occupation*, Simla: Government of India Press, 1943–44, vol. 2, p. 18; D.G.E. Hall, *Burma*, London: Hutchinson's University Library, 1950, p. 173.
11. U Hla Pe, *Narrative of the Japanese Occupation*, Ithaca, NY: Cornell University Southeast Asia Program, 1961, p. 45.
12. *Burma: Japanese Military Administration*, p. 154.

13 M. Longmuir, *The Money Trail: Burmese Currencies in Crisis 1937–1947*, DeKalb: Northern Illinois University Southeast Asia Program, 2002, pp. 30–1.
14 *Burma During the Japanese Occupation*, vol. 1, p. 71; S. Turnell, *Fiery Dragons: Banks, Moneylenders and Microfinance in Burma*, Copenhagen: NIAS Press, 2009, pp. 131–2; Longmuir, *The Money Trail*, p. 42.
15 Longmuir, *The Money Trail*, p. 41.
16 *Burma During the Japanese Occupation*, vol. 1, p. 71, Longmuir, *The Money Trail*, p. 42.
17 Longmuir, *The Money Trail*, pp. 45–56; Turnell, *Fiery Dragons*, pp. 132–3.
18 L. J. Walinsky, *Economic Development in Burma 1951–1960*, New York: The Twentieth Century Fund, 1962, p. 57.
19 *Burma During the Japanese Occupation*, vol. 1, p. 71; Turnell, *Fiery Dragons*, pp. 131–2; Longmuir, *The Money Trail*, p. 41.
20 Turnell, *Fiery Dragons*, pp. 131–2.
21 *Burma During the Japanese Occupation*, vol. 1, p. 71; Turnell, *Fiery Dragons*, p. 133.
22 *Burma During the Japanese Occupation*, vol. 1, p. 133.
23 Turnell, *Fiery Dragons*, pp. 131–2.
24 *Burma During the Japanese Occupation*, vol. 1, p. 71; Turnell, *Fiery Dragons*, p. 132; *Burma: Japanese Military Administration*, p. 245.
25 *Burma during the Japanese Occupation*, vol. 1, p. 71.
26 *Burma: Japanese Military Administration*, pp. 43, 48, 52.
27 Ibid, p. 43.
28 A. Kurasawa, 'Beikoku Mondai ni Miru Senryoki no Tonan Ajia – Biruma, Malaya no Jijo wo Chushin ni', in idem (ed.), *Tonan Ajia-shi no naka no Nihon Senryo*, Tokyo: Waseda Daigaku Shuppanbu, 1997, p. 135; Hla Pe, *Narrative of the Japanese Occupation*, pp. 22, 56.
29 Hla Pe, *Narrative of the Japanese Occupation*, p. 22.
30 *Burma During the Japanese Occupation*, vol. 1, p. 81; *Burma: Japanese Military Administration*, p. 41.
31 Hla Pe, *Narrative of the Japanese Occupation*, p. 22.
32 [Burma Executive Administration], *Season and Crop Report of Burma for the Year Ending the 30th June 1943*, Rangoon: Superintendent, Govt. Printing & Stationery, 1946, p. 9; *Burma under the Japanese Occupation*, vol. 1, pp. 73–4; Hla Pe, *Narrative of the Japanese Occupation*, p. 22.
33 *Burma During the Japanese Occupation*, vol. 1, p. 71, vol. 2, pp. 73–4.
34 *Season and Crop Report of Burma for the Year Ending the 30th June 1943*, p. 8.
35 *Burma During the Japanese Occupation*, vol. 1, pp. 73–4.
36 Hla Pe, *Narrative of the Japanese Occupation*, p. 45.
37 *Burma: Japanese Military Administration*, p. 65.
38 Ibid, p. 41.
39 Ibid, p. 66.
40 *Burma During the Japanese Occupation*, vol. 1, p. 72.
41 Ibid.
42 *Burma: Japanese Military Administration*, pp. 83–4.
43 *Burma: Japanese Military Administration*, pp. 40–1.
44 *Burma During the Japanese Occupation*, vol. 1, pp. 72–3; *Burma: Japanese Military Administration*, p. 96.
45 *Burma: Japanese Military Administration*, p. 96.
46 Boei cho/Boei kenkyujo/Senshi bu, *Shiryoshu Nampo no Gunsei*, p. 206.
47 *Burma During the Japanese Occupation*, vol. 1, p. 74.
48 Ibid, vol. 1, pp. 72–3.
49 Ibid, vol. 1, p. 73.

50 J. Silverstein, 'Transportation in Burma During the Japanese Occupation', *Journal of the Burma Research Society*, 1956, vol. 39, p. 3.
51 *Season and Crop Report of Burma for the Year Ending the 30th June 1943*, p. 9.
52 Silverstein, 'Transportation in Burma During the Japanese Occupation', p. 8.
53 [Burma Government], *Season and Crop Report of Burma for the Year Ending the 30th June 1944*, Rangoon: Superintendent, Govt. Printing & Stationery, 1946, pp. 10–1.
54 *Burma: Japanese Military Administration*, p. 49.
55 *Season and Crop Report of Burma for the Year Ending the 30th June 1943*, p. 12.
56 *Burma During the Japanese Occupation*, vol. 2, pp. 60–1.
57 *Season and Crop Report of Burma for the Year Ending the 30th June 1944*, p. 12.
58 *Burma During the Japanese Occupation*, vol. 2, p. 60.
59 *Season and Crop Report of Burma for the Year Ending the 30th June 1943*, p. 12; *Burma During the Japanese Occupation*, vol. 2, p. 60.
60 *Burma During the Japanese Occupation*, vol. 2, p. 61.
61 Ibid, vol. 1, p. 73, vol. 2, p. 61.
62 G. Huff/S. Majima, 'Financing Japan's World War II Occupation of Southeast Asia', Discussion Papers in Economic and Social History, no. 109 (October, 2012), p. 35; A. Takahashi, 'Regional Differences in Agriculture in Burma During the Japanese Occupation Period', in Nemoto, *Reconsidering the Japanese Military Occupation in Burma*, p. 157.
63 *Season and Crop Report of Burma for the Year Ending the 30th June 1943*, p. 8.
64 *Season and Crop Report of Burma for the Year Ending the 30th June 1943*, p. 3.
65 U Khin Win, *A Century of Rice Improvement in Burma*, Manila: International Rice Research Institute, 1991, p. 38.
66 *Burma During the Japanese Occupation*, vol. 1, p. 81.
67 *Season and Crop Report of Burma for the Year Ending the 30th June 1943*, p. 2.
68 Ibid, pp. 3, 13.
69 *Season and Crop Report of Burma for the Year Ending the 30th June 1944*, p. 12.
70 T. Iwaki, 'Heiho Mobilization and Local Administration in the Japanese Occupation Period: The Case of Pyapon District', in Nemoto, *Reconsidering the Japanese Military Occupation in Burma*, pp. 96–7.
71 *Season and Crop Report of Burma for the Year Ending the 30th June 1943*, pp. 2–3, 13.
72 *Burma During the Japanese Occupation*, vol. 1, p. 82.
73 Hla Pe, *Narrative of the Japanese Occupation*, pp. 18–9.
74 *Season and Crop Report of Burma for the Year Ending the 30th June 1944*, p. 13.
75 *Burma: Japanese Military Administration*, pp. 232–3.
76 Hla Pe, *Narrative of the Japanese Occupation*, p. 45.

17 Indochina during World War II
An economy under Japanese control

Delphine Boissarie

Just before World War II, Indochina had about 25 million inhabitants, including 35,000 Europeans and assimilated persons, who were mainly divided between the two major urban centres, Hanoi (Tonkin) and Saigon (Cochinchina). The prosperity of this French colony was based on the export of rice, pepper, corn and rubber from Cochinchina and coal from Tonkin to France and to neighbouring East Asian countries. Similarly, imports were necessary to the lifestyle of the European community as well as local industry. Because of 'imperial preference', Indochina's foreign trade was mainly oriented towards France.

In June 1940, France's defeat by Nazi Germany and the ensuing breakdown in maritime links between the mother country and the colony left the government of Indochina in an uncomfortable position, both politically and economically. Indochina's government[1] found itself at the mercy of Japan's appetite for conquest. The numerical inferiority of French troops therefore shaped a policy of collaboration with Tokyo which started in June 1940 and resulted in the signing of Franco-Japanese military and economic agreements in July 1941 (Darlan-Kato Agreements). This collaboration apparently gave the Indochina of Jean Decoux, who was loyal to Vichy, the most enviable status among the Japanese-occupied territories, but it was also the most ambiguous. Until the coup on 9 March 1945, Indochina was not, strictly speaking, an occupied country since the French retained an appearance of sovereignty. However, to use a felicitous expression coined by Sébastien Verney, the French actually exercised 'a paper sovereignty', living under an 'unofficial occupation'.[2] In fact, Tokyo gradually took control of the Indochinese economy.

It is possible to identify four distinct phases during this period: from June 1940 to December 1941, Indochina entered a period of 'unwilling concessions' towards Japan.[3] However, it remained free to make choices and sought to strengthen links with its Asian customers and suppliers. After Pearl Harbor, eastern Asia found itself on the front line, and the increasing dependency of the French colony became tougher as Indochina was cut off from France and from its Asian partners. Japan became the only trading partner of Indochina and shaped the local economy to meet its requirements. From 1943, the naval war placed Indochina in a situation of forced self-sufficiency, and the integration into the Japanese coprosperity sphere did not work as agreed. Finally, from *Meigo Sakusen* (Flash Moon Action) of 9 March 1945 and until October 1945 (well after the surrender of Japan on 2 September 1945 and while France was officially freed from German occupation on 8 May 1945), the French totally lost control of the colony, at first in favor of the Japanese, who quickly encouraged the emancipation of the native residents.

Over the whole period, Vietnamese historiography emphasizes that the 'Indochinese' (Vietnamese, Khmers or Laotians) fell under the 'double Franco-Japanese yoke',[4] while French historiography remembers the ambiguous situation which made Indochina both the economic target of the Japanese and the political target of the Allies. Generally speaking, we have to keep in mind that the Japanese occupation of Indochina is an accumulation of the grey zones of colonial history and that of French collaboration, with Germany at home and with Japan in Asia.[5]

We will try to understand how the colony was able to organize its survival though its increased isolation and while satisfying the requirements of the Japanese occupation forces. First, we will see the phases of the control of the Indochinese economy by Hirohito's men before studying thoroughly the impacts of this integration into the Japanese coprosperity sphere on the Indochinese economic organisation. Finally, from the perspective of colonial society and of local companies, we will try to assess the scale of compromises brought about by the isolation of the colony.

Japanese requirements in Indochina

To deprive the Chinese nationalists of their Tonkinese logistics base

Franco-Japanese tensions started from a customs question about the Sino-Tonkinese border, through which cases of goods, including weapons, passed from Haiphong to Kunmin in Yunnan for the Chinese nationalists resisting the Japanese invasion.[6] British Burma and French Tonkin were the only outlets allowing supply to the forces of Jiang Jieshi when all Chinese ports were subject to the Japanese blockade. On 20 June 1940, taking advantage of the fact that France had capitulated to Germany in Europe, the Japanese forced Governor General Catroux to close the border and to allow a Japanese monitoring mission to be stationed there, under the control of General Nishihara. This was the beginning of a long series of ultimatums that gradually subjected the colony to the domination of Japanese troops. Disowned by the French government, Catroux was replaced by Admiral Decoux to head Indochina in July 1940. However, like its previous head, Decoux could only yield to the demands of the Japanese given the weakness of his ability to respond (32,000 men, with 17,000 local auxiliaries, and outdated equipment[7]). Furthermore, on 30 August 1940, an agreement ceded other military facilities to Japan, mainly around the Sino-Tonkinese border, in exchange for recognition of French sovereignty over Indochina and a promise to maintain its territorial integrity. Decoux hoped to temporize in order to avoid the loss of the colony, but hardly a month later, on 22 September 1940, he had to let the Japanese gain use of three airbases, one near Hanoi and two others in the north close to the frontier. Besides this, Admiral Decoux had to accept the stationing of 6,000 troops to the north of the Red River and the potential transit of 25,000 men to Yunnan, as well as the transfer of the Japanese division from Kouang Si to Haiphong for embarkation. Overall, the Japanese secured the free transit of large contingents of the Imperial Army throughout the north of the French colony, unofficially giving them control of the region. Thus Tonkin became a particularly comfortable and welcome rear base for Tokyo within the framework of the war against China.

The signing did not prevent the incident of Lang Son in the week covering 22 through 25 September 1940: 20,000 Japanese soldiers stationed in Yunnan, in concert with the Vietnamese nationalists of Phuc Quoc Dong Minh Hoi (National Restoration), loyal to Prince Cuong De, who had been exiled in Japan since 1915, seized French border crossings in the Lang Son region: 1,900 European and 6,100 Indochinese soldiers were taken by surprise in this air and land attack, with 800 fatalities. The conquered province and the prisoners were then returned by Tokyo, which officially apologised for the unfortunate 'incident', while the Vietnamese nationalists were delivered to French courts, but the warning was noted. The Japanese demonstrated clearly enough to the French that the political stability of the colony depended on the goodwill of the Japanese generals. By October 1940, Japanese troops were permanently present in Tonkin, 600 of whom were stationed in Hanoi.[8]

Japan's first interest was to deprive its Chinese opponents of their supply base, in Indochina and in Burma, and to use Tonkin as a rear base. Once this was achieved, Japan then considered Indochina a reservoir of raw materials directly useful in supporting the Japanese war effort. At this stage, the French collaboration suited Tokyo, since it allowed them to maintain domestic order at little cost. The Japanese still wondered whether they should occupy the country or not. Despite joining the Axis powers on 27 September 1940, Japan still maintained the status quo with the USSR and the United States for one year. Indochina profited partly, and for a limited time, from these uncertainties. However, this apparent freedom came at a cost.

To ensure the maintenance of Japanese troops stationed in Indochina

The military convention of 29 July 1941 (the Darlan-Kato Accords) signed by the Vichy government reinforced Japanese control over the French colony, which agreed to sustain the transit of 50,000 Japanese troops, this time in the south of the colony in Cochinchina. Thus the accord authorised the unofficial occupation of the whole colony from the north to the south and guaranteed free access to the main ports and airfields. At the same time, Indochina was committed to paying an advance on the 'parking fees' of the Japanese, who thenceforward settled their accounts from time to time in gold or convertible currencies until June 1942. These 'allowances of piasters', as Decoux modestly called them in his memoirs, constituted advances on the Japanese military expenses and came to 8 million piasters per month in 1941, to 20 million in the first semester of 1944 and 40 million per month in the second semester of 1944. The transfers were bank transfers from the Indochinese Treasury to a special account of the *Yokohama Specie Bank* (YSB), in 'special yen', dollars or gold. However, from June 1942, the credit that these advances represented was refundable in special yen only, non-convertible and usable only in the territories under Japanese control. Indochina was therefore receiving credits in a currency that it could not use. The *Bank of Indochina* (BIC) was sustaining capital assets representing almost 24 per cent of its balance sheet at the end of 1944, that is to say 716.4 million yen. The BIC was concerned and, through its Saigon Director, Paul Gannay, managed to negotiate guarantees to recover its assets under an agreement signed on 20 March 1943. The YSB agreed to store gold bullion equivalent to the amount of the debt and to pay interest on the advances, which thus become loans. After the coup, the Japanese subjected Indochina and its bank to strict regulation. The total of withdrawals between March and September 1945 amounted to 720 million piasters. For the sake of convenience, the local network of the BIC was placed under the control of the YSB, and Paul Gannay and his officials were imprisoned in Saigon. Even so, at the end of the war, the Americans were to discover 32 tons of gold deposited in the name of the BIC in the vault of the Japanese bank, which had thus respected the letter of the convention of 20 March 1943.[9]

For the Japanese, the aim of these advances was to maintain a military occupation of about 25,000 soldiers, but before *Meigo Sakusen*, this number reached 60,000 soldiers. About 10,000 were based in Tonkin, but a large number of the troops was installed around the colony's economic heart: Saigon and the rice-growing region of Cochinchina.[10] Considering that European population was about 35,000 people at that time, it is easy to measure the vulnerability of the French administration (one or two Japanese soldiers for one European) and the burden on the local budget. However, Decoux, and then his hagiographers stressed it was merely the Japanese 'being there' and denied that there was any form of real occupation before 9 March 1945.[11] According to them, the Indochina government would have succeeded in maintaining French sovereignty to the very last moment, leaving the population with freedom of movement and the local administration with responsibility for internal security. The delicate social and political balance was, however, undermined by Tokyo's stranglehold on the Indochinese economy. A clause in the Darlan-Kato agreement committed both parties to a 'common defence' in the event of potential attacks by either Nationalist China or the Allies, thus ensuring the diplomatic and economic isolation of the entire colony. In this context, collaboration allowed Tokyo to benefit from Indochina, strategic centre of the 'Asian Mediterranean',[12] without having to be too concerned about logistics or internal politics.

Integrating Indochina into the sphere of coprosperity and including it in the war effort

The main goal of the occupation of Indochina was to direct local products such as rice, corn, rubber or wood[13] to Japan and the territories under its influence in order to contribute to the empire's war effort. From 1941, harnessing resources was agreed as part of the Darlan-Kato agreement, renegotiated annually to specify the quantities and the type of products to be exchanged. Rice supply was Japan's primary concern. The agreement of 20 January 1941 states that Indochina would deliver 700,000 tons of rice to Japan – in other words, almost all of the available surplus normally exported. In the agreement, the purchase price per ton was set at the particularly low price of 122 dollars per ton, for a total transaction of 85.4 million dollars.[14] At the time, Indochina produced on average between 5 and 6 million tons of rice per year. The subsequent deal, on 18 July 1942, set the rice export quota at 1.05 million tons, representing all the exportable surplus of rice and corn in the 1942–3 season. The French fulfilled the contract in 1941 and 1942, but in 1943 they only delivered 950,000 tons of rice instead of 1.125 million tons agreed. The poor harvests of 1943–4 and the lack of fertilizer, together with the wear and tear on the machines in the husking plants, reduced the volume of the saleable rice. Poor equipment and climatic uncertainty affected the yield of the rice fields, which dropped by a quarter between 1940 and 1944.

The fall was amplified by both the loss of Cambodian rice-growing territories ceded to Thailand in 1941 after the Franco-Thai conflict and the development of new industrial crops. From 1943, Tokyo demanded an increase in the Indochinese output of cotton, jute, groundnut, rapeseed and minerals, thus pushing Indochinese agriculture in new directions. The area of land devoted to these industrial products increased globally by 317 per cent between 1940 and 1944 (including rapeseed, + 731%; cotton, + 493%; groundnut, + 86%). This 'forced cultivation' also included hemp, mulberry and sesame.[15] The French authorities tried as far as they could to limit the expansion of these crops in the rice-growing areas.[16] Even so, the war and the occupation made Japan into Indochina's sole economic partner. Thus it was vital to respond to the demands of this sovereign-client, even if this despotic reign was hardly a choice.

However, American bombing, from 1942 onwards, particularly of Saigon, Haiphong and Tourane (Da Nang), the main ports in Indochina, decided the Japanese to abandon the export of rice and minerals from June 1944 on. In 1944, Japan collected only two thirds of the required volume of rice (600,000 tons delivered, against 900,000 tons negotiated). Fifteen per cent of the rice acquired by Tokyo was to be sent to Japan and the remaining amount to the territories occupied by the Imperial Army. But in fact, in Saigon and in Cambodia, rice stocks bought by the Japanese were not leaving the quaysides. Meanwhile, the breaking of both land and sea links with Tonkin (which was dependent upon Cochinchina for its rice supply) allowed the exportation of no more than 6,830 tons in 1944, as against 185,620 tons in 1941. Therefore, Tonkin was afflicted by a terrible famine in 1944–5 in which between one and two million people died, while the rice reserves in Cochinchina were rising to almost 304,000 tons. The nationalists took advantage of this to denounce the Vietnamese lot, at the same time suffering from the same colonial situation and occupation.

In general, the circuits of the local economy were profoundly disrupted by the war and the burden of the Japanese occupation.

The organisation of the Indochinese economy

Before Pearl Harbor: redirection of exchange of goods; a short parenthesis

In 1939, France and the French empire accounted for 46 per cent of Indochina's foreign trade, taking in 45 per cent of the rice and 95 per cent of the rubber.[17] The size of these figures owes much to a customs regime which enforced the 'imperial preference', artificially separating the Asian colony and its immediate trading area. In 1931, the piaster was linked to the franc to facilitate commercial relations. However, because of the war at sea, from 1941, Indochina traded with France for only 1 per cent of its exports, and in November 1941, the break was complete: not a single vessel ran between France and Indochina. The high risk of being boarded was added to problems with fuelling the boats (coal and oil).

Indochinese commerce rapidly sought to tighten its links with its regional partners, that is with the markets of the Far East and the Pacific Rim. For instance, half the rubber production for 1940 was sold to the United States. In order to foster Indochina's integration into regional commerce, the Vichy government accorded it customs autonomy from 15 October 1940. Even so, the transition of France, a defeated power, into the camp of collaboration with Germany had a directly negative influence on these new developments. Besides this, the assets of the BIC were frozen by Great Britain in June 1940 and by the United States in February 1941, paralyzing imports.[18] Furthermore, Japan managed to isolate Indochina with the signing of the economic agreements of 6 May 1941, earning there the 'most favoured nation' status. Henceforward Japan had priority for buying rice, maize, coal and so forth. This customs and commercial agreement, matched by a navigation convention, tied the French colony tightly in with the Empire of the Rising Sun. The colony's customs duties, a mainstay of the local budget, also plunged because of the reduction in trade. Besides which, the intensification of the conflict in the Far East ruled out any trade thereafter with Japan's enemies.

This economic isolation was aggravated by destruction and requisitioning afflicting the merchant fleet in Indochina. In 1941, just five freighters, four mixed-cargo vessels and eighteen coasters totalling 131,000 tons remained in Indochina. The Japanese requisitioned eleven of these ships (86,000 tons), while the rest was made available to the Indochinese government. None of these vessels escaped submarines, mines or American aerial bombardment. The Indochinese merchant fleet, already one of the smallest in the Far East, had to be completely rebuilt after the war.[19]

Indochina became progressively dependent on trade with Japan, which had laid hold of most of the colony's external trade from the beginning of 1942.

From Pearl Harbor to 1943: Japan is master of Indochina's foreign trade

The occupation also offered Japanese companies a way to penetrate the Indochinese market. Between 1940 and 1942, the number of Japanese firms present in the colony rose from fourteen to thirty-six. The *Mitsui Bussan Kaisha*, which had long had links with French exporters of rice such as *Denis Frères*, took advantage of this opening up to infiltrate the networks of rice exporting while other *zaibatsu* such as *Mitsubishi*, *Sanko*, *Ataka*, *Taitaku* or *Nakamura* entered the forestry industry. In respect of the agreements of 6 May 1941, the Japanese had access to Indochinese ports, were granted mining and agricultural rights managed by a Franco-Japanese partnership and were able to set up a mission to study Indochinese resources. This was called the 'Japanese economic mission to Indochina' and was supposed to detail very precisely the amenities offered by Indochina. The delegation arrived in October 1941 and was backed by the Ministry of Foreign Affairs and the minister for the Japanese colonies. It included 151 people, divided into fourteen groups (supply, iron, nonferrous metals, food production etc.), led by Yokoyama Masayuki, a career diplomat.[20] Moreover, the setting up of a Franco-Japanese partnership was apparently slowed by the *Bank of Indochina*, which made great efforts to delay the project.[21] The French feared, and rightly so, the domination of Japanese businesses and capital over the local economy, but they were unable to prevent the creation of a few mixed companies (at least three in the mining sector), which were seen as Japanese Trojan horses. From this point of view, playing their role, the professional groups set up by Decoux were able to limit the Nipponese takeover by opposing an administrative front whose task was to slow down any Japanese initiative. However, the sawmills, which were strategically important in shipbuilding, nevertheless passed into Japanese hands, while half of the capital of the Haiphong cement works, essential for major public works, was held by the Japanese. The occupier also infiltrated mining activity by carrying out active research into antimony, manganese, asbestos and saltpetre and by exploiting the tin and tungsten mines in Tonkin.

In 1942, the board of the BIC noted that Japan was virtually the sole purchaser for rice and corn, that 80 per cent of coal exports were sent to Japan and the rest went to countries conquered by them. This way, the Japanese captured 94.6 per cent of Indochinese exports and provided 77.7 per cent of its imports.[22] These figures bear witness to Indochina's integration into the Japanese sphere of coprosperity, which was the final aim of the agreements of May and July 1941. Whether it was wanted or not, the war in the Pacific and the occupation made Japan the only outlet possible for Indochinese productions since the colony's regular customers had gone. In order to prevent the Japanese from entering domestic economic circuits, Decoux decided to centralize the economic management of Indochina by setting up the General Directory of Economic Affairs

(*Direction générale des affaires économiques*), which was charged with negotiating with the occupier and alleviating the shortages. Soon, the mines, agriculture and the forestry service passed into the hands of this body, while the BIC, which was the institution that issued piasters, was placed under the supervision of the colony's government. From that point on, Decoux could appoint the board and the chairman of the bank. The governor of Indochina modelled part of this new organization on Vichy and also by founding six professional groups set up in April 1941 (agriculture and forests, industrial production, mining production, business, transport and credit) under the authority of a central committee and a commissar, also appointed by the admiral. The whole economy therefore passed under the control of the Indochinese government, which accordingly granted import–export licenses and supervised all trade transactions from December 1941 onwards. In 1943, however, we can note that the professional group concerned with business worked exclusively within the framework of the coprosperity sphere under Tokyo's authority.

At the same time, the total amount of currency exchanges with Japan went from 82 to 100 million piasters between 1940 and 1943. Nevertheless, Tokyo, which used to pay its bills in dollars or in 'free yen', began to run short of gold and found a way round this by introducing the 'special yen' in an agreement signed on 30 December 1942. This 'special yen' was based on an overvalued fixed rate with the Peking dollar, and this led to the French colony being robbed of nearly 823 billion 'free yen' between 1942 and 1945. Because of the devaluation of the piaster, Indochina then experienced high inflation, which impacted the cost of living. The monetary mass in circulation jumped from 280.4 million piasters in 1940 to 1,052.3 million in 1944 and confirmed the degradation of the local economy. Moreover, Japan had to compensate for the commercial isolation of the colony by taking the place of the usual suppliers, but this remained an illusion. In 1940, 90 per cent of the oil imported by the colony came from the Dutch East Indies (mainly from the *Société Asiatique des Pétroles*, part of the *Dutch Shell Group*), the rest being bought from the United States (*Standard Oil*), and more than 90 per cent of chemical products, iron and steel came from France. However, Japan, which needed these raw materials to back its war effort, did not put Indochina's needs at the top of its list. The colony received its last consignment of oil in January 1941, which implies that rationing and blockages happened very quickly. In 1943, imports had fallen to a level of about 15 per cent of those of 1939. By 1944, they were only about 2 per cent of the 1939 levels.[23] Indochina was in dire need of everything and entered a 'blockade economy'.

From a blockade economy to the official occupation (end 1943–5)

From the start of the occupation, Indochinese businesses concentrated on exploiting their earlier stocks and on developing local production, especially of substitute products. Spare parts, fuels and oil for engines and divers mechanical pieces were cruelly lacking. As a consequence, the Indochinese government set up a 'council for the industrial development of Indochina', which promoted the building of a chemical production sector. Above all, it was the era of 'make do and mend': reinforced concrete was replaced by lime on bamboo structures, while soaps were made from sodium-laden soils found in the region of Nha Trang. The break in land and sea communications between North and South Vietnam also deprived the Saigon-Cholon electricity station of coal from Hongay, and this had to be replaced by burning wood and rice husks. In rail transport, wood was substituted for coal. Elsewhere, peanut and rapeseed oil replaced industrial oils. In fact, most of the 'forced cultivation' demanded by Japan also answered local demand. Before the war, Indochina only produced 286 tons of raw cotton, which corresponded to only 2 per cent of the needs of the local textile industry. Thus it was that the areas planted with cotton were multiplied by five between 1942 and 1944 (from 10,000 hectares to 52,000 hectares).[24] Once the Japanese quota had been delivered, the producers sold the rest, often at a profit since there was such a need. The ambiguity of the occupation must therefore be highlighted because it was in fact to the benefit of some sectors of the economy.

However, soon, with the war in the Pacific, Indochina found itself deprived of its last client and supplier. At the beginning of 1945, the colony only accounted for 2 per cent of Japanese imports and 14 per cent of its exports. Thus it was of lesser interest to Tokyo, which could no longer organise the transport of Indochinese resources. Moreover, the administrative resistance of the French, who were very imaginative in thwarting the occupier's projects, and then the latent threat of an Allied landing in Indochina, pushed the Japanese into changing strategy. In reality, France had been liberated from the German occupier at the end of 1944. Suddenly Tokyo deemed Indochina an enemy because it was the colony of a state which was now close to the Allies. Ambiguity could no longer prevail. Indochinese resistance was organised under the leadership of General Mordant, head of the French army in the colony. However, Decoux held back from joining de Gaulle and continued with his internal policy of 'National Revolution' and his collaboration with the Japanese even though the Vichy government no longer existed.

During the night of 9 March 1945, the imperial army finally took control of Indochina. Even though they were supported by 30,000 native troops, the 12,000 or so French soldiers could not hold out against the 60,000 Japanese soldiers stationed in the colony. As it was no longer a question of exporting local productions, the army strategy focussed on the colony's financial resources, which it intended to capture in order to manage the financial resources of the conquered territory. The Japanese even invented a new tax, but as bringing it in proved to be extremely difficult, they took a greater interest in gambling activities, which remained lucrative.[25] Moreover, they drained the provisional credits of the colony's general budget and stopped the payment of benefits and in particular those paid to Indochinese and French conscripts. However, Verney notes that expropriations and requisitions were limited in number, and this was probably in order to avoid too deep a disorganisation of the colony. The Saigon Chamber of Commerce became the headquarters of the Kempetaï, symbolising well

Mercury's replacement by Mars in Franco-Japanese relations. Generally speaking, the Japanese did not intend to modify the Indochinese administration, and they kept the colonial structures, judging them to be useful. Minoda, the Japanese governor, only abandoned the federal framework desired by Decoux and instead preferred a clear separation between the Indochinese countries. Otherwise, he appointed and promoted Vietnamese civil servants to management positions which used to be reserved for French executives. This action, which was based on a wider project for the liberation of Asian peoples, was associated with a generous policy towards native agents in terms of payments and gratuities. This was undoubtedly with a view to preparing the postwar situation by encouraging good relations between Japan and the future Indochinese states.

Daily life and work

The wallet of the Indochinese

The Indochinese population were in desperate need of basic goods and medicines. The introduction of rationing for imported products which were reserved exclusively for Europeans and assimilated people who could justify a European lifestyle took place in July 1940. To slow the sharp rise in the price of rice and to limit the growth of a black market, in 1943, the authorities decided that the Cereals Committee would be the sole purchaser of paddy rice from producers and the sole rice broker in Cholon. On the official market, a *quintal* of rice cost 550 piasters in 1945, which was 77 per cent higher than in 1944, when the price was 125 piasters. On the black market, rice sold from 30 to 140 per cent higher. The price rise affected all goods: more than 60 per cent between 1941 and 1945 in Saigon-Cholon. The colonial government's intervention in the economy by fixing prices, quotas and exchange rates was not enough to contain the spiralling market and inflation. In 1944, a European's purchasing power had been divided by three compared to 1940, while that of an Indochinese worker had been divided by five.[26] Moreover, all of the population suffered very steep tax rises decided by the government of Indochina in order to meet the deficit in customs revenues and to ensure financial survival. Living conditions for the local population declined especially from 1943 onwards because of the dismantling of economic circuits and the economy coming under Japanese domination.

Working under the occupation[27]

As they were sensitive to the rigours of the tropical climate, the health of European workers declined due to the lack of Western goods and the impossibility of holidaying in Europe. Their contracts stipulated that every three or four years, they could return to the mother country with their family for six months, to which had to be added the two months of outwards and return voyages by sea. The expatriate generally took advantage of this break to restore his health by taking a thermal cure. This relative reclusion was more or less well tolerated. In most sectors, the slowing down of activity led to situations of overstaffing. Firms encouraged their employees to take their holidays in the colony. Local holidays were therefore more frequent and longer (up to four months) during the occupation. So it was, paradoxically, that the occupation proved profitable to local tourist industries and to the development of colonial sociability. Apart from holidays, textile firms like the *Société Cotonnière du Tonkin* dismissed some of their European and local workforce or suggested voluntary redundancy, with indemnities. Nevertheless, the populations did not suffer too much from the Japanese presence; at least not until the coup. Afterwards, the European population was either interned or confined to residence. In Tonkin, 9,000 of the 12,000 French military personnel were made prisoner. Five to 6 per cent of the French population of Indochina was killed (about 3,000 deaths), and more than a third were imprisoned (about 15,000 prisoners) in appalling conditions (lack of hygiene and food, torture). The violent treatment of the new prisoners went beyond the harsh living conditions experienced by POWs who had been concentrated up till then in Indochina by the Japanese.

From April 1942 onwards, the Japanese had set up a prisoner-of-war camp in Saigon, in an industrial zone near the Saigon River docks. The 1,664 souls who were detained in the camp in 1945 were British (500 prisoners), Dutch (900), American military (209) and Australians (55). The British from Singapore were the most numerous at first. From 4 April 1942, 1,000 were brought from Changi Prison on the *Nisshu Maru*, which was sailing for Saigon. On 22 June 1943, 700 of them were sent to build the Burma Railway. One thousand other POWs of different nationalities were sent to Cambodia to build a road between Phnom Penh and Battambang, while some small groups of about a hundred men were sent to Dalat. Elsewhere, in Saigon, smaller prisons held soldiers from British India. All these men were sent to work either on loading and unloading ships flying the Japanese flag which were moored in Saigon Bay or else on the building of an aerodrome. The working day varied between 11 and 18 hours, with insufficient food rations. Officers received 20 yen per month, even if they had not worked, and the others were paid less than 1 yen per day. The main camp was placed under the orders of Lieutenant Hakuzaki, then Lieutenant Katagiri. The sanitary conditions were dire. Nevertheless, life was made more bearable by the arrival of parcels of food, clothes, medicine and sums of money which the French in Saigon passed on to the prisoners in secret. Towards the end of the war, certain privileged prisoners were even authorised to go out into Saigon in the evening. In short, the living conditions were judged to be tolerable compared to those in other Japanese work camps. The main danger facing the Saigon prisoners was Allied bombing because the camp was within the strategic target of the port.[28] Beyond that, their isolation on French Indochinese territory is supplementary proof of this 'paper sovereignty', which local authorities enjoyed until the coup.

From June 1940 until the coup of 9 March 1945, the French authorities in the Indochinese colony lived in perpetual fear of losing the semblance of sovereignty that Tokyo conceded to them. Until 1944–5, the collaboration policy of the Indochinese government undoubtedly partly convinced the Japanese to go along with this situation in suspension. At the same time, this protected the inhabitants from the harsher effects of the war which were borne in other territories occupied by the imperial army. Tokyo did not care very much about the fate of the populations of the French colony just as long as they contributed to the Japanese war effort. Thus, the economic angle is perhaps the most pertinent point from which to evaluate the potential of the Japanese occupation in Indochina. Gradually, Tokyo managed to take control of Indochina's foreign trade. Japan quickly became the sole trading partner of the colony and could thus force the production of new crops in order to make them match its own needs, within the 'sphere of coprosperity'. On the other hand, Indochina was deprived of its usual suppliers and was quickly obliged to function in autarky, especially from 1943 onwards, when Allied bombing cost Japan its domination of maritime routes. For the Indochinese populations and for local industry, the shortages were hard to manage, and the black market exploded. The famine in Tonkin in 1944–5 announced the end of a precarious balance, and it suddenly raised the human toll of the war in Indochina. The Japanese coup shattered all the illusions of the European community, who became the main target for the atrocities of the imperial army for more than six months.

Also, beyond the strictly economic aspects of the Japanese occupation, the political toll of this episode was very heavy. The Second World War has generally been interpreted by the historiography of the colony as a prelude to the Indochina War. One can look for all the first signs of local freedom movements throughout the history of the colony, from when it was first conquered,[29] but some have focused more closely on the Japanese occupation, which implied a functioning in isolation which was unsustainable from many points of view. The part played by Decoux is still a topic for discussion. Some see him as the protector of French sovereignty, whereas others view him as a collaborator or an impotent puppet in the hands of Tokyo, but his degree of resistance to the occupier, by inertia or by strategy, still poses a problem. Moreover, even though the centralisation of economic functions may have temporarily dissuaded the Japanese from dispensing with their French intermediaries, this eventually played a role in a programme of National Revolution which echoed the political ideology promoted by the collaborationist Vichy government back in France. Recent historiography has tried to measure the impact of this nationalist policy on independence movements and in particular on those of the Vietnamese. However, we can say, without too much debate, that the economic weakening of Indochina through the war and the Japanese occupation undeniably played a part in triggering the independence movement.

Notes

1 The governor of Indochina was, until July 1940, Georges Catroux, and then, until 1945, Jean Decoux.
2 S. Verney, *L'Indochine sous Vichy. Entre Révolution nationale, collaboration et identités nationales, 1940–1945*, Paris: Riveneuve, 2012, pp. 193, 199.
3 P. Lamant, 'La Révolution nationale dans l'Indochine de l'amiral Decoux', *Revue d'histoire de la Deuxième Guerre Mondiale*, 1985, vol. 138, p. 29.
4 Nguyên Khac Viên, *Vietnam, une longue histoire*, Hanoï: The Gioi, 1993 (5th print, 2004), p. 275.

5 Verney, *L'Indochine sous Vichy*, p. 20.
6 Three thousand tons of materials monthly in 1937; 14,000 tons in 1939; 20,000 tons each month in 1940. See J. Valette, *Indochine 1940–1945. Français contre Japonais*, Paris: Sedes, 1993, pp. 14–15. D. Niollet, *L'épopée des douaniers en Indochine 1874–1954*, Paris: Kailash, 1998, p. 533.
7 P. Brocheux/D. Hémery, *Indochina, an ambiguous colonization 1858–1954*, Berkeley: University of California Press, 2009, p. 337.
8 Verney, *L'Indochine sous Vichy*, p. 191.
9 M. Meuleau, *Des pionniers en Extrême-Orient. Histoire de la Banque de l'Indochine. 1875–1975*, Paris: Fayard, 1990, pp. 433–6.
10 This was 56,420 Japanese soldiers by February 1945. Verney, *L'Indochine sous Vichy*, p. 194.
11 J. Decoux, *A la barre de l'Indochine, histoire de mon gouvernement général, j'ai maintenu*, Paris: Plon, 1949, p. 166; P. Devillers, *Histoire du Viêt-nam de 1940 à 1952*, Paris: Seuil, 1952, p. 77; P. Grandjean, *L'Indochine face au Japon 1940–1945. Decoux – de Gaulle, un malentendu fatal*, Paris: L'Harmattan, 2004, pp. 45–51.
12 F. Gipouloux, *La Méditerranée asiatique. Villes portuaires et réseaux marchands en Chine, au Japon et en Asie du Sud-Est, XVIe–XXIe siècle*, Paris: CNRS, 2009.
13 Indochina agreed to provide Japan 200,000 m^3 of wood. Verney, *L'Indochine sous Vichy*, p. 208.
14 Verney, *L'Indochine sous Vichy*, p. 220.
15 See the table drawing the evolution of the acreage dedicated to industrial crops in P. Brocheux, *Une histoire économique du Viet Nam, 1850–2007*, Paris: Les Indes savantes, 2009, p. 163, figures from Bui Minh Dung, 'Japan's Role in the Vietnamese Starvation of 1944–1945', *Modern Asian Studies*, 1995, vol. 29, p. 591.
16 J. Martin, 'Rapport au conseil du Gougal, 3 février 1945', *Revue d'histoire de la Deuxième Guerre Mondiale*, 1985, vol. 138, pp. 71–2.
17 Meuleau, *Des pionniers en Extrême-Orient*, p. 416.
18 Brocheux, *Une histoire économique du Viet Nam*, p. 154.
19 F. Kérisit, 'L'A.M.B.C. en Indochine entre 1939 et 1945', *Bulletin de l'Association Symboles et traditions*, undated; D. Boissarie, *La maison Denis Frères en Extrême-Orient, 1862–1954* (PhD in progress).
20 Le Manh Hung, *The Impact of World War II on the Economy of Vietnam 1939–1945*, Singapore, Eastern Universities Press, 2004, p. 169; Verney, *L'Indochine sous Vichy*, pp. 205, 215, 217.
21 Meuleau, *Des pionniers en Extrême-Orient*, p. 432.
22 Verney, *L'Indochine sous Vichy*, pp. 21, 206, 207. Meuleau, *Des pionniers en Extrême-Orient*, p. 427.
23 Ibid.
24 Brocheux, *Une histoire économique du Viet Nam*, p. 162.
25 Tax from 1.8 piasters to 5.5 piasters upon men more than 18 years old. Verney, *L'Indochine sous Vichy*, p. 437.
26 M. Decaudin, 'Essais de contrôle du marché du riz en Cochinchine 1941–1944', APOM 4, CAOM, quoted by Brocheux, *Une histoire économique du Viet Nam*, p. 160. See also Verney, *L'Indochine sous Vichy*, p. 209.
27 D. Boissarie, 'La maison Denis Frères en Extrême-Orient: l'époque du système D', in H. Bonin/C. Bouneau/H. Joly (eds.), *Les entreprises et l'outre-mer français pendant la Seconde Guerre mondiale*, Bordeaux: Maison des sciences de l'homme d'Aquitaine, 2010, pp. 325–38.
28 J.L. Norwood/E.L. Shek, 'Prisoners of war camps in areas other than the four principal islands of Japan', 1946/07/31, Combined Arms Research Library Digital Library, http://cgsc.cdmhost.com/cdm/ref/collection/p4013coll8/id/3035, viewed in September 2014.
29 C. Fourniau, *Domination coloniale et résistance nationale, 1858–1914*, Paris: Les Indes savantes, 2003.

V
Multinationals acting in occupied economies

18 German steel industry's expansion in occupied Europe

Business strategies and exploitation practice[1]

Ralf Ahrens

There should have been no major German industrial branch which did not attempt to use the military expansion of the Nazi regime for its own economic purposes. This chapter analyses this process using the example of an industry that was of outstanding importance for the armaments industry in the Reich as well as in the annexed or occupied territories since 1938. The German iron and steel industry also enjoyed a reputation of strong political influence, not least because of its high degree of concentration. In the Nazi period, on the other hand, they had to face massive government control attempts and new competition by the state-owned *Reichswerke 'Hermann Göring'*.[2]

Nevertheless, recent research on the prewar years carved out rather high freedom of action for German companies: generally, they had not had to be forced into investing in the autarky and armament production but were sufficiently motivated thereto by economic incentives – that is by the governmental limiting of entrepreneurial risks.[3] The obvious question is to what extent this also applied to the behaviour of companies with regard to the acquisition of foreign enterprises in the German-occupied areas and their operation during the war. From a company-historical perspective, the attention of this chapter is concentrated on the short- and long-term motives and interests of the iron and steel industry and on competition and coordination in accessing the new locations as well as on the reasons for successes and failures in distribution conflicts. Furthermore, it has to be discussed under which general economic and political conditions plus in which contract structures and forms of property the acquisition of foreign industrial premises was put into effect. Finally, there is the question of how relevant these formal property rights were for local business practices and their results. Our knowledge about investments, profits and the conditions of the depreciation allowance but also about the economic performance and the organization of occupied factories is still surprisingly low. The study therefore focuses on three relatively well-researched companies: the *Flick* concern, *Krupp* and the *Gutehoffnungshütte (GHH)*.[4] After some brief notes on the initial conditions arisen in the 'peace years' of the Nazi regime, it examines consecutively the German steel industry's expansion in Western and Eastern Europe.

1. Preconditions: competition and limited capacities

Immediately after the Great Depression, it obviously made sense for the German iron and steel industry to use the armament boom starting in 1933/34 for utilizing and increasing its capacities. However, the extent and speed differed among single companies. The highly concentrated industry, dominated by a series of vertical concerns with their own coal suppliers and manufacturing enterprises, was organized within cartels which highly regulated production and sales. However, within this market regulation, the companies were in competition with each other and pursued different growth strategies.[5] These different strategies also became visible after the Nazi 'seizure of power'. Friedrich Flick, for example, bade intensively for armament orders to employ and even extend the hitherto underutilized capacities of his recently rearranged steel and manufacturing concern. For these purposes, Flick quickly built a new political-military network that soon linked him closer to the Nazi regime than other industrialists. Paul Reusch, chairman of the old-established *Gutehoffnungshütte*, strove toward armament orders as well, but he was willing to risk confrontation with the new regime on other fields. The differences between the two companies became even more visible in dealing with Jewish entrepreneurs, where Flick behaved considerably more aggressively concerning the 'aryanisation' of foreign companies. As a result, Flick's company grew much faster than *GHH* during the prewar years.[6] The leadership of the *Krupp* concern was also much more reluctant than Flick because the company had had bad experiences when a complete orientation towards arms production during the First World War suddenly had to be replaced by civilian product lines afterwards.[7]

The different attitude towards the Nazi regime and its industrial policy also appeared in the exposure to the *Reichswerke AG für Erzbau und Hüttenwesen 'Hermann Göring'* founded in 1937. This government-owned enterprise under the direction of the ambitious National Socialist Paul Pleiger was originally created as a part of the autarky policy under the Four Year Plan to compensate the insufficient supply of the armament industry with iron ore and pig iron by private business. Backed by Göring and his Four Year Plan bureaucracy, the *Reichswerke* quickly evolved into a serious competitor of the old-established coal and steel companies. Flick, however, held considerably less distance to Pleiger than his competitors.[8] The *Reichswerke*'s 'policy of grabbing everything that came its way' in annexed or occupied territories without having to respect the economic calculus of private business did not only result in a 'model of inorganic growth' of the state concern.[9] It was also to become of great importance in the competition for new fabric sites in the annexed or occupied territories since 1938.

The emergence of a new iron and steel concern did not change the fact that after six years of rearmament, industrial capacities and labour force were already utilized to their limits when the Second World War began.[10] The demands on the armaments production of coal and steel companies, however, especially after the failure of the *Blitzkrieg* strategy against the Soviet Union, still increased, although the production of crude steel in the Reich sharply decreased in 1940 and then stagnated because of coal and labour shortages.[11] The seizure of additional raw materials thus became not only a political objective but also a motive for the taking over of facilities in the occupied territories by private enterprises and for respective competition among them. It applies to this industry as well what Peter Hayes has pointed out regarding the chemical giant *IG Farben*: the companies' 'imperialism was the sort that followed the flag', but the resulting opportunities were realized once the conditions seemed profitable.[12] At least in the former German territories in France and Poland, the example of the iron and steel industry indicates that businessmen regarded it more or less as a matter of course to take long-term benefits from the military aggression of the Nazi regime. However, as the following sequences will demonstrate, the problems of the overexpanded heavy industry were not solvable through occupational expansion.

2. The business of occupation

Although fundamental differences based on general political conceptions certainly existed between the occupation and exploitation of Western and Eastern European countries, a closer look reveals the necessity for further regional differentiation. Depending on the countries' industrial levels but also on the racist hierarchies of the Nazis, the ideas about the highly developed Czech complex of armaments and heavy industry, for example, were very different from those on the mining, iron and steel regions of the Soviet Union or the vast rural areas of Eastern Europe. Not least, the permanent changes of the military situation influenced economic planning and practice in the occupied regions. For German companies willing to do business in these countries, relations with the various political leaders on the local level and in the competing centres of power of the Nazi regime were also highly important.[13]

The political and economic conditions of the German business activity in the occupied territories were completed by different legal orders, which in turn arose from the different status of the annexed or occupied territories but also from the national business law partially remaining in force.[14] The acquisition of factories in occupied countries by German companies occurred in very different legal constructs as well. Besides the purchase of capital participations or the 'aryanisation' of Jewish-owned businesses, the deployment of German business representatives as 'trustees' or 'godfathers' was of great importance within the mining, iron and steel industry. In this model, the companies did not receive formal property rights; yet it allowed for a significant influence on production programs, capital stocks and composition of workforce, as will be demonstrated.[15]

2.1 Expanding capacities in the West

Despite institutional differences, the economic policy of occupation in Vichy France, Belgium and the Netherlands was quite similar. In order to include the economies of Western Europe in the preparations for war against the Soviet Union as effectively as possible, the leadership of the Nazi state in the summer of 1940 decided to stop the initial confiscations of raw materials and machinery.

Instead, the companies in these countries were integrated into the war economy by armament orders which they had to assume as subcontractors of German enterprises in the context of 'order relocations' (*Auftragsverlagerungen*). For instance, *Deutsche Werft*, a subsidiary of the *GHH* group, operated the French navy shipyard Toulon in order to 'align to the needs of the German war effort'.[16] The Flick concern from 1943 on supplied fifteen French projectile factories with contracts and with steel from its Rombach plant in occupied Lorraine.[17] To some extent, German trustees or commissioners were installed in Dutch or French companies. But apart from the 'aryanisation' of Jewish-owned businesses, no expropriations of the previous owners took part. Seizures by German companies were performed to some degree through the acquisition of shares, thus preparing for the expected European greater economic sphere under German domination after the war.[18]

Even here, major German major enterprises had to face the limits of their influence; *Vereinigte Stahlwerke*, the largest German steel combine, thus failed with an attempt to take over the majority of the Dutch steel company *Hoogovens*.[19] Especially the big banks benefited from arranging the acquisition of shares in foreign corporations by German companies, though the overall volume remained below political expectations.[20] For German industry, the transfer of orders and later the adoption of 'godparenthoods' could indeed include an interest in future acquisitions to secure the access to the respective markets. For instance, the *Krupp* concern in 1941 kept an eye on how the competitor *Mannesmann* activated political protection for its access to roller and press plants and how the companies *Ferrostaal* and *Otto Wolff* shared the Dutch steel trade with the Soviet Union among themselves.[21] But for the short term, German companies utilized the order relocations mainly so as to balance own shortages in production or in research and development or to avoid investment in new armament capacities whose profitability in the coming postwar period seemed doubtful. Occasionally, relocations or 'godparenthoods' also provided the opportunity to undermine the threat of a forced shutting down of production lines which were not important for war. For the foreign companies, a fundamental interest in acquiring relocation orders existed as they became able to maintain production and to get referred to raw materials and labour force. Depending on market conditions and ownership structures, they could even exert a certain bargaining power on their German contractors.[22]

Regarding Vichy France, a strong overall continuity of corporate structures can be observed despite numerous interventions of the occupation policy and despite the exerted influence of German companies: 'There were neither nationalizations nor privatizations, no big bankruptcy and hardly any mergers'. The elimination of trade unions and communists also promoted the willingness of French companies to fit into the new circumstances.[23] The situation was different in Luxembourg and Lorraine. Partly former German territories, these regions were organized under a German military, later civilian administration and were formally integrated into the Reich's territory in 1942.[24] Exactly these regions stood center of the expansive efforts of German steel concerns. Some of them had already owned plants here which had been confiscated (for compensation) after the First World War. The iron and steel works which now came under German control again had the big advantage that they possessed their own ore base, the Lorraine and Luxembourgian minette ore mines. After the armistice, however, not the German companies but special political appointees received control over the iron ore and coal deposits. Otto Steinbrinck, who beforehand had been chief representative of Friedrich Flick, was nominated as general commissioner for the iron and steel industry in Luxembourg, Belgium and Northern France; the Saar industrialist Hermann Röchling took over the same position in the later annexed 'German-Lorraine' (Moselle) and in the occupied French part (Meurthe-et-Moselle); Paul Raabe from the board of managers of *Reichswerke* became general commissioner for the operation of iron ore in Luxembourg and Lorraine.

The private German iron and steel companies took it for granted to receive Lorraine and Luxembourgian works as property after a final peace settlement. But in June 1940, they declared their preliminary abdication of formal tenures towards the Minister for Economic Affairs of the Reich, Funk, as long as this also held good for the state-owned *Reichswerke*. Instead, they applied to Göring and his staff for provisional trusteeships, out of which a preemption right within the final assignments should arise. One of the most coveted objects was the Luxembourgian *ARBED* concern with its subsidiaries, the core of the Grand Duchy's heavy industry. Right here, however, the competition between the German aspirants and their limited room for manoeuvre clearly crystallized. Gustav Simon, Gauleiter and Head of the Civil Administration, and the private German coal and steel industry agreed over the defence of the claims of *Reichswerke*, which vigorously strove towards an acquisition. Finally, the Luxembourgian management resumed production without a change of ownership but had to come to terms with control by the Gauleiter – as did other Luxembourgian mines and smelting works, too. At the same moment, a complete reorganization of Lorraine and Luxembourgian ore mines by fragmentation and mergers was discussed. But the political stance on the different demands remained dilatory; the regulation of tenures between French or Luxembourgian owners and the German occupiers was adjourned until the postwar term.

Pleiger's *Reichswerke* finally were compensated with two large smelting works in Lorraine. Whilst among private corporations, *Vereinigte Stahlwerke*, *Klöckner*, *Otto Wolff* and *Röchling* got assigned former concern sites in Luxembourg or Lorraine, *Krupp*, *Mannesmann* and *GHH* went away empty-handed. Friedrich Flick, in contrast, received the *Rombacher Hüttenwerke*, although his company had had no presence in Lorraine until then. The private companies had indeed attempted to coordinate the competition with *Reichswerke*, but at the same time they matched each other in a footrace. The loss of former estates after the First World War finally played only a limited role for political decisions on the allocation of 'trusteeships'. At least for the acquisitions of Flick and the *Reichswerke*, the better contacts with Göring and his entourage were the decisive factor. Conversely, the inefficacy of *GHH* within the poker of distribution resulted from a tactical mistake: Paul Reusch also wanted his group to incorporate a Lorraine metallurgical plant. In order to avoid the competition with the former German owners, whose claims he understood as entirely legitimate, he did a priori not centre his interest on any of the originally German, after-the-First-World-War-dispossessed factories. Finally, *GHH* did not receive any trusteeship in the occupied West, as the initially envisaged plant Micheville – which would have increased the crude steel capacity of the group by 40 per cent – lay beyond the intended new German-French border.[25]

After being deployed as trustees by order of Göring in January 1941, the German steel combines had to conclude operating agreements with the German Reich, thus managing the factories 'on behalf of the Reich' but 'on their own account'. They received a preemption right for the postwar period but until then had to pay a production charge to the Reich.[26] The concrete business practice under these conditions so far can only be reconstructed in using the example of the Flick concern.[27] Here, the Rombach capacities were always considered a future part of the concern's industrial production complex. An appropriate design of the operating contracts with the right to property acquisition after the war as well as the decision-making authority over depreciation allowances and capital expenditure was obstinately demanded by Flick and other private companies and finally enforced in 1944. Management and the supervisory board of a company founded specifically for Rombach's operation were filled with management personnel from other subsidiaries of the concern.

Instead of searching for short-term windfall gains, Flick obviously intended a midterm integration of a further concern site. Just like his competitors from the Ruhr and the Saar, he acted on the assumption that Lorraine and Luxembourg would remain part of the Reich and that its iron and steel industry would be included in the German cartel structures after the war. Flick was therefore quite willing to invest own cash resources in the modernization and expansion of the Rombach capacities. He also took between 25 and 50 million reichsmarks into account for a future purchase. But after the new managers had looked more closely at the obtained plant, it quickly emerged that the original assessment of its capability had been greatly exaggerated. Parts of the site were severely obsolete; altogether, the investments in the factory in the 1930s had been far less than the depreciation. In addition, due to a lack of capacity for iron ore production within the plant complex, the steel and rolling mills could not be optimally utilized. Referred to a later presentation, the Flick group therefore invested 16 million reichsmarks in the Rombach plants; and still in March 1944, they calculated with capital investments of more than 12 million up to the end of 1945. The danger of permanently losing this money, indeed, was very low. For as far as the capital expenditure had been approved by the authorities, the Flick concern could demand reimbursement of the residual value from the German Reich if the purchase of the plant fell through after end of war. Ultimately, the entrepreneurial risk of Flick thus was limited to the ongoing operation of the factory. The risk was further reduced by the right to shortly depreciate the capital expenditures for new machinery and buildings from the taxable profits.

However, the profits of the Rombach operation company were kept within tight limits not only on these grounds. The steel production of the plant increased extensively in the short run – Rombach fabricated 600,000 tons in 1943 and thus just under 2 per cent of the Reich's total production – but then decreased significantly in 1944. The proportion of quality steel, which was particularly important for the production of armaments, increased from the original 16 to then 49 per cent until the early stages of 1944. But significant cost increases and a cumulative deterioration of the plants were shrouded by these success figures. Being overexpanded and snowed under with armament orders, the German investment goods industry could not provide enough machines and equipment for new investments. Furthermore, as everywhere in occupied Western Europe, it lacked transport capacity to ensure the supply of coking coal and skilled labour, because a significant part of the French permanent staff was either evicted from German-Lorraine or deported for forced labour into the 'Old Reich'. As a consequence, the proportion of forced labourers in the workforce increased rapidly; in 1944, of the approximately 6,200 workers, only 2,800 were Germans and Lorrainers. About a quarter of the employees were women, among whom especially Russian female workers also had to take over heavy physical work. Within the factory-owned forced labour camps, the harsh working conditions and the insufficient food were attended by a brutal disciplinary regime.

Since the shortage of raw materials, capital goods and labour represented a general characteristic of the German war economy, one may assume that the other plants operated by private mining companies in Luxembourg and Lorraine faced the same problems. Several smelting works were war disabled and would have needed extensive investments. In addition, conflicts of aims erupted within the distribution of ore and coal between German and Lorraine-Luxembourgian sites. The *ARBED* works still operated by the old management also produced far below the prewar level between 1941 and 1944; the targeted modernization of facilities remained selectively.[28]

2.2 (Almost) free rides to the East

Even the conditions for economic expansion in France, Belgium and the Netherlands, that is countries with relatively similar economic structures, were quite different. The situation in Eastern and Central Europe turned out to be even more differentiated. Concerning the status of the various countries, one can follow Richard Overy's basic differentiation between 'incorporated territories' (Austria, the Czech regions and the Silesian part of Poland), 'allies and satellite states' (Slovakia and parts of South-East Europe) and 'colonial regions' (the more eastern parts of Poland, the Baltic states, Serbia and the constituent states of the Soviet Union).[29] In contrast to Western Europe and due to the competition of the *Reichswerke*, the expansion into the annexed territories with industrial structures most similar to the Reich remained inaccessible to the private mining industry, while prospects of an enormous territorial expansion seemed to open up temporarily in the 'colonial' regions.

The highly industrialized Czech territories now labelled Protectorate Bohemia and Moravia in the longer run were to be included in the Reich as one of its core industrial regions. Economic policy therefore tried to stabilize the Protectorate's industrial production and to foster investment, thus producing potential conflict with German business interests. Even the powerful *Reichswerke* occasionally had to stand back with investment plans behind political population considerations. The state-owned concern already had benefited most from the 'aryanisation' and 'Germanisation' after the annexation of Austria and the Sudetenland; the great exceptional case among the private companies was Flick, who could absorb large parts of the two 'aryanised' lignite groups of the brothers Petschek in negotiations with Pleiger. After the German invasion of Prague, Pleiger claimed as well a majority of the major Czech mining, iron and steel, machinery and vehicle manufacturing companies. The *Reichswerke* finally possessed, among others, two thirds of the Czech crude steel capacity and extensive mining operations as well as the Brno munitions plants and the *Škoda* group. The management level of those companies had been almost completely replaced by German managers.[30]

Likewise, the *Reichswerke* had top priority concerning the distribution of the coal and steel industry in Upper Silesia and the new General Government, which had been mainly confiscated after the German invasion. Since the public enterprise was able to monopolize the formerly private Polish-owned stone coal mines, and since the formerly state-run mines devolved to the state-owned enterprise *Preussag*, the originally declared interests of Krupp and Flick vanished quickly. The potentially interesting iron and steel mills would have remained without own coal basis; the private companies thus would have become highly dependent on the public enterprises concerning their fuel supply.[31]

In any case, Friedrich Flick really sprang into action not before a stable interest of the Krupp concern in the Bismarckhütte had become apparent in the summer of 1940 and not before the *Ballestrem* group had reengrossed their former East Upper Silesian sites. Similar to Lorraine and Luxembourg, although to a lesser extent, not only a competition of private mining companies with the *Reichswerke* but also a competition among themselves arose. Even more than in Lorraine, the starting position for the potential division of the markets might have played a significant role after the war. In the interim, the interest of the Flick management was highly kept within a limit, because they feared huge investment needs in the face of the technological obsolescence of the initially envisaged plants. Flick's steel expert Odilo Burkart internally characterized a market entry as 'economic madness'; Hermann von Hanneken, the political plenipotentiary for the iron and steel industry, spoke of a 'heap of ruins'. The Main Trustee Office for the East (*Haupttreuhandstelle Ost*) installed by Göring, which pulled the strings concerning the distribution of the formerly Polish company property, and the Ministry of Economic Affairs tried to ply the private sector with some works.[32]

But in 1941, finally Röchling as well quit the competition for the Upper Silesian iron works. Only two large companies remained: the *Oberschlesische Hüttenwerke AG Gleiwitz*, in possession of the Upper Silesian *Ballestrem* group, and the *Berghütte* group, which combined the slow-selling works without own coal base and whose shares were privatized by a consortium under the leadership of *Deutsche Bank* and *Dresdner Bank* via the stock market in 1942. *Berghütte* and *Oberhütten* produced almost 90 per cent of the Upper Silesian crude steel production in 1942; the works of *Berghütte* group supplied armaments to a great extent already since 1940.[33] For the plants controlled by Pleiger, profitability was subordinated to output. Private entrepreneurs like Flick and Krupp were used to calculating differently, and the experience of a competitor finally proved them right: *GHH* took over a machine factory in the Upper Silesian Tarnowitz in 1941 that potentially could serve as substitute capacity for a German plant in case of war damages. Here, the Nazi economic adviser (*Gauwirtschaftsberater*) was able to disapprove a designated director for political reasons, thus limiting the freedom of action of private business. The number of employees almost doubled between 1941 and 1944, after *GHH* had changed production over to subcontracting for the mining industry. In the longer term, however, extensive investment in modernization would have been required.[34]

The latter problem the Upper Silesian works had in common with those in the occupied Soviet territories, although the situation here was different in many respects. Here, the occupation policy initially tended to the greatest possible exploitation of raw materials and labour in a colonial region but not to a major industry expansion, inherently because of the racist spatial planning of the Nazi regime. In addition, the establishment of state monopoly companies for the East (*Ostgesellschaften*) demonstrated the political intention to organize the access to the major Soviet factories in another manner than in the West. As well as representatives of other companies and industries, German steel industrialists quite early declared their interest in the heavy industrial centres of the Ukraine in the Dnepr and Donezk regions, but the competition initially remained more cautious than in the West. In August 1941, it became apparent that control over the coal mining as well as the iron and steel industry would be completely in the hands of Paul Pleiger, whom Göring forwarded the management of the *Berg- und Hüttenwerksgesellschaft Ost (BHO)*, which held a monopoly on the operation, lease or transfer of mining, iron and steel facilities in the occupied Soviet territories. There were representatives of the private concerns in the supervisory board of this company, but at the same time, Göring also signalized that there would be privatizations of the former Soviet state enterprises after the war. After the failure of the *Blitzkrieg* strategy and in view of urgent staff shortages in the Ukrainian metallurgical plants, the distribution of 'godparenthoods', which were factually a kind of trusteeship in favour of the Reich, began in the fall of 1942. *Krupp*, *Vereinigte Stahlwerke*, *Hoesch*, *Gutehoffnungshütte*, *Klöckner* and *Mannesmann* all benefited from the distribution, but again the main profiteer was Friedrich Flick. In the beginning of 1943, his *Mitteldeutsche Stahlwerke* in cooperation with Pleiger's *Reichswerke* founded the operating company *Dnjepr Stahl GmbH*, which controlled almost all steel mills in the Dnepr bend.[35]

In this case, too, Friedrich Flick had sent his managers seriously into negotiations with the responsible political authorities not until the summer of 1942, when he had found out about serious efforts of Krupp. The competition motive thus played a role in the East as well as in occupied France. The German steel industrialists obviously had no inhibitions about expanding into territories of a war of extermination: already in November 1941, reports of an industrial expert from Military Economic Inspection for the South (*Wehrwirtschaftsinspektion Süd*) circulated among them which reported executions of Soviet POWs, horrific conditions in detention camps and systematic killings of the Jewish population in the Dnepr area. After the Germans had taken the Ukrainian plants, these were to operate only with the massive use of forced labour at all and even then only to a much lesser scale than in the prewar period. The Dnepr steel works, for example, in which about 100,000 people had worked before war, had around 17,000 employees in the summer of 1943. As the previous workforce had been deported to forced labour into the Reich, and since the civilian population of more eastern-situated regions preferably escaped from the labour assignment, the management resorted to all available deportees and prisoners, though these could hardly bear the brunt because of their state of health and abysmal supply.

In addition to the labour shortage, machines and engines had been removed or destroyed by the Red Army before the invasion of the Wehrmacht. Although the operations could be started in May 1943, the crude steel production never reached more than 10,000 tons a month – formerly, the works on the Dnepr had produced 2.8 million tons annually. The investment in the Soviet plants, moreover, very soon turned out to be a losing bargain, because at the end of August 1943, the area east of the Dnepr had to be vacated again. The trip in the Ukraine, however, cost the Flick group solely half the initial capital of *Dnjepr Stahl GmbH* (just 25,000 reichsmarks) plus some office equipment and bicycles out of the *Mittelstahl* plants' stock. The *BHO*, in turn, funded by state loans, bore the cost of the capital expenditures and the ongoing operation of the works; the 'godfathers' were involved neither in profits nor in losses.[36]

The development was not better elsewhere in the Ukraine, but the business risk of the private industry was marginal as well. *GHH*, for example, took over the 'godparenthood' over a machine factory and a metallurgical plant in the Donezk region. Like in the Dnepr region, equipment had to be transferred from Germany (paid for by the *BHO*), as the plant was destroyed to a large part. *GHH* even urged for the right of preemption, obviously willing to invest its own money in case of a successful war in the East. But interim, the Kramatorsk plant produced farm tools and furnaces as well as equipment for an iron work also operated by *GHH*. However, an economically profitable production was hardly possible in the heavily destroyed factory, the more so as the activities ceased about a year later, in September 1943, because of the war's progress.[37]

Likewise, Krupp assumed the 'godparenthood' over an iron work with associated manufacturing plants as well as two further machinery factories, which turned out to be 'sources of loss': 90 per cent of the machines had been dismantled by the Red Army during the withdrawal, and parts of the remaining facilities had been destroyed. A large number of machines had to be brought from Germany and the occupied Western territories; due to the military development, the production, though, was hardly commencing to work. Altogether, the commitment proved to be economically unsuccessful; but the cost for the concern from Essen was very limited because the plants were formally owned by the Reich. At least one of the works could be used for manufacturing ammunition in the 'Ivan program'. In this case, Krupp rented the work from the Reich, operating the plant for the military's account against an 'appropriate remuneration'.[38]

The development of the occupation economy in the Baltic proved to be similar. Though this region was just a sideline for heavy industry, it provides another example of the competition motive in the expansion as well as of the concerns' interest in plants for further processing of their steel production. Being part of Germany's leading wagon manufacturers with its subsidiaries *Waggon- und Maschinenfabrik vorm. Busch* and *Linke-Hofmann*, the *Flick* concern planned to expand this business segment via the acquisition of the Riga wagon factory *Vairogs*. Immediately after the beginning of the war against the Soviet Union, the concern management took the first steps in exploring the factory with about 1,700 employees. But not before June 1942, the political network was activated seriously and in no time – after finding out that the Military Arms Office (*Heereswaffenamt*) wanted to assign the plant for the production of gun carriages to the competitor Krupp.

Three months later, Busch could sign an agreement which almost eliminated any business risk. The German operators received a gratuity for continuing the current production and installing a gun carriage manufacturer. The plant manager also did not further the armament production particularly; any modifications of the facility were made with respect to their future usability for the wagon production in mind. Since the machines for the construction of gun carriers arrived in Riga only with a large delay and since material was lacking, it never came to that armament production Flick had promised the political authorities. Instead, the existing production lines were continued with negligible success and with the work of POWs and deported Jews. Riga had become a central location of the Holocaust shortly after the German occupation, when the majority of the Jewish population had been systematically murdered. Several thousand people constantly having to fear for their lives had been temporarily spared and cooped into ghettos to be used for forced labour. Obviously, there were no moral scruples about doing business in such a location. In the summer of 1943, the plant manager even tried (unsuccessfully) to force the allocation of Jewish workers with the offer of establishing an own concentration camp at the factory premises.[39]

3. Resume

The decline of ethical standards, appearing most clearly in exploiting concentration camp prisoners, was by no means independent of the 'business as usual' carried out in the occupied territories. The German operators perceived themselves as legitimate quasi-owners, which, irrespective of the legal structures of the lease contracts or 'godparenthoods', anticipated formal property rights for the postwar period. In this perception they could feel affirmed by a relative autonomy in the management of the occupied works. German industrialists had not at all to be forced to expand into occupied Europe. Their motive was not short-term profit taking but long-term market expectations for the period after the military reorganization of Europe. Thereby, the steel industrialists just as the chemical managers of *IG Farben*[40] were involved in the murderous 'racial' policy of the Nazi regime, at least accepting the concept of 'Lebensraum' and massively exploiting forced labour.

The acquisitions of foreign works did not take place randomly but in business fields that fit into the concerns' product range. The impulse to take part in the general expansion might have been more or less powerful among different industrialists, but it was undoubtedly boosted by the competition among them and with the *Reichswerke*. The state enterprise whose main objective was maximum output had to be less considerate of economic rationality in its aggressive growth strategy. In contrast, private corporations proceeded with entrepreneurial risk awareness. In occupied Lorraine and Luxembourg, they were prepared to significant investments, which admittedly were safeguarded by governmental refunding guarantees in case the iron and steel plants actually should not pass into private ownership at the end. In the East, one could anyway partake as a free rider in a utopian spatial planning, preliminary contenting oneself with modest expense allowances.

A short-term transfer of capital goods thereby occurred – enforcedly – in the direction of the occupied territories or between them, while raw materials and especially workers preferably were mobilized on the spot. The produced goods, whose amount was temporarily significant in the West and of less importance in the East, subsidized the German war economy. The financial gains of the operating companies, as far as they can be reconstructed at all, remained small. But they were a minor matter within the calculation of German industry as long as no serious losses were incurred. Under the conditions of the war economy, the autonomy of business indeed was considerably constricted with regard to the production program as well as to the supply of raw materials and labour. But the business risks as well remained limited.

Notes

1 Thanks to Marlene Miersch for preparing the English translation.
2 G. Mollin, *Montankonzerne und 'Drittes Reich'. Der Gegensatz zwischen Monopolindustrie und Befehlswirtschaft in der deutschen Rüstung und Expansion 1936–1944*, Göttingen: Vandenhoeck & Ruprecht, 1988.
3 C. Buchheim, 'Unternehmen in Deutschland und NS-Regime 1933–1945. Versuch einer Synthese', *Historische Zeitschrift*, 2006, vol. 282, pp. 351–89; J. Scherner, *Die Logik der Industriepolitik im Dritten Reich. Die Investitionen in die Autarkie- und Rüstungsindustrie und ihre staatliche Förderung*, Stuttgart: Steiner, 2008; see also A. Tooze, *The Wages of Destruction. The Making and Breaking of the Nazi Economy*, London: Allen Lane, 2006, pp. 99–134.
4 K. Priemel, *Flick. Eine Konzerngeschichte vom Kaiserreich bis zur Bundesrepublik*, Göttingen: Wallstein, 2007; J. Bähr/A. Drecoll/B. Gotto/K. Priemel/H. Wixforth, *Der Flick-Konzern im Dritten Reich*, Munich: Oldenbourg, 2008; N. Frei/R. Ahrens/J. Osterloh/T. Schanetzky, *Flick. Der Konzern, die Familie, die Macht*, Munich: Blessing, 2009; W. Abelshauser, 'Rüstungsschmiede der

The German steel industry's expansion 259

Nation? Der Kruppkonzern im Dritten Reich und in der Nachkriegszeit 1933 bis 1951', in L. Gall (ed.), *Krupp im 20. Jahrhundert. Die Geschichte des Unternehmens vom Ersten Weltkrieg bis zur Gründung der Stiftung*, Berlin: Siedler, 2002, pp. 267–472; J. Bähr/R. Banken/T. Flemming, *MAN. The History of a German Industrial Enterprise*, Munich: Beck, 2009; C. Marx, *Paul Reusch und die Gutehoffnungshütte. Leitung eines deutschen Großunternehmens*, Göttingen: Wallstein, 2013.

5 See A. Reckendrees, *Das 'Stahltrust'-Projekt. Die Gründung der Vereinigte Stahlwerke A.G. und ihre Unternehmensentwicklung 1926–1933/34*, Munich: Beck, 2000; idem, 'From Cartel Regulation to Monopolistic Control? The Founding of the German "Steel Trust" in 1926 and its Effect on Market Regulation', *Business History*, 2003, vol. 45, pp. 22–51; C. Kleinschmidt, *Rationalisierung als Unternehmensstrategie. Die Eisen- und Stahlindustrie des Ruhrgebiets zwischen Jahrhundertwende und Weltwirtschaftskrise*, Essen: Klartext, 1993.

6 J. Bähr, 'The Personal Factor in Business under National Socialism: Paul Reusch and Friedrich Flick', in H. Berghoff/J. Kocka/D. Ziegler (eds.), *Business in the Age of Extremes. Essays in Modern German and Austrian Economic History*, Cambridge: Cambridge University Press, 2013, pp. 154–65.

7 Abelshauser, 'Rüstungsschmiede', pp. 272–86, 328–35.

8 Mollin, *Montankonzerne*, pp. 52–147; H. Wixforth/D. Ziegler, 'Die Expansion der Reichswerke "Hermann Göring" in Europa', *Jahrbuch für Wirtschaftsgeschichte*, 2008/1, pp. 257–61. On Flick's and Reusch's reaction to Pleiger's challenges see Bähr, 'Personal Factor'.

9 R.J. Overy, 'Multi-Nationals and the Nazi State in Occupied Europe', in idem, *War and Economy in the Third Reich*, Oxford: Clarendon Press, 1995, p. 336.

10 H.-E. Volkmann, 'Die NS-Wirtschaft in Vorbereitung des Krieges', in W. Deist/M. Messerschmidt/H.-E. Volkmann/W. Wette, *Ursachen und Voraussetzungen des Zweiten Weltkrieges*, Frankfurt am Main: Fischer, 1989, pp. 417–35; Tooze, *Wages*, pp. 303–15, 342–61.

11 Tooze, *Wages*, pp. 497–8, 680–3; Marx, *Paul Reusch*, p. 447; Priemel, *Flick*, pp. 509–16. However, the output of high-quality, electrically smelted steel especially important for armament still increased considerably until 1942.

12 P. Hayes, *Industry and Ideology. IG Farben in the Nazi Era*, Cambridge: Cambridge University Press, 2001 (1st ed. 1987), pp. 213–376, quote p. 264. See also idem, 'Industry under the Swastika', in H. James/J. Tanner (eds.), *Enterprise in the Period of Fascism in Europe*, Aldershot: Ashgate, 2002, p. 33.

13 See the overviews and examples in C. Buchheim/M. Boldorf (eds.), *Europäische Volkswirtschaften unter deutscher Hegemonie 1938–1945*, Munich: Oldenbourg, 2012; H. Klemann/S. Kudryashov, *Occupied Economies. An Economic History of Nazi-Occupied Europe, 1939–1945*, London: Berg, 2012.

14 See J. Bähr/R. Banken (eds.), *Das Europa des 'Dritten Reichs'. Recht, Wirtschaft, Besatzung*, Frankfurt am Main: Klostermann, 2005.

15 See the overviews by W. Röhr, 'Forschungsprobleme zur deutschen Okkupationspolitik im Spiegel der Reihe "Europa unterm Hakenkreuz"', in *Europa unterm Hakenkreuz. Analysen, Quellen, Register. Zusammengestellt und eingeleitet von Werner Röhr*, Heidelberg: Hüthig, 1996, pp. 255–63; and R.J. Overy, 'Business in the *Grossraumwirtschaft*: Eastern Europe, 1938–1945,' in James/Tanner, *Enterprise in the Period of Fascism*, pp. 162–8.

16 J. Bähr, 'GHH und M.A.N. in der Weimarer Republik, im Nationalsozialismus und in der Nachkriegszeit (1920–1960)', in Bähr/Banken/Flemming, *Die MAN*, 2008, p. 301.

17 Priemel, *Flick*, p. 448.

18 Klemann/Kudryashov, *Economies*, pp. 78–97.

19 Mollin, *Montankonzerne*, pp. 223–32.

260 Ralf Ahrens

20 For examples, cf. F. Sattler, 'Der Handelstrust West in den Niederlanden', in H. Wixforth, *Die Expansion der Dresdner Bank in Europa*, Munich: Oldenbourg, 2006, pp. 704–22; and J. Bähr, 'Die Continentale Bank, Brüssel', ibid, pp. 804–14.
21 Extract from a letter from Hans Hermann, technical director of Fried. Krupp AG Rheinhausen, to Krupp board member Johannes Schröder, 4 February 1941, reprinted in *Die faschistische Okkupationspolitik in Belgien, Luxemburg und den Niederlanden (1940–1945). Dokumentenauswahl und Einleitung von Ludwig Nestler*, Berlin: Deutscher Verlag der Wissenschaften, 1990, pp. 140–1.
22 This system has been researched quite intensively for the automotive industry. See P. Lessmann, 'Industriebeziehungen zwischen Deutschland und Frankreich während der deutschen Besatzung 1940–1944. Das Beispiel Peugeot-Volkswagenwerk', *Francia*, 1990, vol. 17, pp. 120–53; N. Gregor, *Stern und Hakenkreuz. Daimler-Benz im Dritten Reich*, Berlin: Propyläen, 1997, pp. 126–30; C. Werner, *Kriegswirtschaft und Zwangsarbeit bei BMW*, Munich: Oldenbourg, 2006, pp. 281–91; E. Dickert, 'Die Rolle der Auto Union bei der "Nutzbarmachung" ausländischer Unternehmen. Auftragsverlagerungen in den besetzten Gebieten während des Zweiten Weltkriegs', *Zeitschrift für Unternehmensgeschichte*, 2013, vol. 58, pp. 28–53; and also M. Schneider, *Unternehmensstrategien zwischen Weltwirtschaftskrise und Kriegswirtschaft. Chemnitzer Maschinenbauindustrie in der NS-Zeit 1933–1945*, Essen: Klartext, 2005, pp. 395–403.
23 H. Joly, 'Französische Unternehmen unter deutscher Besatzung', in Buchheim/Boldorf, *Europäische Volkswirtschaften*, p. 132.
24 The following referred to Mollin, *Montankonzerne*, pp. 220–3, 233–51; H.-E. Volkmann, *Luxemburg im Zeichen des Hakenkreuzes. Eine politische Wirtschaftsgeschichte 1933 bis 1944*, Paderborn: Schöningh, 2010, pp. 100–11, 161–9, 379–424.
25 Bähr, 'GHH', pp. 301–4; Marx, *Paul Reusch*, pp. 455–8.
26 Mollin, *Montankonzerne*, p. 242.
27 The following referred to Priemel, *Flick*, pp. 445–51; Frei et al., *Flick*, pp. 299–309; J. Bähr, 'Die geglückte Expansion im Westen: Der Fall Rombach', in Bähr et al., *Flick-Konzern*, pp. 451–61. The interpretations of these titles regarding Flick's midterm economic interests in Rombach are partly different; the description here follows Frei et al. See also, though very limited in contextualisation and on a small basis of archival research, M. O. Jones, *Nazi Steel. Friedrich Flick and German Expansion in Western Europe, 1940–1944*, Annapolis: Naval Institute Press, 2012.
28 Volkmann, *Luxemburg*, pp. 158–61, 425–33, 511–3.
29 Overy, 'Business', pp. 153–62.
30 R. J. Overy, 'The Reichswerke "Hermann Göring": A Study in German Economic Imperialism' in idem, *War and Economy in the Third Reich*, Oxford: Clarendon Press, 1995, pp. 144–74; Mollin, *Montankonzerne*, pp. 183–92; Wixforth/Ziegler, 'Expansion', pp. 261–72; Wixforth, *Expansion*, pp. 254–304. On general developments, see J. Balcar/J. Kučera, 'Nationalsozialistische Wirtschaftslenkung und unternehmerische Handlungsspielräume im Protektorat Böhmen und Mähren (1939–1945). Staatlicher Druck, Zwangslagen und betriebswirtschaftliches Kalkül', in Buchheim/Boldorf, *Europäische Volkswirtschaften*, pp. 147–71; idem, *Von der Rüstkammer des Reiches zum Maschinenwerk des Sozialismus. Wirtschaftslenkung in Böhmen und Mähren 1938 bis 1953*, Göttingen: Vandenhoeck & Ruprecht, 2013, pp. 22–40, 307–15.
31 Overy, 'Multi-Nationals', pp. 324–6; Mollin, *Montankonzerne*, pp. 192–4; Abelshauser, 'Rüstungsschmiede', pp. 369–71; Wixforth/Ziegler, 'Expansion', pp. 272–5.
32 Frei et al., *Flick*, pp. 285–90 (quotes of Burkart and Hanneken); Priemel, *Flick*, pp. 435–9.

33 Mollin, *Montankonzerne*, p. 194; Wixforth, *Expansion*, pp. 451–60; W. Röhr, 'Grundlinien der Okkupationspolitik des faschistischen Imperialismus in Polen 1939–1945', in *Die faschistische Okkupationspolitik in Polen (1939–1945). Dokumentenauswahl und Einleitung von Werner Röhr*, Berlin: Deutscher Verlag der Wissenschaften, 1989, pp. 41–9.
34 Bähr, 'GHH', pp. 304–5; Marx, *Paul Reusch*, pp. 459–60.
35 D. Eichholtz, *Geschichte der deutschen Kriegswirtschaft 1939–1945*, vol. 2: *1941–1943*, Berlin: Akademie-Verlag, 1985, pp. 392–418, 466–77; R.-D. Müller, 'Von der Wirtschaftsallianz zum kolonialen Ausbeutungskrieg' in H. Boog et al. (eds.), *Der Angriff auf die Sowjetunion*, Frankfurt am Main: Fischer, 1991, pp. 172–98; idem, 'Das Scheitern der wirtschaftlichen "Blitzkriegstrategie"' in ibid, pp. 1116–38; Mollin, *Montankonzerne*, pp. 198–204.
36 Priemel, *Flick*, pp. 459–68; Frei et al., *Flick*, pp. 317–22.
37 Marx, *Paul Reusch*, pp. 461–3; Bähr, 'GHH', pp. 305–6.
38 Abelshauser, 'Rüstungsschmiede', pp. 372–4.
39 Priemel, *Flick*, pp. 455–9; Frei et al., *Flick*, pp. 309–17. On Riga as a Holocaust location and on forced labour of the Jewish inhabitants, see extensively A. Angrick and P. Klein, *Die 'Endlösung' in Riga. Ausbeutung und Vernichtung 1941–1944*, Darmstadt: Wissenschaftliche Buchgesellschaft, 2006.
40 See note 11.

19 The French opportunity
A Danish construction company working for the Germans in France, 1940–1944

Steen Andersen

Introduction

There has been renewed interest in how political risk affects multinationals that operate under dictatorial regimes. For obvious reasons, much of this research has focused on the relationship between companies in Germany during the Second World War and the Nazi regime. But because existing studies lack data about central decision-making processes, they have been able to offer only tentative conclusions about the relationship between dictatorship and political risk.[1] Documentation of discussions within the company, especially at the highest levels, is in many cases absent, leaving only indirect evidence about business strategy in relation to political risk.[2] In this chapter, by contrast, I draw on the minutes of board meetings of a major Danish multinational to show how day-to-day decisions dealt with the opportunities and risks of working in Nazi Germany. I examine how *Christiani & Nielsen* became involved in large-scale building projects in German-occupied Europe, focusing on the strategic planning of its management. The question in focus in this chapter is day-to-day business decisions and the strategies employed by a multinational company to overcome political obstacles on the European market that were implicit in the German New Order. The formation of what became known as *Grossraumwirtschaft* was a result of a coincidence between the ambition of independence and expansion. The goal of the German side was to meet Hitler's desire for a blockade-free economic area in Europe, which should ensure Germany further supplies of strategic materials and commodities such as rubber, aluminium, steel, synthetic oil, coal and food supplies and access to manpower reserves.[3]

Christiani & Nielsen: the pioneers on the international market

Danish entrepreneurial business activity on the international market has to great extent only been represented briefly and in general terms. In this light, it is all the more remarkable that the (albeit sparse) international research into the history of the entrepreneurial business has spoken approvingly of Danish companies, particularly the company Christiani & Nielsen, which is described as 'one of the more remarkable phenomena of pre-World War II international construction'.[4] On the basis of accessible sources, the American Marc Linder has carried out a broadly based analysis of international entrepreneurial projects completed during the last 200 years. Here he emphasises the striking point that during the 1930s, one Danish company in particular succeeded in gaining a solid position on the Latin American market in close competition with the largest German and French entrepreneurial companies. Geoffrey Jones likewise emphasises the international expansion of the Danish entrepreneurial companies, pointing to their significance in the construction of an international global economy after WWI, when cross-border entrepreneurial activity experienced considerable growth.[5]

Christiani & Nielsen had succeeded in setting up profitable branches in South America and Asia and on the Continent already in the 1920s. An expansion-focused business strategy helped the company establish fifteen new branches by 1939, of which the South American market, the Thailand branch and finally the German market were the most lucrative.

The company's high status in Germany is reflected by the fact that a considerable portion of the construction of the Autobahns was handed over to Christiani & Nielsen and the fact that the company was one of the few multinationals that were allowed to transfer their profits out of Germany. In her study of multinational American companies, Mira Wilkins has pointed out that the restrictions forced many companies to invest their frozen surplus in Germany.[6] The special conditions in Germany made it necessary for Christiani & Nielsen to conduct a balanced policy, a classical example of how difficult it is to run a company faced with the political risks of a dictatorial regime. On the one hand lurks the danger of cooperating too much with the regime on its conditions. On the other hand, the company could get into trouble by adopting a collision course with the regime by refusing to adhere to the regime's guidelines. For the individual company, the concern would not just be the reaction of the authorities with regard to a concrete issue but also the views to consolidate and expand on the future market. In an overall perspective, Christiani & Nielsen succeeded in running a business up through the 1930s, which took due account of the company's position on the German market. The company chose an *active* adaptation to Nazi Germany, based on wide local knowledge and a recognition of the fact that the policy of the new regime created the economical and political framework of the company's growth. Part of the company's strategy was to adapt to the Nazi regime's rules by appearing to be 'less' foreign and to a greater extent be perceived as a German company. Finally, Christiani & Nielsen's close cooperation with the Nazi authorities had also given the company a first-hand impression of the radical nature of the regime's policies. Instead, one applied unobtrusive diplomacy when solving the problems and in this way gained a privileged position among the other multinational companies when the flow of surplus to Denmark was opened up. As the political climate in Germany grew still more radical, Christiani & Nielsen developed an ability to cooperate with the German authorities. As early as during the interwar years, the close cooperation with, among others, the Organisation Todt taught Christiani & Nielsen that the company had to choose to act as a loyal player in relation to the political system if the management were to avoid endangering the company. Via its primary ventures, the company had since 1933 become progressively more embedded in the German market. Path dependence had been established, which created limitations in the choices of the company during the five war years.

Existing research generally assumes that companies were left with few alternatives at the outbreak of the Second World War, either because they were bound to traditional markets or because their access to foreign markets was cut off when the pattern of international trade changed overnight.[7] The consensus is that there were no other markets for most firms to conquer and therefore no other actions to take. Alternative viewpoints, it is argued, can only be supported by the benefit of hindsight. But quite a few Scandinavian companies saw the German New Order as it developed from 1940 to 1942 as an opportunity as well as a risk and had more 'freedom of action' than we previously thought.[8] Despite the outbreak of war, production setbacks and manpower shortages, for example, the period proved to be a time of expansion for the international activities of Danish building contractors. The French surrender in June 1940 suggested that Germany would be a future factor of power in Europe, and companies attempted to adjust their long-term strategies accordingly.[9]

The French opportunity

The French construction market had stood idle following France's defeat in June 1940. As in Denmark, the German air force had initiated the construction of air fields immediately after the occupation, while all state and private building enterprise was suspended. Before the outbreak of war, Christiani & Nielsen had invested considerable resources in acquiring a number of large state contracts for harbour developments in Cherbourg and Saint Nazaire. Shortly after the German occupation, the headquarters in Copenhagen had decided to send Rudolf Christiani's youngest son, Alex Christiani.[10]

However, after the German occupation, the greatest problem was not communication with headquarters but the chaos caused by the occupation itself. The French state had been dismembered. The country was bisected by a demarcation line which divided the occupied zone in the North from the free zone in the South. In principle, the Vichy French collaboration government, headed by Marshall Pétain and Prime Minister Laval, governed both zones, but the demarcation line separated the northern zone, comprising Paris and the richest part of France, from the government in the south. Furthermore, Alsace and Lorraine were annexed; two northern departments were governed by the German military administration in Belgium and, last, a corner of south-western France was occupied by Italy. France was subject to Göring's Four Year Plan, which used the Armistice Commission in Wiesbaden as an instrument of pillage; the country was required to pay 20 million reichsmarks a day in compensation.[11]

Construction work had largely been suspended. By the autumn of 1940, the Todt Organisation was already taking delivery of 75 per cent of all French cement production, and, in the occupied zone, all construction work with a value in excess of 5,000 francs had to be approved by the military administration. Thus, the German occupying power had total control of the construction industry and, for political and security reasons, French construction contractors were excluded from military construction work for the occupying power until the autumn of 1942. Instead, they chose to employ their own contractors.[12] By contrast, the highly developed French industrial sector made a significant contribution to the German armament industry from the autumn of 1940, and, aided by the Vichy regime's willingness to cooperate, the majority of French business leaders exhibited considerable adaptability.[13]

Once the construction of the large port and harbour facilities in Cherbourg and Saint Nazaire had been completed, the French department of Christiani & Nielsen only handled small projects. During the autumn of 1940 and the spring of 1941, Christiani & Nielsen succeeded in winning some contracts for the reconstruction of bridges. The contracts were valued at 45 million francs, or approximately 6.5 million Danish kroner, and profits were assessed at 1.3 million Danish kroner.[14]

On 22 August 1941, Alex Christiani travelled to Copenhagen to inform management of the situation in France. He reported that there were opportunities for more large reconstruction contracts but that these would certainly not be financially attractive. The company had chosen to perform the work in order to keep the organisation occupied and because a number of the damaged bridges were originally built by Christiani & Nielsen. For this reason, the company had an opportunity to earn a little extra on the reconstruction work. In spite of the potential increase in government projects, the department's short-term prospects were not particularly promising, as the problem of financing had not yet been solved.[15] However, following Professor Arnold Agatz's tour of inspection of French ports for the German navy, pessimism was replaced by budding optimism in October 1941. The objective of this tour was an investigation of the potential for construction of submarine bunkers. After the Germans had taken the strategically important French Atlantic coast, German submarines were able to reach their theatre of operations without undertaking the dangerous journey through the North Sea. In the summer of 1940, the commander in chief of the German submarine fleet, Karl Dönitz, ordered the construction of bunkers in Lorient, Brest, Saint Nazaire, La Pallice and Bordeaux.[16]

An enthusiastic Rudolf Christiani informed the other members of the management board that Agatz had reported 'that there will be considerable construction work in France in the near future'.[17] The prospect of being among the candidates considered for the construction of the submarine bunkers prompted management to refinance the French department in the same way as it had refinanced operations in Norway. Instead of relying on the French banks, Christiani approached the company's German banker, Dresdner Bank, and implied that the company would soon be working on large construction projects in France for the German state. On Agatz's recommendation, Christiani & Nielsen's French department received an injection of capital from the Dresdner Bank in the amount of 8 million francs on 27 October.

In line with company policy, trade secrets were written down as little as possible. Politically sensitive subjects, in particular, could be intercepted by postal censorship or picked up by other prying eyes. In any event, as a result of the negotiations with the German authorities, Alex Christiani reported in a letter to his father on 30 October that the company was about to sign a contract. The true nature of the contract was the construction of a 245-metre-wide, 162-metre-long and 19-metre-high submarine bunker.[18] When the project was presented to management, all agreed that it was so large that 'C&N Paris would have to form a consortium with other companies' in order to complete it.[19] There was another critical issue: Did the Germans consider Christiani & Nielsen's department a French or a Danish company? The Todt Organisation did not permit direct contact with French companies until after 194.[20] Instead, French companies were forced to work as subcontractors to German companies, which were also responsible for the payment of dividends.[21] In 1921, Christiani & Nielsen's department in France had been converted into Etablissements Christiani & Nielsen SAF, a French incorporated company. Therefore, the Germans most probably considered Christiani & Nielsen a French company during contract negotiations. In any event, Christiani & Nielsen entered into a joint venture with German Leonhard Moll as a result, and the German company acted as the main contractor.[22] The bunker construction was started in the autumn of 1941 and already commissioned in spring 1942. The project was finally completed in January 1943.

Working for Organisation Todt

The construction of the submarine bunkers required skilled engineers, as it was a complicated construction project carried out by highly specialised companies. The project was categorised as *Durcharbeit* – meaning that work on the project continued 24 hours a day until the bunkers, which were of strategic importance, were ready – and, as such, it was one of the Todt Organisation's highest-priority construction programmes. The workforce worked 12-hour shifts and, at night, the construction site was illuminated by large floodlights. Although they had access to mechanical construction equipment and cement pumps, they carried out a good proportion of the work by hand. Part of the workforce attached to the submarine bunker construction was made up of paid workers, for the Todt Organisation had no trouble recruiting contractors who, like Christiani & Nielsen, were interested in making money and finding employment for their workforce. However, the contractors' workers were soon unable to meet the German need for labour, and the Todt Organisation began deploying thousands of prisoners of war and using forced labour. Immediately after the end of the French campaign in the summer of 1940, French prisoners of war were deployed as labourers on the Todt Organisation's construction projects. In 1941, forced labourers were introduced, beginning with 10,000 so-called Spanish Republican

Exiles who were interned in French camps in the German-occupied zone. These were Spaniards who had fought against General Franco's forces during the Spanish Civil War and who had fled to France after the fascist victory. A further almost 30,000 Spaniards were interned in the unoccupied zone of France, and, in the spring of 1941, the Vichy authorities handed over all internees to the German military administration in the occupied zone. They were then deployed as forced labourers on the construction of the submarine bunkers in Bordeaux and La Pallice and, later, on the building of the Atlantic ramparts at La Rochelle.[23] A total of 291,000 workers were attached to the construction of German strongholds; the majority was made up of 191,000 impressed Russians, Poles and Spaniards, and the rest were contract workers from France, Holland and Belgium.[24]

Initially, the forced labourers were interned in camps guarded by the French police, but this task was later transferred to the Todt Organisation's *Schutzkommando*. The construction site in Bordeaux was run by the Todt Organisation's team of engineers, who organised both the workforce and the contractors. A statement by the Todt Organisation's *Einsatzgruppe West* from 15 April 1942 indicates that 2,080 'Spanish Republican Exilse' were deployed during the construction of the submarine bunker in Bordeaux.[25] Compared to the volunteers, forced labourers were very poorly paid and received harsh treatment. Spanish communists, together with Russians, Poles and Czechs, belonged to the second-lowest category in the hierarchy of German forced labourers. Jewish forced labourers were on the third and bottom rung, and in July 1943, all male French Jews between the ages of 20 and 31 were impressed into service for the Todt Organisation. On construction sites in France, forced labourers were either classified as 'owned by OT' or 'belonging to the firm', and in Bordeaux, Spanish workers were deployed under the control of the Todt Organisation. The Todt Organisation set up the 'Lindemann' internment camp close to the building site in the Bouscat district. Spaniards lived here behind barbed-wire fences, without water or electricity and under military guard. Labourers were transported to and from the building site in locked vehicles with bars on the windows.

There is no indication that the German deployment of forced labour caused Christiani & Nielsen any serious moral dilemma, for they chose not to change their strategy towards the Todt Organisation. Profits from work for the Germans made military projects attractive. Based on the archive material available, it is difficult to fix Christiani & Nielsen's exact earnings from the construction work conducted for the Todt Organisation, but French research indicates that the construction of the submarine bunkers returned very high profits. In spite of the fact that the bunkers were different in size and design, construction costs were, on average, 20 million reichsmarks per bunker. Up until the end of 1942, the contractual relationship between the Todt Organisation and contracting firms in France was regulated by a contract which stipulated that the contractor would receive a percentage of the profit, based on construction costs, and a bonus of 4.5 per cent of the construction costs if the bunker was completed on time (*Selbstkostenerstattungsvertrag*). This form of contract enabled contractors to make profits which could be up to 300 per cent higher than profits normally made on government contract work. These high profits are also documented by a French study of 344 contracting firms that built ordinary bunkers in connection with the construction of the Atlantic ramparts in 1942–44 by the Germans. British historian Alan Milward called the construction of German strongholds in France the greatest construction project in French history, and, between 1943 and 1944 alone, the German Ministry of Finance transferred 900 million reichsmark to the Todt Organisation and 717 million to the navy to finance their French installations.[26] In spite of the fact that at this time, profits were adjusted in accordance with the so-called *Leistungsvertrag*, which calculated profit based on a company's wage costs and did not allow for a bonus, the work was highly coveted. In comparison with profits earned by these companies before the war, 153 were able to increase their profits by 50 per cent, 85 companies achieved profits which were 100 per cent higher than in 1939, and 36 contracting firms earned 200 per cent more than before the outbreak of war. One of Christiani & Nielsen's smaller competitors, Sainrapt & Brice, who were also experts in the use of reinforced concrete, had a turnover of 45 million reichsmarks from the construction of military depots and small bunkers on the Atlantic coast between 1940 and 1944. In 1940, Sainrapt & Brice's equity amounted to 150,000 reichsmarks and, in 1944, it had increased to two million reichsmark.[27]

A discrete business

During the spring of 1942, Christiani & Nielsen increased endeavours, both in Denmark and in France, to take over more of the French stronghold construction work. Before Engineer Cardinal, head of the Todt Organisation in Denmark, set off for France, he managed to find time to discuss new contracts with Christiani, and he promised the company that he would put in a good word for them. There were also direct negotiations between Christiani & Nielsen and the German authorities in France. Following a request for Christiani & Nielsen to 'take a look at some work in France', as Christiani laconically put it in his report to the other members of the management board on 13 April 1942, Director Emil Blunk travelled to Paris for a series of meetings with the Todt Organisation and the Military Economic Staff (*Wehrwirtschaftsstab*) in April 1942. Blunk had received Christiani's permission to make the necessary contacts in Germany and France, but beyond that, Alex Christiani was the only other person involved in the decisions.[28]

The ground was prepared for the department in Paris to accept new assignments and, in addition, the German department began work in France during April 1942. The company's French department had accumulated a great deal of machinery during the construction of the large harbour and port facilities in the thirties. Thus, there was no lack of technical capacity following the decision to allow the German department to work in France. Management had made this decision to circumvent German requirements which stipulated that the French company would only be permitted to operate as a subcontractor to a German company. By handing over the construction work to Blunk and the German department, Christiani & Nielsen was able to obtain approval as a German company, and the French department could act as a subcontractor to its own company. The first assignment assumed by the German department was the repair or reconstruction of the enormous entrance lock at Saint Nazaire. Christiani & Nielsen had built the lock, which could also be used as the world's largest dry dock, between 1930 and 1932. The lock was badly damaged during a British raid on Saint Nazaire on 26 March 1942, and the Germans wanted the damage repaired as quickly as possible.[29]

Blunk's next move was to negotiate a contract with the Todt Organisation, which accepted Christiani & Nielsen as the main contractor to extend the existing submarine bunker at La Pallice/La Rochelle, which was made up of seven quays and commissioned by the Third Submarine Flotilla on 27 October 1941. It later became evident that three new quays would be needed. Blunk and Alex Christiani began work on the 'construction site in La Pallice' together, as it required the efforts of the whole organisation. Back in Copenhagen, management was informed that the French department had made its workforce available to Blunk. There was a short, fundamental discussion at the management meeting on 22 June 1942 which confirmed the company's previous strategy, as the French department also reported that many government assignments had been suspended and, therefore, they would 'try to obtain work for the Todt Organisation in France' via Blunk.[30] Management was fully aware of the fact that this work would involve the construction of strategic bunkers which would be used to protect the German submarines whose job it was to sink Allied war and merchant ships. At an organisational level, the company made arrangements to continue conducting large construction assignments for the occupying power in France; on 10 July, Christiani and Blunk agreed to appoint Oberbaudirektor Dr Gedes as the German department's new board member and head of German naval construction in France.[31]

During his deliberations, Christiani wondered 'whether this was the right move on grounds of principle'. He came to the conclusion with the rest of the management board that the decision was fundamentally sound, as they had already decided that the company's European subsidiaries/departments should be financially self-supporting. The fact that they might be actively supporting German warfare was less important than the financial stability of the company. The conclusion was that 'they should attempt to benefit as much as possible from Director Blunk' and attract as many construction assignments as they could manage.[32] It is remarkable that the company did not give more consideration to the risks involved in construction work of this nature. This policy meant that there was a risk the Allies would consider all company subsidiaries/departments in Allied areas part of an enterprise which was working actively for the victory of the Axis Powers. The political situation in the summer of 1942 should, perhaps, have caused the management board to doubt some of their previous decisions, but Christiani's unshakeable belief in Germany's eternal position of power overshadowed the political reality.

The headquarters in Copenhagen further believed that the Allies would not discover the company's involvement in the bunker construction or, if they did, they would be able to overlook it, as other European businesses also dealt with the Germans. Even though they attempted to conceal their activities by avoiding any mention of the construction projects for the Germans in mail which risked interception by the Allied censors, management had no intention of admitting that the principles of Allied warfare also applied to a Danish company. They reasoned that as long as they worked discretely for the Germans, they would not come into conflict with the Trading with the Enemy Act.

The German department played a key role in the strategy for the large military building projects for the Germans. Management claimed that the department was considered a German company and, as such, was required to act in the German interest. In France, this strategy apparently contributed to the fact that, after the war, Christiani & Nielsen's French department avoided addition to the list compiled by the *Ministère des travaux publics et des transports* of companies excluded from public projects due to collaboration with the occupying power.[33]

In the eyes of the management board, the fact that the Hamburg department had its own German board of directors and was registered as *Ingenieurbaugesellschaft Christiani & Nielsen mbH* formally legitimised the company's transactions. This quest for legitimacy may seem illusory considering the fact that headquarters owned all shares in all subsidiaries/departments and the Hamburg department was under the control of Christiani himself. Nevertheless, it was of crucial significance to the company's own self-image as an international enterprise with an openly national flavour. In spite of the war, Ørstedhus claimed that Christiani & Nielsen was still working 'to build a greater Denmark'. Christiani & Nielsen's management was given many opportunities to work for the Germans, and they chose more often than not to say yes. Their arguments were powerful and, within the company, choices were legitimised in order to avoid facing the fact that they could have acted differently.

The bunker constructions and the company's future transactions in France were again brought up at the management meeting on 13 July. The progress in Saint Nazaire provided them with hope of more assignments, and the following short note was recorded in the minutes of the meeting: 'Besides, C&N Hamburg is building a submarine dock in La Pallice'. In addition to extensions to the existing bunker, Christiani & Nielsen took on the construction of a bomb-proof generator hall in La Pallice.[34] The company's German department acted as the main contractor on the construction work, and 'Dr. Christiani had requested Director Blunk to take on C&N Paris as a "*discrete business*" if at all possible'. No one in the boardroom doubted that the matter required great discretion. The involvement of the French department ensured efficient use of the company's large stock of machinery, and the German department acquired large numbers of personnel from French operations. The involvement of the German department, on the other hand, increased the parent company's potential for repatriating some of the profit from the bunker constructions.

Company strategy in France was to adopt a low-key approach. It was strongly emphasised that no one outside the boardroom should have any information on the construction work in France, and the company had also introduced new communication procedures which circumvented the Danish mission in Berlin. Correspondence was conducted by means of the foreign post censorship. There was no reason to provide the Foreign Ministry with more information about their French business than necessary.

Following the British raid on Saint Nazaire, Hitler gave orders to improve the protection of the submarine bunkers against attack.[35] Initially, the Germans chose to reinforce the lock at Saint Nazaire, and Christiani & Nielsen succeeded in winning the contract. Several of the submarine bunkers were located in the inner part of the harbour and, due to the tides, the submarines had to pass through the locks before they were able to moor at the quays under the thick concrete ceilings. The bunkers themselves were resistant to air attacks, but the locks were the Achilles heel. If the Allies were to damage a submarine in the lock, it would block the entrance to the bunker. Therefore, the Germans were interested in building a protected lock next to Christiani & Nielsen's old Normandy lock. The bunkers were usually built by the *Marinebauwesen*, and plans of the submarine bases were classified material. However, Christiani & Nielsen was given the task of preparing a proposal for a new lock.[36]

From a technical point of view, the assignment was rather difficult. However, the engineers believed that they had found a solution to the large spans involved. The final version was increased to 155 metres in length, 25 metres in width and 14 metres in height. With this construction, Christiani & Nielsen had developed a concept for concrete locks which could be applied to other bunker constructions. Management was aware that the company had discovered a solution which would be coveted by the Germans, and Christiani made it clear that 'a profit of at least 25 per cent was expected'. On evaluation of Christiani & Nielsen's

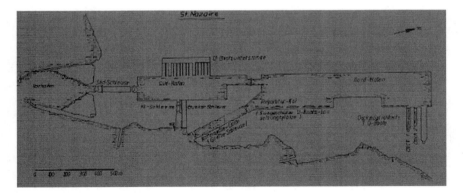

Figure 19.1 Plan of the submarine bunker construction in Saint Nazaire
Source: S. Neitzel, *Die deutschen Ubootbunker und Bunkerwerften*

dedication to the project, it is clear that they were mainly driven by an ambition to earn money; however, there was also a significant amount of prestige linked to construction work of this kind.

The prospect of future work in France was discussed at an extraordinary meeting of the management board on 21 December 1942, held because Alex Christiani was in Copenhagen to submit his reports. The extension to the submarine bunker in La Pallice posed many challenges, as the first part of the bunker, which was 235 metres in length, covered the whole width of the harbour. Christiani & Nielsen had to blast and dig away between 8,000 and 10,000 cubic metres of rock in order to create space for the three new wharves. They had also taken on the construction of the concrete lock in La Pallice, which was to be based on the Saint Nazaire concept. According to Alex Christiani's provisional assessment, it would bring in a profit of around 10 million francs once they had concreted the 6,000 cubic metres required for a 167-metre-long and 26-metre-wide bunker lock. In the absence of the accounts, the total profit is not known, but in a letter to the Crisis Squad on 31 August, Christiani readily reports that the company's French department had completed projects in La Rochelle amounting to 1,032,000 Danish kroner.[37] It is not likely that Christiani exaggerated the company's profit, and he deliberately omitted the fact that the Hamburg department had acted as the main contractor.

The threat from the Allies

In spite of the suspension of civil construction work, company prospects were bright, and at this meeting, Alex Christiani asked the management board whether 'C&N should take on yet another assignment for the Todt Organisation'. Payment for the German projects was considered 'very reasonable', and, after the Todt Organisation introduced the concept of '*Leistungsvertrag*', burdensome financing was not required as building materials were supplied by the Germans. The only factor restricting the acceptance of more assignments was the lack of construction machinery. Concerning the legitimacy of continuing to construct massive platforms for German offensive weapons, everyone agreed that they would carry on. This decision would have no effect on the progress of the war, and, in any case, continuation would not contain any political risk in the company's estimation. In summary:

> In principle, Dr Christiani believed that C&N Paris was entitled to engage in any German projects sanctioned by France's own contractors. In Dr Christiani's opinion, turnover would have to amount to 20–30 million francs for the department to survive; turnover would have to be as high as 40–50 million francs for the department to make a profit.[38]

As long as French companies were also working for the Germans, and provided the company was able to realise a turnover of between 5.7 and 7.2 million Danish kroner, management agreed that they should continue. Even though Christiani &

Nielsen only carried out construction work in the German-occupied zone, the company's strategy was partly legitimised by Marshall Pétain's declaration that it was in the French interest to support the construction of the Atlantic ramparts. Up until November 1942, the declaration by the Vichy regime contributed to the stance taken by French contractors and helped create informal ground rules for these companies that claimed that their work aided the protection of French sovereignty by averting an Allied invasion.[39] In order to understand the rules governing the actions of the players, it is important to note that Christiani clearly differentiated between the opportunities open to 'C&N Paris' and those open to 'C&N Hamburg' on the French market. In Christiani's opinion, it was not as necessary to legitimise the German department's intervention on the French market, but the French department's work for the Germans was only considered legitimate as long as other French companies were building for the occupying power.

Political developments and the incipient Allied control of the war were factors which the company was increasingly required to consider in its strategic planning. In spite of an abortive raid on Dieppe on 19 August 1942, the Allies had already

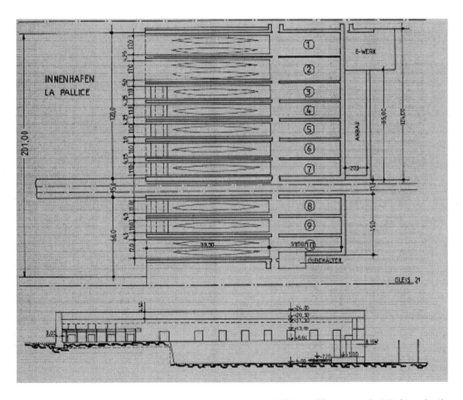

Figure 19.2 Plan of the submarine bunker at La Pallice (Christiani & Nielsen built wharves 8–10); source: S. Neitzel, Die deutschen Ubootbunker und Bunkerwerften.

clearly indicated that they intended to stage a landing on the French coast. In January 1943, management carried out an assessment of the risks faced by the company. They concluded that

> Considering the progress of the war, Dr Christiani believed that the company would soon reach a stage at which it would be necessary to be very careful when taking on work in places where there was a danger of future difficulties.[40]

Management frequently made reference to the 'progress of the war' during the occupation when assessing the outcome of the war. In this case, Christiani hinted that the prospect of a German victory was no longer as realistic as it had been and, therefore, one ought to anticipate a separate peace agreement or an Allied victory. In any event, the company ought to be prepared for the fact that the market on which it had been operating was facing a potential change. In the worst case, there could be trouble if the Allies began working side by side with the French resistance movement. However, there is no indication that this scenario was considered particularly likely. Initially, political and military developments gave rise to fears of financial loss if the war ended before the company was able to complete its assignments for the Germans. Therefore, it was important to exercise caution in order to avoid a situation in which the company had profits outstanding when peace was negotiated. The fact that the political development was, primarily, considered a financial risk was reflected in the assessments of future projects. The company differentiated between the projects the Germans would cancel and those they would continue.

In the view of the company, continuation – and even expansion – was legitimate as long as there were French companies building for the Germans. It was quite clear that the work of the French companies was used to internally legitimise company decisions. The motto was that, if there was a potential for profit, they would prefer to do well rather than badly; the financial survival of the company had a higher priority than political and moral considerations. The only time during the winter of 1943 at which the company expressed reservations about the bunker constructions was when the French government decided to stop financing the Todt Organisation's projects in the country. Christiani & Nielsen did not want to end up in a situation in which financial risk could be transferred to the company. The political risk attached to the construction work had no influence on the decisions. On the contrary, they continued to explore the potential for new assignments and, when the Germans came up with a new project to convert the Rove Tunnel in Marseille to submarine bunkers, Christiani & Nielsen submitted a proposal.[41] Even though Christiani & Nielsen was the target for the Allied bomb attacks, management estimated that the money compensated for the risks involved in continuing work for the Germans in the French harbours. At the management meeting on 17 August 1943, a telegram from Blunk was discussed, and Christiani assessed that 'there would be a lot of work for C&N Hamburg as large sections of the quays and buildings for which C&N Hamburg had acted as contractor were gone'.[42] The destruction caused by the bomb attacks on the harbour facilities gave rise to copious construction work, and the company's German department continued to work in the French harbours for the German navy. Management assessments concentrated purely on potential income, and records do not give any indication of any management evaluation of the military risks attached to work in a war zone.[43]

Summary

Christiani & Nielsen's principal interest in France after the German occupation in 1940 was the maintenance and expansion of its business. During the second half of the 1930s, France was the company's least lucrative market, and the German occupation posed further limitations on construction work. After the Armistice in June 1940, the company's greatest political risk was the occupying power's control of the construction market. Building materials were considered strategic commodities, and Germany only permitted a limited number of reconstruction projects. The occupying power took delivery of the greater part of French cement production and allocated military construction work to its own companies. In spite of the fact that the company succeeded in securing a share of some of the reconstruction projects, from 1940 to 1941, management was forced to admit the prospect of a loss of income from the French market. In an attempt to find a solution to the risks created by the war, and as a result of group strategy which stipulated that subsidiaries/departments should be financially self-supporting, the company chose to take on work for the occupying power. Christiani & Nielsen emerged as a company which did *not* simply react to political upheaval; by taking a proactive stance, it was able to create new opportunities as well as a situation which enabled compliance with the company's overall strategy. It was not German policy to allocate military construction projects to French companies before the spring of 1942, and, as Christiani & Nielsen was registered as a French company, it was excluded from this type of work. In order to overcome this obstacle, the company moved its Hamburg department into the French market and allowed the local department to work as a subcontractor to the German department. This decision proved to be profitable, as it enabled the company to attract German orders. However, in the longer term, it also meant that the main responsibility lay with the German department, and the French department did not appear responsible for the company's large military contracts. Christiani & Nielsen succeeded in acquiring some of the construction work on the large installations with the help of the company's German advisor, Arnold Agatz, who was in charge of the construction of submarine bunkers for the Navy construction office (*Marinebauamt*).

Even though management had decided that it was group policy to build military installations for the Germans, it was of vital importance that as few people as possible were aware of the company's activities. Not even the heavy Allied bombing of the French harbours caused the group to pull out. There was good money in taking on the risk and continuing work.

Notes

1 The concept of 'political risk' has been systematically discussed in relation to business history and dictatorship in the interwar period in C. Kobrak/P.H. Hansen, *European Business, Dictatorship and Political Risk 1920–1945*, New York: Berghahn, 2004, pp. 3sq. and in F.-P. van der Putten, *Corporate Behaviour and Political Risk. Dutch Companies in China 1903–1941*, Leiden: Research School for Asian, African and Amerindian Studies, 2001, pp. 5–6.
2 Gerald Feldman has emphasized the lack of detailed studies of business decisions during the Second World War. See G. Feldman, 'Historical Sources for Business History: Problems and Prospects'. Paper presented at the 10th Annual European Business History Conference 2006.
3 R.J. Overy, 'The Economy of the German "New Order"', in idem/G. Otto/ J. Houwink ten Cate (eds.), *Die 'Neuordnung' Europas. NS-Wirtschaftspolitik in den besetzen Gebieten*, Berlin: Metropol, 1997, pp. 11–28; H. Schröter, *Außenpolitik und Wirtschaftsinteresse – Skandinavien im außenwirtschaftlichen Kalkül Deutschlands und Großbritanniens 1918–1939*, Frankfurt/Main: Peter Lang, 1983.
4 M. Linder, *Projecting Capitalism – A History of the Internationalization of the Construction Industry*, Santa Barbara: Greenwood Press, 1994.
5 G. Jones, *Multinationals and Global Capitalism – from the Nineteenth to the Twenty-first Century*, Oxford: Oxford University Press, 2005.
6 M. Wilkins, *The Maturing of Multinational Enterprise: American Business Abroad from 1914 to 1970*, Cambridge, MA: Harvard University Press, 1974.
7 Peter Hayes states that from 1937, the relationship between business life and the Nazi regime was characterized by a policy of 'carrots and sticks'; see P. Hayes, *Industry and Ideology IG Farben in the Nazi Era*, Cambridge: Cambridge University Press, 1987, p. 169. Martin Fritz claims that the possibilities for private firms from the neutral countries had limited room for acting independently; see M. Fritz, 'Swedish adaptation to German domination in the Second World War', in J. Lund (ed.), *Working for the New Order – The European Business under German Domination 1939–1945*, Copenhagen: Copenhagen Business School Press, 2006, p. 136.
8 C. Buchheim/J. Scherner, 'The Role of Private Property in the Nazi Economy: The Case of Industry', *The Journal of Economic History*, Vol. 66, pp. 410–12; J. Scherner, 'The beginnings of Nazi autarky policy: the "National Pulp Programme" and the origin of regional stable fibre plants', *Economic History Review*, 2008, vol. 61, p. 894; N. Forbes, 'Multinational Enterprise "Corporate Responsibility" and the Nazi Dictatorship: The Case of Unilever and Germany in the 1930s', *Contemporary European History*, 2007, vol. 16, pp. 166–7.
9 T. Bergh/H. Espeli/K. Sogner, *Brytningstider – Storselskabet Orkla 1654–2004*, Oslo: Orion Forlag, 2004; K.G. Andersen, *Flaggskip i fremmed eie. Hydro 1905–1945*, Oslo: Pax, 2005, pp. 384–9; I. Karlsson, 'Sveriges Ekonomiska Relationer med det ockuperade Norge', in M. Fritz et al.(eds.), *En (O)moralisk Handel – Sveriges ekonomiska relationer med Nazityskland*, Stockholm: Forum för levande historia, 2006, pp. 117–52; P. Sandvik, *The Making of a Department, Falconbridge Nikkelverk 1910–1929–2004*, Trondheim: Norwegian University of Science and Technology, 2008, pp. 99–107; M. Fritz, 'Swedish Ball-Bearings and the German War Economy', *Scandinavian Economic History Review*, 1975, vol. 23, pp. 15–35; M. Fritz/B. Karlsson, *SKF i stormaktspolitikens kraftfält – Kullagereexporten 1943–1945*, Göteborg: SKF, 1998.
10 Christiani & Nielsen, board meeting minutes, 12 September 1940. Archive no. 10.557.RA.

11 Hitler's resolve that the victory in France avenge the humiliating Versailles Treaty had a significant impact on German occupation policy in France during the first phase. It was important that the French feel defeat, and this also applied to the French business community. However, more rational forces in Berlin, as well as the developments of the war, made the Germans realise that French businesses held armament potential; cf. E. Jäckel, *Frankreich in Hitlers Europa. Die deutsche Frankreichpolitik im Zweiten Weltkrieg*, Stuttgart: DVA, 1966, pp. 13sq.
12 D. Voldman. 'Le bâtiment, une branche sollicitée', in A. Beltran/R. Frank/H. Rousso (eds.), *La vie des entreprises sous l'Occupation*, Paris: Belin, 1994, pp. 98–9.
13 R. Vinen, *The Politics of French Business*, Cambridge: Cambridge University Press, 1991, p. 102.
14 Christiani & Nielsen, board meeting minutes, 22 July 1941. Archive no. 10.557. RA.
15 Christiani & Nielsen, board meeting minutes, 22 August 1941. Archive no. 10.557.RA.
16 F.W. Seidler, *Die Organisation Todt. Bauen für Staat und Wehrmacht 1938–1945*, Koblenz: Bernard & Graefe, 1987.
17 Christiani & Nielsen, board meeting minutes, 10 October 1941. Archive no. 10.557.RA.
18 S. Neitzel, *Die deutschen Ubootbunker und Bunkerwerften – Bau, Verwendung und Bedeutung verbunkerter U-Bootstützpunkte in beiden Weltkriegen*, Koblenz: Bernard & Graefe, 1991, p. 83.
19 Christiani & Nielsen, board meeting minutes, 10 October 1941. Archive no. 10.557.RA.
20 Handbook of the Todt Organisation by the Supreme Headquarters Allied Expeditionary Force Counter-Intelligence Sub-Division MIRS/MR-OT/5/45.
21 Handbook of the Todt Organisation by the Supreme Headquarters Allied Expeditionary Force Counter-Intelligence Sub-Division MIRS/MR-OT/5/45, p. 59.
22 'Der Bau des Ubootbunkers begann im September 1941 durch die Baufirmen Leonhard Moll und Christiani & Nielsen', in Neitzel: *Die deutschen Ubootbunker*, p. 83; Employés du 'Marinebauamt Bordeaux'. Director of Naval Intelligence: France: Bordeaux: U-Boat bases; operational orders and bomb damage. 1941–1944. ADM 199/2470. The French intelligence service revealed a fairly precise picture of the construction of the bunker in Bordeaux based on information from workers at the construction site. In a report from 5 December 1943, they mention the contractors working on the bunker and named Germans in senior positions in the Todt Organisation.
23 Seidler, 'Die Organisation Todt, pp. 140–1.
24 Voldman, 'Le bâtiment, une branche sollicitée', p. 99.
25 Belegschaftstand der OT-Einsatzgruppe West am 15. April 1942, reprinted in Neitzel, *Die deutschen Ubootbunker*, p. 211. This document reports that 2,931 Frenchmen, 2,080 Spaniards, 396 Belgians, 138 Italians and 67 Dutch worked on the Bordeaux bunker. As a result of wartime events, the archives of the Todt Organisation in France and of the *Marinebauamt* were lost. Thus, it is difficult to determine the exact number of forced labourers deployed on the construction of the submarine bunkers. Neitzel has published an authoritative work on the German submarine bunkers based on records available in the *Bundesarchiv* and, in a letter to this author, dated 22 November 2002, he states that he considers it improbable that a company such as Christiani & Nielsen would not have deployed forced labour.
26 A.S. Milward, *The New Order and the French Economy*, Oxford: Clarendon Press, 1970, p. 278.

278 Steen Andersen

27 R. Desquesnes, 'Atlantikwall et Südwall' – La Defense Allemande sur le Littoral Francais (1941–1944), Caen: Thèse de Doctorat d'Etat Université de CAEN, Mention 'Histoire', 1987, p. 239sq., vol. 1, and document no. 77, 'La collaboration avec l'occupant (branche des travaux publics)' in vol. 2, p. 96; Handbook of the Todt Organisation by the Supreme Headquarters Allied Expeditionary Force Counter-Intelligence Sub-Division MIRS/MR-OT/5/45, p. 62.
28 Christiani & Nielsen, board meeting minutes, 13 April 1942. Archive no. 10.557. DIF.
29 In 1942, the dry dock in Saint Nazaire was the only facility capable of accommodating the German battleship *Tirpitz*. Therefore, the British admiralty launched a bold attack on the dry dock. An outdated British frigate, *HMS Campbeltown*, was equipped with 4.5 tons of explosives and sailed into the harbour of Saint Nazaire. The ship rammed the dry dock on 26 March 1942. In addition, commando soldiers were landed, their assignment being to destroy the infrastructure of the harbour and the docks. The ignition of the explosive charge on board the *Campbeltown* was delayed until the Germans thought the raid was over. A large number of Germans were killed, and around 100 labourers also lost their lives in the explosion. The dry dock remained unusable until 1948, and the attack prevented the *Tirpitz* from further action in the Atlantic.
30 Christiani & Nielsen, board meeting minutes, 22 June 1942. Archive no. 10.557. DIF.
31 Christiani & Nielsen, board meeting minutes, 10 July 1942. Archive no. 10.557. DIF.
32 Christiani & Nielsen, board meeting minutes, 22 June 1942. Archive no. 10.557. DIF.
33 Copy (unconfirmed) of a declaration by the *Ministère des travaux publics et des transports*, 5 December 1945, annex Y 7. Rigsadvokatens P-sager, journal no. P.16.457. RA.
34 Christiani & Nielsen was registered as the main contractor on the construction site Porta in La Pallice/La Rochelle by the Todt Organisation's site supervision (*Oberbauleitung*); cf. H. Singer (ed.), *Quellen zur Geschichte der Organisation Todt, vol. 3, Die Organisation Todt im Einsatz 1939–1945, dargestellt nach Kriegsschauplätzen auf Grund der Feldpostnummern*, Osnabrück: Biblio, 1987, p. 234.
35 Neitzel, *Die deutschen Ubootbunker*, p. 82.
36 Christiani & Nielsen, board meeting minutes, 23 November 1942. Archive no. 10.557.RA.
37 Letter from Rudolf Christiani to the Copenhagen Crisis Squad, 31 August 1945. Rigsadvokatens P-sager, journal no. 16457. RA.
38 Christiani & Nielsen, board meeting minutes, 21 December 1942. Archive no. 10.557.RA.
39 D. Voldman, 'Le bâtiment, une branche sollicitée', p. 101; K.-V. Neugebauer, *Die deutschen Militärkontrolle im unbesetzten Frankreich und Französisch Nordwestafrika 1940–1942. Zum Problem der Sicherung der Südwestflanke von Hitlers Kontinentalimperium*, Cologne: PhD thesis, 1977, pp. 186sq.
40 Christiani & Nielsen, board meeting minutes, 4 January 1943. Archive no. 10.557. RA.
41 Christiani & Nielsen, board meeting minutes, 7 May 1943, 2 July 1943, 13 July 1943, 5 August 1943. Archive no. 10.557.RA; Neitzel, *Die deutschen Ubootbunker*, pp. 141sq.
42 Christiani & Nielsen, board meeting minutes, 17 August 1943. Archive no. 10.557.RA
43 Director of Naval Intelligence: France: St. Nazaire and La Pallice: U-Boat bases; operational orders and bomb damage including location of wreck of HMS Campbeltown, 1942–1945. ADM 199/2469; Report on details of U-Boat Shelters,

25 June 1943, Naval Intelligence Department. U-Boat Bases in Occupied France 1942 Apr. 1943 Apr. Air 15/199; Bombing of St. Nazaire, N.I.D. U.C. Report, 3 April 1943; Bombing Attacks on La Pallice and St. Nazaire, 7 June 1943. ADM 199/2470; Bombing of U-Boat Bases by the 8th U.S. Air Force, 3 July 1943; Results of bombing of Bordeaux: CX/27216/A, 25 May 1943; Bordeaux: Submarine Base: CX/12304, 24 August 1943. ADM 199/2470.

20 Management of the South Manchuria Railway Company

Tsutomu Hirayama

Introduction

The Manchurian Incident had a strong impact on Imperial Japan and Manchuria; it expanded Imperial Japan's sphere of influence, founded the puppet government of Manchukuo, and framed and enforced a new economic system. The South Manchuria Railway Company (SMR), established in 1906, had been forced to change under this influence due to varied expectations of different entities.

Most previous studies of SMR show that it cooperated closely with the Kwantung Army in planning Manchuria's regulation policy and acted as the centrality of Manchurian economic development by investing in new companies with the Manchukuo government. With the first phase of planning completed, the Kwantung Army and the Japanese government reorganized SMR into a railway company without the function of a holding company. SMR spilt off heavy-industry businesses as well as many of its subsidiaries to the Manchuria Heavy Industrial Development Company (MHID), losing its central position in Manchuria.[1]

These previous studies revealed that the Kwantung Army and the Japanese government altered politically SMR's position in the Manchurian economy. These studies seek to describe how SMR was given a drubbing by the national policy of Imperial Japan, especially focusing on the relationship between SMR's top management and the senior government officials; however, we are only given a final conclusion that political power broke up SMR, and there is no explication of how SMR had run a business under wartime control.

The purpose of this chapter is to show why SMR a semigovernmental company had changed its approach toward economic control policy in Manchuria in not political but economic and managerial contexts and how SMR managed itself as a private company rather than a government-controlled company under the conflict between public interests and private company's profit in the 1930s.

1. SMR's capital increase in 1933 and private-sector stockholders' pressure

The Manchurian Incident made SMR active in the Manchuria economy. The increasing capital requirements of SMR led the company to issue stocks in 1933, which increased capital from 440 million yen to 800 million yen.

The vice president, Yoshiaki Hatta, announced the 10-year investment plan in heavy industries at the extraordinary general meeting of stockholders in March 1933.[2] The private-sector stockholders (the stockholders) approved his plan as well as the capital increase of 360 million yen, which allotted 180 million yen to the Japanese government, 110 million yen to the stockholders, 10 million yen to the staff and 60 million yen to the public offering.[3]

The public offering of 60 million yen (1.2 million stocks) had a bidding process, and the subscribers had to put a premium on the new stocks. SMR's documents show that the total number of subscribers was 23,941; the total number of subscribed stocks was 3,518,220; and the number of successful bidders was 9,910. The total premium was 6,215,394 yen, and the highest and lowest subscription price was 80.5 yen and 54.9 yen. This meant that the public offering was successful as a preliminary step.[4]

This public offering had sixty-five reception offices securities firms, stockbrokers and banks. The central metropolises had fifty offices in Tokyo, Osaka and Nagoya, among others; the regional cities had eleven offices in Otaru, Kanazawa and Nagasaki, among others; and the colonial cities had four offices in Dalian, Shengyang, Changchun and Seoul.[5]

Figure 20.1 plots the rate of successful bids and the weighted average subscription price. It shows that most successful bidders who paid a high contract price lived in the regions mentioned. In addition, the total number of subscribed stocks per capita was 224 in the central metropolises, 50 in the regional cities and 111 in the colonial cities.[6] The public offering indicates that the successful bidders in the regions took smaller stock subscriptions at a higher contract price.

The capital increase in 1933 had been paid for in instalments of 10 yen per stock each year until 1937. We turn to the fluctuation in the number of stockholders and stock holdings in the term concerned. Table 20.1 plots the number of stocks and applications for transfers. It shows that the success of the official offering was temporary. The stockholders got new stocks through a capital increase in 1933 (1933 stocks), and they began simultaneously to transfer their stocks in January 1934. Table 20.2 plots the number of stockholders and the ration of share in private stocks. Table 20.2 shows that staff, seeming to have no loyalty toward SMR, released not only 1933 stocks but also the paid-up stocks. The stockholders in urban areas did release stocks, which were bought by regional stockholders, increasing the number of stockholders in regional areas and the ration of shares.

Coincidentally, the numbers of stockholders were increasing in urban areas, decreasing the per-capita stocks in the regions. Furthermore, the number of large stockholders who had more than 5,000 stocks decreased from 221 stockholders in November 1935 to 124 stockholders in May 1938. Moreover, the loyal stockholders of SMR, who had kept more than 5,000 stocks during the same period, bought 31,125 '1933 stocks' but released 83,594 paid-up stocks.[7] This meant that the size of SMR stockholders was shrinking and the new stockholders were littler than the existing ones.

It is noteworthy that the stock price of SMR declined after the capital increase in 1933,[8] indicating that stock supply exceeded stock demand. Certainly, the

282 Tsutomu Hirayama

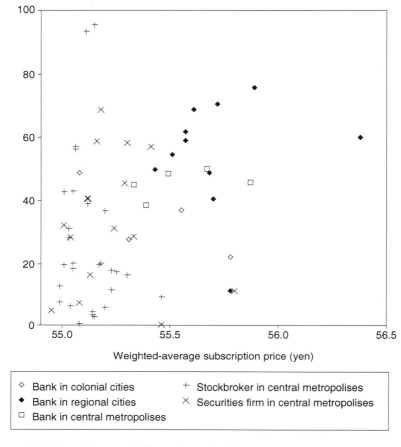

Figure 20.1 Rate of successful bits and weighted-average subscription price

Sources: SMR, 'Daini Shinkabushiki Bonyu Soukeihyo, Hoka' (Tabulation of Confirmed Subscription for 1933, Public Offering), DCI, Before: 17A-226

Notes: 'Central metropolises' were Tokyo, Osaka, Nagoya, Yokohama and Kobe. 'Regional cities' were Otaru, Akita, Sendai, Mito, Kanazawa, Kyoto, Yokkaichi, Hiroshima, Shimonoseki, Moji and Nagasaki. 'Colonial cities' were Dairen, Shengyang, Changchun and Seoul.

capital increase got the approval of the extraordinary general meeting of stockholders, and the public offering was successful. However, this approval was from their real shareholders, who could not oppose the increase due to their small stock holdings and, thus, had to release them.

Why did stockholders in urban areas release their SMR stocks that were kept or allotted? The stock price of SMR was as high as that of other major companies, for example, Kanebo, Nihon Yusen, Tokyo Dento and Nihon Sangyo. Furthermore, the yield on one SMR stock was higher than that for the other companies, because the stock price of SMR was lower after April 1934.

Table 20.1 Number of stocks and applications of transfers

Year	Number of paid-up stocks of transfer	Number of 1933 stocks of transfer	Sum	Number of applications of transfers
1933	1,731,364	0	1,731,364	38,312
1934	862,279	1,671,551	2,533,830	57,519
1935	782,647	1,025,376	1,808,023	29,089
1936	674,394	883,722	1,558,116	31,265
1937	800,047	857,260	1,657,307	31,549
1938	732,961	220,707	953,668	21,050

Sources: SMR, 'Kabusu oyobi Jinin Zengetsu tono Hikakuhyo' (The table for the number of stocks and stockholders compared to the previous month), DCI, Before: 17A-229.

Table 20.2 Number of stockholders and ration of share in private stocks

			1933	1934	1935	1936	1937	1938
Stockholders (person)								
		In urban area	11,941	16,971	18,830	20,355	21,507	22,505
		In regional area	14,784	21,425	25,188	28,192	30,694	33,971
		In colonies	3,941	8,520	3,103	3,182	3,165	3,667
		Staff of SMR		17,238	8,175	7,469	6,501	6,466
		sum	30,666	64,154	55,296	59,198	61,867	66,609
Stocks (%)								
	Paid-up stocks							
		In urban area	54.5	54.9	52.8	51.8	51.3	49.9
		In regional area	34.5	35.2	36.3	38.2	39.0	40.3
		In colonies	11.0	9.0	10.4	9.6	9.4	9.4
		Staff of SMR		0.9	0.5	0.4	0.3	0.4
	1933 stocks							
		In urban area		58.6	54.4	49.9	49.5	46.4
		In regional area		26.8	34.4	39.7	42.0	43.1
		In colonies		10.2	8.4	7.7	6.7	7.7
		Staff of SMR		4.4	2.8	2.7	1.8	2.9

Sources 1: as for Table 20.1.
2: Kabunushi Seimeihyo (The list of stockholders), SMR, as of June 1933.

Notes 1: 'Urban area' were prefectures of Tokyo, Oosaka, Aichi, Kanagawa and Hyogo. 'Regional area' were other prefectures in Japan.
2: All numbers are as of 31 January, but the year 1933 is as of 1 July.

It was the prominent media coverage in Asahi Shinbun, the oldest and largest national daily newspapers, that led those in urban areas to release their stocks. Asahi Shinbun Database hints that, from December 1926 to December 1945, the number of headlines for SMR was 2,033, of which 754 were front-page headlines, and of these, 243 occupied the front pages with the headlines about politics, diplomacy and the military in Manchuria.[9] These numbers distinguished SMR from the other companies.

Asahi Shinbun had not only given prominent coverage but also repeatedly changed the information for the fundraising and reorganization of SMR. For example, President Uchida Yasuya announced that SMR would concentrate on core railway business in December 1931, but the next president, Hayashi Hirotaro, announced that he would like to extend SMR's businesses in August 1932. In April 1932, Vice President Eguchi Teijo announced the capital increase plan on dividend guarantee by the Japanese government; however, just after Eguchi's replacement in April 1932, the next vice president, Yoshiaki Hatta, announced that they had deliberated Eguchi's plan carefully and preferred to apply for a bank loan.

The more coverage SMR was given, the more difficult it was for the stockholders in urban areas to anticipate SMR's potential actions. Therefore, not only did they refrain from further investment in SMR stocks, but they also released some of their previous stock holdings. Consequently, intensive coverage by Asahi Shinbun from the Manchurian Incident to April 1934 made the stock price of SMR fluctuate violently.

Why did the remaining stockholders in regional areas underwrite SMR stocks that the others had parted with? It is believed that this was because there was no asymmetric information between urban areas and regional because there was no difference in the coverage about SMR between nationwide newspapers and local papers; moreover, a nationwide radio broadcast had provided the people with most of the common information about SMR in the 1930s.[10]

What made the regional stockholders underwrite the released SMR stocks was the difference in opportunity to invest in a major company stock. It is true that stock exchanges were already established in that region of Japan and that stock exchange trading was flourishing; however, there was not much stock transfer, which implied a change of stockholders due to a short sale and margin buying. Also, because the stock exchange could not increase the supply of stocks, it was difficult particularly for those demanding them in the region to get hold of these major company stocks.[11] The stockholders of SMR and the regional investors had sought the opportunity to invest in the major company stock. In other words, SMR could raise funds from the stockholders for the capital increase in 1933, because the stock market in Japan at the time was imperfect in the sense that there was the barrier to entry.

This meant that the new stockholders were different from the existing ones in both behaviour and thinking. For instance, the new holders were novice stock investors and did not display sufficient loyalty toward SMR. Furthermore, it was not believed that their financial resources were strong. What it all means is that the existing stockholders' dislike of SMR after the Manchurian Incident had caused the fluctuation in the number of stockholders and stock holdings, making SMR's equity financing so fragile. Thus, SMR had to stabilize the stockholders.

President Yosuke Matsuoka disclosed the information about SMR and its subsidiary through the media, as this would help gain support from the stockholders. He made a strong appeal to them and stated that SMR and its subsidiaries made a profit in cooperation with the Japanese and Manchukuo governments. However, his attempt was a failure. Since the information about SMR and its subsidiary appeared in *Economist* and *Toyo-Keizai-Shinpo*, famous economic journals, in September 1935,[12] the number of stocks transferred was increasing and the stock price was declining. At last, SMR's stock fell below per in September 1937. The stockholders believed that SMR and its subsidiaries were under the Japanese government and sacrificed profit to national policy.

On the other hand, with new measures, the stockholders had put pressure on SMR, which wanted to act as the centrality of Manchurian economic development. The stockholders who were large, individual and loyal organized themselves in August 1934 and enrolled the stockholders who were new, small and disloyal.[13] The association was named Mantetsu-Kabunushi-Kai.

According to an opinion poll by Mantetsu-Kabunushi-Kai, most stockholders feared that SMR could not manage itself under national policy. They preferred nonintervention in SMR management by the Japanese government. Also, they desired that SMR seek profit as a private company, not a government-controlled company, and the provision of a fixed dividend rate of 8 per cent with a stoppage on declining stock prices.[14]

2. Activities and thoughts of middle management of SMR

The stock market, in which there was a change of stockholders through a sacrifice sale, had conflicted with SMR under national policy and argued that SMR had inefficient management. The question now arises about how SMR managed itself after Mantetsu-Kabunushi-Kai had applied the pressure; that is, it is important to clarify who had influence in decision making of administration of SMR after the Manchurian Incident. We concentrate our discussion on personnel matters of the top and the middle management, especially on activities and thoughts of SMR's middle management.

The feature of personnel matters in SMR was that the terms of office for the top management were very short under the party governance.[15] Although the regulatory terms of the presidents and vice presidents were for five years, only few actually served the entire term. The trend of short terms among SMR's top management raises the question of who actually managed SMR and made constant decisions to change leadership. In fact, the same concern was felt by some of SMR staff, who then delivered a statement with a pamphlet in July 1924. Those concerned were staff members who had entered SMR after graduating from university in the 1910s and were promoted to section chief (we called them Old Generation Staff). They criticized the frequent changes and the short years of service by the top management, most of whom lacked career experience in the Manchurian economy. They proclaimed that the promotion of staff members to top management should be reserved for those with thorough knowledge of Manchuria and not based on the change of government in Japan.[16]

Figure 20.2 plots the average term in office and the number of middle management – the department head and the section chief – who were full-time staff from SMR's establishment in 1906 to its reorganization in 1937. According to the figure, the average term in office had increased since the establishment of SMR. This meant that SMR's middle management could have participated in management activities while working as business staff. The average term peaked in fiscal 1916/17 and began to drop until fiscal 1919/20. This trend of declining term length reflected the extensive promotion to middle management in SMR. Old Generation Staff had been promoted to chief after this drastic change.

In addition, the younger staff members, who had joined SMR in the 1920s, took a more radical approach (we call them New Generation Staff). They proposed the establishment of an association comprising the staff themselves for the purpose of managing SMR. Shinji Okumura, a role model to New Generation Staff, claimed that it was indispensable for the nation to regulate the industry for the purpose of rationalization. He also insisted on staff participation in SMR's management to efficiently and intensively rationalise the industry.[17]

Eventually, a consensus was reached between Old and New Generation Staff; they established Mantetsu-Shain-Kai in April 1927. But they did not declare that SMR was managed by their staff, but rather the staff continued to work under SMR and therefore took on SMR's mission. In other words, the radical thoughts

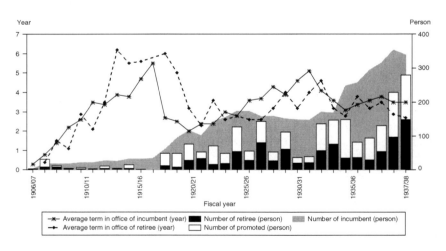

Figure 20.2 Average term in office and number of middle management

Sources: Mantetsu Kai (Association for the retired staff of SMR and the people concerned), ed. *Minami Manshu Tetsudo Kabushiki Gaisha Kakyu Ijo Soshiki Kiko Hensen Narabini Jinji Ido Ichiranhyo* (Diagram for Change in the Organization and Staff of SMR), reprinted, Tokyo: Ryukei Shosha, 1992.

Notes: 'Number of incumbent' was as of end of fiscal year.

of New Generation Staff were suppressed by Old Generation Staff. Jotaro Yamamoto, who was appointed president with the Friends of Constitutional Party, Rikken-Seiyu-Kai, as a backer in July 1927, accepted Old Generation Staff's demands, especially those regarding management participation. Therefore, those who had staff careers were promoted to directors and did not double as the department heads.[18] This meant that the promotion of qualified internal staff to top management had brought about stability in SMR's management.

However, in August 1929, Mitsugu Sengoku was appointed president with the Constitutional Democratic Party, Rikken Minseito, as a backer. Shortly after, the stability achieved under Yamamoto crashed due to drastic reform. Sengoku made bold personnel changes and hired new recruits as directors in 1930 who had no career experience in SMR. New directors doubled as the department heads.[19] This meant that Sengoku had rejected the idea of allowing old staff participation in management and promoting Old Generation Staff to top management.

It is noteworthy that President Sengoku had a clear policy for SMR's management. In a speech to the staff, Sengoku declared his aspiration to operate of SMR in the form of Taylorism and scientific management. Sengoku considered Old Generation Staff agents for lax management who had supported Yamamoto in his diversification of SMR and the founding of many subsidiaries, which is why he dismissed several old staff.[20] Therefore, he made Mantetsu-Shain-Kai issue a special article titled 'An increase in efficiency of SMR' in their bulletin, *Kyowa*, primarily to express his thoughts.[21] Sengoku made his followers, for example, Director Takao Godo, appeal that the management of SMR needed to be efficient under industrial rationalization based on unification of standards. So Sengoku's vision of industrial rationalization could be collaboration with the thoughts of New Generation Staff who had before been suppressed by the old generation.

According to Figure 20.2, the average term in office for middle management was declining until fiscal 1932/33, that is, after Sengoku's retirement, because – similar to Hirotaro Hayashi – the next president, Yasuya Uchida, dismissed Old Generation Staff. Thus, New Generation Staff were promoted to middle management in the 1930s. In parallel with the promotion of them, SMR's staff was promoted to top management again and did not double as the department heads. Moreover, the directors who had staff careers with SMR had commanded an absolute majority of top management under President Yosuke Matsuoka, who was appointed in August 1935. (The information disclosure in *Economist* and *Toyo-Keizai-Shinpo* took place against a background of not only Matsuoka's assumption but also New Generation Staff's internal promotion.) Furthermore, for the first time, Director Oojiro Sato, who had a staff career with SMR, was appointed vice president under the next president, Takuichi Oomura, who was promoted from vice president.[22] New Generation Staff, who occupied SMR's middle and top management, acquired the position to manage SMR based on their ways of thinking.

New Generation Staff who differed from Old Generation Staff had clear beliefs and clever vision. They wanted to manage SMR by themselves, thereby regulating the economy in Manchuria and Japan. Therefore, after the Manchurian Incident, they played an active role in the research department of SMR (Keizai-Chosa-Kai; that is, SMR upgraded the research section to the department in January 1932), as they wanted to contribute to the planning and control by Imperial Japan. The staff in Keizai-Chosa-Kai had cooperated with the Kwantung Military and planned the economic control policy in Manchuria, as is generally known.

New Generation Staff were promoted to middle management, and the internal staff promotion changed the top management in the 1930s. Thus, SMR wanted to act as the centrality of Manchurian economic development at the expense of stockholders' profit; therefore, the stockholders had desired that SMR seek profit as a private company, not a government-controlled company. In other words, the Manchurian Incident and the capital increase in 1933 intensified the conflict between the top and middle management and the stockholders of SMR.

3. Capacity for statistical survey in SMR's research

The question arises, finally, about why the top and middle management of SMR did not refuse the request of stockholders and how SMR's profit for the stockholders took precedence over public interest under Imperial Japan's policy. To begin from the conclusion, it was because SMR had the limited capacity for statistical survey from the viewpoint of public uniform survey standards.

The statistical survey was essential to planning economic control policy. In fact, Keizai-Chosa-Kai implemented many statistical surveys in Manchuria and published numerous statistical books on the Manchurian economy. It should be noted that SMR's guidebook indicated that the traditional method of statistical survey adopted by SMR's research section was to collect statistical books edited and published by other research institutes, for example, the Eastern Chinese Railway Company and the Chinese government.[23] They filtered many data from the massive collections and tabulated accounts for their intended purpose. SMR's research section would typically create a desktop survey based on the statistical survey administered by others. Moreover, SMR's research staff had done these surveys without consulting anybody else, relying on intuition and experience.[24]

Certainly, before the Manchurian Incident, SMR's research section had no problems regarding their sharp style of statistical survey. In general, their collection was highly acclaimed rather than criticized in Japan. However, when Keizai-Chosa-Kai, which had drafted the first plan for controlling the Manchurian economy, wanted to plan a uniform economic policy for Manchuria and Japan in 1936, the Japanese government, especially the Ministry of Finance, rejected this plan under SMR's research. The Ministry of Finance officials insisted that the research and planning by Keizai-Chosa-Kai lacked statistical *basis*. They criticized the method of statistical survey by SMR's staff, because they could not understand how the tabulations were made and repeat the same experience in statistical aggregation by SMR's research section.[25]

On the other hand, the Japanese government had adopted the method of statistical survey which distinguished it from SMR, training statistical researchers constantly.[26] The government had established the rigid method of statistical survey used in national research, for example, the census in 1920. It is important that its statistical surveys were done with questionnaires under the law that had established the formal procedure. Therefore, anyone could understand the proceedings of statistical aggregation by the Japanese government, and if there was a doubt about aggregation, anyone could reaggregate the data on these questionnaires. Moreover, the Japanese government could get various statistical data daily, weekly or monthly; that is, it could modify the economic control plan in accordance with the real situation, because most statistical surveys were done with questionnaires under instructions from the Japanese government.

It is well known that SMR had employed many Marxists with records of arrest and published several investigation results in various fields; therefore, SMR's research activities were deemed brilliant by many historians in later ages.[27] When they carried out their biggest surveys – the research for wartime inflation in Japan, Manchuria and China and the survey for powers of resistance on the Chinese military — the results strongly opposed the military authorities in Imperial Japan, so that they were oppressed by the military-police unit for being communist. But the other side of this oppression would indicate that Imperial Japan did abandon them due not only to their thought but also to their capacity for statistical survey.

SMR's research department – Keizai-Chosa-Kai – could not change its traditional method and sharp style of statistical survey and, therefore, contribute to the planning and control in Imperial Japan. In other words, New Generation Staff, who played an active role in Keizai-Chosa-Kai, could not promote SMR as the centrality of economic control to the mainstay of Imperial Japan due to their limited capacity for statistical survey and policy analysis. They could not manage SMR as a national-policy company in spite of commanding a majority of the top and middle management. New Generation Staff experienced a setback.

However, it is noteworthy that it was the criticism of statistical surveys in Keizai-Chosa-Kai that could recover SMR's management under New Generation Staff's setback. SMR's research department had a few staff who made a specialty of statistics and could understand the value of the rigid method of statistical survey with questionnaires. These statistical researchers in SMR already had some doubts about its desktop survey when New Generation Staff played an active role in Keizai-Chosa-Kai. Those who had been ignored due to minority held the course on the method of statistical survey in August 1939, under Dai-Chosa-Bu, which was a successor of Keizai-Chosa-Kai.[28]

They lectured SMR's research staff about the rigid method of statistical survey and insisted that it was important for SMR's research department to carry it out based on questionnaires. They also pointed out that SMR had collected the original statistical data filled in on the questionnaires for the company's business, especially railways and coal-mining businesses.[29] This meant that there were the informative data in SMR which made it possible for SMR's statistical researchers to conduct a macro-analysis of the industries of railway and coal mining in the Manchurian economy and assess the cause-and-effect relationship at the micro level on the job site of these businesses. In other words, SMR could manage these businesses more efficiently due to their statistical survey based on questionnaires which had collected the original data.

More importantly, a few statistical researchers in SMR could recognize anew from the results of rare and superior statistical surveys that it was the railways and the coal-mining businesses that were the core profitable sectors of SMR. Therefore, it is believed that they supported the corporate reorganization of SMR. The course in 1939 was the opportunity to thoroughly give a better understanding of managerial merit of the corporate reorganization of SMR to not only research staff but also the middle and top management. Consequently, it was the capacity for statistical survey that made SMR stop managing itself as a national-policy company and seek profit for the stockholders as a private company.

4. Concluding remarks

SMR transferred its administrative power over the land attached to railways to the Manchukuo government and sold most of its subsidiaries to MHID in December 1937. SMR finished acting as the centrality of Manchurian economic development. But this meant that SMR concentrated its power on the sound businesses that were highly lucrative and that the stockholders could participate in. Therefore, this corporate reorganization of SMR was broadly welcomed. The sharp rise of SMR stock prices after its reorganization indicated that the stockholders supported the reformation of SMR. Consequently, the fluctuation of stockholders and the spread of stocks were more moderate in the capital increase in 1940, and the stockholders could get their stable dividend rate of 8 per cent until the end of SMR.

It was the important problem that the stockholders increased their stock holdings with SMR's declining stock price. This situation required SMR to be an independent stock-based company rather than a national-policy company. In other words, SMR was dependent on not only the Japanese government as the largest stockholder but also the stockholders in the private sector.

However, only the pressure of the stockholders and stock market did not change a national-policy company into a private company. The outside pressure is no guarantee of success in an organization's change. It is indispensable for somebody on the inside to be in cooperation with the outsider. SMR had New Generation Staff who had clear beliefs and clever vision, wanted to manage SMR by themselves for regulating the economy in Manchuria and Japan, obtained the internal staff promotion and occupied SMR's top and middle management.

More importantly, when they played a responsible role in managing SMR, they had to acknowledge that SMR's research could not fulfil the demand of the Japanese government due to their limited capacity for statistical survey; New Generation Staff saw that their attempt and activities were a failure. This setback made them regain their presence of mind; therefore they could deal with fluctuating stockholders when stock prices were declining. Also, the staff who could not admit their failure, specifically Shinji Okumura, transferred to MHID with SMR's reorganization. In other words, they find out the way of making the best use of their limited capacity for statistical survey, because they could respond to criticism of statistical researchers positively.

Consequently, pressure of stockholders and stock market, internal promotion of staff and their capacity for statistical survey made SMR change its approach toward economic control policy in Manchuria.

Notes

1 See, for example, A. Hara, '1930 Nendai no Manshu Keizai Tosei Seisaku (Economic Control Policies in Manchuria in the 1930s)', in Manshu Shi Kenkyukai (ed.), *Nihon Teikokushugika no Manshu (Manchuria under the Japan Empire)*, Tokyo: Ochanomizu Shobo, 1972; idem, 'Manshu ni okeru Keizai Tosei Seisaku no Tenkai (Development of Economic Control Policies in Manchuria)', in Y. Ando (ed.), *Nihon Keizai Seisaku Shiron (History of Economic Policies in Japan)*, vol. 2, Tokyo: Tokyo University Press, 1976; K. Kato, *Mantetsu Zenshi (Complete History of the South Manchuria Railway)*, Tokyo: Kodansha, 2006.
2 'Rinji Kabunushi Sokai Fukusosai Setsumei' (Explanation by the Vice President at the Extraordinary General Meeting of Stockholders), *Hatta Yoshiaki Monjo* (Document of Yoshiaki Hatta, DYH), No. 0310, 6 March 1933, p. 5.
3 'Rinji Kabunushi Sokai Ketsugi Jiko' (Resolution at the Extraordinary General Meeting of Stockholders), DYH, No. 0322, 6 March 1933, p. 2.
4 South Manchuria Railway Co. (SMR) 'Moshikomi Kakakubetsu Meisaihyo' (Detailed Price List of Subscription for the 1933 Public Offering) *Heisa Kikan Shiryo (Document of the Closed Institution*, DCI), Before: 17A-28.
5 SMR, *Daini Shinkabushiki Kobo Boshu Seisekihyo (Tabulation of Subscription for 1933, Public Offering)*, DCI, Before: 17A-125.
6 SMR, *Daini Shinkabushiki Bonyu Sokeihyo, Hoka (Tabulation of Confirmed Subscription for 1933, Public Offering)*, DCI, Before: 17A-226.
7 SMR, *Oo-kabunushi Hyo (List of Large Stockholders)*, DCI, Before: 17A-196; SMR, *Oo-kabunushi Hyo (List of Large Stockholders)*, DCI, Before: 17A-23; SMR, *Oo-kabunushi oyobi Jiko Meibo (Name Cards of Large Stockholders with Incident Record)*, DCI, Before: 12–22.
8 *Tokyo Kabushiki Torihikijo Geppo (Monthly Report of Tokyo Stock Exchange)*, various issues.
9 *Asahi Shinbun Senzen Shimen Database (Database for Asahi Shinbun in the prewar period), 1926–1945*, Ver. 1, Asahi Sinbun Co., 2002.
10 *Rajio Nenkan (Year Book of Radio Broadcasting)*, 1938, Nihon Hoso Kyokai (The Broadcasting Corporation of Japan), pp. 58–9.
11 See in particular K. Chosakai (ed.), *Kabuya no Karakuri (The Tricks of Stockjobber)*, Tokyo: Nogeisha, 1934.
12 'Mantetsu no Kokkateki Shimei to Sono Jittai (National Mission at SMR and its Details)', *Ekonomisuto (Economist)*, No.13–26, 11 September 1935, pp. 17–25. 'Minami Manshu Tetsudo no Kaibo (Business Analysis of SMR)', *Toyo Keizai Shinpo*, No. 1673, 28 September 1935, pp. 79–84.
13 *Kabunushi Kakui ni Uttau (Statement for All Stockholders of SMR)*, Mantestu Yushi Kabunushi Kai (Voluntary Organization of SMR's Stockholders), 1934, pp. 8–11.
14 'Mantetsu Kabuka no Konmei Riyu' ('Why is the stock price of SMR lower?') *Mantetsu Kabunushi-kai Kaiho (Newsletter of SMR Stockholders Association)*, No. 1, December 1937, p. 22.
15 The top management of SMR consisted of the president, one or two vice presidents and the directors (min. four, max. nine).
16 *Mantetsu no Shimei ni Kangamite Gojin no Chujo wo Hirekisu (We would like to open up our hearts for everyone in view of SMR's mission)*, Minami Manshu Tetudo

Kabushiki Gaisha Shain Kanbu Ichido (All Company Executives of SMR), 8 July 1924.
17 S. Okumura, 'Shain-Kai Mondo (Questions and Answers on Voluntary Association for SMR's Staff), part 3', *Kyowa (Bulletin of Shain-Kai)*, No. 4, July 1927, pp. 26–7.
18 Mantetsu Kai (Association for the retired staff of SMR and the people concerned) (ed.), *Minami Manshu Tetsudo Kabushiki Gaisha Kakyu Ijo Soshiki Kiko Hensen Narabini Jinji Ido Ichiranhyo (Diagram for Change in the Organization and Staff of SMR)*, reprinted, Tokyo: Ryukei Shosha, 1992.
19 Ibid.
20 Mitsugu Sengoku, 'Sosai yori Shain ni Gosoudan (President's Notice to Staff of SMR)', *Kyowa*, No. 26, 15 May 1930, pp. 4–5.
21 *Kyowa*, No. 43, 1 February 1931.
22 Mantetsu Kai, *Minami Manshu*.
23 SMR (ed.), *Mantetsu Chosa Kikan Yoran (General Survey of Research Sections in SMR)*, 1935.
24 *Dai Gokai Tokei Zadankai Sokkiroku (Shorthand Record of the 5th Discussion Meeting for Statistical Survey)*, MT/A06/1, 1935, (Collection of National Science Library, Chinese Academy of Sciences, CLCAS), p. 25.
25 A. Hara, 'Manshu', p. 67.
26 See for example M. Sato, *Kokusei Chosa to Nihon Kindai (National Census and Japanese Modern)*, Tokyo: Iwanami Shoten, 2002.
27 See for example J. Young, *The Research Activities of The South Manchurian Railway Company, 1907–1945*, New York: East Asian Institute, Columbia University, 1966; K. Hara, *Gendai Ajia Kenkyu Seiritsu Shiron (Historical Essay on the Basis for Modern Asian Studies)*, Tokyo: Keiso Shobo, 1984; T. Ito, *Life Along the South Manchurian Railway*, New York: M. E. Sharpe, 1988.
28 Mantetsu Chosabu (SMR research department) (ed.), *Dai Ikkai Shanai Tokei Koshukai Yoroku (Digest of the first Lecture for Statistical Survey)*, MT/Z90/1, 1939, CLCAS, p. 2.
29 Ibid, p. 37.

21 Shanghai's cotton textile industry during the Pacific War

Exploring relations with Japan and the transformation of the economic structure

Narumi Imai

Introduction

The objective of this chapter is to reveal in part the Shanghai economy during the Sino-Japanese War, using as its subject matter the cotton textile industry, which was representative of Shanghai industry and which had enjoyed a strong relationship with Japanese companies since before the war. In particular, the chapter aims to investigate additional study on changes in the operating environment, reorganization of the industrial organization and changes in the attitude of capitalists towards Japan following the outbreak of the Pacific War.

I wish to highlight the following three points within the context of previous research.

The first is the development of empirical research on Shanghai's wartime economy. The impact of inadequacies in various economic statistics due to the chaos of war means that many details of Shanghai's wartime economy remain unknown. As described in what follows, political issues of collaboration with Japan may also be involved; until recent years, no thorough examination of commerce and industry or of foreign trade in wartime Shanghai had been made in China.[1]

Second, I would like to further examine the attitude of Chinese capitalists towards Japan and changes in such attitudes. Particularly after the outbreak of the Pacific War, Chinese capitalists had to resort to some form of contact with Japan for business operations and also as a necessity of daily life. Due to the sensitive political nature of the issue, studies into collaboration with Japan have long been shunned; however, these days, many researchers have tried to demonstrate such behaviour by referring to the intentions of these capitalists.[2] Moreover, prior to the war, Japanese citizens and Japanese companies had made many inroads into Shanghai and had formed many interrelationships, ranging from confrontation to collaboration, with Chinese society.[3] Although we cannot ignore the specific political characteristics of China's relationship with Japan during the war, we need to bear in mind that it was built on the accumulation of prewar economic relations between the two countries.

The third point is connected with the second, but rather than just looking at the social role of capitalists in terms of business operations, I also want to consider their various activities from a wider angle. It is the duty of a capitalist to make a profit from economic activity. Analysis of a capitalist's economic activity within a certain industry must be premised on a thorough understanding of the structure of that industry and the economic environment surrounding it. The activities of the capitalists that are revealed in this process, while not ignoring political factors, need to be fundamentally analysed on the basis of 'economic logic'. On the other hand, China's capitalists originate from the landed gentry of the premodern era, and it is not appropriate to regard them simply in terms of economic rationalism. The case of Shanghai in particular is a city that, on the one hand, developed around foreign concessions amidst an 'absence of government' for the Chinese and with little history of provincial administrative structure from China. So capitalists became the leaders in control of Shanghai's Chinese society. They improved the legal and social status of the Chinese and controlled social unrest while negotiating with various foreign powers. By means of such activities, the capitalists themselves and the people of Shanghai fostered a sense of sharing a Shanghai consciousness, and this led to the formation of anti-Japanese nationalism.[4] The pursuit of profit through corporate operational activities also evolved amidst the era of enhanced ethnic consciousness. The basic position of the author's research, including this chapter, is to consider the wartime capitalists as having both 'economic logic' and 'ethnic rationale'.

1. The Shanghai economy during the Sino-Japanese War and occupation by Japan

The controlled economy pervaded China during the Sino-Japanese war despite the fact that the executive body and specific economic developments were separate in China. The Sino-Japanese conflict had become outright war, and national economic activity as a whole was placed under direct control, which widely affected the Chongqing National Government and 'Manchuria' and the Japanese-occupied territories.

Within this environment, the city of Shanghai held a unique position. Modern Shanghai was a city that had developed within an open economy where the state was little involved in economic activities and in which free markets played a major role. The city was mainly composed of private-sector companies with ties to the domestic and international markets, and it experienced ongoing growth in a 'free' environment. So, even after an outbreak of Sino-Japanese conflict, Japanese military control was weaker in Central China, which included Shanghai, than in North China, and it tended to be confined more to major cities, roads and railways. And above all, even after the outbreak of the Sino-Japanese conflict, those settlements in Shanghai where Japanese occupational rule had not reached (i.e. locations within the joint concession territories excluding the Security Area of Japan, as well as the French Concession) still maintained ties with both domestic and international markets, making occupational rule centralized under a controlled economy difficult.

Shanghai's prominent position in the Chinese economy since the prewar period and its complex interweaving of international relationships meant that Japan could not invade the Shanghai concessions and brought the city economic prosperity during wartime. Many studies have already pointed out the economic realities of this so-called 'island of prosperity'. However, the activities of Japanese companies also relied on the concession's economy in a variety of ways, and we cannot ignore this more complicated aspect of the occupied-land policy. For example, as described in what follows, in the cotton industry, textile operations located in China and backed by Japanese capital had increasingly come to rely on raw cotton imported from overseas via the concession (Table 21.1). And Chinese capital within the concession and the links with domestic and foreign markets beyond the concession were both essential in terms of the sale of the end product.[5]

Even the institutions involved in the occupying government had not evaluated the overall impact of such aspects of the concession economy on Japan's occupational policies. For example, the view of the concession in Japan's military went as follows:

> If the concessions (including Hong Kong) take on the role of headquarters of the Chongqing administration's government *in absentia*, they also become the hot-bed of schemes to disrupt public security. . . . The concessions are an ever growing enemy, inhibiting a number of our measures to implement control, in particular with regard to economic measures on the control of the inflows and outflows of finance and currency for manufactured materials in the occupied territories.[6]

Table 21.1 Consumption of raw cotton by Japanese spinners in Shanghai (dan)

Year	North China Cotton	Central China Cotton	Total Chinese Cotton	Total Import Cotton	Utilization Rate of Import Cotton
1935	965,410	680,453	1,645,863	641,996	28.1%
1936	1,175,259	695,045	1,870,304	423,498	18.5%
1937	1,036,496	527,889	1,564,385	152,833	9.0%
1938	974,356	545,383	1,519,739	221,103	12.7%
1939	387,730	682,127	1,069,857	2,128,255	66.5%
1940	42,508	716,541	759,049	2,104,104	73.4%
1941	No data	860,550	860,550	1,182,782	57.8%

Sources: From 1935–1938: T. Tatani, Jihengo no Shina niokeru Bosekigyo: shutoshite sono suji teki shiryo (The cotton spinning industry under the Sino-Japanese War: with central focus on statistics), p. 250.
From 1939–1941: Toakenkyujo (ed.), *Shina Senryochi Keizai no Hatten* (The Economic Development of Occupied Shanghai), Tokyo: Ryukeishosya, 1978, reprinted (The original was published at 1944, p. 241.
※ After 1937, Chinese mills occupied by Japanese spinners are included.

On the other hand, on 3 October 1940, the decision of the East Asia Development Board regarding the Shanghai Concession went as follows.

(i) The Shanghai Concession should of course also be subject to recovery for the sake of building a new order in East Asia, on the same principle as all other Chinese concessions; the method and timing of this should be decided by reflecting on trends in the world political situation and the enhancement of the imperial defence force
(ii) In light of the Shanghai Joint Concession's position in the world economy and in view of its purpose as a base from which to acquire resources lacking in the Empire, for the time being it should maintain its traditional international flavour, and its stability should be held static.[7]

The one hand pointed out the evils of the existence of the concession and the economic activity conducted therein, and the ultimate aim seemed to be the return of the concession to the pro-Japanese regime and the inclusion of the concession in the controlled economy for the purpose of procuring goods and unifying the monetary and financial process. The other hand seemed to be of the opinion that the special characteristics and international nature of the concession, with its links to domestic and foreign markets, should be preserved, and Japanese needs, such as the acquisition of resources, should be extracted.[8]

I leave a more detailed study for another paper, but given that direct intervention was virtually impossible, the evaluation and treatment of the Shanghai concession was certainly a very sensitive issue for the Japanese. The economy of the Shanghai concession could be said to encapsulate the challenge of two conflicting systems of economic management (namely a controlled economy and an open economy) and, moreover, how to incorporate them into policies for the occupied territories overall.

The outbreak of the Pacific War in December 1941 saw Japanese troops deployed to the concession, and the Shanghai concession's base for free economic activity came to an end. However, although the business environment changed drastically, Japan was unable to fully introduce a controlled economic system and bring Shanghai under its control. This chapter seeks to reconsider the controlled section of the economy while monitoring the activity of capitalists in the cotton textile industry in Shanghai during the Pacific War.

2. Developments in 1942

2.1 *The cotton textile industry and capitalists in the period preceding the Sino-Japanese conflict*

Many previous studies have discussed the cotton textile industry during the period between the outbreak of the Sino-Japanese conflict and the start of the Pacific War.[9] In contrast with factories outside the concession that were destroyed and occupied by the Japanese army, the factories inside the concession saw a recovery in industrial production fuelled by the special demand of wartime (Tables 21.2 and 21.3). In addition, as long as the concession continued to exist as a base of operations, only a very small proportion of capitalists openly cooperated with Japan.

I would like to point out that, compared to elsewhere, the textile industry in Shanghai used a high proportion of raw cotton from overseas. Looking at the use of raw cotton in the prewar cotton textile industry backed by Chinese capital (hereafter referred to as 'Chinese textile operations'), I find that almost 100 per cent of the factories in North China used Chinese raw cotton; in comparison, all the factories in Shanghai were heavily dependent on raw cotton from overseas, with no more than approximately 50 per cent of the raw cotton sourced from China. The American variety of raw cotton was suitable for the production of fine yarn, which was developing at the time, and the fact that its cultivation was virtually nonexistent in the Shanghai area, together with increasing transportation costs for domestic raw cotton and the relatively low cost of procuring foreign imports of raw cotton, meant that the proportion of raw cotton sourced from America grew.[10]

Next, let us look once again at the changes associated with the outbreak of the war. Before the Sino-Japanese conflict, about 80 per cent of the demand for raw Chinese cotton came from Japanese textile operations in China; however, from the Second Shanghai Incident in 1937 onwards, the rate of dependency on foreign cotton increased rapidly (the temporary dip in 1937 was doubtless due to the impact of the Second Shanghai Incident). This was due to the fact that demand within Japan for cotton from North China was gradually increasing, making it more difficult to use this source for Japanese textile operations located in Shanghai[11]; production of cotton in Central China was also decreasing, and the obliteration of the logistics system by Japanese military rule meant that it

Table 21.2 Cotton yarn and cloth output of Shenxin Mills No. 2 and No. 9

年	Shenxin mill no. 2			Shenxin mill no. 9			
	Yarn (jian)	index	Yarn (jian)	index	Cloth (1000m)	index
---	---	---	---	---	---	---
1937	26301	100.0	63914.59	100.0	13065.78	100.0
1938	33271	126.5	81326.05	127.2	19847.29	151.9
1939	36716	139.6	96560.73	151.1	21535.23	164.8
1940	37716	143.4	97144.71	152.2	17922.55	137.2
1941	30781	117.0	41184.79	64.4	5430.78	41.6
1942	2624	10.0	4621.95	7.2	250.82	1.9
1943	2258	8.6	5809.05	9.1	1578.32	12.1
1944	.	.	2016.95	3.2	630.13	4.8
1945	.	.	2537.27	4.0	260.93	2.0

Sources: *Rongjia qiye shiliao*, vol. 2, p. 73.

Table 21.3 Cotton yarn and cloth output of Yong'an Mill No. 3

年	Yarn (jian)		Cloth (pi)	
	Output	Index	Output	index
1936	29501	100.00	119832	100.00
1938	52271	177.18	192086	160.30
1939	50117	169.88	215174	179.56
1940	41743	141.50	178411	148.88
1941	33298	112.87	144540	120.62
1942	2633	9.02	11090	9.25
1943	3056	10.35		
1944	1379	4.67		
1945	377	1.27		

Sources: *Yong'an fangzhi yinran gongsi,* pp. 255, 258.
1945: By August, blank columns are no data or no output.

had become difficult to ship domestic cotton to Shanghai. Compared to data on Japanese textile operations in China, sufficiently reliable data on Chinese textile operations during the war are scarce. For example, *Yong'An Mill 3*, which was operating in the concession at the time, was using raw cotton at a domestic-to-foreign ratio of 52:48 in 1938.[12] I cannot tell the regions in which Chinese raw cotton was grown from this historical data. However, the impact of Japanese rule was significant, and as it seems that it was difficult to ship cotton from North China for use in Shanghai's Chinese cotton, it is more likely to have been cotton from Central China, which was geographically closer.

In any event, following the outbreak of the Sino-Japanese conflict, the cotton textile industry in Shanghai became more dependent on foreign cotton. However, the situation changed completely with the outbreak of the Pacific War in December 1941. Imports of raw cotton from the United States and British-controlled India were disrupted by the start of Japan's war with Britain and the United States, and thereafter the industry had to rely on cotton from Central China alone.[13] This was a major turning point for Shanghai's cotton textile industry, which had developed by sourcing its raw cotton from overseas. In particular, the need to secure raw cotton from Central China was shared by both Japanese and Chinese capitalists, leading to the start of business collaboration with Japan.

2.2 The collaboration initiatives of Chinese spinners

FCCM, founded in 1917 by Chinese textile manufacturers, saw its organizational activities gradually stagnate in the wake of the Second Shanghai Incident.[14] After the outbreak of the Pacific War, those in the industry renewed their affiliation and once again worked together in earnest. With the loss of the concession as a base for activity and imports of raw cotton impossible to obtain, it became important for Chinese spinners to build relations with Japan and form alliances with the Wang Jingwei government.

In March 1942, textile industry capitalists from the Jiangnan region, around Shanghai, met and founded CMARC. The association's president was Wen Lanting (from Shenxin 9th mill), its vice president was Jiang Shangda (from Changzhou Minfeng) and its executive directors were Liu Jingji (Anda and Dacheng) and others. It was Vice President Jiang Shangda who held the real authority in the dealings of the Association.[15]

Jiang Shangda was born in Wujin, Jiangsu Province, in 1893 and became Deputy of Accounts at Changzhou Mingfeng cotton mill, which was founded by his father-in-law in 1920. When the Sino-Japanese conflict began and Japan occupied the Central China zone, Jiang wanted to protect his own personal assets, so he had his acquaintances appointed to the offices of the (pro-Japanese) Jiangsu provincial government to try to foster contacts with Japanese organizations; he also had many personal interactions with Japanese people.[16] With the start of the Pacific War, in addition to CMARC, Jiang also became president and member of the General Assembly for the Control of National Commerce and CCRW, set up under the auspices of the Wang administration. He played a prominent role as the representative of Chinese textile in negotiations between Japan and the Wang government. Jiang took advantage of his personal connections with the Japanese and was successful in his efforts to return mills under the management of the Japanese military to the Chinese spinners. In any event, the timing of the association's formation and its choice of personnel show that attitudes towards Japan and the Wang government were important. The association's brief included the following: (i) promotion of raw cotton improvement, acquisition and distribution; (ii) development and improvement of cotton goods production methods; (iii) sale and transportation of goods; (iv) training of professional staff and technological research; (v) statistical surveys and publication; and (vi) mediation of problems between parties within the industry.[17] In addition, RCC was also instituted with the remit of acquiring raw cotton purchase rights and promoting improvements in cotton production operations. Unlike the Cotton Mill Association, RCC invited to its board power-brokers from the mill industry, the financial sector and the raw cotton industry; the head of the committee was Guo Shun, with Jiang Shangda appointed as deputy head.[18]

Their attitudes and proposals with regard to securing raw cotton are shown in the minutes of the 'MIPRC' held by the Wang government (May 23, 1942). The details are as follows:

- To increase production of raw cotton by restoring cultivation acreage in the provinces of Jiangsu, Zhejiang, Anhui and simultaneously reclaiming wasteland
- To undertake research into the rural economy in order to establish a fair price for raw cotton and protect the interests of cotton farmers
- To provide a training institute in order to train experts in cotton production
- To plan for increased production of raw cotton by constructing new waterways and installing irrigation equipment

- To institute a central board to manage the quality of raw cotton and establish laws to maintain quality of the same
- To establish an agency to centrally manage policies aimed at increasing raw cotton production around the country, to be constituted by those in charge of cotton trade administration, various related organizations, textile industry associations, textile industry experts and the like.[19]

In this way, the Chinese textile industry aimed for projects to improve the production environment such as quantitative and qualitative improvements in the raw cotton supplied, surveys of actual conditions in the agricultural economy, the establishment of related mechanisms and human resource training. We can trace the tendency for Chinese spinners to seek improvements in the production environment with a view to improving this kind of overall process in the textile industry back to the formation of FCCM. For example, Chinese spinners also played an important role in operations to spread improvements in cotton seed cultivation at the time of the Republic of China, as in the case of their operations to introduce and spread raw cotton cultivated in America and suitable for use in machine-made fine yarn production.[20] It should not be forgotten that the activities of Chinese spinners, ongoing since before the war, continued to be exhibited in their 'collaborative' attitude.

Next, let us look at Chinese spinners' attitudes towards the purchase of raw cotton. Documentation from Japanese spinners in China states that 'a certain influential Chinese spinner in Shanghai represents the opinion within the industry'.[21]

According to this documentation, as shown in Figure 21.1, the specific method proposed was that 'full responsibility for raw cotton production under the supervision of the military' should be entrusted to 'Chinese merchants' and that 'qualified Chinese merchants should be placed between the military and the producers as mediators'. Here the term 'Chinese merchants' referred to 'Chinese cotton spinners with previous experience and proven results in the areas of raw cotton purchase and cotton cultivation initiatives'.[22] The Japanese military commissioned the purchase of raw cotton to 'Chinese merchants' and, in consultation with the Chinese banking industry, the 'Chinese merchants' made loans to farmers and guaranteed them a minimum price come harvest time. Then the 'Chinese merchants' purchased raw cotton from the farmers and handed it over to the army. Under this conception, Japanese spinners in China would be completely excluded from the raw cotton purchase process. The point of this was that 'even if the Japanese cotton spinners desired to participate, they would be at a major disadvantage and unable to do so'.

This conception does not mean that Chinese spinners refused collaboration projects with Japan across the board. It was more that Chinese spinners were reluctant to allow Japanese spinners located in China to purchase raw cotton.

But, in reality, we can trace different developments with regards to the attitudes and expectations of Chinese spinners towards Sino-Japanese 'collaboration'. 'Meetings to Increase Production of Raw Cotton' were held on a regular

Shanghai's cotton textile industry 301

basis thereafter; but there is no evidence of such matters being enforced in actual policy. Furthermore, the might of Japanese spinners in China was not actually eliminated.

2.3 The collaboration initiatives of Japanese spinners in China

Because efforts to purchase cotton from Central China in the previous year (1941) met with little success, Japanese spinners in China were worried by the raw cotton situation in Central China.[23] The reasons cited for the decline in purchases were reduced cultivation due to bad weather, an excessively low official price for raw cotton and 'a break-down of the relationship between raw cotton and manufactured products'.

Its 'break-down of the relationship' means the fact that in the Changzhou, Wuxi and Suzhou areas, Chinese spinners faced no restrictions on sale price or volume of manufactured products. So '[Chinese spinners] take advantage of the good profits they make from high quality products and buy up large amounts of Chinese cotton at high prices, meaning that most of the output of these regions is absorbed by Chinese cotton spinners', while the amount of raw cotton acquired by the Japanese side remains sluggish. Therefore, it was vital to subject Chinese spinners to 'the same restrictions and controls' that were imposed on Japanese spinners, and it was necessary to 'allow joint use of such capital and manpower with leading Chinese merchants' and 'establish a system of inspection and penalties in order to stop the loss of raw cotton by Chinese cotton merchants'.[24]

Such policies differ from the context in which the Chinese textile manufacturers of the time intended to implement a comprehensive policy to increase production of raw cotton. The objective of 'collaboration' for the Japanese spinners in China was to continue collaboration with the military and to purchase raw cotton to satisfy the immediate needs of the Japanese side. The reason for collaboration with the Chinese side was to 'regulate' their independent behaviour by using their networks to purchase raw cotton.

Figure 21.1 Raw cotton initiatives of Chinese spinners
Sources: 'Kachu homen menka zosan ni tsuiteno gutaian' (The concrete plan on increasing output of raw cotton in central China), *23 January, 1942* in the document of MAJSC R-15.

With the approach of the 1942 raw cotton purchase season, the Japanese side brought together the Japanese and Chinese raw cotton suppliers and announced a policy to establish a centralized agency for the control of raw cotton, and in September 1942 ACRCC was formed. ACRCC comprised not only eleven Japanese textile companies and fifteen Japanese raw cotton trading companies but also twenty-two Chinese textile companies and nine Chinese raw cotton traders. It was established with a 4-million-yuan fund, with 1 million yuan raised from each of the following: Chinese spinners (i.e. Cotton Mill Association of the Republic of China), Japanese spinners in China (i.e. the Shanghai Branch of MAJSC) and both Chinese and Japanese raw cotton traders.[25] Japan took the lead role in developing the organizational structure for the purchase of raw cotton.

ACRCC decided that the centralized purchase of raw cotton in 1942 would be conducted by the Japanese side in the Jiangbei region and the Chinese side in the Jiangnan region.[26] In response to this decision, the Chinese spinners decided to institute six cotton firms for the purchase of raw cotton (see Table 21.4) At the same time, CMARC set up *yintuan* (i.e. organizations to provide joint lending from several different banks) that jointly served Chinese spinners and raw cotton traders, with investment in the six cotton firms made in the name of these finance groups. In this way, the Chinese spinners developed a system for the purchase and distribution of raw cotton. However, in the final instance, the remit of ACRCC was to purchase raw cotton and not to increase overall production of raw cotton.

2.4 Cotton purchasing: the case of the Changtai Cotton Corporation

The Chinese side had been allocated the Jiangnan district as its purchase region, and it organized six cotton purchase organizations there. The Jiangnan district had traditionally been an area where Japanese trading companies had their branches or local offices, and it was an area where a lot of purchasing activity was conducted. The Japanese penetrated the Chinese-controlled purchase area,[27] and it is said that most of the raw cotton purchased by the Chinese side ended up being snatched up by the Japanese side.[28] Here I consider the case of the Changtai Cotton Corporation in detail.

The Changtai Cotton Corporation met with Japanese intervention because it happened to develop 'Qingxiang' operations in the Changshu and Taicang districts. 'Qingxiang' operations was implemented mainly in the Jiangsu and Zhejiang provinces by the Wang regime with collaboration from the Japanese military and was a policy that aimed at overall public security and consumer stability in the regime's areas of governance. It was also regulated in terms of private company activity to ensure tax revenues and a thorough economic blockade.[29]

Around one month after the purchase system had been finalized, on 23 October 1942, the 'JCSIQD' held a meeting under the auspices of ACRCC which was attended by parties connected to the cotton industry from both Japan and China.

Table 21.4 The stock of central China cotton investigated by ACRCC as of 30 June 1943 (dan)

Name of company	Amount purchase by the end of June	Stock by the end of May	Stock in June	Amounts	Stock in up-country
Jiangbei	241775.57	164348.14	47053.16	211401.30	30374.27
Shanghai	39293.97	31843.97	6023.00	37866.97	1427.00
Pudong	85897.50	72754.86	11262.80	84017.66	1879.84
Ningbo	1463.00	9965.93	2654.80	12620.73	2016.27
Changtai	18696.71	9828.06	300.00	10128.06	8568.65
Nanjing	4017.81	2849.55	100.34	2949.89	1067.92
Purchased directly	362.73	No data	362.73	362.73	No data
amounts	404681.29	291590.51	67756.83	359347.34	45333.95

Sources: The documents of MAJSC, R-9.

At the event, the following decisions were taken with regard to 'reorganizing the Changtai Cotton Corporation into an organization with a new mechanism to purchase raw cotton by means of collaboration between Japan and China'.

- While not changing the root structure of the Changtai Cotton Corporation, in addition to the existing purchase regions of Changshu and Taicang districts, the 'Qingxiang' operations of the Taihu Lake South East area which was under the jurisdiction of Suzhou-based institutions shall be included.
- Taihu Lake South East shall be a district where purchase associations from the Japanese side are authorized to make purchases for the Changtai Cotton Corporation and, as such, permanent liaison officers shall be stationed at the Changtai Cotton Corporation and, at the same time, Japanese advisors ratified by ACRCC shall be invited to the Corporation.
- The Corporation shall be responsible for shipping a quantity of 250,000 *shidan* of raw cotton to Shanghai.[30]

Prior to this, on 20 October 1942, raw cotton purchase plans had been finalized under the jurisdiction of the Changtai Cotton Corporation for fiscal year 1942. According to these plans, the addition of Taihu Lake South East as a new area of jurisdiction gave a cotton production forecast for the jurisdiction area of 530,000 *shidan*. Takashi Tsutsumi, who was a representative of ACRCC, deemed the amount of raw cotton to be shipped to Shanghai 250,000 *shidan* and suggested that the remainder to be used to supply cotton mills within the said districts. Interestingly, following this, there was an exchange between Japan's head of the secret service in Suzhou and Jiang Shangda:

(Head of the Secret Service) 'The occupied territories of Central China have a population of around 50,000,000 which, with current consumption of raw cotton divided, makes more than 1 *jin* per capita. Even after shipping out 250,000 *shidan*, there will still be 280,000 *shidan* left, so there will likely be no objection (to Mr. Tsutsumi's proposals)'.

(Jiang Shangda) 'The Chinese may be poor, but they consume around 2 *jin* of raw cotton per capita. 1 *jin* is not enough, so if the region is to be self-sufficient we need to request 2 *jin*'.

(Head of the Secret Service) 'However, there is a shortage of raw cotton at the present time and so, you must persevere with 1 *jin*. Allowing 2 *jin* to be consumed within the region would cause unwelcome trouble for other regions and, at present, we cannot allow the attitude that consumption should be extra just because this is a production zone'.[31]

I assume that the head of the secret service on the Japanese side was able to acquire all of the 530,000 *shidan* of the raw cotton production forecast, despite the fact that the purchasing track record for the previous fiscal year had not been good. Meanwhile, Jiang Shangda, with no real awareness of the daily life of the Chinese populace, claimed that he was determining their rations. In this manner, the purchase forecasts for raw cotton and allocation plans were made on the basis of a very sketchy outlook.

There are some statistics still in existence which record the purchasing results of the period by cotton firms; let us check these (Table 21.4). Of the forecasts for cotton production and cotton purchases (530,000 *shidan* = 150,000 *dan* of spun cotton) made by the head of the secret service, the quantity purchased by the Changtai Cotton Corporation amounted to less than 19,000 *dan* in total, which was a weak result.

3. Developments in 1943

3.1 Reorganization and further reorganization of the structure of the cotton industry

The year 1943 saw the implementation of the 'New Policy on China', and on 15 March, GARNC (the Assembly for the Regulation of Commerce) was established as Central China's centralized agency for the regulation of goods under the auspices of the Wang administration. The Assembly for the Regulation of Commerce was given authority over the purchase and distribution of all controlled goods, not just raw cotton, and from the textile sector Jiang Shangda, Tong Lu Qing, Guo Shun and Wen Lanting all served on its board. Lower down the structure, the Assembly for the Regulation of Commerce was reorganized into separate Japanese and Chinese trade federations comprised of trade guilds, based on the principle of one industry, one guild. However, because raw cotton was a vital commodity, it was decided to institute SCC with a raw cotton division and a cotton goods division, and representatives from Japan and China participated in both (Figure 21.2). But by this stage, there was a whole series of organizations formed in 1942, namely, CMARC and RCC, as well as ACRCC, in which both the aforementioned participated, along with the Japanese spinners located in China. Apart from these institutions, there was also now the addition of the group known as RCG, which was organized by the raw cotton merchants, and friction ensued between the individual groups. Subsequently, the Wang administration determined the Sino-Japanese cooperative associations outlined in Figure 21.2 to be unnecessary, and in August 1943, after compulsory purchases of cotton cloth were carried out, these associations were abolished.[32]

On 27 November 1943, the structure was once again reorganized. The existing Association for the Control of Raw Cotton in Central China was reorganized, both the Japanese and Chinese Raw Cotton Federations were broken up, and CCRW was newly established. This committee was an auxiliary body of the Assembly for the Regulation of Commerce, and below it were APRC and a finance corporation known as RCMU. Cotton goods were also similarly reorganized, but this was a subordinate organization of the Assembly for the Regulation of Commerce (Figure 21.3). The duties of CCRW were as follows: (i) the supply of raw cotton for military use by the Japanese army and for export to Japan; (ii) the consolidated purchase and distribution of raw cotton from Central China; (iii) the determination of the purchase and distribution price of raw cotton; (iv) the procurement of funds for the purchase of raw cotton; (v) the establishment of plans for exchange commodities necessary for the purchase of raw cotton; and (vi) the screening and issuance of raw cotton registration cards and distribution permits.[33]

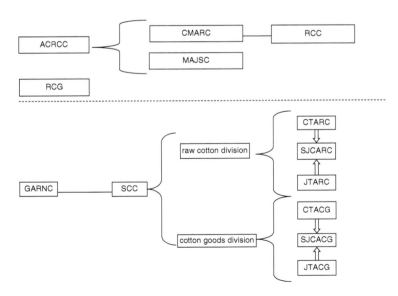

Figure 21.2 Establishing GARNC and reorganizing the structure of the cotton industry (15 March 1943)
Sources: J. Tsukamoto, 'mengyo tosei ichigenka no gutai hosaku' (The concrete measure for unifying the cotton industry control), *Syogyo Tosei Kaikan*, Vol. 5, July 1943.

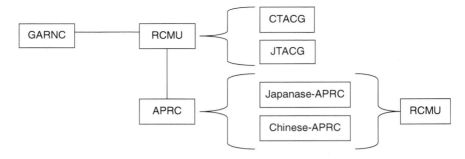

Figure 21.3 Further reorganization of the cotton industry's structure (27 November 1943)
Sources: Tsukamoto Jotaro, "mengyo tosei ichigenka no gutai hosaku", *syogyo tosei kaikan*, Vol. 5, July 1943.

It entailed very complicated discussions, and after its establishment, the Assembly for the Regulation of Commerce spent eight months or more reorganizing the structure.

3.2 Stagnation of purchasing operations

Underlying the very slow progress in the reorganization of the structure of the cotton industry was the conflict of interest between the Chinese spinners and the Japanese side. First, little of the Chinese equity plant that had been requisitioned by the Japanese at the start of the Sino-Japanese conflict was returned to the Chinese. Negotiations between Chinese and Japanese textile capitalists for the return of Chinese spinning factories were held in parallel with the reorganization of the raw cotton regulatory structure taking place at the time. The return of Chinese spinning factories across the board was determined under the New Policy on China at the start of 1943. However, the Japanese spinners in China to whom management had been delegated did not readily relinquish their interests, and they tried to retain their influence regarding the return of such factories through various means such as joint ventures and acquisitions. Consequently, the handover was slow to progress and led to distrust on the Chinese side.

Second, there were issues surrounding the compulsory purchase of cotton cloth in Shanghai, a policy implemented by the Assembly for the Regulation of Commerce in August 1943. In the city of Shanghai, cotton cloth was a scarce, precious commodity. This fact plus an accelerated rate of inflation made cotton cloth subject to speculative buy-outs, and from early spring 1943 this had already become a social issue. In May 1943, the Wang administration brought into force the 'Provisional Regulations on Major Commodity Hoarding Offences', which imposed the death penalty as the maximum punishment for speculative buy-outs. Following this, the administration instituted CIB.[34] However, these steps were not very effective, so the Wang administration decided to take measures to purchase the cotton fabric in Shanghai district in one fell swoop in order to curb soaring prices and allow the regime to acquire the important commodity for the Japanese side.[35] There was considerable resistance by the Chinese spinners to these compulsory purchases.[36] Moreover, the following excerpts are taken from the minutes of a meeting on the compulsory purchase of cotton cloth attended by Sino-Japanese capital interests from the textile industry.

> It is essential to solve the pricing problems in the cotton cloth issue. If the issue of pricing is not resolved rationally, ultimately we will not be able to solve the cotton cloth issue. Speaking from the producer side, we are unable to make shipments because the former prices of cotton cloth are already inappropriate for current conditions and new prices are yet to be published. But our intention has never been to hoard the cloth.
> (Takashi Tsutsumi)

> Looking at it from the Japanese perspective, the first priority should be to decide a plan for the distribution of cotton cloth, then (having done that) determine the prices and immediately distribute the cotton cloth.
> (Liu Jingji)

> The situation in China is that there are thousands of cotton cloth merchants who adjust supply and demand between themselves. In the absence of a decision on pricing that everyone feels to be reasonable, there is no clue of how to make these adjustments.
> (Oyama Hayao/Hishita Itsuji)

> The original cause of these failures is that no one put a proper structure in place beforehand. Even if you first decide the price of cotton cloth, there are problems with the distribution; consequently it is better to first determine the structure. Japan has already organized a structure with our consuls in individual regions leading local teams, and we have drafted proposals on shipment methods. (*truncated*)[37]

This clearly shows the difference between the Chinese side, whose first concern was the circumstances of cloth producers and merchants and who wished to determine reasonable prices to such end, and the Japanese side, who wished to prioritize structural developments in order to allow efficient purchasing.

So it took time just to reorganize the structure, with little substantive progress in collaboration. Purchase operations under the new system finally started on 20 December; however, at 3,200 yuan, the official price for raw cotton in the Shanghai Finance Corporation was less than the current market price, which stood at 4,000 yuan, and this led to a slump in purchase offers. Ultimately, amounts purchased were higher than the previous year, but this was only achieved due to an outflow of raw cotton held by Chinese spinners in the hinterland (Hankou district).[38]

3.3 Exploring Chinese company management

During and after the Pacific War, Sino-Japanese cooperative operations showed poor results in the purchase of raw cotton and also saw a significant fall in the production of cotton cloth compared to before the war (Tables 21.2 and 21.3). It seems that the situation was one in which company management was unable to function properly. So, in light of this, what paths for survival did the Chinese capitalists explore? I would like to examine this, using historical archives that remain in existence.

Small-scale cotton mills

Small-scale cotton mills were small spinning factories set up by Chinese spinners in the face of a series of increased controls on Central China's raw cotton and were implemented following the outbreak of the Asia-Pacific War. Japan and the Wang administration held tight control of the cotton industry in the city of Shanghai. However, their control was weaker in rural communities. So from around 1943, there was a substantial trend to establish small cotton mills, mainly along the Beijing-Shanghai railway route, smuggling out equipment from existing Shanghai factories that had lain idle and unused due to raw cotton shortages and so on. The decline in the cultivation of raw cotton caused by war in the rural outskirts of Shanghai meant that the areas along the Beijing-Shanghai railway route essentially became the leading cotton-producing zones in Central China.[39] For example, Shenxin company, the largest in the industry, moved some of the facilities of its No. 3 Plant in Wuxi to Changshu, a cotton-producing area, where it established a branch factory.[40]

CCRW tried to crack down on these small-scale cotton mills in the form of the 'Draft Regulations on Small Scale Cotton Mills'.

> Article 1: CCRW hereby enacts these regulations for the purpose of realizing the unified purchase and the unified distribution of raw cotton.
>
> Article 2: Factories in the 4 provinces of Jiangsu, Zhejiang, Anhui, Huai'an and those within the cities of Nanjing and Shanghai using automated equipment for the production of cotton yarn that have fewer than 800 spindles shall be deemed small-scale cotton mills.
>
> Article 3: Application for registration shall be made to CCRW when establishing small-scale cotton mills and, upon passing inspection, the party concerned shall be issued a registration card and allowed to operate the business. Those small-scale cotton mills already established prior to the promulgation of these regulations shall apply for registration within 20 days of the promulgation of these regulations.

Article 4: Small-scale cotton mills shall not independently purchase raw cotton. The raw cotton to be used shall be distributed by CCRW in accordance with the number cotton spindles, under a separately determined method. Small cotton mills that are located far from cotton producing areas and the cotton corporations may make representative purchases of raw cotton after undergoing inspection by the Committee for the Control of the Cotton Industry. The Committee for the Control of the Cotton Industry shall separately prescribe such methods.[41]

However, these regulations do not seem to have been effective. That is to say, there were members of CCRW within the Chinese spinners, and the chief committee member that the administration (i.e. the Wang government) petitioned in the making of this document was Wen Lanting, who also had strong links with the capitalists on the Chinese side. Such people would surely have also been familiar with the practice of evading regulation using the establishment of small-scale cotton mills. Furthermore, there is also evidence that the creation of small-scale cotton mills involved the Japanese spinners in China.[42] In short, on the one hand, members were involved in setting up small-scale cotton mills to avoid the regulations of the Japanese military and the Wang regime. On the other hand, they themselves were cracking down on such practices under the Wang administration's system.

The shift to investment in the financial sector

Figure 21.4 looks at the accounts of the Yong'an Textile Corporation and shows the ratio of operating income to nonoperating income for each year. With steep wartime inflation, it is hard to analyse the actual management conditions from the figures alone, and I would like to give this full consideration at another time. However, inflation aside, it is possible to compare (i) the operating income of the core business, which was generated mainly from the production and sale of cotton fabric, and (ii) the nonoperating income, which mainly comprised financial gains such as the sale of securities and real estate rentals.

Prior to the start of the Pacific War, the proportion of operating income at the Yong'an Textile Corporation had been higher, with the main source of earnings being the production and sale of cotton cloth. However, if we examine the historical archives still in existence, this apparently did not mean that financial income was unimportant. For example, following the outbreak of the Sino-Japanese conflict, new cotton mills were built in the concession one after another, and by 1941, the number of spindles in operation amounted to 228,000. However, Yong'an textile mill No. 3 located in the concession had production facilities of 63,184 spindles in 1937, and by 1942, these had only grown to 65,104 spindles. It was called 'an island of prosperity', but the amount of funds invested in production equipment was not as much as originally thought. Profits gained were directed towards financial activities. Testimonies from parties connected to Yong'an Textiles state that 'The spread of false currency (i.e.

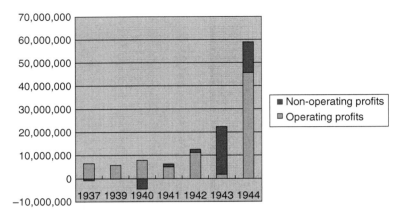

Figure 21.4 The operating profits and non-operating profits of Yong'an cotton mill
Sources: Shanghaishi dang'anguan, the documents of Yong'an fangzhi yinrangongsi Q197–1–464, 465, 466.

banknotes issued by the Japanese military and the pro-Japanese government) meant inflation of prices, so in order to sustain monetary values and make big profits, the capitalists began to shift the main focus of their operations from industrial production to commercial speculation. This was a common theme amongst those in the industry'. And, 'As for the range of speculative activities, it could be said that "*anything went*", but this approach was mainly done on an individual basis. On a company basis the main activities were speculation in shares and cotton cloth'.[43] At Yong'an Corporation, no more than a mere 28.84 per cent (1938 figures) of available capital was invested in the production of cotton cloth.[44]

From 1942 onwards, the production of cotton cloth stagnated and, as shown in the accounts, on the whole, firms shifted their operations to speculative trading in securities and currencies, real estate and commodities (starting with cotton fabric). Especially, the period 1942–43 was an era of unique prosperity for the Shanghai economy, centred on financial services, even as industrial production saw a significant fall. Vast quantities of idle capital flowed into the buying and selling of goods, real estate, stocks and so on. Against this backdrop, financial institutions such as banks and investment companies were set up in rapid succession. The overheating of the economy at this time had very little to do with developments in the real economy.[45]

The profits made from the trading of raw cotton and cotton cloth were nominally entered in operating income. However, production operations had stagnated, as shown in Table 21.2, and on top of this was the previously mentioned compulsory purchase of cotton cloth. This combination of factors meant that, in actual fact, the profits could also be regarded as originating from financial speculation rather than from normal production and sales operations. The trend at the time for companies to shift from manufacturing to finance was also evidence that Japan and the Wang regime's reform of the cotton industry and financial regulations were not functioning well.

Conclusion

Table 21.5 shows the cotton production volumes for Central China and the purchase quantities of the Japanese side following the start of the Sino-Japanese conflict. If we look at the relationship between the projected acquisition amounts and the amounts actually purchased, the combined results of Chinese and Japanese purchases made after the outbreak of the Pacific War were poor. Even when the Pacific War started, the Japanese side was unable to incorporate the Shanghai economy, which was based on a system of open economy, into the controlled economy. Certainly, this chapter only dealt with the cotton industry. However, it was, after all, the cotton industry that saw robust development while representing the Shanghai economy and providing ties to suburban towns and rural areas; it also had many influential capitalists in the business sector. For these reasons alone, the Japanese military's inability to secure the collaboration of the cotton industry capitalists had a major impact on its ability to dominate the economy, because it was these capitalists who held the real power in the Shanghai economy and who were very familiar with the economic situation in the local regions, including rural areas.

Table 21.5 Raw cotton output and purchase by Japan in central China (dan)

Cotton year※	Purchase planning	Purchase	Output
1937 (Minguo26)	No data	No data	2,790,000
1938 (27)	No data	No data	2,412,000
1939 (28)	No data	No data	2,082,000
1940 (29)	No data	858,000	3,321,000
1941 (30)	No data	694,000	1,128,061
1942 (31)	2,390,000	404,681	1,568,219
1943 (32)	900,000	605,000	1,196,304
1944 (33)	320,000	209,400	1,218,620

Sources: The purchase planning in 1942: '17,18 menka nendo chushi men demawari-ryo' in the documents of MAJSC, R-9.
The purchase amount in 1942 The documents of MAJSC R-9 equal to Table 2.
The planning and amount of purchase from 1943 to 1944: Asada Kyoji Nihon teikoku shugi ni yoru chugoku nogyo shigen no syudatsu katei (the plundering process of Chinese agricultural resources by Japanese imperialism) in Nihon Teikoku Shugi kano Chugoku (China under Japanese imperialism), pp. 145,155 and 160.
The output from 1937 to 1940 Toa kenkyujo ed., *Shina senryochi keizai no hatten*, pp. 74–75.
The output from 1941 to 1944 Su-zhe-wan mianhua tongjibiao ji shangtonghui yu quanguo jingji weiyuanhui tongjiju you mianchantongji dewenjian (zhongguo di'er lishi danganguan wanwei quanguo shangye tongzhi zonghui dangan 2086–1676).
The others Takamura Naosuke Kindai nihon mengyo to chugoku (Modern Japanese cotton industry and China), University of Tokyo Press, 1982, p. 241.
※ from August 1 to July 31 of next year

After the Pacific War ended, China's cotton textile capitalists began to participate in cooperative operations with Japan. However, this did not mean an across-the-board acceptance of Japanese rule. As cooperative initiatives related to the cotton industry clearly demonstrate, while they cooperated with the Japanese for raw cotton purchase operations on the one hand, on the other they set up small-scale cotton mills and moved into the financial service sector and other areas. In so doing, they acted with determination to maintain conditions in the management of their corporations, even at a time of war.

List of Abbreviations

ACRCC 華中棉花統制会 huazhong mianhua tongzhihui
the Association for the Control of Raw Cotton in Central China

APRC 棉花収買協会 mianhua shoubai xiehui
the Association for the Purchase of Raw Cotton

CCRW 棉花統制委員会 mianhua tongzhi weiyuanhui
the Committee for the Control of Raw Cotton

CIB 物資調査委員会 wuzi diaocha weiyuanhui
the Commodity Investigations Board

CMARC 中華民国紗廠連合会 zhonghua minguo shachang lianhehui
the Cotton Mill Association of the Republic of China

CTACG 華商棉製品業同業連合会 mianzhipin tongye lianhehui
the Chinese Trade Association of Cotton Goods

CTARC 華商棉花業同業連合会 mianhuaye tongye lianhehui
the Chinese Trade Association of Raw Cotton

FCCM 華商紗廠連合会 huashang shachang lianhehui
the Federation of Chinese Cotton Mills

GARNC 全国商業統制総会 quanguo shangye tongzhi zonghui
the General Assembly for the Regulation of National Commerce

JCSIQD 清郷地区紡績連合委員会 qingxiangdiqu fangji lianhe weiyuanhui
Joint Committee for the Spinning Industry in Qingxiang District

JTACG 日商棉製品同業連合会 mianzhipin tongye lianhehui
the Japanese Trade Association of Cotton Goods

JTARC 日商棉花同業連合会 mianhuaye tongye lianhehui
the Japanese Trade Association of Raw Cotton

MAJSC 在華日本紡績同業会 zaika nihon boseki dogyokai
the Mutual Association of Japanese Spinners in China

MIPRC 棉花増産会議 mianhua zengchang huiyi
Meeting to Increase Production of Raw Cotton

RCC 原棉委員会 yuanmian weiyuanhui
the Raw Cotton Committee

RCG 棉花同業公会 mianhua dongye gonghui
the Raw Cotton Guild

RCMU 棉花管理処 mianhua guanli suo
the Raw Cotton Management Unit

SCC 棉業専業委員会 mianye zhuanye weiyuanhui
the Special Committee of Cotton

SJCARC 中日棉花協議会
the Sino-Japanese Cooperative Association of Raw Cotton

SJCACG 中日棉製品協議会
the Sino-Japanese Cooperative Association of Cotton Goods

Notes

1 There are some recent studies, for example, J. Wu et al., *Kangzhan Shiqi de Shanghai Jingji (Shanghai Economy during Sino-Japanese War)*, Shanghai: Shanghai renmin chubanshe, 2006; S. Zhang, *Shanghai 'Gudao' Maoyi Yanjiu* (The Study of Shanghai 'Solitary Island'), Beijing: Zhishi chansheng chubanshe, 2006; S. Zhang, *'Gudao' Shiqi de Shanghai Gongye (Shanghai Industry during 'Solitary Island' Time)*, Beijing: Zhongguo yanshi chubanshe, 2007.
2 W. Yeh (ed.), *Wartime Shanghai*, London: Routledge, 1998; P. M. Coble, *Chinese Capitalist in Japan's New Order: The Occupied Lower Yangzi 1937–1945*, Berkeley/Los Angeles: University of California Press, 2003.
3 T. Kubo, 'Qingdao kashin bo: Nihon shihon tono kyocho to kyoso' (Competition and Cooperation between a Chinese-owned Qingdao-Huaxin Mill and the Japanese mills in Qingdao), in idem, *Senkanki Chugoku no Mengyo to Kigyo Keiei (Chinese Cotton Industry and Its Business between the Two World Wars)*, Tokyo: Kyuko shoin, 2005.
4 M. Kohama, *Kindai Chugoku no Kokyosei to Kokka* (The 'Public' and the State in Modern Shanghai), Tokyo: Kembun shuppan, 2005.
5 'Some of the cotton yarn from Japanese spinners in Shanghai is exported to the South Seas, but the majority is intended for domestic Chinese consumption, with the markets in the hinterlands and non-occupied territories playing an important part'. T. Nawa, 'Senji Shina bosekigyo no dotai to sono mondai' (The Dynamics and problems of the wartime Chinese spinning industry), in Dainippon Boseki Rengokai (ed.), *Toa Kyoeiken to Sen'i Sangyo (The Greater East Asia Co-Prosperity Sphere and the Textile Industry)*, Osaka: Dainippon Boseki Rengokai, 1941.
6 Daihon-ei Rikugun-bu/Daihon-ei Kaigun-bu, '"Shina-jihen shori yokou" ni kansuru shoyou jiko no setsumei nitsuite' (Explanation of the necessary matters on the 'Guidelines for dealing with "the China Incident"'), November 1940, in T. Shimada et al.(ed.), *Gendai-shi Shiryo*, vol. 9, *Nicchu Senso No. 2 (Source Materials on the Contemporary History, vol. 9, Sino-Japanese War, No. 2)*, Tokyo: Misuzu shobo, 1964.
7 Ministry of Foreign Affairs (ed.), *Nihon Gaiko Monjo: Nicchu-senso* 4 (Documents of Japanese Diplomacy) Tokyo: Rokuichi shobo, 2011, p. 2791.
8 Hirofumi Takatsuna classifies the situation mentioned with regard to the concession into the 'hard-liners' and the 'international school'; see H. Takatsuna,

'Nicchu Sensoki ni okeru Shanghai Sokai mondai' (The Shanghai settlement issue during the Sino-Japanese War), in idem, *Kokusai Toshi Shanghai nonakano Nihonjin (Japanese in the International City Shanghai)*, Tokyo: Kembun shuppan, 2009.
9 For example, W. Xu/H. Huang, *Rongjia giye Fazhanshi* (A History of the Development of the Rong Family Enterprises), Beijing: Renmin chubanshe, 2000, Zhang, *'Gudao' shiqi*.
10 T. Kubo, 'Chugoku mengyo no chitai kozo to keiei ruikei' (Types of management and Regional Differences in the Cotton Industry in Modern China), in idem (ed.), *Sen kanki chugoku no mengyo to kigyo keiei*.
11 N. Takamura, *Kindai Nihon Mengyo to Chugoku (Modern Japanese Cotton Industry and China)*, Tokyo: University of Tokyo Press, 1982, pp. 242–6.
12 Zhongguo kexueyuan jingji yanjiusuo, Zhongyan gongshang hangzheng guanliju zibenzhuyi jingji gaizao yanjiushi (ed.), Yong'an Fangzhi Yinran Gongsi (Yong'an Spinning and Textile Company), Beijing: Zhonghua shuju, 1964, p. 256.
13 N. Takamura, *Kindai*, p. 288.
14 C. Sun, 'Kangri zhanzheng shiqi de su-zhe-wan shachangye tongyegonghui he yuanmian weiyuanhui' (The guild of the spinning and textile industry and the Raw Cotton Committee in the Jiangsu, Zhejiang and Anhui areas during the Sino-Japanese War) in Shanghai-shi zhengxie wenshiziliao weiyuanhui (ed.), *Shanghai wenshiziliao cungao huibian*, vol. 7 *(Selections of Literary and Historical Materials of Shanghai)*, Shanghai: Shanghai guji chubanshe, 2001, p. 412.
15 C. Sun, 'Kangri', p. 414.
16 Ibid, pp. 414–18.
17 'Zhonghua minguo shachang lianhehui lishihuiyi jilu', 2 March 1943, in Shanghai-shi dang'an guan, *Shanghaishi Mianfangzhi gongye Tongyegonghui Dang'an*, S30-1-47.
18 C. Sun, 'Kangri', pp. 413–4. The Cotton Mill Association of the Republic of China had its name changed by the Wang administration's commerce department and was renamed the Trade Guild of the Jiangsu, Zhejiang and Anhui Cotton Mills in August 1943.
19 '1942 nian wangwei-shiyebu zhaokai mianhuazengchan huiyi de wenjian he mianlianhui chaozhuan youguan mianchandiaocha he zengchan deng youguan wenshu' (Wang government convenes meeting to increase production of raw cotton and investigating cotton increasing produce cotton) in Shanghai-shi dang'an guan, *Shanghaishi Mianhua Shangye Tongyegonghui Dang'an*, S233-1-116.
20 Y. Iitsuka, 'Chugoku kindai ni okeru nogyo gijutsusha no keisei to mensaku kairyo mondai' (The formation of agriculturists and the cotton breeding problem in modern China), *Ajia-keizai*, 1992, vol. 33.
21 'Kachu homen menka zosan ni tsuiteno gutaian' (The concrete plan on increasing output of cotton in central China) 23 January 1942 in Zaika Nihon Boseki Dogyokai Shiryo (Documents of MAJSC), held by the library of Institute of Social Science, the University of Tokyo. All the descriptions on the cooperation planning that follow are based on this material.
22 The usual process of purchasing raw cotton prior to the war was that Chinese spinners purchased it from Chinese raw cotton dealers rather than going directly to the cultivation zones. (For example, the case of Shanghai Xin Yu (Pu Yi) Spinning Company, see Kubo, *Senkanki*, pp. 36–7.) Therefore, we should possibly include raw cotton dealers along with 'Chinese cotton spinners' in the definition of 'Chinese merchants'. And, in fact, when the ACRCC was formed, its members included raw cotton merchants as well as cotton traders.
23 'Chushi-men demawari sokushin hoho ni tsuite' (On promoting the supply of Chinese raw cotton), 15 April 1942. Addressed to Mr. Morita, the accounts manager of Japanese army, from Hishita Itsuji, the head of the Shanghai Branch of MAJSC.

24 Ibid.
25 Zhonghua minguo shachang lianhehui lishihuiyi jilu, 2 March 1943.
26 K. Asada, 'Nihon teikokusyugi niyoru chugoku nogyo shigen no shudatsu katei' (Exploitation of Chinese Agricultural resource by the Japan Empire: 1942–45), in idem (ed.), *Nihon Teikokushugi kano Chugoku (China under the Japan Empire)*, Tokyo: Gakuyu shobo, 1981, p. 129.
27 Naka Shina Keizai Nenpo Kanko-kai, *Naka Shina Keizai Nenpo* (Annual Report on the Central China Economy), vol. 2, 1942, p. 281.
28 Yong'an fangzhi yinran gongsi, p. 257.
29 T. Furumaya, 'Nihongun senryochi no seikyo kosaku to kosen' (The Qingxiang operation in occupied area by the Japanese Army and the resistance by the Chinese people) in idem (ed.), *Nicchu Senso to Shanghai soshite Watakushi* (Sino-Japanese War, Shanghai and I), Tokyo: Kembun shuppan, 2004.
30 'Seikyo chiku bosekigyo rengo iinkai dai san-ji iinkai ketsugiroku' (Records of resolutions by Joint Committee for the Spinning industry in Qingxiang District), 23 October 1942, in *Shanghai shi Dang'anguan Shanghaishi Mianfangzhi Gongye Tongyegonghui Dang'an*, S30–1–120. The original document was written in Japanese.
31 Seikyo chiku mengyo tosei kondankai, 'Seikyo chiku no menka shubai oyobi haikyu ni tsuite' (On purchase and distribution of raw cotton in Qingxiang District), 20 October 1942, in *Shanghai shi Dang'anguan*, S30–1–120.
32 J. Tsukamoto, 'Mengyo tosei ichigenka no gutai hosaku' (The concrete measure for unifying the cotton industry controls), *Syogyo ToseiKaikan*, vol. 5, July 1943, p. 4.
33 Y. Yuan, 'Riben jiaqiang lueduo huazhong zhanlue wuzi paozhi "shangtonghui" de jingguo' (The plundering process of strategic commodities in Central China by Japanese and "Shangtonghui"), in M. Huang (ed.), *Weitingyou yinglu* (Recollecting Wang Government), Beijing: Zhongguo wenshi chubanshe, 1991, p. 208.
34 'Busshi Chosa Iinkai wo sosiki' (Setting up the Commodity Investigation Board), *Tairiku Shimpo*, 14 May 1943.
35 N. Takamura, *Kindai*, pp. 295–8.
36 C. Sun, 'Kangri', p. 417.
37 'Mianye zhuanye weiyuanhui di shisi ci changwu huiyi jilu' (The record of 14th executive committee of the Association for the Control of Raw Cotton), 29 July 1943, in *Zhongguo di'er Dang'anguan Wangwei Quanguo Shangye Tongzhi Zonghui Dang'an*, 2086–1063. Hishita Itsuji was the chairman of the Shanghai Branch of MAJSC, and Oyama Hayao was the chairman of the Shanghai Branch of Ito-chu Shoji Co.
38 N. Takamura, *Kindai*, p. 294.
39 Y. Yuan, 'Riben jiaqiang lueduo', p. 209.
40 Shanghai shehui kexue yuan jingji yanjiusuo (ed.), *Rongjia qiye shiliao, vol. 2* (Document Collection of the Rong Family Enterprises), Shanghai: Shanghai renmin chubanshe, 1980, pp. 145–7.
41 The document from Wen Lanting to Executive Yuan, 9 October 1944, in Shangtonghui miantonghui jiu xiaoxing shachang qudiguize caoan gei xingzhengyuan de han (The National Commerce Control Commission send official documents about regulating small-scale cotton mills to Executive Yuan), zhongguo di'er dang'anguan wangwei quanguo shangye tongzhi zonghui dang'an, 2086–562.
42 Zhongguo kexueyuan jingji yanjiusuo, *Yong'an*, p. 258.
43 Ibid.
44 Ibid, p. 256.
45 T. Kubo 'Senji Shanghai no shogyo keiei' (Management of commercial business in Shanghai during Sino-Japanese War) in Ibid, *Senkanki*.

22 Conclusion

Differences and similarities of the two occupation regimes

Marcel Boldorf and Tetsuji Okazaki

Administrating occupation

The area which formed the Greater East Asia Co-Prosperity Sphere was vaster and more populated than the European territories under German control. Many chapters of this book had a closer look at the administrative side of occupation and the economic penetration.

With regard on the willingness to cooperate, the Japanese could hope for local support that the German *Wehrmacht* could hardly expect: in most of the occupied East Asian countries, there were at least small groups within the national elites who welcomed the Japanese as liberators from European colonialism. Indeed, the Japanese Empire held out the prospect of a great future for the Asians after the withdrawal of European powers, which was symbolized by the slogan *Hakko Ichiu* ('the world under the one roof'). This facilitated the installation of so-called puppet governments in the occupied territories. In Europe, however, the occupiers could only rely in selected cases such as Norway or France on collaborating parties that were willing to support the National Socialist conglomerate of racial and inhumane policies.

The two ways of expansion were different. The National Socialists were gaining territorial control by land warfare, starting with the attack on neighbouring countries which partly should be Germanised. This aggressive strategy resulted in fighting in all the parts of Europe. The land forces took over the task of administrating the occupied territories with the support of delegated officials from the Berlin ministries of finance and of economics. Competing Nazi organisations were formed which tried to interfere on the spot, especially the organisation Todt and the SS troops which executed Sauckel's orders of recruiting the labour force. With the Main Trustee Office for the East (*Haupttreuhandstelle Ost*), a special administration was formed for the exploitation and devastation of Eastern Europe. All these organisations tried to interfere in the governance of the occupied countries.

In the chapter on the organisation of Nazi rule in occupied Europe, we saw that there was a range of possibilities for organising the administration. In exceptional cases such as Denmark and France, the occupied country could maintain its own government, thus allowing self-administration to a certain degree. Most of the industrialised countries under German occupation at least had a small elite that maintained room for manoeuvre for companies relevant for the war. On the other hand, the Middle East European and East European countries were put under complete oppression, their elites were erased and their economies reduced to a status of food and raw material supplier.

In most of the Asian occupied countries, 'puppet governments' were installed. Only the Thai government and the French colonial regime in Indochina remained in place. Malaya, Indonesia, the Philippines and Burma were administered by military governments. Japan exercised control through these governments and different administrative bodies which were collaborating with the Japanese military forces.[1] Also, in the north east part of China, called 'Manchuria' in the early 1930s, the Japanese army established a puppet country, 'Manchukuo', installing the descendant of the Qing Dynasty Aisin-Gioro Puyi as the emperor. Concerning the other part of China, in 1937 after the Japanese army occupied Beijing, the Provisional Government of the Republic of China was established as a puppet government. In 1940, this government was integrated by the government of the Republic of China in Nanjing, led by Wang Chao-Ming, which was totally depending on Japan as well. However, as its governmental powers were limited, the Japanese army basically ruled the occupied territories directly.

With the exception of the Chinese territories which were put under the direct rule of the Japanese army, the organisation of collaboration was the same as in the European countries that maintained governments of their own. That meant notably for the companies that some freedom of action was maintained, although the whole economic situation has to be characterized as a policy of exploitation. On the other hand, rival organisations like in the German occupied territories which were based on a racial background were unknown in Japan's hegemonic sphere. In both forms of occupation, the ministries in the capitals of Berlin and Tokyo sent military specialists but also economic experts to the occupied country in order to promote the exploitation of the occupied economies by own administrative bodies.

Structure of trade

Under both hegemonic regimes, foreign trade was extremely concentrated on the occupied territories. The largest share of German foreign trade (81 per cent) took place with neighbouring countries, as Table 22.1 on German imports shows.

The most important German trade partners were inside its sphere of influence. Countries outside the *Grosswirtschaftsraum* were of minor importance, such as the other East and South East European countries, Switzerland or fascist Spain. However, some countries – such as Sweden for iron ore or Norway for aluminium – were of sectoral importance. The rest of the world, including Japan, had almost no significance for Germany's foreign commerce during wartime. Geographically, one can notice that there were hardly any long-distance transports. Thus, the transaction costs of trade for Germany were low in comparison to Japan's Greater East Asia Co-Prosperity Sphere.

Table 22.1 German import structure 1940–1944 (100% = 83.3 billion RM)

Protectorate	19.8%	Greece	4.1%
France	15.3%	General Government	4%
Belgium	9.7%	Hungary	3.6%
Italy	9.4%	Romania	3.5%
Netherlands	7.2%	Other European Countries	17.9%
Denmark	4.3%	Rest of the world	1.2%

Source: J. Scherner, 'Der deutsche Importboom während des Zweiten Weltkriegs. Neue Ergebnisse zur Struktur der Ausbeutung des besetzten Europas auf der Grundlage einer Neuschätzung der deutschen Handelsbilanz,' *Historische Zeitschrift*, 2012, vol. 294, pp. 112–13.

Compared to Japan, the German Reich had a high trade deficit towards the occupied countries. Officially it amounted to 5 billion reichsmarks, but recent research has shown that the deficit was much higher. A recalculation reveals that the German deficit between 1940 and 1944 cumulated to a sum of 42 billion reichsmarks.[2] Apparently, Germany was successful in directing the war goods into its war economy without compensating the imports with exports. This led to permanent arguing with the collaborating regimes, especially with France, where regular negotiations were held.

For Japan, the organisation of foreign trade was logistically more difficult than for Nazi Germany. For the transport of goods to the Japanese mainland, a large commercial fleet was needed which had to be protected by the navy. The transfer of resources from occupied areas to Japan depended very much on the capacity of marine shipping for civil use.[3] Indeed, in deciding to start the war with the United States and the United Kingdom, the prospect of availability of the marine shipping capacity for civil use was one of the most important issues to consider for the military authorities and the government, and in the end, decline of that capacity was the fundamental condition which caused the collapse of the Japanese war economy.

Japan's trade with the occupied territories was not as unilateral as in German-dominated Europe. In some cases such as Manchuria, exports from Japan were even more important than imports. This was because Japan intended to develop the munitions industry and industries of basic materials there, and for that purpose, export of capital goods was needed. Altogether, during the Pacific War, Japanese foreign trade was centred on Chinese territories. In 1943, the share of China proper and Manchuria was 80 per cent of the exports and 69 per cent of the imports. Before the war, Japan heavily depended on imports from the United Kingdom, the United States and their colonies, especially India and Australia, for basic raw materials, such as raw cotton, wool and iron ore. Hence, the embargo by these countries caused serious damage to the Japanese industries. Given this situation, China and Manchuria were expected to be the alternative sources of those materials.

Conclusion 319

Requisitions and plundering?

Like belligerent Germany, Japan was short of raw materials except for coal since the first day of the war.[4] Among the most required goods were strategic goods such as nickel, mercury and rubber, which were almost entirely imported. Among the other goods that were imported to a large extent were iron ore (83 per cent), crude oil (79 per cent), tin (71 per cent), zinc (61 per cent), aluminium (59 per cent) and copper (37 per cent).[5] Japan had to use up its stockpiles and depended for tin and nickel on Indonesia, for oil on East Kalimantan and South Sumatra and for zinc on Burma. Hence, the Japanese army tried to acquire these resources by integrating those areas into its sphere of influence, the Greater East Asia Co-Prosperity Sphere.

The situation of the German Reich was quite similar to that of the Japanese: the German war economy needed more or less the same raw materials, and Nazi administrators planned to fill the existing gaps in supply by appropriating the needed goods in the occupied areas. The initial strategy to cover the shortages was to plunder the occupied areas. Therefore, requisitions without payments were often used to bring the needed materials to the German Reich. Until September 1940, the German troops acquired 135,000 tons of copper (100,650 tons from France), 20,860 tons of lead (11,288 tons from Belgium), 9,300 tons of tin (6,280 tons from France) and 8,890 tons of nickel (8,725 tons from France).[6] Although the system of exploitation changed to a strategy which was more based on stimulating the companies by incentives, ruthless plundering remained characteristic for the Nazi rule until the end of the occupation. In the course of the war, the *Wehrmacht* changed to the practise that the companies were paid with money derived from the huge amounts of occupation fees that were raised on the occupied countries.

In contrast to that, in the majority of the Asian countries, outright plundering did not happen on a large scale after the arrival of the Japanese army. The occupiers tried to maintain the initial goodwill of large segments of the societies, as can be noticed in the case of Indonesia. However, Dutch-owned economic resources were rapidly claimed.[7] In Indochina, requisitions also remained limited in number.[8] Only in occupied China were strategic resources plundered on a larger scale.[9] It is likely that the Japanese armed forces wanted to avoid disorganisation of the occupied countries. The occupation was rather led by a sense of rationality without giving up the aim of taking advantage of the occupied economies. Japan founded the central bank that issued its own bank notes in each occupied territory, such as the Manchuria Central Bank (*Manshu Chuo Ginko*) in Manchuria, the Chinese Alliance Reserve Bank (*Chugoku Rengo Junbi Ginko*) in North China, the Central Reserve Bank (*Chuo Chobi Ginko*) in Middle China and the South Asia Development Bank (*Nanpo Kaihatsu Kinko*) in South East Asia. Besides the bank notes of these organisations, military scrip circulated simultaneously. Using those currencies, the Japanese occupation force procured goods from the occupied territories, which caused hyperinflation there. This implies the inflation tax was the major tool for exploitation.

In addition, in the course of the war, the Japanese Military Administration admitted the seizure of goods for the maintenance and feeding of the armed forces. In Burma, for example, the Japanese army placed a heavy demand on cattle and pig stocks for the war effort against British India.[10] This was because the belligerent zone was far from the Japanese mainland and a lot of manpower and resources were needed for the military operation. This kind of appropriation was also implemented in occupied Europe, in the East more than in the West, by using military violence. Especially in the Soviet territories, a systematic looting was organized which led to a devastation of large areas. Payments for requisitions were only introduced gradually.

Both occupation regimes tried to direct export trade to their war economies. The Japanese developed plans for resource procurement, exploitation and management that were set up by the Cabinet Planning Board (*Kikaku In*) or the Ministry of Munitions (*Gunju Sho*), which was established by integrating the Cabinet Planning Board and a major part of the Ministry of Commerce and Industry (*Shoko Sho*) in November 1943. However, it was sometimes difficult for them to control the trade, because the army and the navy had large powers and discretion in managing the territories they had occupied. The occupation forces would also control trade and exchange and make certain that no valuable resources, including tungsten, quinine, rubber, tin or oil, would reach the enemy. Existing currencies would be used as much as possible, supplemented where necessary by the use of military scrip made out in the units of the local currency.

The German occupiers introduced a special institution, the Central Contracts Offices (*Zentralauftragstellen* or *Zast*), to direct trade to German importers. The *Zast* gathered all the orders from German companies and transferred them to exporters in the occupied territories. It controlled the entitlement of resources as the pivotal input factor for industrial production. The amount of raw materials and semimanufactured products that was necessary to carry out the German importers' orders was allocated to the exporting companies. Only when the exporters submitted his specific delivery bill to the Central Contracts Office could they receive the wanted inputs. At the end, the exporting company issued an invoice, which the German recipient had to pay in reichsmarks, the exporter receiving in his country the equivalent in the local currency.

The institutional arrangement achieved by the Germans was more sophisticated than the Japanese control of trade. This was an effect of the different industrial structure of the countries occupied by Germany and Japan. As will be explained, exports in strategic sectors were put under the control of Japanese companies through monopolies established over commodity distribution.

Support of the war industry

The countries that Germany occupied in Western and Middle Eastern Europe were among the first industrialised areas of the world. Most noteworthy were the Protectorate of Bohemia and Moravia, then since 1940 France, Belgium, the Netherlands and finally Northern Italy towards the end of the war. These occupied areas had a diversified industrial structure and were able to support the German war effort by an own armament production. For reasons of precaution and secrecy, the *Wehrmacht* preferred to produce semifinished goods in the occupied territories,[11] but nevertheless the support of the war economy was quite important, as Table 22.2 shows.

Although the shares of non-German contribution to the war industry are quite impressive, the table does even not reveal that a lot of semifinished goods could be used for armament purposes. The crucial role of the French industry for Germany's war effort appears as clearly as the impact of the Belgian and Dutch shipbuilding and communication equipment industries. Moreover, the German Reich had incorporated neighbouring areas with considerable steel production, in particular Austria, Northern Bohemia, Lorraine and Luxembourg, and had occupied Poland, Northern France and Belgium.

Even if the Japanese had wanted to act in a similar way, they did not have the opportunity to occupy such industrial areas in East Asia. This is the main reason the Japanese army drew up a grand plan for industrial development in Manchuria in the 1930s. Instead of occupying industrial areas, they intended to build up the industries themselves. However, the breakout of the Sino-Japanese War and mobilization of resources for the war made implementation of this plan difficult, and as a result, the contribution of Manchukuo for war production in the Japan Empire was mainly in producing raw materials. Indeed, 80 to 90 per cent of the industry of the Greater East Asia Co-Prosperity Sphere were on the Japanese mainland.[12] The occupied territories had no heavy industries at all, and the only noteworthy industrial branches were cotton and rubber industries.

Expropriations

Some of the country studies reveal that Nipponisation and Germanisation were used as methods of cultural infiltration. In the German occupation policy, this method also had an economic impact. We could see in the case of the Protectorate of Bohemia and Moravia that the expropriation of companies and the appointment of trustees were facilitated by aryanisation and Germanisation. The racial policy served as a means for gaining control over the war-relevant industrial sectors.[13] In the annexed parts of Poland and in the General Government, the expropriation policy was even more ruthless, with countless cases of asset confiscations.[14]

In the occupied countries of Western Europe, the sequestration policy was more cautious. In 175 studied cases in the French industry, the plans of German entrepreneurs of acquiring shares of seized or aryanised firms were hardly successful.[15] However, some industrial plants in strategic branches were set under sequestration, for instance the steel works in Lorraine and Northern France, the Norwegian aluminium branch or Dutch chemical works.[16] The German aggressors even respected enemy property, at least for a certain period. In 1938, the government decided to confiscate assets only as retaliation for measures against German property abroad. This principle was held on in the decree on foreign

Table 22.2 Shares of occupied countries on the German war production of 1943 (in per cent)

	Arms	Ammunition	Vehicles	Shipbuilding	Aviation industry	Communication equipment	Optical equipment
France	1.5	1.4	11.9	6.4	6.5	5	2.8
Belgium/Northern France	0.8	0.7	1.3	11.9	0.1	10.7	0.2
Netherlands	0.1	0.1	0.8	14	1.1	8.3	3.5
General Government	1.8	3.9	1.2	—	1	3.6	1.6
Denmark	0.3	—	0.3	1.5	0.1	0.5	—
Norway	0.3	0.3	0.7	1.9	—	0.5	—
TOTAL	4.8	6.4	16.2	35.7	8.9	28.6	8.1

Source: Eichholtz, *Die deutsche Kriegswirtschaft*, vol. 2, p. 508.

assets in January 1940. However, Göring's Four Year Plan administration aimed at reducing the number of foreign (non-European) companies on the Continent.[17] With the changing war fate, his policy was enforceable when in 1942/43 the argument of the 'risk for German warfare' became more obvious. Enemy asset administrators were introduced to lead US firms such as Ford France.[18]

In the occupied territories of Southeast Asia, compulsory changes in asset ownership also happened through confiscation of enemy property. Mainly companies that were necessary for the prosecution of the war were set under Japanese control.[19] In Indonesia, such takeovers included the oil industry, the banks and some agricultural estates, especially when producing rubber. Mostly affected were properties held by Dutchmen and Indonesians of mixed descent. The enemy-held property was entrusted to the Japanese Military Administrator's Office.[20] In Indochina, some foreign, mostly French groups were able to oppose Japanese expropriations, relying on their contacts with French governor Jean Decoux. However, some strategically important industries (sawmills, cement works, mining companies) were taken over by the Japanese military forces.[21]

More radical were the Japanese forced expropriations of factories and mines in occupied China. In Manchuria, the government confiscated the assets of the Chinese military clique government. The acquired assets contributed in kind to found special corporations, collaborating with the South Manchurian Railways Company (SMR), a huge Japanese semipublic conglomerate that invested in railways as well as in various industries.[22] They developed in industrial sectors such as electricity, iron, steel and aluminium production, coal and petroleum mining and refining. Driven by the will to industrialize Manchuria and receiving high investments from Japan, the Kwangtung Army gained control over the heavy industrial sector with the help of the Manchukuo government and SMR. Each special corporation was given the authority to monopolize a certain industrial branch where it operated. Because of this 'one corporation, one industry' policy,[23] there were no corporate groups needed in Manchuria such as existed in Germany and in most occupied European countries.

Also, in North China and Middle China, semipublic holding companies, the North China Development Company (NCD, *Kita Shina Kaihatsu Kabushiki Gaisha*) and the Middle China Promotion Company (MCP, *Nakashina Shinko Kabushiki Gaisha*), were established respectively, to which the Japanese government contributed in kind the assets confiscated from the Republic of China government.[24]

Governance of the occupied economies

Various publications, among them the chapters on European countries in this book, have shown that central planning played a minor role in the control of occupied economies. The Nazi propaganda emphasized the role of planning, pretending the all-competence of the regime. The institutional effects of the Speer reorganisation of 1942 have been overestimated. Even after that, there was hardly any centralised planning – on the contrary, his reforms promoted the self-organisation of the armament industry.

As has been shown in the chapter on the Nazi reorganisation of Europe, an important outcome of the late Speer reforms in summer 1943 was the establishment of direct trade relations between German importers and exporting companies in the occupied countries. The Zast lost its former function as an institution for establishing economic transactions between exporting companies and German importers. Instead, 'relocation communities' (*Verlagerungsgemeinschaften*) between the involved companies were designated to improve the transfer of orders to the occupied countries. The German contractors were considered 'leading firms', giving direct instructions to their partners abroad. Thus, they were responsible for the production requirements and sometimes even provided skilled workers or technical know-how. The institutional arrangement was regarded as a self-organisation of the economy; it was first developed in the Reich and then transferred to the occupied economies. Prominent examples in the automotive industry were Renault and Volkswagen, who created, since November 1943, a potentially effective cooperation.[25] Hence, such arrangements lasted only for a short time because the course of the war changed and Germany found itself on the losing side.

The Japanese spoke about planning as well. Indeed, strict planning and control were implemented in Japan itself and in Manchuria, where the governance by Japan was fairly stable and civil governments worked.[26] However, in the other territories, real planning was reduced to an efficient resource allocation: on the spot, the Commodities and Pricing Committee (*Busshi Bukka Iinkai* in Indonesia) was charged with that task. The guidance of exports via a shift of orders was not practised in Japanese occupation. Japan's exploitation of the occupied countries was based on financing the needed imports with the creation of new currencies, as stated earlier.

In the Japanese occupation regime, the *zaibatsu* played a crucial role which was in some respects comparable to the relocation communities of the Speer reform in summer 1943. However, the role of *zaibatsu* in the occupied economies changed over time. In the early stage, the army ideologically refused *zaibatsu*, because they were accused of exploiting people, and indeed, the army first excluded them from Manchuria. However, the army gradually learned that it was difficult to manage occupied economies without the help of *zaibatsu*. Hence, in 1937, the Kwantung Army invited Yoshisuke Ayukawa, the president of *Nissan zaibatsu*, to Manchuria, and in the occupied areas in South East Asia, many *zaibatsu* firms engaged in development of natural resources from the beginning.

Thus, the Japanese government delegated the monitoring of contractual relations between Japanese *zaibatsu* and overseas partners to the executive managers. Numerically, the presence of major companies including those affiliated with *zaibatsu* was very important in territories such as Indochina, Indonesia and Burma, especially since 1942. In semioccupied countries such as Indochina, mixed companies were created in the mining sector which were regarded as Japanese 'Trojan horses'.²⁷ Moreover, *zaibatsu* such as *Mitsubishi, Sanko, Ataka, Taitaku* or *Nakamura* entered the forestry industry. In Indonesia, new types of business corporations, the so-called *kumiai*, were introduced according to Japanese models in order to promote cooperation between private Japanese businessmen and Indonesian entrepreneurs.²⁸ In Burma, *zaibatsu*-controlled associations dominated rice and timber production as well as the distribution of commodities.²⁹ In many cases, *zaibatsu* managed to monopolize foreign trade, thus making an important contribution in directing war-relevant goods and raw materials to Japan.

The German and the Japanese armies were the main consumers in both systems of war economy. In order to procure war-relevant goods and material while maintaining market-like economies, they needed large amounts of local money. Imperial Japan as well as Nazi Germany erected new central banks in the occupied territories. On the one hand, these financial institutions managed the funds which were transferred via occupation costs, and on the other hand they issued new currencies by introducing military scrip or currency equivalents like the RKK vouchers. This method of money creation allowed the German and Japanese armies to finance a large part of military expenses in the occupied territories. However, the emitted currencies were paper credits, since they could not be spent to finance imports from the occupiers' countries. Moreover, the issue of new money led to rapid inflation, which makes it difficult to draw an accurate picture of the real balances. Many chapters of this book take a closer look at the implications of this kind of financial policy.³⁰

Synthesis

In both occupation regimes, company-centred models of economic cooperation prevailed, at least towards the end of the war. The economic advisers of Imperial Japan preferred such collaboration from the very beginning of the occupation of South East Asia, whereas in Nazi Germany, the state did not refrain from monitoring economic transactions. Under the supervision of the Central Contracts Offices (*Zast*), a system of direct contacts between trade partners was established. At a late stage of the war, the Speer reform of June 1943 introduced a system of self-determination. In Japan proper, where a relatively strict planning and control system had been enforced especially since 1941, the government officially came to use profit incentives as a tool for promoting war production, and furthermore, the Munitions Company Law, which approved of larger discretion of the companies designated by that law, was legislated in October 1943.³¹

These processes in Germany and Japan show that the mechanisms which were the most conforming to a market economy were the best for achieving high-output results. The simulation of market transactions in a restricted economic framework was the optimal response to entrepreneurial profit seeking. Governance was easier to manage than in a economic system which was administratively and militarily dominated. In both cases, war financing was covered with occupation costs which were imposed to the occupied countries. The effect was that the occupied territories financed their exploitation to a large degree themselves. Furthermore, the oppressed populations in the occupied countries were obliged to support Germany's and to a lesser extent Japan's warfare by the use of forced labour.

Notes

1. See the chapter by Charney/Naono on Burma.
2. Scherner, 'Der deutsche Importboom', p. 106.
3. See Figure 1 in Okazaki's chapter on the Greater East Asia Co-Prosperity Sphere.
4. T. Okazaki, 'Productivity Change and Mine Dynamics: The Coal Industry in Japan during World War II', forthcoming in *Jahrbuch für Wirtschaftsgeschichte*.
5. G. Daniels, 'Japan – Domestic life, economy and war effort', in I.C.B. Dear/ M.R.D. Foot (eds.), *The Oxford Companion to the Second World War*, Oxford: Oxford University Press, 1995.
6. R.-D. Müller, 'Die Mobilisierung der deutschen Wirtschaft für Hitlers Kriegsführung', in B. Kroener et al.(eds.), *Das Deutsche Reich und der Zweite Weltkrieg, vol. 5, 1: Kriegsverwaltung, Wirtschaft und personelle Ressourcen 1939–1941*, Stuttgart: DVA, 1988, p. 524.
7. See Lindblad's chapter on Indonesia.
8. See Boissarie's chapter on Indochina.
9. See Imai's chapter on the Shanghai textile industry.
10. See the chapter of Charney/Naono on Burma.
11. Scherner, 'Europas Beitrag zu Hitlers Krieg', p. 82.
12. J.F. Dunnigan, *The Pacific War Encyclopedia, vol. 1*, New York: Facts on File, 1998, p. 213.
13. See Wixforth's chapter on the Protectorate and Ahrens's chapter on the German steel industry.
14. See Lehnstaedt's chapter on Poland.
15. P. Verheyde, 'Vichy, die deutsche Besatzungsmacht und ihre wirtschaftlichen Beziehungen im Rahmen der "Arisierung" der großen jüdischen Unternehmen', *Zeitschrift für Unternehmensgeschichte*, 2005, vol. 50, pp. 218–31.
16. A. Tooze, *Ökonomie der Zerstörung*, p. 452.
17. M. Horn/T. Imlay, *The Politics of Industrial Collaboration during World War II. Ford France, Vichy and Nazi Germany*, Cambridge: Cambridge University Press, 2014, p. 58.
18. Ibid, p. 152.
19. See Sicat's chapter on the Philippines and Charney/Naono's chapter on Burma.
20. See Lindblad's chapter on Indonesia.
21. See Boissarie's chapter on Indochina.
22. A. Hara, *Nihon Senji Keizai Kenkyu (Research on the Japanese War Economy)*, Tokyo: University of Tokyo Press, 2013, p. 92. Concerning SMR, see Hirayama's chapter.
23. See Okazaki's chapter on Manchuria.
24. T. Nakamura, *Senji Nihon no Kahoku Keizai Shihai (Control of the North China Economy by Japan during the War)*, Tokyo: Yamakawa Shuppansha, 1983, p. 168.
25. Horn/Imlay, *Politics of Industrial Collaboration*, p. 233; P. Lessmann, 'Industriebeziehungen zwischen Deutschland und Frankreich während der deutschen Besatzung 1940–1944. Das Beispiel Peugeot-Volkswagenwerk', *Francia*, 1990, vol. 17, pp. 120–53.
26. T. Okazaki/M. Okuno-Fujiwara (eds.), *Contemporary Japanese Economic System and Its Historical Origins*, New York: Oxford University Press, 1999; see also Okazaki's chapter on Manchuria in this book.

27 See Boissarie's chapter on Indochina.
28 See Lindblad's chapter on Indonesia.
29 See the chapter by Charney/Naono on Burma.
30 See the chapters of Scherner and Huff/Majima as well as the country studies on France, Norway, Burma and Indonesia.
31 Okazaki/Okuno-Fujiwara, *Contemporary Japanese Economic System*.

Index

agriculture 19–20, 73, 107, 112, 148, 150–2, 155, 161, 168, 173, 194–7, 208–9, 213, 219–20, 222–3, 225–9, 236, 238–9, 300, 323
aircraft 17, 27, 101, 180–4
Alsace 8, 10, 99, 264
aluminium 12, 18, 76, 106, 141, 180–2, 262, 317, 319, 321
Antwerp 121–2, 124
armament 7, 11–12, 14–18, 20–1, 41, 44, 53, 74, 77, 82, 99, 101–4, 106–8, 123, 141, 148, 150–5, 161, 166–7, 169–70, 247–50, 253, 255, 257, 265, 277, 321, 324
aryanisation 12, 100, 163, 166, 171–2, 174, 248–50, 254, 321
Association for the Control of Raw Cotton (Central China) 305, 312
Atlantic Wall 44, 47, 131, 137, 267–8, 273
Auschwitz 81–3
Australia 56, 220, 242, 318
Austria 7, 8, 18, 64, 73–4, 161, 163, 166, 170, 253–4, 321
autarky 7, 28, 35, 65, 105, 197, 243, 247–8
automobile (automotive industry) 16, 26–7, 101, 180–4, 224, 260, 324
aviation 16, 20, 134, 219, 322; *see also* aircraft
Ayukawa, Yoshisuke 27, 183–5, 187, 324

Ba Maw 218, 220–2, 227, 229
banking (banks) 13, 18, 41, 45, 52, 56–7, 61, 66, 104, 113, 115, 118–20, 135–6, 138, 161–2, 165–6, 170–2, 192, 199, 207–8, 219–22, 250, 265, 281, 300, 302, 310, 323, 325

Banque de l'Indochine (Bank of Indochina) 56, 235, 238
Bawdwin Mines 244
Beijing 29, 308, 317
Belgium 2, 8, 13, 18–19, 41, 43, 45, 47, 50, 52, 73, 77, 80–1, 112–26, 141, 249, 251, 253, 264, 267, 277, 318–22
Berlin 11–12, 14, 20, 78, 106, 124, 128, 133, 135, 140, 150, 152, 156–7, 162–3, 165–6, 168–70, 173, 271, 277, 316–7
Bertsch, Walter 169
Best, Werner 10, 99
Bichelonne, Jean 79, 101, 103, 106
Black market, 13–14, 17, 44, 46–7, 49, 53, 105, 120, 122, 124–5, 139–40, 153–4, 198, 208, 211, 214, 241, 244
Blitzkrieg 7, 20, 76, 150, 248, 255
Bohemia 2, 7–8, 10, 18, 40, 110, 161–3, 165–71, 173, 254, 320–1
bombing 63, 150, 169, 198, 214, 225, 227, 236, 242–3, 275
bonds 39–40, 56, 60–1, 118, 136, 172
booty 130–1, 133–4, 143
Bordeaux 265, 267, 277
bread 105, 153
Brussels 13, 99, 113–4, 117, 119–20, 123, 126
Burma 3, 25, 56, 59, 61–3, 65–7, 218–29, 233–4, 242, 317, 319–20, 324–5

capital 2, 25–6, 29, 32, 52, 78, 95, 100, 104, 119, 124, 137, 141, 166, 170–1, 180, 183–5, 188, 195–7, 200–2, 221–2, 235, 238, 249, 252–3, 256, 258, 266, 280–2, 284, 288, 290, 295, 297, 301, 307, 310, 318

330 Index

capital stock 16, 195, 197, 201–2, 249
cement 16, 106, 134, 186–7, 225, 238, 265–6, 275, 323
central banks 2, 26, 41, 57, 90, 104, 113, 118–20, 130–1, 135, 142, 208, 221, 319, 325
Central Contracts Office (Zentralauftragsstelle) 13, 15, 17, 102–3, 108, 141, 169, 320, 324–5
central planning 11–12, 20, 27, 35, 42–3, 85, 107, 140, 143, 148, 166, 170, 179, 183, 185–8, 219, 249, 255, 258, 262, 273, 280, 288–9, 320, 323–5
chemicals 1, 12, 26, 30–2, 76, 82, 121, 180–1, 187, 239–40, 249, 258, 321
China 3, 24–5, 28–30, 32–5, 56, 64, 86–90, 92, 95, 178, 186, 188, 224, 234–5, 289, 293–314, 317–19, 323
Chinese Communist Party 32, 86
Chinese Nationalist Party 29, 32–3
Christiani & Nielsen 262–78
clearing 11, 13, 40–1, 46, 50, 55, 68, 103, 108, 113, 118–20, 128, 130–33, 136, 138, 141, 143
clothing 30–1, 65, 67, 80, 131, 124, 134, 141, 150, 197, 214, 226, 242
coal 26, 28–9, 32, 76, 92, 101–3, 105–6, 112–15, 117–18, 121–2, 124–6, 141, 180–2, 184–5, 187, 197, 209, 211, 213, 232, 237–8, 240, 248, 251, 253–5, 262, 289–90, 319, 323
coal mining 26, 29, 32, 76, 92, 112–15, 117–18, 121–2, 125–6, 180, 184, 209, 211, 254–5, 289–90
Cochinchina 61, 232, 234–7
coercion 15, 20, 64, 67, 99
collaborating 2, 10, 13–4, 21, 25, 102, 179, 186, 218, 316–8, 323
collaboration 3, 8, 10, 99, 104, 106–7, 115–6, 120–1, 126, 130, 161, 164–5, 193, 207, 232–5, 237, 240, 242–3, 264, 270, 287, 293, 298, 300–3, 307, 311, 317, 325
Comité Central Industriel (CCI, Belgium) 113–17, 127
Committee for the Control of Raw Cotton (CCRW, China) 299, 305, 308–9, 312
Commodity Distribution Association (Burma) 223
communists 32, 86, 207, 250, 267, 289

conglomerate 27, 34, 182, 184, 187, 213, 316, 323
consumption 7, 35, 39, 45, 48–9, 51, 66, 105, 137, 143, 167, 173, 181, 195, 199, 209, 295, 304, 313
contract 1, 11–13, 15–17, 76–7, 81, 101–3, 105–8, 132, 138, 166, 169, 201, 212, 236, 241, 247, 250, 252, 255, 257, 264–73, 275, 277–8, 281, 320, 324–5
control, administrative 10, 14, 27, 35, 42–3, 45, 56, 75, 80, 86–95, 99–100, 114, 118, 122, 163–4, 166–9, 174, 185–8, 192–4, 209, 213, 218–24, 233, 239, 247, 251, 267, 280, 285, 288–9, 294–6, 317, 323–5; economic 2, 3, 11, 13–14, 16, 18, 42, 47, 99–100, 103, 107–8, 112–15, 118–19, 121–4, 162–6, 171–4, 179, 185–8, 192, 207–9, 219–24, 226, 229, 232–5, 243, 251, 255, 265, 270, 280, 288–9, 291, 294–6, 299, 301–9, 311–12, 320–3, 325; institutional 2, 12, 14, 18, 100–5, 115, 119, 169; price 2, 13, 19, 61, 67, 105, 107, 124, 135, 185, 192, 196, 223; territorial 7–8, 10, 18, 20, 57, 68, 80, 99–100, 130–1, 147, 155, 161, 178–9, 183, 186, 191, 211, 213, 225, 232–5, 240, 273, 275, 298, 302, 316
Copenhagen 264–5, 269–70, 272
copper 18, 100, 319
cotton 100, 209, 223–4, 226–7, 236, 240, 293, 295–314, 318, 321
Cotton Mill Association (Republic of China) 299, 302, 305, 312, 314
credit 39–41, 46, 50, 57–8, 60, 119, 130–5, 142–3, 162, 166, 207, 219, 235, 239–40, 325
currency 11, 34, 40–2, 45, 51–2, 55–7, 59, 61–7, 90, 103–4, 132–3, 166–8, 185–6, 192, 199, 219–21, 227, 235, 239, 295, 309–10, 319–20, 324–5

Daluege, Kurt 169, 177
damage 2, 29, 133, 191, 194–5, 197, 200–3, 214, 225, 255, 265, 269, 271, 278, 318
Darlan-Kato agreement 232, 234–6
decolonisation 205
Decoux, Jean 232–5, 238–41, 243, 323
Denis Frères 238

Denmark 8, 10–2, 19, 78, 80, 99, 133, 141, 263–4, 268, 270, 316, 318, 322
diamonds 112–3, 117, 121–2, 209
distribution 29, 87, 91–2, 101, 118–9, 122, 152, 185–6, 198–9, 208–9, 222–3, 226, 247, 251, 253–5, 299, 301–2, 304–5, 307–8, 320, 325
Dnjepr-Stahl (steel company) 255–6
Dresdner Bank 255, 265–6

economic groups (Wirtschaftsgruppen) 101, 113, 168
electricity 25–6, 29, 32, 103, 180–2, 240, 259, 267, 323
elite(s) 2, 8, 12, 112–22, 126, 164–5, 316–7
embargo 11, 34, 318
emigration 89, 172
entitlement 2, 14–5, 102, 155, 320
entrepreneur 12, 27, 100, 112, 114–6, 121–2, 124, 167–8, 170, 183–4, 210, 213, 223, 247–8, 252, 255, 258, 262–3, 321, 325
exploitation 1–2, 11–13, 17, 19–20, 39–42, 46, 50–1, 55, 57–8, 91, 99, 103, 105–7, 112–3, 118–9, 124, 126, 130–1, 133–4, 139, 141–2, 148–51, 155–6, 163–5, 169, 173, 219, 223, 247, 249, 255, 316–7, 319–20, 324, 326
export 13, 15–17, 19, 27–8, 32–3, 39, 56–7, 65, 67, 102, 104, 131–3, 141, 144, 151, 155, 166–8, 183, 185–6, 194–6, 209, 214, 222–7, 232, 236–40, 305, 313, 318, 320, 324
exporter 17, 102, 209, 223, 225, 238, 320
expropriation 172, 240, 250, 321, 323

Falkenhorst, Nikolaus von 137, 141–2
famine 212, 236, 243
farmer 19–20, 66, 79, 81, 95, 138, 151–2, 173, 211, 299–300
field post transfers 139, 143
Five Year Plan (Manchuria) 25, 27, 86–8, 92, 95, 179–83, 186–7
Flick, Friedrich (concern) 247–8, 250–2, 254
food 2, 16, 19, 26, 34, 63, 65–7, 78, 80, 108, 116, 124–5, 131, 134, 141, 150–6, 173, 192, 195–9, 211, 223, 238, 242, 253, 262, 317

Index 331

forced labour 2, 20, 73–7, 80–2, 87, 106–8, 112, 116, 123, 132, 148, 150–1, 154, 156, 196, 212, 253, 256–8, 266–7, 277, 326
Four Year Plan (Germany) 11, 18, 45–6, 82, 107, 125, 148–9, 152, 157, 162, 165–6, 170, 248, 264, 323
France 2, 8, 10–11, 13, 15, 41, 43–53, 57–8, 64, 73, 77–81, 99–108, 118, 123, 140–1, 143, 150, 171, 232–3, 237, 239–40, 243, 249–51, 253, 256, 262, 264–72, 275, 277, 316, 318–23, 327
Frank, Hans, 147–50, 153–4, 156, 157
Frank, Karl Hermann 163–5, 169, 173
Fuji Gas & Spinning KK (Burma) 225, 227

Galicia 76, 147–8
Galopin, Alexandre 13, 112, 115–7, 119–21, 127–8
General Government 3, 8, 10, 12, 17, 19, 77, 80–1, 147–57, 165, 254, 318, 321–2
Germanisation 8, 150, 165, 168, 171–3, 254, 321
ghetto 81, 83, 151–3, 155, 158, 257
gold 57, 60, 64, 69, 166, 172, 235, 239
Göring, Hermann, 11, 102, 149, 159, 165–6, 170, 248, 251–2, 254–5, 264, 323
governance 192, 285, 302, 316, 323–4
Greater East Asia Co-Prosperity Sphere 1–2, 24–5, 28, 30, 34–5, 67, 193, 206, 219–20, 233, 239, 316–7, 319, 321, 326
Greater Economic Sphere (Grosswirtschaftsraum) 1–2, 7, 10, 140, 167–8, 250, 317
Greece 8, 64, 76, 80, 136, 318
Gross Domestic Product (GDP) 2, 55, 57–8, 169, 200–2, 210, 213, 227
guerrilla 65, 194, 211
Gutehoffnungshütte (GHH) 247–8, 250–2, 255–6

Hacha, Emil 162–4, 172, 175
Hanneken, Hermann von 254
Hatta, Mohammad 207, 210, 213, 215
Hatta, Yoshiaki 281, 284

Index

hegemony 1, 74–5, 82, 164–5, 167, 169, 191
Heydrich, Reinhard 164–5, 169, 172, 177
Himmler, Heinrich 148, 153
Hitler, Adolf 7, 10–11, 48, 53, 76–7, 79, 81, 131, 138, 140, 148–50, 161–65, 169, 262, 271, 277
holding companies 27, 29, 36, 112–3, 116, 118–21, 124, 187, 280, 323
holocaust 156–7, 257
Hungary 9, 10, 73, 75, 80, 167, 318

Iida, Shojiro 219, 222, 226
immigration 86–8, 91, 219
import 1, 2, 11, 16, 18–19, 27–30, 33–4, 40–1, 46, 49, 53, 57, 61, 67, 104–5, 130–3, 136–8, 141, 151, 166, 168, 179, 183, 185–8, 195–6, 205–7, 210, 212, 214, 221–3, 226–7, 232, 237–41, 295, 297–8, 317–19, 324–5
importer 14, 21, 75, 141, 320, 324
incentive 12, 14–16, 19, 64, 102, 104–5, 108, 130, 152, 154, 196, 247, 319, 325
India (Indians) 1, 56, 218, 221–7, 242, 298, 318, 320
Indochina 3, 25, 33–4, 55–63, 65–7, 232–44, 317, 319, 323–4, 326–7
Indonesia 3, 56–8, 61–3, 65, 205–15, 317, 319, 323–7
industrialist 12–16, 114–6, 121, 164–5, 167, 169–70, 174, 248, 251, 255–8
industry 2–3, 7, 12–21, 24–7, 29, 32, 34–6, 39, 45, 76–9, 82, 86–8, 91–5, 99–103, 105–8, 112–18, 120–3, 126, 132, 138, 140–1, 149–50, 152, 154–5, 160–74, 178–85, 187, 192, 194–6, 198, 205, 209–11, 219–20, 223–5, 227, 232, 236, 238–40, 242–4, 247–60, 265, 280–1, 286–7, 289, 293–312, 317–18, 320–6
institutions 2, 12–14, 21, 46, 79, 99, 101, 103, 107–8, 112–24, 126, 131, 134, 141, 148–9, 155, 162, 169, 193, 205–6, 208, 210, 215, 222, 239, 249, 295, 303, 310, 320, 323–5
investment 7, 12, 15–16, 25, 29, 33–4, 36, 66, 103, 123–4, 130, 140, 150–1, 161, 171, 184, 223, 247, 250, 252–6, 258, 281, 284, 302, 309–10, 323

iron 12, 28, 32, 101–2, 105, 162, 180–2, 184–7, 224, 238–9, 247–9, 251–2, 254–6, 258, 323
iron ore 28, 32, 181–2, 248, 251–2, 317–19
Italy (Italians) 8–9, 17, 34, 41–2, 49–50, 74–5, 78, 80, 110, 264, 277, 318, 320

Japanese army (Imperial Japanese Army, IJA) 86, 178, 184, 206, 208–9, 218–20, 225, 229, 296, 301, 305, 317, 319–21
Japanese Military Administration (JMA) 56, 193, 219–24, 226–9, 320
Jewish property 41, 52, 100, 124, 171–2, 248–50
Jews/Jewish 12, 41, 52, 80–3, 100, 121–2, 124, 149–57, 160, 170–2, 248–50, 256–7, 267
Jiang, Shangda 299, 303–4

kabushiki kaisha (commercial concern) 29, 223
Kehrl, Hans 107, 170
Keynes, John Milnard 59, 66
Konoe, Fumimaro 184
Korff, Hans Claussen 47–8, 137–40, 143
Krakow 147, 149, 151–2, 154, 159
Krupp 247–8, 250–1, 254–7
Kwantung Army (Japan) 86–9, 95, 178–80, 182–4, 186–8, 280, 288, 324

labour 2, 11, 14, 20, 55, 57, 73–83, 86–95, 99, 102, 106–8, 112, 116, 123, 125, 131–4, 137–40, 143, 147–56, 164, 169, 173, 196, 205, 207, 211–12, 215, 223–9, 248, 250, 253, 255–8, 261, 266–7, 277–8, 316, 326; *see also* forced labour
labourer 39, 41, 65, 73–4, 77, 80–1, 107, 112, 132, 148, 150, 152–6, 212, 228, 253, 266–7, 277–8
Lehideux, François 101
Liaison Conference: Government – Imperial Head Quarters (Japan) 33–4, 218–9
Liu, Jingji 299, 307
loan 40, 125, 222, 226, 235, 256, 284, 300–1
London 119, 166, 170

Lorraine 10, 12, 99, 250–4, 258, 264, 321
Lublin 80–1, 147
Luxembourg 10, 18, 250–4, 258, 321
Lyon 100

Malaya 56, 61–3, 65–6, 209, 225, 228, 317
management 14–15, 89, 91, 93–4, 101, 116, 119–20, 123, 151, 178, 184, 199, 209–10, 218–20, 224, 227, 238, 241, 251–7, 262, 264–6, 268–72, 274–5, 280, 285–91, 296, 299, 306, 308–9, 312, 320
Manchukuo 24–5, 27, 86–92, 178–80, 182, 184–8, 280, 285, 290, 317, 321, 323
Manchuria Heavy Industrial Development Company (MHID) 27, 29, 184, 187, 280, 290
Manila 66, 193–4, 197–200
manufacture, manufacturing 15, 17–18, 26, 28, 30–1, 33, 67, 93, 100–2, 107, 123, 184, 210, 224, 228, 248, 254, 256–7, 295, 298, 301, 311
Marseille 16, 274
Material Mobilization Plan 27, 32, 185–6
Matsuoka, Yosuke 1, 285, 287
merchant 57, 59, 222, 237, 269, 300–1, 305, 307, 314
Middle China Promotion Co. (MCP) 29, 32–3, 323
military scrip 2, 55–6, 65–6, 68, 192, 194, 219–20, 319–20, 325
mining 18, 26, 29, 32, 73, 93, 103, 112, 114–5, 117–8, 121–2, 126, 162, 170, 180, 184, 194–5, 209, 219–20, 222, 224–5, 227, 238–9, 249, 253–5, 289–90, 304, 323–4
Mitsubishi 209, 223, 225, 238, 325
Mitsui 208–9, 223, 238
mobilisation (resources) 7, 12, 27, 32, 86–92, 94–5, 108, 150–1, 153, 185–7, 192, 198, 212, 215, 219, 229, 321
monopoly 25, 55, 65, 76–7, 113–4, 152, 170, 180, 209, 212, 222–4, 254–5, 320, 323, 325
Moscow 1, 165

Nakamura (zaibatsu) 238, 325
Nampo (Southern occupied areas) 218, 221

Nanjing 29, 184, 303, 308, 317
National Banks 41, 45, 52, 104, 118–9, 166–7, 192
National Mobilization Law (Manchuria) 86–7, 89
navy 8, 29, 34, 44, 76, 138–9, 206, 250, 265, 268, 275, 318, 320
Netherlands 8, 10–12, 16–17, 19, 40, 43, 49–50, 77, 80, 118, 141, 155, 206, 208–10, 215, 249, 253, 318, 320, 322
Neurath, Konstantin von 163–5
New Labour System (*Romu Shintaisei*, Manchuria) 86–7, 89–90, 92–4
nickel 209, 319
Nissan 27, 183–4, 324
Nord (France) 8, 18, 99
Nordag AS (Norway) 134
Norges Bank 41, 134–6, 141–2
North China Development Co. (NCD) 29, 32–3, 323
Norway 2, 8, 10, 12, 19, 41–3, 45, 47–50, 53, 75–6, 80–1, 130–44, 155, 265, 316–7, 322, 327
Nuremberg 77, 172
nutrition 19–20, 66, 148, 151–3, 155–6, 159

occupation account 42, 44–6, 131, 134–7, 142
occupation costs 2, 11, 13, 20, 39–60, 68, 100, 103–4, 108, 118, 120, 126, 128, 131, 136–7, 142–3, 156, 325
Ogawa, Gotaro 220, 229
oil 30–1, 57, 101, 182, 197, 206, 208–9, 211, 213–4, 219, 223, 227, 239–40, 262, 319–20, 323
Okumura, Shinji 286, 290
one industry one corporation policy (Manchuria) 25, 180, 187
Operation Reinhard 153
Organisation Todt 14, 16, 77, 131, 134, 138–40, 264–9, 272, 274, 277–8, 316
Ostland (Reich Commissariat) 8, 19, 165

Pacific Ocean 1, 57, 59, 197, 203, 213, 237, 240
Pacific War 34–5, 182, 202, 205, 211, 237–8, 293, 296, 298–9, 308–9, 311–2, 318
paddy 211, 223, 225–8, 241

Paris 13, 68, 99, 170, 264, 266, 268, 270, 272–3
Pas-de-Calais 8, 18, 99
Pearl Harbor 34, 191, 232, 237–8
petroleum 26, 33–4, 57, 180, 209, 211, 233, 239, 323
Philippines 3, 25, 56, 61–3, 65–6, 191–203, 220, 317, 326
planning *see* central planning
Pleiger, Paul 171, 248, 251, 254–5, 259
plundering 2, 12–13, 16, 20, 100, 124, 126, 149, 164, 207, 319
Poland 3, 12, 18, 50, 73, 77–80, 133, 147–52, 154, 156, 249, 253, 321, 326
polycracy 14, 107–8, 166
prices *see* control (price)
prisoners of war (POW) 2, 73–4, 81–2, 88, 90–2, 107, 112, 122, 132, 206, 221, 226, 242, 256–7, 266
property rights 2, 12, 16, 100, 170, 220, 247, 249, 252, 257
Prytz, Fredrik 136, 142
puppet government 24, 29, 79, 192, 243, 316–7

Qingxiang operations 302–3, 312

railways 24–5, 29, 32, 42, 76, 87, 94, 100, 131, 134, 152, 178–80, 184, 188, 212, 218, 220, 225, 228, 242, 280–1, 284, 288–90, 294, 308, 323
raw materials 1–2, 12–15, 17, 44, 76, 100–3, 108, 113, 122–3, 131, 148, 158, 166–7, 169, 182, 185, 194, 214, 224–5, 234, 239, 249–50, 253, 255, 258, 317–21, 325
recruitment (labour) 8, 75–80, 87–94, 106, 154
Reichskreditkasse (RKK) 13, 41, 104, 133, 135, 146
Reichswerke Hermann Göring 148, 171–2, 247–8, 251, 253–5, 258
Reitz, Erich 123–4
Renault 324
requisition 14, 20, 25, 29, 34, 57, 100, 104–7, 130–1, 133–5, 137–8, 142–3, 179, 197, 211, 225, 237, 240, 306, 319–20
Reusch, Paul 248, 251
revolution 64, 113–4, 205, 207, 213, 240, 243

rice 57–8, 63, 65–7, 197–8, 211–14, 223, 225–7, 232, 235–8, 240–1, 325
risk 61, 74, 153, 237, 247–8, 252, 256–8, 262–4, 269–70, 272, 274–6, 323
Röchling, Hermann (industrialist) 251–2, 254
Rombach (steel works) 250–3
romusha 212, 214
rubber 1, 33, 58, 65, 82, 208–13, 219, 232, 236–7, 262, 319–21, 323

Saar 251–2
Sanko 223, 238, 325
Sauckel, Fritz (Plenipotentiary for Labour Deployment) 14, 76–9, 106–8, 111, 132, 154, 316
seigniorage 55, 64–5, 67–8
Sengoku, Mitsugu 287
sequestration 12, 124, 140, 321
Serbia 8, 18, 76, 80, 253
Shanghai 29, 56, 293–300, 302–3, 306–8, 310–1, 326
Shell 239
shipbuilding 17, 224, 238, 321–2
shipping 34–5, 57, 59, 135, 196, 209–11, 213, 303–4, 318
shortage 15, 28, 33, 59, 76, 87, 90, 92, 99, 102, 104–6, 153, 166, 183, 186, 203, 210–14, 227–8, 239, 243, 248, 250, 253, 255–6, 264, 304, 308, 319
Škoda 166–7, 170, 254
Société Asiatique des Pétroles 239
Société Cotonnière du Tonkin 242
Société Générale (Belgium) 112–3, 119–22, 124
Solvay 121
South Manchuria Railway Company (SMR) 179–80, 280–91, 323, 326
Soviet Union (USSR, Soviets) 1, 7, 18–19, 73–4, 76–82, 120. 128, 131–2, 147, 150–1, 156, 171, 180, 248–50, 253, 255–7, 320
special corporations (Manchuria) 25–7, 34, 179–80, 183–4, 186–7, 323
Speer, Albert 11–12, 14, 17–18, 20, 77, 79, 103, 106–8, 138, 140, 143, 323–5
Sperrbetriebe (S-Betriebe) 15, 79, 107–8
spinning 225, 227, 295, 298–302, 305–9, 312–14
SS ("Schutzstaffel" of the NSDAP) 8, 14, 75, 148–9, 153–4, 156, 164, 173, 316

Index 335

standard of living 39, 58, 197, 211–12, 214
Standard Oil 239
state-owned enterprise 100, 170–1, 192, 247, 251, 254
steel 1, 12, 18, 20, 26, 32, 34, 106, 112–15, 121, 124, 134, 162, 180–2, 184–7, 225, 239, 247–59, 262, 321, 323, 326
stockholder 280–5, 288, 290–1
stock market 56, 255, 284–5, 290–1
stockpiles 135, 137, 319
sugar 58, 65, 155, 195–6, 198–9, 209, 211, 213, 223
Sukarno 206–7, 212, 214–5
Sweden 75, 141, 317
Switzerland 75, 317

Taitaku 238, 325
Takashi, Tsutsumi 303, 307
taxation 39, 52, 55–6, 59, 65, 67, 104, 118, 133, 140–1, 145, 172, 198, 207–8, 220, 224, 240–1, 244, 302, 319,
Terboven, Josef 140–2
textiles 16, 29, 44, 100–2, 107, 112–16, 121–4, 162, 205, 209–12, 214, 226–7, 240, 242, 293–312, 326
Thailand 25, 34, 56–63, 65–7, 228, 236, 263
timber 223–4, 227, 325
tin 58, 65, 102, 209, 219, 225, 238, 319–20
Todt, Fritz *see* Organisation Todt
Tokyo 56–7, 206, 208, 210, 219, 224, 232, 234–6, 239–40, 242–3, 281–3, 317
Tonkin 232–6, 238, 242–3
transport 11, 20, 26, 29, 32, 44, 76, 80–1, 93, 100, 108, 131, 134, 138, 150, 154, 156, 160, 167–8, 172, 194, 197, 210, 218–20, 223–5, 239–40, 253, 267, 270, 297, 299, 317–8
trusteeship 12, 123, 140, 171–2, 249–52, 254–5, 316, 321
tungsten (Wolfram) 1, 219, 225, 238, 320

Ukraine (Ukrainians) 8, 10, 19, 76, 149, 151, 255–6
unemployment 75, 78, 88, 132, 150, 227
United Kingdom (UK) 33–4, 131, 318
United States of America (USA) 24, 33–4, 64, 183, 185, 191–4, 197, 200, 202–3, 234, 237, 239, 298, 318

Vereinigte Stahlwerke (steel plant) 167, 250–1, 255
Vichy (French Government) 18, 57, 79, 103, 106, 232, 234, 237, 239–40, 243, 249–50, 264–5, 267, 273
village 66, 76, 80, 88, 152, 173, 226–8
Vitkovice Mining and Foundry Works 162, 170
Vlaams Economisch Verbond (VEV, Flemish Economic League) 113–16
Volkswagen 260, 324

wages 2, 13, 45, 75, 78, 105, 113, 117, 123–6, 138, 151, 154, 161, 167–8, 212, 227
Wang, Chao-ming 29, 317
Wang, Jingwei 298–9, 302, 304–9, 311, 314
war damage *see* damage
Warsaw 80, 147–51, 153–5, 194
Wehrmacht 1, 8, 11, 13, 15–17, 19–21, 41–3, 46–50, 54, 75–6, 81, 99–101, 103–5, 107–8, 131–43, 145, 148–9, 152–5, 256, 316, 319, 321
Wen, Lanting 299, 304, 309, 315
Wiesbaden (Armistice Commissions) 104, 264
Wirtschaftliche Forschungsgesellschaft (Economic Research Company) 100

Yamamoto, Jotaro 287
Yokohama Specie Bank (YSB) 56–7, 208, 221–2, 235
Yong'an Textile Corporation 309

zaibatsu 27, 34, 183, 208, 238, 324–5
Zentralauftragsstelle (Zast) *see* Central Contracts Office
zinc 181, 224–5, 319